Pension Tax Guide

2017-18

Robert Gaines

Disclaimer

This publication is sold with the understanding that neither the publishers nor the authors, with regard to this publication, are engaged in providing legal or professional services.

The material contained in this publication does not constitute tax advice and readers are advised that they should always obtain such professional advice before acting, or refraining from acting, on any information contained in this book. Readers are also advised that UK tax law is subject to frequent and unpredictable change.

Every effort has been taken to compile the contents of this book accurately and carefully. However, neither the publisher nor the author can accept any responsibility or liability to any person, whether a purchaser of this book or not, in respect of anything done or omitted to be done by any such person in reliance, partly or wholly, on any part or on the whole of the contents of this book.

Pronouns

For simplicity and elegance, the male pronoun is generally used in this book to cover references to both male and female (unless the context indicates otherwise).

2013-14 edition August 2013
2014-15 edition September 2014
2015-16 edition September 2015
2016-17 edition September 2016
This edition September 2017

Pension Tax Guide

2017-18

Robert Gaines

Published by:

Claritax Books Ltd
6 Grosvenor Park Road
Chester, CH1 1QQ

www.claritaxbooks.com

ISBN: 978-1-908545-99-2

Other titles from Claritax Books

Other tax titles from Claritax Books include:

- A-Z of Plant & Machinery
- Capital Allowances
- Construction Industry Scheme
- Discovery Assessments
- Employee Benefits & Expenses
- Employment Status
- Entrepreneurs' Relief
- Financial Planning with Trusts
- Furnished Holiday Lettings
- Main Residence Relief
- Research & Development
- Residence: The Definition in Practice
- Stamp Duty Land Tax
- Tax Chamber Hearings
- Tax Losses
- VAT Registration Handbook
- Venture Capital Schemes

See www.claritaxbooks.com for details of these and of our other forthcoming titles.

About the author

Robert Gaines LL.B has had practical experience of working with pensions for over 30 years, originally as a senior manager, but latterly as a self-employed consultant and author. He has advised a number of financial institutions and other firms and spoken at numerous events. He has also contributed pension chapters to a range of books that deal with private and public sector employment as well as individual tax planning.

Robert was for more than 25 years the author of *The Pensions Factbook* (published by Wolters Kluwer). He has also written and updated material for other publishers such as *Pensions and Retirement Planning* (Taxbriefs), and he contributes to the online service *Perspective* (Pendragon).

About the publisher

Claritax Books publishes specialist tax titles, complementing what is on offer from the larger tax publishers. Typically, our books cover niche topics in greater depth or take a more practical approach to particular tax issues. Our titles are written for accountants (both in-house and in practice), tax advisers, employers, lawyers and other professionals. Our authors include barristers, solicitors, accountants and other experienced tax specialists.

Claritax Books titles cover (among other topics) tax appeals, capital allowances, the statutory residence rules, CGT reliefs, the CIS scheme, pensions and trusts, stamp duty land tax, VAT, employment taxes and furnished holiday lettings. Visit www.claritaxbooks.com for details of all our books.

Claritax Books is a trading name of Claritax Books Ltd (company number 07658388, VAT number 114 9371 20). The company is based in Chester, England.

Abbreviations

AUA	Assets under administration
AVC	Additional voluntary contribution
BCE	Benefit crystallisation event
BIM	Business Income Manual
CEP	Contributions equivalent premium
CGT	Capital gains tax
Ch.	Chapter
CPI	Consumer prices index
CTA	Corporation Tax Act
DC	Defined contribution
DOTAS	Disclosure of tax avoidance schemes
DWP	Department for Work and Pensions
EFRBS	Employer-financed retirement benefit schemes
EIM	Employment Income Manual
EIS	Enterprise Investment Scheme
ESC	Extra statutory concession
FA	Finance Act
FAD	Flexi-access drawdown
FATCA	Foreign Account Tax Compliance Act
FCA	Financial Conduct Authority
FP	Fixed protection
FSA	Financial Services Authority
FSCS	Financial Services Compensation Scheme
FSMA 2000	Financial Services and Markets Act 2000
FURBS	Funded unapproved retirement benefit scheme
GAD	Government Actuary's Department
GDCV	Genuine diverse commercial vehicle
GMP	Guaranteed minimum pension
HMRC	HM Revenue & Customs
ICR	Initial capital requirement
ICTA 1988	Income and Corporation Taxes Act 1988
IHT	Inheritance tax
IHTA 1984	Inheritance Tax Act 1984
IHTM	Inheritance Tax Manual
IP	Individual protection
IPTM	Insurance Policyholder Taxation Manual
ISA	Individual savings account
ITA 2007	Income Tax Act 2007
ITEPA 2003	Income Tax (Earnings & Pensions) Act 2003
ITTOIA 2005	Income Tax (Trading & Other Income) Act 2005
LLP	Limited liability partnership
MPS	Money purchase scheme

NEST	National Employment Savings Trust
NIC	National Insurance contributions
PA	Pensions Act
PCLS	Pension commencement lump sum
PIB	Pension income builder
PIE	Pension increase exchange
PLA	Purchased life annuity
POAT	Pre-owned assets tax
PPF	Pension Protection Fund
PPP	Personal pension plan
PSA	Pension Schemes Act
Pt.	Part
PTM	Pensions Tax Manual
QNUPS	Qualifying non-UK pension schemes
QOPS	Qualifying overseas pension scheme
QROPS	Qualifying recognised overseas pension scheme
RAS	(Tax) relief at source
REIT	Real estate investment trust
RII	Retirement income insurance
ROPS	Recognised overseas pension scheme
RPS	Registered pension scheme
RPSM	Registered Pension Schemes Manual
RVF	Relevant valuation factor
S.	Section
SAYE	Save As You Earn
Sch.	Schedule
SDLT	Stamp duty land tax
SERPS	State Earnings-related Pension Scheme
SI	Statutory instrument
SIPP	Self-invested personal pension
SLA	Standard lifetime allowance
SSAS	Small self-administered scheme
TCGA 1992	Taxation of Chargeable Gains Act 1992
TIOPA 2010	Taxation (International and Other Provisions) Act 2010
ToPA 2014	Taxation of Pensions Act 2014
TSEM	Trusts, Settlements and Estates Manual
UFPLS	Uncrystallised funds pension lump sum
UKSC	United Kingdom Supreme Court
UURBS	Unfunded unapproved retirement benefit scheme
VCT	Venture Capital Trust

Table of contents

1. The tax benefits of registration

1.1 Overview

Pensions are often described as "deferred remuneration", a description which is helpful when explaining the way tax rules are applied to them. In effect, UK tax relief defers the tax that would otherwise be charged on income allocated to pension contributions rather than removing the charge altogether.

A pension may be payable to the individual who has been employed in the service of the state or a private enterprise or it may be paid to a dependant such as a surviving spouse or partner or a nominated beneficiary. It may be paid to an individual who is or has been self-employed or to his or her dependant or nominated beneficiary.

So far, so relatively straightforward, but the real difficulties with pensions derive not so much from the payment of the benefit (although the increasing range of benefit options has made that difficult enough), but the means of accruing or accumulating the retirement benefit. The vehicle for accruing and paying benefits is, of course, the pension scheme or policy.

This book will not spend much time describing public sector or public service schemes because for tax purposes, they are generally treated in the same way as private schemes. Their "constitution" is determined by legislation (mainly statutory instrument) and described in guides. Most public service schemes are "unfunded" rather like the state pension scheme under which we all benefit if we pay National Insurance contributions. This means that benefits, rather than being provided from a fund, are paid out of current tax revenues.

Most schemes are "registered" for tax purposes. The resistance to registration by members of some public service schemes has centred on the inevitable restrictions that this will bring. Never was there a better demonstration of the "carrot and stick" approach of pension tax rules.

References

Throughout this book there are references to legislation (mainly FA 2004 as amended). Reference is also made to guidance in HMRC manuals, mainly the *Registered Pension Schemes Manual* (RPSM) and *Pensions Tax Manual* (PTM) but also the *Employment Income Manual* (EIM) and the *Business Income Manual* (BIM). The RPSM has now been archived by HMRC.

A list of abbreviations is included at the start of the book.

Law date

The text is based on the law as at 1 August 2017. A consequence of the announcement of the 2017 General Election was the withdrawal of a number (but not all) of pension-related provisions that had been included in the *Finance (No. 2) Bill* (which became the *Finance Act*). Before Parliament was dissolved, the government indicated that if it won the General Election, the provisions would be reintroduced and in some cases backdated in effect to 6 April 2017 and this intention has subsequently been confirmed by a written parliamentary answer and publication of the draft *Finance Bill (No. 2)* 2017.

The previous government's proposals are described in the relevant text.

1.2 Statutory definitions of a pension scheme

Definitions of pension schemes appear in the *Pensions Acts* (sponsored by the DWP and concerned with the protection of members) and in FA 2004 (sponsored by the Treasury and concerned with the protection of tax revenues).

There are differences between the definitions, but none that need concern us in this book.

1.2.1 Definition for tax purposes

FA 2004, s. 150 describes a pension scheme as:

> "……… a scheme or other arrangements, comprised in one or more instruments or agreements, having or capable of having effect so as to provide benefits to or in respect of persons:

a. on retirement,
b. on death,
c. on having reached a particular age,
d. on the onset of serious ill-health or incapacity, or
e. in similar circumstances."

The section determines that an "occupational pension scheme" means a pension scheme established by an employer or employers and having or capable of having effect so as to provide benefits to or in respect of any or all of the employees of:

a. that employer or those employers; or
b. any other employer,

(whether or not it also has or is capable of having effect so as to provide benefits to or in respect of other persons).

The *Finance Act* 2013 recognised that the wording allowed the growth of so-called "family pension plans". They offered membership of an employer scheme and employer contributions for the employee's family as part of the employee's benefit package. The family members were not employed by the sponsoring employer and the plans were a way of circumventing the member's annual allowance (**Chapter 2**). The 2013 Act (amending ITEPA 2003, s. 308) requires the individual for whom the employer contribution is made to be employed by the sponsoring employer (although there may be a number of sponsoring employers who have established a single scheme together, typically an "industry-wide" scheme). The measure was effective from 6 April 2013.

Law: FA 2004, s. 150; FA 2013, s. 11

1.2.2 Definition for DWP purposes: occupational scheme

Under the *Pensions Act* 2004, if an occupational pension scheme has its main administration in the UK, the trustees or managers of the scheme must secure that the activities of the scheme are limited to retirement-benefit activities. There are civil penalties for a trustee or manager who does not observe the requirements of the section. Although compliance with the *Pensions Acts* is not directly a concern of HMRC, a tax-advantaged scheme is not otherwise sustainable unless it does comply.

Retirement-benefit activities are described in PA 2004 s. 255 as operations related to retirement benefits and activities arising from operations related to retirement benefits. Retirement benefits are in turn described as:

a. "benefits paid by reference to reaching, or expecting to reach, retirement, and
b. benefits that are supplementary to benefits within paragraph (a) and that are provided on an ancillary basis:
    i. in the form of payments on death, disability or termination of employment, or
    ii. in the form of support payments or services in the case of sickness, poverty or need, or death."

Law: PA 2004, s. 255

Interpreting s. 255

The reference to ancillary benefits has caused difficulties of interpretation in the past and the Pensions Regulator has provided guidance.

It remains possible to include the death benefit arrangement under the same trust as the retirement benefits, but the scheme cannot include death benefits for employees who will never qualify for retirement benefits (they are not "ancillary"), perhaps because the scheme is closed to new members and retirement benefits are provided under a personal pension scheme.

The Pensions Regulator's view is that:

a. Life cover can be provided under the same scheme as the retirement benefits even if the scheme is closed to new members and/or future accrual.
b. Life cover may not be provided for new members after the retirement benefits section has closed to new members.
c. It is possible for death benefits to be included under the same scheme as retirement benefits, even if the member does not qualify for the retirement benefits if retirement benefits are provided under another linked scheme. The link would have to be stronger than sharing a sponsoring employer.

d. The scheme may include members for death benefits only if they have opted-out of the retirement benefits section of the occupational scheme or declined to join.

e. Employees in a waiting period may join the death benefit section if they will realistically be able to join the retirement benefit section.

In order for an occupational scheme to be able to accept funding payments and to qualify for the tax benefits of a "registered pension scheme", it must be established under a trust. This is primarily to ensure that the employer is immediately "alienated" (as the pre-2006 Inland Revenue Practice Notes used to describe it) from contributions paid. Personal pension schemes may be subject to a trust or established under a contractual arrangement (which is effective because the contract is between the member and the provider even if the employer contributes).

The reference to reaching retirement in the *Pensions Act* has now been complemented by the reference in FA 2004, which also envisages benefits being taken on reaching a particular age. This is a significant change from the pre-2006 rules that unsuccessfully attempted to draw a link between retirement and taking benefits.

Law: PA 2004, s. 252(2)

1.3 Features of a registered pension scheme

Membership of an occupational scheme may be confined to employees of a single sponsoring employer or of a group of sponsoring employers who may have a common interest such as the industry in which they participate or location. Membership may also extend to self-employed individuals such as contractors. The most obvious example of self-employed individuals being members of an employer-sponsored scheme is that of NHS general medical practitioners and NHS dental practitioners although of course their scheme is the statutory NHS Pension Scheme. The change in legislation in 2004 obviated the need for extra-statutory concession A9, which allowed general practitioners to be members of the NHS Scheme although they were not NHS employees, and the concession was withdrawn.

A feature of occupational schemes is that they are established by the employer so their design, cost and benefits are determined by the employer. There is no formal way of setting up an occupational scheme, but if it is to accept further funding payments, it must be established under a trust.

A personal pension scheme is established by a provider or "establisher" and membership of the scheme is evidenced by an arrangement or arrangements between the scheme and the individual. It is described in PA 2004, s. 239(3) as a registered pension scheme that is not an occupational scheme. The law does not recognise the concept of a "plan" or "policy". This is a term used by providers and advisers to denote an arrangement or collection of arrangements. An employer may pay a contribution, but has no other formal involvement. Personal pension schemes may be established under trust or perhaps more commonly by way of a deed poll. A deed poll is simply a declaration and establishes a contractual relationship. The significance of the difference is not that great for most of us, but it could have an impact on the way death benefits are paid and taxed and in the area of personal bankruptcy.

The expression "work-based" scheme has only recently been widely recognised in the UK, but is widely used in EU legislation. It refers to any scheme, occupational or personal pension scheme, to which the employer provides access through a "direct payment facility". A direct payment facility is a facility for the employer to collect personal contributions from payroll and pass them directly to the scheme or scheme provider. Direct payment contributions may or may not supplement employer contributions.

A work-based scheme can therefore refer to an occupational scheme or a personal pension scheme. The distinction has more relevance to DWP rules than to tax rules.

Since the implementation of FA 2004 on 6 April 2006, there has been very little difference between the tax rules that apply to occupational schemes and personal pension schemes. The real distinctions become obvious in the areas of member protection (where the occupational scheme is mainly supervised by the Pensions Regulator) and consumer protection (where the marketing and management of personal pension schemes is supervised by the Financial Conduct Authority, previously the Financial Services Authority). Work-based schemes and their sponsors are further supervised by the DWP or Department for Business, Energy & Industrial Strategy under "pay and benefits" legislation such as the *Equality Act* 2010.

Law: PA 2004, s. 239(3); FA 2004

1.4 Registration of pension schemes

1.4.1 Requirement to register

In order to enjoy the full range of reliefs and allowances, the scheme must be registered with HMRC. An application to register may be made by an occupational scheme as described above or by a personal pension scheme (or stakeholder scheme) that has been established by a firm with permission to do so under the *Financial Services and Markets Act* 2000 and *Financial Services Act* 2012. This legislation was extended to self-invested personal pension schemes (investment-regulated schemes) in 2007, a development which prompted the Financial Services Authority (now the Financial Conduct Authority) to conduct a series of "thematic reviews" between 2009 and 2012, followed by "alerts" and letters, the latest being published on 21 July 2014. FCA intervention has led to a more conservative approach to investment by administrators of these schemes. The overriding theme of the correspondence from the FCA in particular is that the administrator has a duty of care and diligence in respect of the SIPP investments and cannot rely on the liability of the adviser (or the decision of the member).

Schemes that were approved for tax purposes immediately before 6 April 2006 were automatically registered the next day although they had an option to de-register within three months.

A feature of the 2004 tax legislation (as amended) is that it is far more prescriptive than was previously the case. There is little room for discretion on the part of HMRC. The legislation is supplemented by the HMRC *Pensions Tax Manual* (PTM) (previously *Registered Pension Schemes Manual* (RPSM, now archived by HMRC)) which is part of a library of manuals designed originally to provide support for HMRC staff.

Under the pre-2006 rules, occupational schemes were individually subject to "mandatory approval" (usually confined to investment companies), "discretionary approval" or "discretionary exempt approval" (allowing the full range of tax reliefs) by HMRC. Personal pension schemes were, in effect, authorised by the FSA (except investment-regulated schemes) and "approved by" HMRC.

1.4.2 *Instantaneous registration*

The system of registration introduced under FA 2004, s. 153 was far more streamlined. The scheme administrator made an application online and providing the procedure was followed and the questions on the form were answered, HMRC were required to register the scheme and this was instantaneous. The administrator was given a Pension Scheme Tax Reference (PSTR). HMRC did not wish to see the scheme documentation such as the rules. This is known as "process now, check later".

The registration requirements were accompanied by provisions for de-registration (FA 2004, s. 157) if the application for registration was inaccurate or if certain conditions were breached.

The application for registration had to be made when the scheme had been established and required the scheme administrator to make a declaration that:

- the scheme met all the conditions to be a registered pension;
- information supplied in the application was correct and complete to the best of the scheme administrator's knowledge and belief;
- the scheme administrator understood that false statements could lead to a penalty and/or prosecution, and could lead to the scheme being de-registered; and
- the instruments or agreements by which the scheme was constituted did not entitle any person to unauthorised payments.

Application for registration could only have been made by the scheme administrator, but many of the administrator's obligations to HMRC may subsequently have been delegated to a "scheme practitioner". Tax relief was allowed from the date of registration. HMRC guidance in the *Registered Pension Schemes Manual* stated that tax relief on contributions would not be available until the scheme was registered.

There was a right to appeal against a refusal to register in FA 2004, s. 156. However, this section did not anticipate the regulations which allowed electronic application. Under this process, an error message would have responded to any field not appropriately completed and the application would not have been treated as having been made until it had been corrected. Registration was then automatic and the need for an appeal process was obviated (because the application had not been refused).

It is the scheme that is registered and this entitles all members of the scheme (for example, an occupational scheme or a personal pension scheme) to tax relief. However, there are "special cases" for these purposes and the most notable is the "section 32" or "buy-out" policy. This is a deferred annuity offered by a life assurance company to which accrued rights may be transferred when a member leaves the scheme voluntarily or in the event of the scheme being wound up. The legislative reference is to FA 1981, s. 32. These arrangements will automatically be treated as registered pension schemes if the funds came from a registered pension scheme (which they will). There is no need to go through the registration process.

The policy will again be treated as automatically registered if:

- the buy-out policy existed before 6 April 2006;
- the benefits are not in payment; and
- the funds came from a tax-privileged scheme.

The tax rules for buy-out policies also cover policies under occupational money purchase schemes that have been assigned to the member after leaving pensionable service.

Law: FA 1981, s. 32; FA 2004, s. 153, 156, 157

1.4.3 Delayed registration – the 2014 Finance Act

The growth in so-called "pension liberation" schemes, and the practical difficulties in controlling them, forced the government to introduce measures in FA 2014 which hark back to the cumbersome and time-consuming process of approval. Indeed, one of the earliest provisions of the schedule is to allow HMRC time to consider new registration applications. The measures appear in FA 2014, s. 46 and Sch. 7.

Paragraph 2(3) of the schedule provides that HMRC may refuse to register a pension scheme where it appears to HMRC that the main purpose of the scheme is not to provide pension benefits or that the scheme administrator is not a fit and proper person to be the administrator. Existing provisions relating to failure to provide information, the provision of inaccurate information and obstructing HMRC officials are extended to cover documents provided in support of the application. HMRC are given further powers to request information and documents, and a power to enter business premises. An information notice may be served on an administrator or third party (copy to the administrator). Non-compliance may lead to registration being refused. Third parties may be subject to a financial penalty.

There are substantial penalties if the application to register contains a material inaccuracy or a false declaration and the administrator did not take reasonable care, or was aware of the inaccuracy but did not inform HMRC.

If the administrator does not receive a decision within six months, then he or she may appeal as if the application had been refused. All these measures include an appeal process.

The measures are effective for any application on or after 20 March 2014.

Complementary measures allow a scheme to be de-registered if the main purpose of the scheme is not to provide pension benefits or if the adminstrator is not fit and proper. These measures are also effective from 20 March 2014 although deregistration on grounds of the administrator not being fit and proper is only effective from 1 September 2014.

Law: FA 2004, s. 153; FA 2014, s. 46 and Sch. 7

1.5 Registration – transition in 2006

1.5.1 Automatic registration

Schemes that enjoyed tax privileges at 5 April 2006 were automatically registered the following day under FA 2004, Sch. 36, para. 1(1)(a-g). As part of the simplification agenda, a range of schemes previously treated as different from each other were combined under the same set of rules without the need to apply for registration. They comprised:

a. A retirement benefit scheme (also known as an occupational pension scheme) approved under ICTA 1988, Pt. 14, Ch. 1. If part of the scheme was approved, then that part of the scheme was treated as registered.
b. A personal pension scheme approved under ICTA 1988, Pt. 14, Ch. 4. This category included stakeholder and group personal pension schemes.
c. A retirement annuity contract or retirement annuity trust (for groups of individuals) approved under ICTA 1988, Pt. 14, Ch. 3.
d. Relevant statutory schemes that are not approved schemes (public sector schemes such as the NHS Pension Scheme. It also includes some schemes that were not statutory schemes, but were treated as if they were).
e. Parliamentary pension funds or schemes.
f. Superannuation schemes approved before 1970 ("old code" schemes) that had been adopted as new code schemes if contributions had been paid since 5 April 1980.
g. Certain deferred annuities such as buy-out policies.

Law: FA 2004, Sch. 36 para. 1(1)

1.5.2 Opting out

Scheme administrators were able to opt out of registration if they gave written notice before 6 April 2006. There would have been significant tax consequences, partly because the only way to opt out was to request HMRC to withdraw registration. The scheme administrator was subject to a de-registration charge of 40 per cent of the value of assets immediately before 6 April 2006 and possibly other charges.

Schemes that were not approved at 5 April 2006 or had previously lost approval were not automatically registered, but could apply for registration after that date.

1.5.3 *Importing pre-2006 rules*

The changes introduced with effect from 6 April 2006 were so radical that they were bound to be inconsistent with some scheme rules drafted under the previous tax regime. In particular there would have been instances when a previously allowable transaction was no longer allowed under the new rules or where an earlier rule was unduly restricted under the new rules. *The Registered Pension Schemes (Modification of the Rules of Existing Schemes) Regulations,* 2006 (SI 2006/364) had the effect of treating a number of features of the tax approval rules as being automatically imported into the rules of existing pension schemes that automatically became registered pension schemes on 6 April 2006. The effect was to preserve the way in which the scheme rules were applied before 6 April 2006.

By way of example, the approval rules may have included an earnings cap as a reflection of legislation at the time. The effect of the regulations was to preserve the earnings cap in the scheme rules although it had been lifted generally by FA 2004. This measure was very important to defined benefit schemes that would have had to change their rules with undue haste or seen their scheme funding increase as high-earning members observed the cap being removed from their pensions. The regulations did not apply to the following existing pension schemes that automatically became registered pension schemes:

- schemes that adopted rule amendments before 6 April 2006 that came into effect on and after that date, where those amendments had a corresponding effect to all of the modifications in the regulations;
- schemes with rules that were framed in such a way that no amendment was necessary to reflect all of the modifications in the regulations; or
- schemes that made rule amendments during the transitional period that stated that all of the modification regulations that applied to that scheme no longer applied to the scheme.

The regulations modified the rules of an existing pension scheme that automatically became a registered pension scheme on 6 April

2006 for a transitional period. This transitional period ended on the earlier of:

- the first date after 5 April 2006 on which rule amendments in relation to such an existing scheme took effect that stated that the modification regulations no longer applied to the scheme; and
- the end of the tax year 2010-11.

A rule amendment adopted on or after 6 April 2006 and which stated that the modification regulations no longer applied could only mean that none of the modifications applied. The regulations did not allow a selective approach by disapplying just some of the modifications: they take an "all or nothing" approach.

1.6 The benefits of registration

The tax benefits of registered pension schemes are famously generous within the allowances specified in FA 2004.

1.6.1 Employer contributions

Employer contributions may be treated as a deductible business expense for the employer if they can be shown to be for the purposes of trade (or in the case of an investment company, for the management of the business). The basic rules of deductibility of employer costs appear in ITTOIA 2005 Part 2 (trading income) and CTA 2009 Parts 2 (investment business) and 3 (trading), but those sections are specifically applied to pension contributions by FA 2004, s. 196; this also includes a provision that contributions may be deductible even though they may otherwise have been treated as being of a capital nature (and therefore not otherwise deductible against trading income). In effect, HMRC will use their discretion, as discussed in **Chapter 2**.

Law: FA 2004, s. 196; ITTOIA 2005, Pt. 2; CTA 2009 Pt. 2, 3

1.6.2 Tax on the member

Employer contributions will not be taxed on the member to the extent that they fall within the annual allowance.

Member contributions may be relieved against the individual's highest marginal rates of income tax to the extent that they fall within the annual allowance and the annual limit for relief.

The principle behind the operation of tax relief on pension schemes is often described as "exempt, exempt, taxed" referring chronologically to input, fund and benefits. At the time of the 2015 summer Budget, the Treasury issued a consultation ("Strengthening the incentive to save: a consultation on pensions tax relief") that proposed a review of the way tax relief operated. One of the options proposed is that relief should be withdrawn from input and benefits should be exempt (similar to the Individual Savings Account). This would require significant transitional effort and a supplement to the benefit to compensate for loss of 25% of the benefits which are relieved at the input stage *and* benefit stage (tax-free pension commencement lump sum).

In his 2016 Budget, the Chancellor of the Exchequer appeared to withdraw the option to change the incidence of tax, but introduced the "lifetime ISA", described later in this chapter and implemented on 6 April 2017. The relevant legislation is the *Savings (Government Contributions) Act* 2017

Law: FA 2004, s. 188, 201; ITEPA 2003, s. 307, 308

1.6.3 Taxation of pension funds

Pension funds are not generally subject to UK tax on income from investments and capital gains. In effect, this provision also applies to funds managed by life assurance companies under the heading of "pensions business" although the authority falls under different tax legislation. Funds are accountable for tax on overseas investments over which UK tax law has no jurisdiction and are also subject to VAT and stamp duty.

Law: FA 2004, s. 186, 187; TCGA 1992, s. 271

1.6.4 Taxation of member benefits

There are generous tax-free lump sums available to the member in the event of the member taking "retirement" benefits to the extent that they are within the lifetime allowance.

Law: FA 2004, s. 166

There are generous tax-free lump sums payable to beneficiaries on the death of the member before taking those benefits and before age 75 to the extent that they are within the lifetime allowance.

Law: FA 2004, s. 168

The pension is taxed as pension income (the same as earned income), and is not subject to National Insurance contributions. The main significance of this treatment is that it is taxed as income immediately after application of the personal allowance, but before savings and investment income. Pension income therefore, just like earned income, will erode the savings rate band, but the personal savings allowance (£1,000 for a basic rate taxpayer and £500 for a higher rate taxpayer) will be unaffected.

Law: ITEPA 2003, s. 579A-579D, 683(3)

1.7 Disclosure of tax avoidance schemes

The requirement to disclose certain schemes to HMRC was introduced in August 2004 and extended in August 2006.

It is commonly said that tax avoidance is lawful and evasion is illegal. This is far too simplistic and unhelpful and the subject is too complicated to discuss in this chapter. Broadly speaking, individuals are allowed to structure their affairs in a way which would, amongst other objectives, minimise their exposure to tax. However, tax avoidance measures will not succeed if their predominant objective is to save tax rather than to further a commercial objective. There is a raft of cases that have determined the boundaries and many disputes are well-intentioned differences of opinion. The "penalty" for losing the argument with HMRC in these cases (most of which do not reach the courts) is likely to be a tax bill, interest and a civil penalty.

Evasion implies fraudulently breaking the tax code and certain required disclosures that may accompany it and there may be criminal penalties.

As a means of reducing legal fees, the DOTAS (disclosure of tax avoidance schemes) regime was introduced. There is detailed guidance on the HMRC website.

The tax arrangement must be disclosed if:

- it will or might be expected to enable a person to obtain a tax advantage;
- the tax advantage is or might be expected to be one of the arrangement's main benefits; and
- it falls within one or more "hallmarks".

The hallmarks are:

- wishing to keep the arrangements confidential from a competitor;
- wishing to keep the arrangements confidential from HMRC;
- arrangements for which a premium fee could be expected;
- arrangements that are standardised tax products;
- arrangements that are loss schemes;
- certain leasing arrangements.

Disclosure is normally required of the "promoter".

Registered pension schemes are either schemes that were originally approved prior to 6 April 2006 or schemes that have been registered and in respect of which declarations and disclosures have been made. They are not required to be disclosed although, if they are part of a larger arrangement, the arrangement might have to be disclosed. In general, however, retirement planning with the use of registered pension schemes does not require disclosure.

1.8 Key features

1.8.1 Scheme constitution

Rights and obligations under trust-based schemes are described in the scheme rules which will also include a description of tax rules and allowances. The trust is a shorter more technical document that describes the terms of the trust by reference to employer, trustees, members and beneficiaries.

Under contract-based schemes, the scheme rights and obligations are again described in the rules and the scheme is usually established under a deed poll (which enables it to avoid the onerous requirements of a trust, but also some of the requirements of a more conventional contract).

Deferred annuity contracts (retirement annuity contracts and "buy-out" policies) are simply evidenced by policies and subject to policy provisions.

1.8.2 Sponsors of pension scheme legislation

Pension scheme legislation is largely sponsored by two government departments.

The Department for Work and Pensions is concerned with scheme governance and the protection of members of "work-based" schemes. Put simply, it wants to ensure that employers deliver on their promise. Supervision of work-based schemes is undertaken by the Pensions Regulator although individual activities such as investment may fall under the control of the Financial Conduct Authority.

The DWP is also responsible for the provision of state scheme benefits and by implication, contracted-out benefits (where benefits from the state second pension or SERPS are forgone when an individual is a member of a contracted-out occupational scheme).

The Treasury and HMRC are responsible for building, maintaining and enforcing a framework of tax reliefs and charges. The Treasury has overall responsibility for financial services legislation that deals with the marketing and conduct of investment firms and has established the Financial Conduct Authority.

The topic of pensions is so far-reaching, however, that it involves other governing institutions. The Department for Business, Energy & Industrial Strategy inevitably has a say in the running of pension schemes because occupational schemes and other work-based schemes are part of the employment contract and more specifically, as the case of *Barber v GRE* 1990 confirmed, a pension benefit falls under the definition of "pay" to which the *Equal Pay Act* 1970 and many other equality measures such as the *Equality Act* 2010 apply.

The occupational pension rules may be resolved by internal resolution (*Pensions Acts* 1995 and 2004), by the Pensions Advisory Service, employment tribunals, the Pensions Ombudsman, the Financial Ombudsman, the UK courts (if you have substantial resources) and the European Court. Although much of pension law is encoded in statute, many disputes involve the more general rules of contract and trusts.

Tax disputes, on the other hand, will be determined by HMRC and the tax Tribunals or again, the courts.

Disputes involving personal pension schemes are most likely to be resolved by the Financial Ombudsman.

1.8.3 Funding bases

A fundamental distinction between different types of occupational scheme can be made in respect of funding. The two main options have been "defined benefit" - which includes final salary and career average schemes - and "defined contribution". Part 1 of the *Pension Schemes Act* 2015 added a third category, defined ambition schemes, and broadened the definition of defined contribution schemes to enable them to pool investment risk. Although it has hitherto been common to interchange the terms "money purchase" and "defined contribution", the facility to pool investment risk is incompatible with the definition of money purchase funding as described by the 2011 *Pensions Act* (see below).

The categorisation of schemes in this way follows that of DWP legislation. The tax legislation takes a slightly different route. In particular, whereas the DWP legislation distinguishes between defined contribution and money purchase schemes, tax law regards them as the same.

Defined benefit schemes

Simply described, a defined benefit scheme defines the member's retirement benefit in the scheme rules according to a formula which will comprise an accrual rate, years of pensionable service and pensionable pay. Inherent in the description are a number of definitions that are described by the scheme rules such as pension age, pensionable service and pensionable salary.

The defined benefit scheme does not define the emerging pension in cash terms (it cannot without knowing what pensionable pay will be at the benefit date), but it can target a pension as a proportion of pay. With the introduction of legislation in the 1980s and 1990s to protect the benefits of the early leaver, nearly all the risk associated with these schemes falls on the employer, and in particular the risk that investment returns will fall short of expectations and will require a higher contribution and the risk that members will live longer than expected, requiring the pension to be paid for longer, also causing stress on the fund.

A feature of defined benefit schemes is that they do not earmark specific pension "pots" for individual members. Rather there is one fund, the required size of which is determined by the scheme liabilities ("technical provisions" in the legislation) including future benefits.

Money purchase schemes

These schemes (also described as "defined contribution" or "DC" schemes) allow the employer to define a contribution, usually as a percentage of current pay, and benefits will be dependent on the size of the accumulated fund at retirement and the rate at which it is converted to pension. The size of the fund is in turn a product of the value of contributions paid and when they are paid and investment returns after charges. The rate of income will depend on the type of pension taken: an annuity rate will be determined by mortality risk, overheads and the performance of the underlying, generally fixed interest investments such as gilts and other bonds.

Under FA 2004, money purchase schemes that are not cash balance schemes are described as "other money purchase schemes".

The definition for tax purposes appears in FA 2004, s. 152 and is not very helpful (and to an extent has been overtaken by events):

> "(2) For the purposes of this Part an arrangement is a 'money purchase arrangement' at any time if, at that time, all the benefits that may be provided to or in respect of the member under the arrangement are cash balance benefits or other money purchase benefits."

and

> "(4) In this Part 'money purchase benefits', in relation to a member of a pension scheme, means benefits the rate or amount of which is calculated by reference to an amount available for the provision of benefits to or in respect of the member (whether the amount so available is calculated by reference to payments made under the pension scheme by the

> member or any other person in respect of the member or any other factor)."

The contrasting feature of a money purchase scheme is that each member will usually be allocated a specific "pot" or arrangement.

Pensions Act 2011, s. 29 added a definition of money purchase benefits as *Pension Schemes Act* 1993, s. 181B. The section was commenced on 24 July 2014 but is backdated to January 1997.

The definition states that:

> "2. A benefit other than a pension in payment falls within this section if its rate or amount is calculated solely by reference to assets which (because of the nature of the calculation) must necessarily suffice for the purposes of its provision to or in respect of the member.
>
> 3. A benefit which is a pension in payment falls within this section if:
>
>   a. its provision to or in respect of the member is secured by an annuity contract or insurance policy made or taken out with an insurer, and
>
>   b. at all times before coming into payment the pension was a benefit falling within this section by virtue of subsection (2).
>
> 4. For the purposes of subsection (2) it is immaterial if the calculation of the rate or amount of the benefit includes deductions for administrative expenses or commission.
>
> 5. In this section references to a pension do not include income withdrawal or dependants' income withdrawal (within the meaning of paragraphs 7 and 21 of Sch. 28 to the FA 2004)."

A feature of the definition is that it is impossible for a money purchase scheme to fall into deficit because the pension may only be calculated by reference to assets etc. The scheme may invest in assets that offer a protected or guaranteed return, but this will not create a *scheme* deficit.

Note that regulations allow existing schemes time to manage the change of definition.

For tax purposes there are real consequences of a scheme being treated as a defined benefit scheme, not least of which is that the pension may only be a scheme pension and this is discussed at **4.5.3**.

Law: *Pensions Schemes Act* 1993, s. 181B; *Pensions Act* 2011, s. 29; *The Pensions Act* 2011 *(Transitional, Consequential and Supplementary Provisions) Regulations* 2014 (SI 2014/1711)

Cash balance schemes

The statutory definition of a cash balance scheme appears in FA 2004, s. 152:

> "(2) For the purposes of this Part an arrangement is a 'money purchase arrangement' at any time if, at that time, all the benefits that may be provided to or in respect of the member under the arrangement are cash balance benefits or other money purchase benefits."

and

> "(5) In this Part 'cash balance benefits' means benefits the rate or amount of which is calculated by reference to an amount available for the provision of benefits to or in respect of the member calculated otherwise than wholly by reference to payments made under the arrangement by the member or by any other person in respect of the member (or transfers or other credits)."

A cash balance scheme is one under which a lump sum (but not a pension) is defined and allocated from time to time to members by the employer according to the performance of the employer over a year. The fund is then re-valued to pension age. When benefits are taken, the fund comprising the accrued lump sum payments is converted to providing a pension. The cash balance scheme is not that common and tends to be industry-specific such as the banking industry and the retail industry. For tax purposes it is usually treated as a money purchase scheme, but for DWP purposes members of the cash balance scheme enjoy all the (more rigorous) protections of a defined benefit scheme.

A further complication is that the tax legislation, in order to distinguish cash balance schemes from other money purchase schemes uses that terminology: "cash balance schemes" and "other money purchase schemes". Most commentary will be about "other money purchase schemes" because they are by far the most common variant.

Hybrid schemes

A hybrid scheme is a scheme that offers a mixture of money purchase and defined benefits. So, for example, the member may accrue pension based on a fraction of remuneration with the addition of a type of "bonus" in years in which investment returns have been especially good. The additional pension is sometimes referred to as an "underpin". Alternatively, the scheme may offer a benefit based on the size of a fund subject to a minimum pension being available (that might be a guaranteed minimum pension as a consequence of the member having been contracted-out of the state scheme before April 1997).

Unfunded schemes

It is rare to come across unfunded schemes in the private sector. Their use is restricted to "top-up" benefits for senior managers and the schemes are little more than a promise to pay directly from the employer's resources at retirement. These schemes are not registered (employer-financed retirement benefit schemes).

Shared risk (defined ambition) schemes

The *Pension Schemes Act* 2015 addresses the difficult choice that the sponsor of an employer-sponsored scheme faces: either to establish a scheme on a defined benefit basis (where the pension "promise" requires the sponsor to carry the risk of adverse investment returns, costs and improved mortality) or to establish a scheme on a defined contribution basis (where the risks are undertaken by the member, because there is no benefit promise).

The Act replaces the two statutory categories of money purchase and non-money purchase with defined benefit (full pensions promise during accumulation), shared risk (pensions promise related to some of the benefits during accumulation and also known as "defined ambition") and money purchase (no pensions promise during accumulation). Regulations were to be made to ensure that other designs would have been included within the statutory framework. The government has suspended legislative progress because of the burden already placed on the administration of schemes by recent legislation.

The Act envisages that pension promises may be made by a third-party and regulations will seek to enforce these obligations.

Some of the designs envisaged in the consultation document that preceded the Bill and which were largely identified in other jurisdictions are:

Money-back (MBG) or capital investment return guarantees

These ensure that members receive the same as they contributed, or their contributions plus a minimum investment return.

There are ways in which the guarantees can be provided relatively cheaply, but only if assumptions about minimum years of contributions and a pre-set investment strategy are maintained. The guarantees only relate to size of fund and not the retirement income.

Retirement income insurance (RII)

This uses part of the fund to purchase an income insurance that in turn insures a minimum level of income. It will grow each year as further insurance is purchased. At retirement, the insurance is triggered if the member lives long enough to exhaust his or her fund.

The pension income builder (PIB)

Part of the contribution purchases a guaranteed deferred annuity and the balance goes to a common pooled fund that is invested in riskier assets. The consultation paper suggests that the annuity would be provided by the fund, not an insurance company. This model implies risk-sharing in respect of the pooled fund.

The collective benefits scheme

The legislation allows for the development of collective (defined contribution) benefits.

This scheme pools all member contributions in a single fund.

Where, in all circumstances, the rate or amount of the benefit payable to or in respect of a member depends entirely on:

(a) the amount available to pay that member's and other members' benefits; and

(b) factors used to determine what proportion of that amount is available for the provision of the particular benefit,

these benefits are defined as "collective" in the Act. The definition also provides that a benefit which is a money purchase benefit is not a collective benefit (because a money purchase arrangement is a defined contribution arrangement that provides benefits only for the designated member and only to the extent of the value of the assets in the arrangement).

The Act provides that regulations may require that trustees or managers of pension schemes offering collective benefits set targets in relation to the rate or amount of those benefits. In particular, regulations can be made about, amongst other things, the way that targets are expressed, recorded and published. The intention is that members of a scheme with collective benefits should be provided with a reasonable estimate of the benefits that they can expect to receive from the scheme; in the absence of a well defined pot over which the individual has clear ownership, the target is a way of illustrating for the member what they might receive. The Act provides for regulations to require trustees or managers of a scheme to obtain an actuarial certificate confirming that the actuary is of the opinion that the probability of the assets being sufficient to meet the initial targets is in line with the level set out in the regulations.

Most of the options include holding lower-risk assets during the growth phase and close to retirement. The PIB and collective benefit structures do hold higher risk assets which could offset the impact of holding low-risk assets earlier. Most of the models involve a trade-off between average returns and upside and downside risk which is the risk that individuals would have an income in retirement that is higher or lower than expected.

Law: *Pensions Act* 2011, s. 29; *Pension Schemes Act* 2015, Parts 1, 2

1.9 Terminology and FA 2004

There is a great deal of terminology in FA 2004 with which the practitioner must become familiar. Equally important, though, is to become familiar with the terminology in the legislation. There are many examples of misunderstanding being caused by an irrepressible urge to paraphrase legislative terms which though occasionally ugly do have the merit of representing a "common language".

The scheme: The scheme is the means by which the trustees or scheme manager (contract schemes) accumulate contributions, transfer values and investment returns, and provide members and dependants with retirement and death benefits.

The arrangement: There is no helpful definition of "arrangement" in the tax legislation as it relates to pensions although there are many references (such as FA 2004, s. 152 which describes the types of arrangements to which the legislation refers rather than what an arrangement is). An arrangement is simply an entity that can be treated differently from other arrangements. A scheme may comprise more than one arrangement. Note that the DWP does not recognise the sub-division of schemes into arrangements. In other words, under DWP rules there is never any sub-division of schemes.

The policy or ***plan***: The policy or plan as a term has no significance in tax legislation. An individual who applies for membership of a personal pension scheme, for instance, will be allocated one or more arrangements and membership will be evidenced by the policy (plan) schedule.

Rights and ownership: This is especially important in the area of money purchase schemes that invest in member-directed investments such as SIPP and SSAS (where direct investment has been directed or influenced by a member). It is for the trustee or manager to deliver a benefit according to the scheme rules and if appropriate the policy provisions. A means of delivering the benefit is to invest the proceeds of contributions and realise the value of assets when benefits become payable. However, the member does not have proprietary rights in the assets of the scheme, but beneficial rights which may be calculated by reference to assets and the scheme rules. In other words, although it may be convenient so to do, an individual's benefit may not necessarily be paid from a specific asset.

1.10 Other categorisations

1.10.1 Contributory or non-contributory

A contributory scheme is a work-based scheme where the employee is required to make a contribution as a condition of membership and entitlement to employer sponsored benefits.

1.10.2 Contracted-out or not contracted-out

The facility for employers to contract occupational pension schemes out of the state earnings-related pension (the additional pension) was withdrawn with effect from 6 April 2016 when the new single-tier state pension was implemented. Individuals who were entitled to guaranteed minimum pensions on that date retained those rights. The government would like to have abolished guaranteed minimum pensions, but was unable to surmount the technical hurdles and opted instead for making a streamlined "modification" process available.

Under a contracted-out scheme, the employer elected to contract out members of a defined benefit scheme from the additional (earnings-related) state pension. The "contract" allowed the employer and employee to pay lower rates of National Insurance (reduced by a "rebate") on the condition that alternative benefits were provided by the private scheme. Until April 1997, the alternative benefit had to be in the form of a guaranteed minimum pension (GMP) which roughly equated to what the state would otherwise have provided in addition to the basic state pension. Those benefits are preserved, but the requirement from April 1997 has been for the scheme as a whole to meet a reference scheme test. The test is more a test of quality (the range of benefits) rather than quantity (which was the case with the GMP test).

1.10.3 Retirement annuity contract or personal pension scheme

Personal pension schemes are the successors to retirement annuity contracts. Retirement annuity contracts are individual deferred annuity policies and were introduced by FA 1956. They were replaced in 1988 by personal pension schemes although contributions could continue to the original arrangements. Each provider will generally offer one scheme and invite individuals, employed or self-employed to become members. Personal pension arrangements are similar in effect to retirement annuity contracts, but are different in one important respect which is that contributions may be made by employers rather than just the plan holder. The significance is that employer contributions are not subject to National Insurance (because contributions are not treated as "pay").

1.10.4 Integrated scheme

The scheme is designed to provide a total defined benefit based on combining the state scheme and the private scheme.

1.10.5 Stakeholder pension schemes

Stakeholder pension schemes were introduced in 2001. They were money purchase in design and mostly established as personal pension schemes. A few were set up as occupational schemes. They had three distinguishing features:

a. They were subject to a "CAT standard". The acronym referred to charges, access and terms. Charges were restricted to being a percentage of fund (originally 1% of fund a year taken daily, latterly 1.5% of fund a year in the first 10 years and then 1% of fund again taken daily). Access could not be denied to any applicant who paid £20 singly or regularly on the grounds that the contribution was too small. The scheme could not apply any penalties for early retirement, stopping contributions or transferring funds to another tax-advantaged scheme.
b. Most employers with five or more employees were required to provide access to a stakeholder scheme or a suitable alternative. This meant the provision of a direct

payment facility and designation of a scheme and employee access to information about it. The legislation did not require the employer to pay a contribution and indeed this obligation (to designate a scheme) was abolished on 1 October 2012 to coincide with the start of automatic enrolment (although the payment facility must continue to be provided for those who were contributing before that date).

c. The Financial Services Authority introduced a streamlined computer-based means of applying for membership of a stakeholder scheme.

Stakeholder schemes targeted the modestly paid who, it was thought, were unfairly disadvantaged by the charging structures of conventional products. They did drive down charges and changed the types of charge, but did little to improve the number of savers.

It is always important to remember that stakeholder pension schemes were treated for tax purposes as any other type of registered pension scheme.

1.10.6 Automatic enrolment and NEST

Automatic enrolment is being introduced in stages (by employer size and, latterly, PAYE reference) from 1 October 2012. It requires nearly all jobholders who are aged at least 22 and no more than state pension age to be automatically enrolled in a qualifying scheme. Individuals who are directors of companies to which the automatic enrolment scheme relates need not be automatically enrolled, and nor do office-holders such as police officers in England and Wales. Similarly, members of limited liability partnerships may be invited to join at the employer's discretion if they are not treated as employees by HMRC.

The qualifying scheme is simply one that can meet the requirements of automatic enrolment and that has been registered with the Pensions Regulator. One of those requirements is that the employer must ensure that a contribution is paid to the scheme although some of that contribution can be recovered from the member and HMRC.

The automatic enrolment requirements and the National Employment Savings Trust (NEST) were created by DWP policy and legislation. They do not in any way amend or modify the tax legislation for pensions. Both NEST and other qualifying schemes are subject to the same tax rules as other pensions which may not so qualify.

The qualifying scheme may be a defined benefit, defined contribution, cash balance or hybrid occupational scheme established by the employer or it may be a work-based personal pension scheme, that is a grouped personal pension scheme for which the employer provides a facility to collect contributions through a payroll facility.

NEST is a registered pension scheme and enjoys all the tax reliefs available to registered pension schemes. It is established on a money purchase basis and on which charges are especially low (0.3% of the fund per annum taken daily and a single contribution charge of 1.8% of the contribution until the NEST Corporation has paid off establishment financing from the government). The scheme offers a range of target date funds and also bespoke funds.

NEST does not offer a member-directed investment facility and does not offer loans.

NEST was restricted in its early years. It could not accept transfers from other schemes, and contributions were limited to £4,900 in 2016-17. The significance of this is that worthwhile provision for higher earners would have required contributions to be made to other schemes either instead of or in addition to NEST contributions. The restrictions were lifted on 1 April 2017.

Automatic enrolment differs from employer stakeholder obligations in two main ways:

- the worker is automatically enrolled before he or she has a chance to opt out (rather than being invited to join); and
- the employer is required to make a contribution and can require one from the member as a condition of membership.

The introduction of automatic enrolment means that the employer must identify at least five categories of employee in order to comply with the legislation:

- jobholders already in a qualifying scheme;
- eligible jobholders who working or ordinarily work in the UK, aged at least 22, but under state pension age and with earnings of at least £10,000 (the earnings "trigger") in 2017-18 (these employees must be automatically enrolled);
- non-eligible jobholders between the ages of 16 and 74 who usually work in the UK and who have qualifying earnings that are below the earnings "trigger". They may opt in to the scheme in which case the employer must make a contribution;
- non-eligible jobholders who are between the ages of 16 and 22 or who are between the ages of state pension age and 74 with earnings that are at least the earnings "trigger". The employer may choose to admit these individuals to the scheme. An employee can demand to be admitted in which case the employer must make a contribution;
- entitled workers who are aged between 16 and 74, who ordinarily work in the UK, but who do not have qualifying earnings (£5,876 in 2017-18). The entitled worker has a right to join a scheme, but the employer is not required to contribute although the employer must provide a means of deducting contributions and paying them to the scheme.

These groups are known as "jobholders".

The earnings "trigger" is £10,000 in 2017-18, but the contribution is based on earnings between £5,876 and £45,000 in 2017-18.

Earnings in this context are defined as any of the following payable in connection with the person's employment:

- salary, wages, commission, bonuses, overtime;
- statutory sick pay, statutory maternity pay, statutory adoption pay;
- statutory shared parental pay.

However, like stakeholder pension schemes, there are no special tax considerations that apply to automatic enrolment schemes or NEST that do not apply to other registered pension schemes.

Law: PA 2008, Part 1; SI 2010/772 *(The Occupational and Personal Pension Schemes (Automatic Enrolment) Regulations* 2010) (as amended); SI 2015/178 *(The National Employment Savings Trust (Amendment) Order* 2015); SI 2017/394 *(The Automatic Enrolment (Earnings Trigger and Qualifying Earnings Band) Order* 2017); SI 2016/311 *(The Occupational and Personal Pension Schemes (Automatic Enrolment) (Miscellaneous Amendments) Regulations* 2016)

1.11 What makes pension schemes different from other forms of saving?

Pension schemes are simply another form of long-term saving, but they have distinctive features that mark them out as being different from other savings vehicles:

1. The range of tax reliefs is unique as befits a set of incentives that is designed to encourage saving for terms that could be at least 40 years.
2. A condition of tax reliefs is that the rules applying to how and when benefits are taken is relatively prescriptive (and indeed retirement benefits are generally only available from at least age 55).
3. There are strong protections for members of occupational schemes that are designed to ensure that each period of active membership carries an entitlement to benefits that is protected by legislation and supervised by the DWP, the Pensions Regulator and the Pensions Ombudsman.
4. Employers may make contributions directly to a registered scheme without there being a liability to National Insurance or tax.

On the whole, the debate about whether a registered pension scheme offers the best solution for an individual (or employer) is not so much between right and wrong as what is appropriate for a particular individual. Having been appraised of the individual's circumstances and objectives, it may be useful to consider a number of questions:

Feature	Registered Pension Scheme	Comments
Is income tax/corporation tax relief available on input or output?	Relief within allowances on all contributions. 25% of the fund is relieved on input, within the fund and on output.	ISAs offer tax relief on output. EIS and VCT can offer limited relief on input.
Are funds tax-advantaged in respect of income and capital gains?	Free of UK tax on income and capital gains, but dividend tax credits are not recoverable.	ISAs similar to pensions. Limited relief for EIS/VCTs.
Are the funds IHT-advantaged?	Generally free of IHT and payments by-pass the estate. On death before 75, benefits are also generally free of income tax.	ISA funds go to the estate or may be inherited by a spouse or civil partner (by increasing the survivor's allowance to the value of the "inherited" fund).
How flexible are the investment options?	Investments may be collectives or member-directed. The latter are controlled e.g. generally no residential property or other assets used by the member or connected persons.	ISA funds are more limited.
How convenient are the input facilities?	Very flexible – monthly, quarterly, annual or single contributions.	Generally flexible as pensions, but more sophisticated investments require large lump sums.

Feature	Registered Pension Scheme	Comments
How flexible are the "benefit" facilities?	Fairly inflexible: benefits not generally available until at least 55. Benefits must be restricted within fairly narrow parameters e.g. generally lifetime income, but up to 25% lump sum. Rules introduced in 2015 have relaxed some of these restrictions for money purchase schemes, for which the only real restriction is when benefits may be taken.	Most other investments allow proceeds as a lump sum at any time (subject to a minimum short term to be tax-efficient in the case of VCT/EIS).
Can the employer provide direct input?	Yes.	The input will either be treated for tax purposes as a gift or remuneration.
Are there protections for members/ investors?	Under the *Financial Services Act* 2012, the Pensions Regulator, Pensions and Financial Services Ombudsman, Pension Protection Fund (defined benefit schemes only), Financial Services Compensation Scheme.	Most of these apply to other forms of saving excepting Pensions Regulator.
Are there benefit restrictions/caps?	Yes. (See annual allowance, annual limit and lifetime allowance, for example.)	Generous reliefs, outside the general £50,000 cap on income tax reliefs, also apply to other investments.

In its 2016 Budget and in the *Savings (Government Contributions) Act* 2017, the government proposed the introduction of "lifetime ISAs" to be available from April 2017. At the same time, the government appeared to withdraw its proposal to change the basis of tax relief on pension arrangements (from "exempt, exempt, taxed" to "taxed, exempt, exempt").

The lifetime ISA offers tax-advantaged funds and tax-free output whether taken as income or as a lump sum. However, input to a maximum of £4,000 a year (no monthly maximum) will be supplemented by a 25% "government bonus".

The lifetime ISA account must be opened between the ages of 18 and 40 and the bonus will be available on input before age 50.

The lifetime ISA limit will be part of the overall ISA limit, which is £20,000 in 2017/18.

The lifetime ISA fund may be used towards the deposit on a first home valued at up to £450,000.

Alternatively it may be used to provide a retirement fund. This means that it will be available for any purpose from age 60. It may be withdrawn earlier than age 60 and other than to provide a first home deposit, but the bonus (and any growth on it) will be lost and there will be a 5% charge on the value of funds.

1.12 Death benefits

It is normal to distinguish between "death in service" (more accurately death before retirement benefits are taken) and "death in retirement" (death after retirement benefits are taken) benefits. Death in service benefits in respect of a defined benefit scheme are provided by a separate group life assurance contract. The sum assured is applied to providing lump sums and/or dependants' pensions.

In respect of a money purchase scheme, the lump sum benefit is usually represented by a payment of the value of the accumulated fund. This may be supplemented by a lump sum paid from a group life assurance plan and applied to the provision of a dependant's pension.

On death in retirement, the principal benefit will be a dependant's pension – or in the case of money purchase benefits, a dependant's, nominee's or successor's pension. This will be provided by the investment scheme if the scheme is a defined benefit scheme, but under a money purchase scheme it will depend on the option chosen by the member when benefits are taken. So, for example, the benefit may continue from a pension annuity or may be paid as a lump sum from a drawdown plan.

1.13 The approach of tax legislation

FA 2004 (implemented on 6 April 2006) made radical changes to the way tax was charged in relation to pension schemes. The 2004 Act was a brave attempt to simplify tax legislation and remove one of many barriers to saving. Although many commentators and practitioners have complained that it did anything but simplify matters, the application of pension tax rules is much more straightforward for the government's target audience. The rules become more complicated with the introduction of more sophisticated planning strategies, but these apply to the minority of the target group.

It is also worth remembering that the tax rules were part of a wider simplification agenda which included stakeholder pension schemes and automatic enrolment.

The legislation starts by applying the tax benefits to registered pension schemes. The model ("exempt, exempt, taxed") is very simple:

- Input enjoys a number of tax benefits and is controlled. Excessive input is disqualified from tax relief or is taxed.
- Pension funds enjoy UK tax benefits.
- Output enjoys a number of tax benefits and is controlled. Excessive output or output not taken in a prescribed form is taxed quite heavily to recover reliefs given and in some cases to penalise the member (which indeed at one time raised the prospect of legal action under human rights legislation).

The key to this approach is not to prohibit, but to tax transactions that contravene the legislation and exceed allowances. So, for example, there is no limit on the size of contribution that can be made, but the tax consequences are unlikely to make it financially worthwhile to exceed the relevant allowances.

1.14 Schemes that are not registered

The benefits of tax registration are generous to the extent that it is almost inconceivable that an employer or pension provider would not apply for registration. However, since a change in the legislation that accompanied the introduction of an earnings cap in 1989, employers have used the facility to top up retirement benefits by way of a scheme that originally was not approved for tax purposes and latterly is not registered. The term used to describe these schemes has developed from "funded (or unfunded) unapproved retirement benefit schemes" (FURBS or UURBS) to non-registered schemes or "employer-financed retirement benefit schemes".

Unfunded schemes are little more than an employer promise to pay from the employer's resources when the member retires.

Funded schemes offer the employer the opportunity to pay contributions to a discretionary trust in order to provide benefits on retirement or death. Members enjoy some of the protections of the *Pensions Acts*.

The legislation dealing with the taxation of these arrangements has changed in a relatively short space of time:

a. In their original form, employer contributions were deductible (and originally not subject to National Insurance), but were immediately taxed on the member as a P11D benefit.
b. Employer contributions were then subjected to National Insurance contributions from 1998. (The *Forde and McHugh Ltd* case in 2014 confirmed that no liability applied before then. See also **12.9.1**).
c. Retirement benefits were tax-free if they were paid as a lump sum at retirement age to the extent that contributions providing those benefits had been taxed.
d. There were special concessions for the taxation of investments held by the scheme.
e. The value of the lump sum death benefit could have been distributed without being subject to inheritance tax on the death of the member. There were no periodic charges.

f. These rules were turned on their head with the introduction of the 2004 regime for registered pensions. The fundamental change was that the member was not taxed on contributions, but was taxed on the benefit. There may also have been a liability to National Insurance if the member continued to be employed by the scheme sponsor.
g. The inheritance tax exemptions were removed although benefits accrued until 5 April 2006 could have been exempt to the extent that they could have been ring-fenced.
h. The tax privileges for investments were removed.
i. From 6 April 2011, the rules have, in effect, reverted. Under a complicated series of provisions relating to disguised remuneration (which includes, but is not exclusive to, EFRBS), the member is taxed on employer contributions (which are also subject to National Insurance) and the benefits are tax-free to the extent that they derive from contributions that have been taxed and providing they are paid as a lump sum. The provisions relate to funded money purchase schemes. The schemes are described in the legislation as "employment income provided through third parties".

The consequence of the latest rules is that EFRBS are less popular and incentives are now more likely to take the form of, for instance, share schemes.

EFRBS are described in more detail in **Chapter 12**.

Law: FA 2011, Sch. 2 inserting ITEPA 2003, Part 7A
Case: *HMRC v Forde and McHugh Ltd* [2014] UKSC 14

1.15 General tax and tax avoidance measures

The government announced in its 2012 Budget that from 2013 there would be a limit on the amount of income tax relief available to an individual where the tax relief was not already restricted by legislation. The legislation appeared in FA 2013, s. 16. The limit was set at £50,000 or, if greater, 25% of adjusted total income. This proposed measure has no impact on pension rules. They are already subject to a legislative framework of allowances, reliefs and taxes.

Pension scheme planning is not required of itself to be separately disclosed under the proposed DOTAS rules (Disclosure of Tax Avoidance Schemes) under the authority of FA 2004, s. 309-319 and supporting regulations.

However, as established in the case of *Roux Brothers (ex parte Waterside Inns)*, HMRC may attack any series of transactions where the transaction is of negligible commercial value, being established predominantly with a view to avoiding tax.

Law: FA 2004, s. 309-319; FA 2013, s. 16
Case: *R v IRC, ex parte Roux Waterside Inn Ltd* [1997] STC 781

1.16 Recent history

For tax purposes, recent history starts in 1956 and ends on 5 April 2006.

Early in the last century, a succession of court cases had confirmed the deductibility of employer contributions to a pension scheme for employees on the grounds that, like pay, they were incurred wholly and exclusively for the purposes of trade.

ICTA 1970

In 1956, the tax system recognised "self-employed retirement annuities" later to be known more popularly as retirement annuity contracts. These were simply deferred annuity arrangements that enjoyed a number of tax reliefs, most notably tax relief at marginal rates on contributions paid within certain limits. Contributions could only be paid by the individual policyholder. Contracts were between the policyholder and the provider.

In 1970, pension tax legislation was consolidated in ICTA 1970. This included a statutory framework for occupational schemes, but initially, 20% controlling directors were excluded from membership of occupational schemes. This was reversed by FA 1971.

Input to retirement annuity contracts was limited to a scale of percentages of "net relevant earnings" dependent on age (higher contributions for older ages). Relevant earnings were earnings from a trade or profession that were not already pensioned by an occupational scheme. Identifying "net" earnings required a number of deductions to be made.

The legislation for occupational schemes was brief, but supplemented by a large framework of discretion afforded to the then Inland Revenue. In order to attract a generous array of tax reliefs the scheme was required to be approved or, even better, exempt approved.

Approval

Approval could have been discretionary or mandatory. Discretionary approval allowed more generous reliefs and the way in which the Inland Revenue was likely to exercise its discretion was described in the Inland Revenue Practice Notes (IR12).

Mandatory approval gave the Inland Revenue no discretion and benefits were consequently much more restricted. The only regular application of mandatory approval was to the approval of schemes for shareholding directors of investment companies who were not allowed to be members of a discretionary approved scheme.

The thrust of the tax restrictions on occupational schemes was that however the funding basis was designed (e.g. money purchase or defined benefit), the primary limit was on the emerging benefit. Usually this meant that the scheme could provide a fraction of final pay (e.g. 1/60) for each year of service. The Inland Revenue could, however, allow the rate of accrual to be accelerated to provide as much as two thirds of final remuneration providing the member had reached normal retirement date and completed ten (later 20) years' service. For short periods there was a corresponding reduction in the accelerated maximum.

The retirement lump sum was also limited by reference to an accrual table, usually 3/80 of final pay for each year of service, but again this rate could be accelerated subject to the accrual period not being less than 20 years.

Personal pension schemes and FA 1987

Retirement annuity contracts were succeeded in the 1987 *Finance Act* by personal pension schemes although contributions could continue to be paid to the former. Personal pension schemes allowed the various services inherent in a personal arrangement to be "unbundled". The scheme became a means of accumulating funds which could then be used to purchase an annuity as a separate contract. There were three enhancements to personal pensions compared to their predecessors:

- the contribution limits were amended and made simpler (still based on age);
- the scheme was able to accept employer contributions; and
- the scheme enabled the member to contract out of the earnings-related state pension. This option was withdrawn from 6 April 2012.

ICTA 1988 was another consolidating measure. It was accompanied by a revised set of Practice Notes and guidance for personal pension schemes.

At the same time, the government introduced freestanding additional voluntary contribution schemes to enable members of occupational schemes to top up their scheme benefits in a type of personal pension that was independent of the main scheme. For practical purposes, these have been succeeded by personal pension schemes since 6 April 2006.

Measures in FA 2004 dealing with the reform of pension scheme tax were implemented on 6 April 2006. The changes to the regime were radical, but there were substantial transitional protections.

The "highlights" of the 2004 Act (implemented on 6 April 2006) were:

- the tax rules for occupational and personal pension schemes were harmonised (there are now very few points of difference);
- the contribution allowances were changed;
- the benefit allowances (and treatment for tax purposes) were changed;
- the rules have been subject to amendment in every year since 2004.

Law: FA 2004, Pt. 4 and Sch. 28 to 36 and 42, amended by every Finance Act to 2012 and supplemented by a long list of statutory instruments and Orders in Council

1.17 The state scheme and the pension credit

1.17.1 State pension changes: 2016

This is not intended to be a detailed description of the state pension scheme, rather a summary in order to provide a context. For most people, their retirement provision will comprise a state pension and private provision. For those individuals at the lower income levels, the state scheme will represent a significant proportion of their retirement provision and there may be little or no private provision. For others, the state scheme may be relatively insignificant and meaningful retirement provision will consist of any or all of retirement pensions, other retail savings vehicles, property and business income.

The state pension scheme underwent a significant change on 6 April 2016. In summary:

The basic state pension and the additional (earnings-related pension) were abolished for those who had not yet reached state pension age.

The savings credit element of the pension credit was abolished.

For those claimants who had reached state pension age on or before 5 April 2016, their entitlement to the basic state pension and the additional pension and accompanying options did not change. That meant that the options to defer taking the pension were unchanged even if deferment was to a date beyond 5 April 2016.

Individuals whose state pension age was beyond 5 April 2016, became entitled to the new state single-tier pension in respect of any accrual after that date. Furthermore, any accrual before that date was converted to the state single-tier pension. In order to determine the value of pre-2016 accrual, the new basis of calculating the state single-tier pension will be applied and compared with accrual calculated on the previous basis. The claimant will be entitled to the higher amount which will be regarded as state single-tier pension.

In order to qualify for the full single-tier pension, the individual must have paid or been credited with National Insurance contributions for 35 years (previously 30 years). They must have contributed for at least 10 years to qualify for any benefit and between 10 and 35 years the benefit is time-proportionate.

The facility to contract out of part of the state scheme was abolished on 6 April 2016 although guaranteed minimum pensions accrued before April 1997 are preserved.

If an individual has been contracted out for part of his or her working life, the pre-2016 benefit will inevitably be reduced. This is a complicated calculation.

The amount by which the pension under the old rules excceeds the pension under the new rules is known as the "protected payment". Whereas the single-tier pension is generally reviewed each year in line with the "triple lock" (increasing by the greatest of the increase in national average earnings, the consumer prices index and 2.5%), the protected payment is only increased with the consumer prices index (as the additonal pension before).

From 6 April 2016 it is not possible to claim a state pension on the contribution record of another individual (i.e. "category B pensions") except for some transitional provisions.

The single-tier pension may not be shared on dissolution of marriage, but the protected payment may be.

If the start of the state single-tier pension (where state pension age is after 5 April 2016) is deferred beyond state pension age it will be increased by 5.8% (simple interest formula) for each year of deferment (time apportioned for part-years). There is no option to take an alternative lump sum.

1.17.2 Contributory benefits pre-6 April 2016

This section has been retained (albeit slightly updated) for historical purposes and because it remains relevant for those who had accrued substantial benefits before 6 April 2016, either because they reached state pension age before 6 April 2016 or because the single-tier pension may be based in part on pre-2016 benefits. It should be read with the previous section.

The state scheme is a contributory scheme. The pre-2016 scheme included a basic state pension payable at a flat rate from state pension age or later state retirement age chosen by the contributor. In payment it increased each year (from April) by the greatest of the annual increase in the Consumer Prices Index, the increase in national average earnings (both to the previous September) and 2.5 per cent.

It was funded on a pay as you go basis which means that today's contributions paid today's benefits. The pension represented the first layer of income to be taken into account in the tax calculation, which means that in effect it was likely to be paid tax-free.

The contributions were National Insurance (NIC) contributions. The contributions that counted were flat rate Class 2 contributions for the self-employed and Class 1 employee and Class 1 employer contributions in respect of employees who earned above the primary and secondary thresholds. National Insurance contributions qualified the contributor and dependants for benefits other than just the state retirement pension.

In order to qualify for the full basic rate pension, the contributor must have paid NI contributions for at least 30 years. For contribution periods of less than 30 years, the pension was proportionately reduced. Generally speaking, no lump sum was payable, but if the pension was postponed, it was increased by one fifth of one per cent for each week of postponement (simple interest formula) which was 10.4% a year; an alternative option was to take a lump sum instead of the increase. The lump sum was taxed at marginal rates that would apply to income for the year before addition of the lump sum. The lump sum was withdrawn in April 2016 and the uprating of the deferred pension was reduced from 10.4% to 5.8%, but the reduction only applied to individuals who reached state pension age on or after 1 April 2016 (so it did not reduce for existing claimants).

1.17.3 Additional pension for employees

Employees also qualified for the earnings-related additional pension. There was no minimum qualification period, but the pension could have been reduced by periods in which the contributor was contracted out or simply not contributing. Contracting out was restricted to members of contracted-out defined benefit schemes after 5 April 2012.

Until April 1997, contracting-out on a defined benefit basis required the employer to provide a guaranteed minimum pension (GMP) for members through a defined benefit scheme. The consequence was that National Insurance contributions for employer and member were reduced and the member did not qualify for a proportion of the additional pension (state earnings-related pension or SERPS). The facility to contract out on this basis was abolished from 6 April 1997 and contracting out was abolished altogether from 6 April 2016. As a protection for members, schemes continue to maintain GMPs although members' rights have been modified by legislation with the introduction of the single-tier pension.

The additional pension was made up of:

- a "fixed rate accrual amount" (£93.60 a week in 2015-16) in respect of earnings between the lower earnings limit (£5,824 in 2015-16) and the lower earnings threshold (£15,300 in 2015-16); and
- 10% of earnings between the lower earnings threshold and the upper accrual point (fixed at £770 a week).

The lower earnings threshold did not increase to the level of the upper accrual point because the state pension was set to change in 2016.

The additional pension increases in payment each year in line with the Consumer Prices Index.

For those whose benefits from private and state pensions did not reach a threshold, the state pension credit may have been available. This comprised two elements: the guarantee credit and the savings credit.

The guarantee credit was designed to ensure that all pensioners had an income at least equal to the guarantee. This maximum credit, which is a means-tested benefit, is retained after 5 April 2016 (£159.35 per week for a single person, £243.25 per week for a couple, in 2017-18).

To remove the disincentive to save, the savings credit provided a top-up which increased the total pension credit with savings, but then reduced. The savings credit is unavailable after 5 April 2016 for new claims. Savings credit in payment on that date may continue.

The key weekly figures (to give an idea of the part played by the state) are:

Single-tier pension 2017-18	£159.55*
Pension credit guarantee credit – standard minimum guarantee 2017-18 (single person)	£159.35

* In individual cases the figure may be higher (because rights under the previous framework are in effect protected) or lower (because the individual has been contracted-out or has otherwise not made sufficient National Insurance contributions).

Subject to a transitional period, there is no dependant's state pension for dependent spouses or civil partners. Each can accrue a pension in his or her own right.

If the contributor dies before state pension age there are number of available death benefits:

- a bereavement payment is a tax-free lump sum of £2,000 payable subject to certain conditions;
- a taxable bereavement allowance is available if the widowed spouse or civil partner is at least 45 years old. It reduces the younger the dependant and is only payable for 12 months;
- the widowed parent's allowance is payable until the youngest child is 16, or 19 if remaining at school. It comprises a basic allowance and earnings-related addition. It is taxable.

The *Pensions Act* 2014 replaces the death benefits with a bereavement support payment with effect from 6 April 2017. The benefit is not included in the benefit cap and is not part of the universal credit. It provides a benefit for the 12 months following death. It is not age dependent.

2. Contributions and input

2.1 Overview

The 2004 pension tax regime works within a basic model of reliefs and allowances. The allowances control input through the annual limit for relief on personal contributions and the annual allowance which regulates input from all sources.

Quite separately, there are rules regarding deductibility of contributions made by an employer for its employees.

2.2 The controls on input

There are no limits on contributions (input) that can be made to a registered pension scheme. Rather, there are controls on the extent to which tax relief will be available on contributions. It may be worth reminding ourselves of the reliefs available in respect of contributions:

1. Employer contributions may be treated as a deductible business expense to the extent that HMRC regard them as incurred solely for the purposes of trade (trading businesses) or management (investment companies). A specific provision allows a contribution to be deductible even if, but for the section, it would be regarded as a payment of a capital nature (and therefore not a deductible expense of the business). The effect is to reduce the business's exposure to corporation tax or income tax (FA 2004, s. 196).
2. Employer contributions within the member's annual allowance will not be subject to income tax (the annual allowance charge) on the member (FA 2004, s. 201 and ITEPA 2003, s. 307 and 308).
3. Member contributions will be allowed tax relief at marginal rates of income tax if they are relievable contributions made by a "relevant UK individual" and within the annual limit for relief (FA 2004, s. 188).

4. Member contributions will not be subject to the annual allowance charge if they fall within the annual allowance (FA 2004, s. 227).

There are two main controls on input to a registered pension scheme and they are both personal allowances available to the member.

The annual limit for relief refers only to personal contributions in a tax year and limits the amount of relief available by reference to size of contribution.

The annual allowance refers to aggregate contributions from all sources in respect of a tax year.

Their interaction is described in more detail below (section **2.5.3**).

The annual cap on income tax reliefs (the greater of £50,000 or 25% of income) was introduced in FA 2013, s. 16, and has been effective since 6 April 2013. The restriction broadly applies where reliefs and allowances are not already capped and, as such, has no application to registered pension schemes which have their own regime for capping reliefs.

2.3 The annual limit for relief

2.3.1 Eligibility for relief on personal contributions

The annual limit for relief is an allowance that applies to personal contributions. Contributions are measured over tax years.

To qualify for this allowance, the member must be a relevant UK individual and an active member. Contributions may be made by someone (other than an employer) on behalf of the member, but it is the member who must be the relevant UK individual and who will attract tax relief.

Law: FA 2004, s. 188
Guidance: PTM 044100

Relevant UK individual

A relevant UK individual is an individual who is under the age of 75 and:

a. has chargeable relevant UK earnings in the tax year;
b. is UK tax resident at some time in the tax year;
c. has been UK tax resident at some time in the previous five tax years and when he or she joined the scheme (which need not have been in the previous five years);
d. has for that tax year general earnings from overseas Crown employment subject to UK tax (as defined by ITEPA 2003, s. 28); or
e. is the spouse or civil partner of an individual who has for the tax year general earnings from overseas Crown employment subject to UK tax (as defined by ITEPA 2003, s. 28).

In its consultation document "Freedom and choice in pensions" (March 2014), the Treasury proposed removing the age limit of 75 on making personal contributions. It subsequently withdrew the proposal.

In its consultation document "Strengthening the incentive to save: a consultation on pensions tax relief", the Treasury started a debate on how tax relief should be allowed on pension schemes. At present, the model is based on "exempt, exempt, taxed" and this descibes chronologically the incidence of tax and allowances. The consultation suggests a number of alternatives for the future including allowing no relief on input, but relief on benefits ("tax, exempt, exempt" – resembling an individual savings account) which would be supplemented by the Treasury on crystallisation.

In 2016, the Chancellor did not pursue the option, but instead announced the introduction of a "lifetime ISA" from 6 April 2017. This has been described in **Chapter 1**. The lifetime ISA may provide a cash benefit in later life or the deposit for a first-time house buyer. It may be taken out between the ages of 18 and 40.

The contribution (up to £4,000 a year and part of the general ISA limit of £20,000 in 2017/18) will be supplemented by a 25% bonus for contributions paid before the age of 50. This resembles reinvested basic rate tax.

The cash benefit may be withdrawn at any time, but if it is taken before the age of 60 the bonus (and growth on the bonus) will be clawed back and there will be a 5% charge.

The benefit will be tax-free although on death, assets held in the ISA will fall into the investor's estate for IHT purposes.

The consultation made no mention of withdrawing tax relief although many have speculated that higher rate relief is at risk.

Law: FA 2004, s. 189
Guidance: PTM 044100

Relevant UK earnings

Relevant UK earnings are defined as:

- employment income such as salary, wages, bonus, overtime and commission providing it is chargeable to tax under ITEPA 2003, s. 7(2);
- income chargeable under ITTOIA 2005, Pt. 2, that is income derived from the carrying on or exercise of a trade, profession or vocation (whether individually or as a partner acting personally in a partnership);
- income which is chargeable under ITTOIA 2005, Pt. 3 and is immediately derived from the carrying on of a UK furnished holiday lettings business (whether individually or as a partner acting personally in a partnership);
- income which is chargeable under ITTOIA 2005, Pt. 3 and is immediately derived from the carrying on of an EEA furnished holiday lettings business (whether individually or as a partner acting personally in a partnership);
- income arising from patent rights and treated as earned income;
- general earnings from an overseas Crown employment which are subject to tax in accordance with ITEPA 2003, s. 28.

Law: FA 2004, s. 189
Guidance: PTM 044100

Where relevant UK earnings are not taxable in the UK due to TIOPA 2010, s. 2(1) (double taxation agreements), those earnings are not regarded as chargeable to income tax and so will not count towards the annual limit for relief.

There are special considerations to be made for overseas income and income derived from investment companies.

Relievable contributions include contributions paid by the member or on behalf of the member by some person other than an employer where they:

- are paid before age 75; and
- do not represent life assurance premium contributions.

They will *not* include:

- contributions paid when or after the member reaches the age of 75. There is no minimum age;
- life assurance premium contributions;
- contributions paid by employers;
- transfers of rights to the scheme;
- pension credits awarded on dissolution of marriage.

Law: FA 2004, s. 188 and 195A
Guidance: PTM 044100

2.3.2 Amount of the annual limit

The annual limit for relief restricts tax relief on personal contributions to the greater of:

- 100% of relevant UK earnings; and
- £3,600 (before tax relief).

There is no facility under the tax legislation to carry forward unused annual limits or to carry back contributions to an earlier tax year.

If the member's chargeable relevant UK earnings are less than £3,600, relief will only be available on a contribution of £3,600 if it is paid on a "relief at source" basis. Relief at source will be examined shortly, but in summary allows the member to pay a contribution which is supplemented by basic rate relief claimed from HMRC and invested by the pension provider.

The facility to contract out of the state second pension on a money purchase basis was abolished on 6 April 2012. Until that date, minimum contributions recovered from the employee by the employer as part of the contracting-out process were not measured against the annual limit.

Law: FA 2004, s. 190
Guidance: PTM 044100

2.3.3 Effect of personal contributions on allowances

If a member is entitled to an age related personal tax allowance their total income for the purposes of section ITA 2007, s. 36 and 37 (level of income where age related personal allowance may be reduced) is reduced by the amount of the grossed up contribution paid to a scheme operating tax relief at source (RAS: see **2.3.7** below). In other words, the age allowance will not be jeopardised by income allocated to a pension contribution in these circumstances.

Similarly, where a personal contribution is paid by an individual who has adjusted net income of between £100,000 and £122,000 (2016-17), the grossed up contribution may be deducted from the net adjusted income for the purposes of "reinstating" the personal allowance (at a rate of £1 for every £2 of contribution). This will usually mean that relief is being claimed at a rate of 60%.

Example: contribution of £10,000

Net adjusted income before contribution is paid	£110,000
"Reinstated" personal allowance	£5,000
Reduction in tax (at 40%) from reinstated personal allowance	£2,000
Marginal rate relief on contribution	£4,000
Total tax relief	**£6,000** (60%)

2.3.4 Tax relief at source (RAS)

There are three different ways in which personal contributions can be allowed tax relief. The appropriate means is determined by the scheme or plan provider.

Under this method, personal contributions are paid to the scheme or plan after deduction of basic rate tax. The basic rate tax is then claimed from HMRC by the provider and used to supplement the "net" contribution. If the member is a higher rate taxpayer, he or she will make a claim for higher rate relief from the local inspector, usually through the self-assessment process.

The provider may invest the "gross" contribution value immediately the net contribution is received and in anticipation of receiving the basic rate relief from HMRC, but this is not a legal necessity (and is unlikely to be the case in respect of providers with more limited resources).

Higher rate relief is given by expanding the basic rate tax band by the amount of the gross contribution. The effect is to reduce the higher (or additional) rate band by a corresponding amount or less where the amount straddles the bands.

RAS must be used when a member wishes to pay a contribution of £3,600 (or less) because earnings are lower than that figure or there are no earnings at all.

Law: FA 2004, s. 192
Guidance: PTM 044230

2.3.5 Net pay arrangement

This method has a longer history than RAS and was originally confined to occupational schemes. Under this process, the employer deducts the gross contribution from the employee's pay before tax is applied, but after the National Insurance contribution has been calculated. So, the contribution attracts no relief from National Insurance, but it does reduce the income tax liability for the member. This is not the same as salary sacrifice where pay is actually reduced in advance of entitlement.

The employer then passes the personal contribution to the pension arrangement.

The employer may offer RAS or the net pay arrangement, but not both in respect of the same scheme. Most occupational schemes offer the net pay arrangement for reasons of history (they offered it before RAS was introduced in 1987).

There are no significant advantages and disadvantages of the two methods. However:

- only RAS can provide tax relief for the non-taxpayer (an unusual set of circumstances); but

- higher rate relief is available more quickly under the net pay arrangement.

Law: FA 2004, s. 193
Guidance: PTM 44230

2.3.6 Relief on making a claim

This method is rarely used nowadays. It requires the member to claim relief from the local tax office once the contribution has been paid. It is allowed by adjusting the tax computation.

Relief on making a claim will generally arise in two sets of circumstances:

1. Some providers have not changed their systems to accommodate RAS for retirement annuity contracts.
2. Where an individual is paying contributions under the net pay arrangement, it may be that a contribution (for example, annual) is paid near the end of the tax year when earnings are insufficient to cover the whole of the contribution that would otherwise be deducted. The allowance cannot be carried into the next year and relief on making a claim becomes the only viable option.

Note that relief is only available on making a claim to the extent that the member would otherwise pay tax.

Migrant member relief is made available by granting relief on making a claim. The relief is available to some members of overseas pension schemes who are tax resident in the UK (see **2.3.9** below).

Members who are self-employed, and members of a statutory superannuation scheme (such as general medical and dental practitioners: see below), are allowed relief on making a claim as a consequence of the statutory basis of dealing with their situation which replaced extra-statutory concession A9 (see **2.3.10**).

If contributions in a tax year exceed the annual limit for relief, no tax relief is available on the excess: the appropriate relief at source is recovered by HMRC from the provider and any higher rate relief is either:

- not given (by reducing the increase in the basic rate band) to the extent of the excess; or
- reclaimed from the taxpayer through self-assessment.

The member may then leave the excess invested in the scheme (with the balance of contribution) or may request a refund of the excess contribution. The refund is a specified authorised payment (a refund of excess contributions lump sum) from a registered pension scheme, but not a benefit crystallisation event (BCE).

Law: FA 2004, s. 193(4) and Sch. 33, para. 1(3)
Guidance: PTM 044240

2.3.7 Contributions for others

If a contribution is made on behalf of the member (such as for a minor child or non-working spouse), the contribution is paid net of basic rate tax, but then enhances the member's basic rate band (not that of the payer) because relief is only available to the member.

Note that if a contribution is paid on behalf of a member, it will constitute a potentially exempt transfer (so equally could form part of the estate) for inheritance tax (IHT) purposes. However, there are numerous reliefs that should prevent the risk of the contribution falling into the estate:

- The contribution could be offset against the IHT annual allowance of £3,000 (which can be supplemented by unused annual allowance from the previous tax year).
- The contribution may be a gift from normal expenditure and therefore exempt from IHT. This is a specialist area, but broadly requires the contribution to be from regular income and not to reduce the donor's standard of living.
- The gift may be covered by the inter-spouse exemption.
- The gift may be a potentially exempt transfer.

In calculating the value of the "gift" for inheritance tax purposes the net contribution is taken if the contribution is paid under the RAS process. This is because the value of the gift is based on the loss to the donor's estate rather than the gain to the recipient.

The employer then passes the personal contribution to the pension arrangement.

If the contribution is paid for a minor (under the age of 16), the applicant is the individual who makes the contribution and is the party to the contract. This must be a parent or guardian. When the member reaches the age of 16 if employed (18 if not employed), the member automatically becomes the owner of the policy or arrangement (although there is no reason why contributions should not continue "on behalf of…").

2.3.8 Risk benefits and the annual limit

Waiver of contribution

Personal pension schemes issued before 6 April 2001 and retirement annuity contracts were able to include a waiver of contribution facility. In effect an insurance underwritten in a similar way to permanent health insurance, a claim can be made when the member has had to give up their job (or any job) because of ill-health or accident. There would be a deferment period of (usually) three or six months.

If the individual makes a claim under a "waiver of contribution" insurance, the value of contributions is credited to the scheme as if they had been paid. However, these are not paid contributions as such and do not attract tax relief. The addition to pension contributions representing the cost of the insurance would have been relievable with the pension contribution.

Providing the insurance premium (and associated pension contribution) is maintained, the facility continues to be available on these arrangements although it was generally withdrawn on 6 April 2001. There is no reason why contributions should not be funded by the proceeds of a permanent health insurance (also described as "income protection") policy in respect of later arrangements. However, the benefit from permanent health insurance funds real contributions which are subject to the same tax and allowance rules that would ordinarily apply to personal contributions.

Life assurance

The rules relating to life assurance policies are complicated and represent a rare example of a distinction between rules for occupational schemes and rules for schemes that are not occupational schemes (principally personal pension schemes).

Under the rules in place to 5 April 2006, premiums to certain life assurance policies attracted relief at highest marginal rates. There were restrictions on the type of policy which had to be a term assurance with no available surrender value or indeed any other options or "rider" benefits, and contributions were subject to the overall contribution allowances.

The life assurance could have been written under the personal pension scheme legislation as an individual policy or it could be written under an occupational scheme trust on a group basis. It could even be established as a "stand-alone" group policy for employees who might not be accruing retirement benefits or who might be accruing benefits during the period of cover under a group personal pension scheme (for which the tax rules at the time were separate from those relating to occupational schemes).

Individual or group policies

The starting point of the legislation implemented on 6 April 2006 is that tax relief is unavailable to members on premiums they pay to individual term assurance policies, but may be available when life cover is written under the trust deed and rules of an occupational pension scheme. As such, group life cover written under the occupational scheme trust provides benefits on death as part of the activities of an occupational pension scheme. However, if the provision of life cover is not accompanied by the accrual of occupational scheme retirement benefits, then tax relief is not available.

The position is complicated by the transitional arrangements and provision for "protected policies". Any contributions paid before

- 1 August 2007 to an occupational pension scheme; or
- 6 April 2007 to a scheme that is not an occupational pension scheme

cannot be life assurance premium contributions and so can be relievable pension contributions eligible for tax relief.

The legislation distinguishes between life assurance premiums paid by a member to a registered pension scheme (that do not qualify for tax relief) and premiums paid under the pension relief rules (that do). The former are treated as premiums to a non-group life policy.

Even premiums to a non-group life policy attract relief if the policies are protected, however.

The restrictions do not affect the tax relief available to an employer on payment of premiums to a non-group life policy by the employer and treated as a business expense.

Non-group life policies

A non-group life policy is defined as a policy of insurance under which the only benefits which may become payable are benefits payable in consequence, or anticipation of:

- the death of the individual;
- the death of one of a group of individuals which includes the individual (e.g. a policy that covers a number of individuals but only pays a benefit out on the first death or last survivor's death); or
- the deaths of more than one of a group of individuals (e.g. a policy that pays a benefit out on the death of each of the individuals),

where:

- the group includes the individual; and
- all the other members of the group are connected with the individual.

Law: FA 2004, s. 195A(8)

So a policy that will pay out on the death of only one individual (regardless of how many individuals may be "covered" by the policy) will be a non-group life policy.

A policy that will pay out benefits on the death of more than one individual will only be a non-group life policy where the individuals "covered" by the policy are all connected. (Connected has the meaning as given in FA 2004, s. 195A(8), that is broadly as members of the same family.)

Contributions paid by or on behalf of the *member* for these types of policy will not be *relievable pension contributions* and so cannot receive tax relief.

A policy that will pay out benefits on the death of more than one individual and where the individuals covered by the policy are not connected will not be a non-group life policy. Contributions made by or on behalf of the member, aged under 75, to pay premiums to this type of policy may be a relievable pension contribution.

Law: FA 2004, s. 195A

Protected policies

Some pension schemes allow members to pay for additional death in service benefits through additional voluntary contributions (AVCs). Where cover is provided on a group basis tax relief will continue to be available for contributions made to such schemes because the policies will not be non-group life policies.

A policy is protected under an occupational scheme that is a registered scheme if it is:

1. issued in respect of insurances made and became held for the purposes of that registered pension scheme before 21 March 2007;
2. issued in respect of insurances made and became held for the purposes of that registered pension scheme after 20 March 2007 but before 1 August 2007, where:
    - the insurer received the application for the policy before 29 March 2007, and
    - the amount and term of the payable benefits under the issued policy are no greater than as set out in the application to the insurer; or
3. to replace a policy that was previously in existence but had subsequently lapsed, and
    - the new policy is made on the same terms and conditions as the lapsed policy;
    - the new policy was merely re-instated and was not the subject of a new insurance proposal;
    - the lapsed policy would have been eligible for relief had it stayed in force (i.e. it was a "protected policy" under the legislation); and

- the new policy is made and held within the pension scheme before 1 August 2007.

A policy will usually lose its protection if benefits under the policy are increased or if the policy term is extended. The exceptional circumstances (when protection is not lost) is if the change is made in order to comply with age equality legislation.

Protected policies – not occupational schemes

A policy under a registered scheme that is not an occupational scheme is protected if:

1. it is issued in respect of insurances made and became held for the purposes of a registered pension scheme before 6 December 2006; or
2. it was issued in respect of insurances made on or after 6 December 2006, and
    - the insurer received the application for the policy before 14 December 2006;
    - the insurance was made and became held for the purposes of a registered pension scheme before 1 August 2007; and
    - the amount of the benefits and period for which they are payable is not greater than as set out in the application; or
3. it was issued in respect of insurances made on or after 6 December 2006, and
    - the application was received by the insurer after 13 December 2006 but before 13 April 2007 and on the day the insurance was made the individual also had an actual or prospective entitlement to a pension under the same scheme;
    - the insurance was made and became held for the purposes of a registered pension scheme before 1 August 2007; and

- the amount of the benefits and period for which they are payable is not greater than as set out in the application.

Law: FA 2007, Sch. 18, para. 4, 5
Guidance: PTM 044100

Losing protection

A protected policy will cease to be protected only if there is a variation to the policy terms which:

- increases the benefits payable under the policy; or
- extends the period during which benefits are payable.

Where the policy of insurance was issued in respect of insurances made before 6 April 2006 only variations made after 20 March 2007 can cause loss of protected status.

Where the policy was issued in respect of insurances made after 5 April 2006 but before 6 December 2006 only variations made after 5 December 2006 can cause loss of protected status.

If benefits are altered because the policyholder exercises an option that cannot be refused by the insurer, HMRC takes the view that this is the exercise of an option, not a variation, and protected status is not jeopardised.

Law: FA 2004, s. 195A, and Sch. 36, para. 37; FA 2007, Sch. 18, para. 4, 5
Guidance: PTM 044100

2.3.9 Contributions to overseas schemes and the annual limit

Members of overseas pension schemes may claim tax relief on contributions to such a scheme if they meet all of the criteria for migrant member relief. These are:

- the member is resident in the UK when the contribution was made;
- the member has relevant UK earnings chargeable to UK tax;
- the contribution is paid to a qualifying overseas pension scheme;

- the member was a member of the qualifying overseas pension scheme before becoming resident in the UK, and continued to be a member of that scheme on becoming resident and made contributions to that scheme;
- the member was at any time in the 10 years before the beginning of residence in the UK entitled to tax relief in respect of contributions to the scheme under the law of the country or territory in which the member was then resident;
- the scheme manager has notified the member that he will advise HMRC of any benefit crystallisation events in respect of that member; and
- the member has notified the scheme manager of an intention to claim relief.

This is "migrant member relief" and is a continuation of what was known as "corresponding relief" prior to 6 April 2006. If migrant member relief is available, the maximum relievable personal contribution is the annual limit for relief.

Law: FA 2004, s. 243, and Sch. 33, para. 1, 4, 5; SI 2006/212 *(The Pension Schemes (Relevant Migrant Members) Regulations* 2006), reg. 2
Guidance: PTM 044100

2.3.10 Personal contributions in special circumstances

Doctors and dentists

General medical and dental practitioners who are contracted to the NHS are self-employed, but have a statutory option (previously ESC A9) to be members of the NHS Superannuation Scheme. The NHSS Scheme does not operate the "relief at source" basis and the member, as a self-employed individual, is unable to pay contributions via the "net pay arrangement". Tax relief must therefore be claimed by the member through the self-assessment process.

Payment dates

The date a personal contribution is paid can be problematic. The principle is that it will usually be the date of receipt of the contribution by the scheme. If an employer deducts contributions from pay and passes them to a group personal pension scheme, then the date of receipt is again the payment date. However, if the contribution is collected under the net pay arrangement, HMRC take the view that the contribution is "paid" when it is deducted from pay. If the scheme administrator has difficulty establishing the facts, he may use the date the money was received or an estimated date. Difficulties are more likely to attend historic dates in which case a "notional credit date" may be adopted.

Refunds

There are rare circumstances when personal contributions may be refunded:

- When a member has completed less than two years' service in an occupational defined benefit pension scheme and the scheme rules allow it. This is a short service lump sum and is taxed. The two year vesting period is reduced to 30 days in respect of money purchase schemes by the *Pensions Act* 2014, s. 36. This means that refunds will only be available if the member has completed less than 30 days' membership of the scheme.
- When a member exceeds the annual limit for relief in a tax year, a lump sum representing the excess may be paid to the member at the request of the member. The refund is tax free. Until early 2015 the "refund" was treated as an authorised payment of lump sum and not as a refund. This meant that once paid, the contribution reduced available annual allowance even if "refunded". This position has now been reversed by HMRC and the contribution does not reduce available annual allowance if refunded.
- There were circumstances when a refund could have been made when the special annual allowance charge would otherwise apply. The special annual allowance charge was withdrawn in 2011. No refund is allowed to remedy an excess over the annual allowance: such a refund would be an unauthorised payment.

Law: FA 2004, s. 166, Sch. 29, para. 5, 6 and Sch. 35, para. 15; PA 2014, s. 36

Guidance: PTM 044100, 045000

Short service refund

The conditions for this payment to be made are:

- the registered pension scheme making the payment is an occupational pension scheme and the refund is allowed by the scheme rules;
- the member has not completed the two-year vesting period (30 days for a money purchase scheme when this measure was implemented on 1 October 2015);
- the member's "pensionable service" under the scheme was terminated before "normal pension age" and the member is not entitled to a "short service benefit" because, in effect, benefits have not vested;
- the member has not previously been subject to a lifetime allowance test in relation to that scheme, and so there have been no previous benefit crystallisation event (BCEs) triggered under that scheme in relation to that individual. Whilst payment of some "authorised" lump sum payments does not trigger a BCE, all such payments (except a refund of excess contributions lump sum) will extinguish the member's entitlement under the scheme; and
- the payment is made before the member reaches his or her 75th birthday.

The maximum amount that can be treated as a short service refund lump sum for tax purposes is an amount equal to the total amount of the actual contributions paid by the member to the scheme.

Where the scheme has been a contracted out scheme, and is required to pay a contributions equivalent premium (CEP) to HMRC to buy back the member into the State scheme (in respect of service before 6 April 2016), the scheme administrator may deduct the employee's share of the CEP from the member's contributions. Whether or not such a deduction is made, payment of a CEP by a registered pension scheme is an authorised member payment in its own right.

Under PA 2014, s. 36, there will be an entitlement to a short service benefit after a member of a money purchase scheme has completed 30 days' qualifying membership of the scheme.

This means that the option of a refund will expire at the end of the 30 days.

The measure will be effective from 1 October 2015 and is only mandatory for a member whose qualifying service started on or after that date. It will only apply where all the benefits are money purchase within the new definition.

Law: FA 2004, Sch. 29, para. 5; FA 2006, Sch. 23, para. 27; PA 2014, s. 36.
Guidance: PTM 045000

Refund of excess contributions lump sum

The refund of excess contribution lump sum must be paid within six years of the end of the tax year in which the excess was paid, but need not be paid before age 75. It is tax-free when paid.

Law: FA 2004, s. 188(2), 190; Sch. 29, para. 6

Payments of interest on lump sums

The payment may include interest that may be treated as part of the refund if it is within the refund limit (e.g. no more than the excess contribution less any refund already made) or it may be interest in addition to the limit in which case it will be treated as a scheme administration payment and therefore authorised. The rate of interest must be calculated on a commercial basis.

In the case of a short service refund of personal contributions, the scheme administrator will be responsible for deducting a tax charge from the payment and passing it on to HMRC. The tax payable is 20% on the first £20,000 and 50% on any excess over the £20,000.

Law: FA 2004, s. 205, as amended by *The Taxation of Pension Schemes (Rates etc.) Order* 2010 SI 2010/536; ITTOIA 2005, s. 369
Guidance: PTM 045000

2.4 Employer contributions

2.4.1 A business expense

Contributions by an employer to a registered pension scheme (or an employer-financed retirement benefit scheme) will be treated as a deductible business expense in computing its exposure to corporation tax or income tax if the expense can be demonstrated to have been incurred wholly and exclusively for the purposes of the trade or profession. There is a parallel provision for investment businesses which requires the expense to have been incurred in the management of the business (rather than derived from investment income). Registration of the pension scheme is not a requirement of deductibility.

Unlike the situation before 6 April 2006, there is no special pension tax regime if shareholding directors of an investment company are included in the membership of a registered pension scheme. However, as a general rule, HMRC will expect to see the proportion of income allocated to pay and benefits as modest.

For a contribution to be treated as a deduction in a trading or accounting year, it must actually have been paid in that year. This requirement appears in FA 2004, s. 196 although that section only extends to registered pension schemes. Contributions cannot be carried back or forward in this context, but there is nothing that prevents a loss created by a contribution from being carried back or forward.

FA 2004 introduced a small variation to the statutory basis of allowing contributions to be deducted for both trading and investment companies. FA 2004, s. 196(2) provides that contributions will not be disallowed on the grounds of being capital expenditure in computing profits. FA 2004, s. 196(3) similarly provides that contributions will, for companies with investment business, be treated as management expenses to the extent that they would otherwise not be. This treatment (which is in each case confined to registered pension schemes) is important for those employers who may wish to make a one-off payment for a variety of reasons such as to remedy an underfunding.

Fees associated with establishing a pension fund are not treated as contributions and, as capital expenditure, are not deductible.

There is a parallel set of rules for contributions made by life assurance companies (for their employees).

Whether a contribution is allowable as a deduction or not has nothing to do with the framework of personal allowances such as the annual allowance that applies to the member.

Law: FA 2004, s. 196; ITTOIA 2005, Part 2; CTA 2009, Part 3
Guidance: PTM 043200

2.4.2 Required liabilities of the employer

If an employer is required to make a "deficiency payment" under PA 1995, s. 75 to remedy a funding shortfall on the winding-up of a defined benefit scheme, that payment will be treated as a contribution. In these circumstances, the contribution may be made after the sponsoring business has discontinued and the contribution will be assumed to have been made on the last day of trading (and therefore in the last trading year).

The Pension Protection Fund (PPF) was established by PA 2004. It provides assistance when a sponsoring employer becomes insolvent and a defined benefit scheme is underfunded. The scheme and its assets may be taken over by the PPF. The PPF is funded by a system of levies on employers.

Statutory levies paid by employers to these funds are not contributions made to a registered pension scheme and so would not normally qualify for relief under FA 2004, s. 196. However, the *Pension Protection Fund (Tax) Regulations* 2006, reg. 21 provides that the *Pensions Act* levies will be deemed contributions under FA 2004, s. 199. This means that tax relief will be given for such levies.

The provision in reg. 21 means that any relief given to a sum paid by an employer on account of any of the *Pensions Act* levies will not be spread (see **2.4.4**).

Law: PA 1995, s. 75; FA 2004, s. 199; SI 2006/575, reg. 21

2.4.3 Is the employer contribution deductible?

The fundamental rules appear in CTA 2009, s. 54(1)(a) (corporation tax) and ITTOIA 2005, s. 34 (income tax). To be treated as a deductible business expense, it must have been incurred wholly and exclusively for the purposes of trade or, in the case of an investment company, wholly and exclusively for the purposes of management. Furthermore, it must actually have been paid.

The deduction is made against the financial year in which it is actually paid. If the contribution is paid under the winding-up requirements of PA 1995, s. 75 and after the business of the sponsoring employer has ceased, the contribution is treated as having been paid in the last year of trading. This is the only set of circumstances when a contribution can be paid and deducted after business cessation. The section requires that when the scheme is wound up, all remaining liabilities of the employer to the scheme be satisfied. The scheme is not a preferential creditor, but the liability may be secured, and frequently will have been, in order to satisfy the Pensions Regulator in the period running up to the failure of an employer subject to the prior demands of lenders (such as the banks).

Note that a specific provision under FA 2004 allows a contribution to be treated as deductible notwithstanding the fact that, but for the provision, it would be regarded as a payment of a capital nature and therefore not a deductible expense.

The assumption made by HMRC will be that a contribution to a registered pension scheme is deductible. It will be exceptional for a contribution to be disallowed wholly or in part. If a local tax office has doubts about deductibility, it must refer the case to HMRC (PSS) in Nottingham. If the contribution is regarded as excessive for these purposes, only the excess will be disallowed.

Law: FA 2004, s. 196; ITTOIA 2005, s. 34; CTA 2009, s. 54(1)(a)

Wholly and exclusively

Guidance is provided in the *Business Income Manual,* but it will always be difficult for HMRC to determine that a contribution is not wholly and exclusively for the purpose of trade without becoming involved in inappropriate judgements of what an individual should be paid. Nevertheless, it is possible to identify areas of greater risk and some principles that are likely to be applied. An example concerns shareholding directors of close companies and those connected to them (i.e. relatives). The focus in these circumstances will primarily be on the relatives: HMRC will consider their commitment to the business and what an individual in a comparable job in a different business would expect to be paid. Even this may be difficult. As for the director, in this example, the difficulty for a full-time director is identifying what is the "rate for the job" and, within reason, HMRC are unlikely to challenge it.

What is true is that pension contributions are simply part of the remuneration package and, again within reason, HMRC will not attempt to judge what should be the split between salary and pension contribution (or current versus deferred remuneration). Unlike the pre-2006 regime, there is no formal connection between the size of contribution, age and remuneration. HMRC have made ill-defined comments about the contribution not being excessive to provide a pension commensurate with pay, but there is little logic to this:

- a formal connection would require funds and contributions to be projected as under the previous system on which this was supposed to be a simplified improvement;
- even under the previous regime, it was accepted that single contributions could be used to make up for past underfunded service;
- an owner director is quite within his or her rights to suppress salary for a range of commercial reasons.

Having noted these points, the literal response would be that the pension is intended to represent a continuation of earnings and by implication neither a continuation of investment income in the form of dividends nor a significant increase in income derived from employment.

HMRC point out that expenses incurred "for the purposes of going out of business" could not normally be regarded as incurred for carrying on the business.

Pension contributions do not fall under this heading if they are contractual. Indeed, if they are not a contractual obligation, the contributions will often be deductible because (for instance) they preserve morale in other companies in the trading group.

The most likely example in the context of tax planning is the large contribution paid to a shareholding director when a company ceases to trade. This will depend on the facts, but if the contribution is not contractual (as it probably will not be) there is a significant risk that it will not be allowed as a deduction.

Contributions enabled by means of a remuneration sacrifice will always be assumed to have been incurred wholly and exclusively for carrying on the trade.

Levies to the Pension Protection Fund are treated as contributions and as incurred wholly and exclusively for the trade by virtue of SI 2006/575, reg. 22. These are not subject to spreading.

Law: ITTOIA 2005, s. 34; CTA 2009, s. 54; SI 2006/575 (*The Pension Protection Fund (Tax) Regulations* 2006), reg. 22
Guidance: BIM 46020, 46065; PTM 043200

2.4.4 Spreading

The "tax spreading" rules identify the dilemma that faces the Treasury. On one hand it wishes to prevent transactions undertaken for the purposes of avoiding tax, but on the other hand, it wishes to encourage a commercial transaction (making pension provision) with the use of tax incentives. As part of the process of meeting the objectives, the Treasury will also wish to maintain a steady, predictable stream of tax revenues.

More specifically, the tax spreading rules are designed to smooth the availability of tax reliefs where contributions are especially uneven. The rules only apply to employer contributions and are unlikely to have any impact on personal tax and retirement planning. They do not directly withdraw or reduce the tax relief available in respect of business expenses, rather they reallocate a proportion of exceptional contributions to chargeable or accounting periods other than those in which the contributions were paid. This can have the effect of reducing the overall relief available.

The principal calculation is to compare contributions actually paid (in other words, not deemed to have been paid under a previous spreading calculation) to a scheme in the current period with contributions actually paid to the scheme in the previous period of similar length. If the excess in the current year is at least £500,000, then relief may be spread over more than one year. Note that the calculation is performed in respect of each scheme of an employer, not aggregate contributions to all schemes.

The requirement to compare contributions for a period of similar length is met simply by applying a factor to contributions paid in the previous period, i.e.

$$\frac{\text{number of days in current period}}{\text{number of days in previous period}} \times \text{contribution paid in the previous period}$$

Certain contributions do not need to be spread. These are contributions to pay for:

- cost of living increases to pensions in payment to pensioner members; and
- benefits for future service for members joining the scheme in the current chargeable period.

The spreading provision will only be applied if the contribution in the current period is *more than* 210% of the contribution in the previous period and *at least* £500,000. The period over which relief will be spread is determined by FA 2004, s. 197(4), (5).

Amount of excess	**Period of spread (includes year of payment)**
£500,000-£999,999	Two years, spread equally
£1,000,000-£1,999,999	Three years, spread equally
£2,000,000 or more	Four years, spread equally

There are special rules for allowing relief to be given in full when an employer ceases trading during a spreading period.

HMRC have the power to restrict tax relief on employer contributions paid in respect of members where:

- any of the benefits which the member may receive from a registered pension scheme are dependent on the non-payment of a benefit that the member was expecting to receive from an employer financed retirement benefits scheme; or
- payment of benefits to the member from an employer financed retirement benefits scheme would reduce the transfer value of any rights in a registered pension scheme.

The details of when and how such a restriction will take place are set out in *The Registered Pension Schemes (Restriction of Employers' Relief) Regulations* 2005 (SI 2005/3458).

To establish the tax relief restriction on the employer's contributions in respect of a member, the pension input amount for each of the member's arrangements under the scheme is calculated in relation to the employer's period of account in which the contributions are paid. The amount of the restriction on the relief is an amount equal to the aggregate of the pension input amounts for the period of account in question in respect of each arrangement under the scheme relating to the member.

Law: FA 2004, s. 197; SI 2005/3458
Guidance: PTM 043400

2.5 The annual allowance

2.5.1 Amount of the allowance

The annual allowance is, in effect, a limit on aggregate input from all sources to all registered pension schemes in respect of an individual. It is a personal allowance. Contributions in excess of the annual allowance are subject to an annual allowance tax charge.

In its relatively short history, the annual allowance has undergone a number of changes and these are described in this chapter. A significant change introduced in 2015-16 was the alignment of "input periods" with tax years. In their original form, annual allowances were determined for tax years and this remains the case. However, to identify how much annual allowance was used in a tax year, reference was made to input for all input periods that ended in the tax year. Input periods were determined by arrangement and were of varying lengths, but usually no more than 12 months.

By way of example, if a contribution was paid to a money purchase scheme on 1 December 2013, but in an input period that ended on 31 May 2014, that contribution would have been measured against the annual allowance for 2014-15 (even though it was paid in the tax year 2013-14). For the purposes of the annual limit, it would have been set against the 2013-14 tax year (i.e. the tax year in which it was paid).

In 2015-16, all input periods that were "open" on 8 July 2015 were closed on that date and a new input period started on 9 July 2015 which closed on 5 April 2016. All subsequent input periods run from 5 April to 6 April. This is described below.

Personal contributions paid at or after age 75 and contributions that are not otherwise relievable (such as to most life assurance policies) are not included in the aggregate. Relievable pension contributions that are paid by, or on behalf of, the individual, but are subsequently returned to the individual by way of a refund of excess contributions lump sum that is made in a pension input period ending in the tax year 2014-15 or a later tax year, are not regarded as input for these purposes. The rule, published by HMRC in early 2015, represents a reversal of the rule that applied to input for tax years to 2013-14.

The annual allowance operates separately from, and in addition to, the annual limit for relief on personal contributions. It is therefore possible to breach the annual limit for relief, but to be within the annual allowance or to breach the annual allowance, but to be within the annual limit for relief. Furthermore, the method of recovering excessive tax relief differs in each case.

The amount of the annual allowance was set at £215,000 for the tax year 2006-07 and increased each year to £255,000 in 2010-11. From the following tax year, it was set at £50,000, but with a facility to carry forward unused allowance from previous years. In 2014-15, the annual allowance reduced to £40,000.

The annual allowance has therefore been set at:

2006-07	£215,000
2007-08	£225,000
2008-09	£235,000
2009-10	£245,000
2010-11	£255,000
2011-12	£50,000
2012-13	£50,000
2013-14	£50,000
2014-15	£40,000
2015-16	£80,000 (see below)
2016-17	£40,000 *
2017-18	£40,000 *

*From 2016-17, the annual allowance may be reduced for those with high "adjusted income" (see **2.13** below).

The 2015 summer Budget proposed a number of changes to the operation of the annual allowance. As a consequence, the 2015-16 tax year was sub-divided into two notional tax years (6 April 2015 to 8 July 2015 – the "pre-commencement tax year" and 9 July 2015 to 5 April 2016 – the "post-commencement tax year") and the aggregate annual allowance for the tax year as a whole was £80,000 (subject to a maximum of £40,000 for the period 9 July 2015 to 5 April 2016 (the "post-alignment tax year"). This is described below.

The Budget also proposed a scaling back of the annual allowance for high earners from the 2016-17 tax year: the £40,000 allowance is reduced by £1 for every £2 by which the adjusted income of the member (including employer pension contributions) exceeds £150,000. In order for the measure to apply, income excluding pension contributions ("threshold income") must exceed £110,000. The measures are described below at **2.13**.

The rules applicable from 2016-17 and the transition to those rules are described in paragraph **2.13** below.

Increases to the annual allowance may be made by Treasury Order, but the allowance may only be reduced by primary legislation.

The sharp underlying reduction in the annual allowance has been alleviated by a facility to carry forward unused allowance for up to three years to increase the allowance in a later year. The facility was introduced in 2011-12 allowing unused allowance to be carried forward from 2008-09. At the end of that tax year the facility to use 2008-09 expired. The carry forward is automatic and does not have to be claimed. The conditions for its use are:

- the current year's allowance must first be exhausted;
- relief from the oldest year is carried forward before any other;
- to calculate the amount of available relief, current rules and allowances must be used. So, if the allowance in 2010-11 was £255,000, any unused allowance from that year had to be calculated as £50,000 minus allowance already used in that year;
- benefit accrual for the purposes of determining input to a defined benefit scheme is discounted by applying the increase in the CPI to the value at the start of the input period (not otherwise introduced until 6 April 2011). In 2015-16, the increase was fixed at 2.5% rather than the CPI;

- the member must have been a member (not necessarily "active") of a registered pension scheme in the year from which unused allowance is to be carried forward;
- the tax year 2015-16 was a transitional year during which input periods were aligned with tax years. There are special rules for the carry-forward facility in this year (described below).

FA 2013, s. 49 reduced the annual allowance still further to £40,000 in 2014-15. The three-year carry forward facility was retained on broadly the same basis as had subsisted until then except that the annual allowance in the previous three years is assumed to have been £50,000 (not £40,000). For input periods ending in the 2015-16 tax year and later, the allowance for 2014-15 is assumed to have been £40,000.

Law: FA 2004, s. 227A, 228, and Sch. 34, para. 9; FA 2013, s. 49; *Finance (No. 2) Act* 2015, Sch. 4; SI 2015/80

Guidance: PTM 053000, 058000

2.5.2 Special annual allowance

In 2009, the government introduced anti-forestalling legislation prior to the implementation of a special annual allowance for "high earners", but this was complicated and was abandoned in favour of a lower standard allowance in 2011-12.

2.5.3 Annual allowance v annual limit

There are two main controls on contributions and they are both personal allowances available to the member.

The annual limit for relief refers only to personal contributions in a tax year and limits the amount of relief available by reference to size of contribution. Briefly, relief is limited to contributions of £3,600 or 100% of earnings, whichever is the greater.

The annual allowance refers to aggregate contributions from all sources in respect of a tax year. In 2017-18 (and 2016-17) it is £40,000 and under special rules applying for 2015-16, it was £80,000. If the annual allowance (and any carried forward allowance) is exceeded in a tax year, the member is taxed at marginal rates on the excess.

For the avoidance of doubt, an individual may be within the annual limit on personal contributions, but exceed the annual allowance for aggregate contributions, in which case there will be an annual allowance tax charge (even if contributions are only paid by the individual).

An individual may be within the annual allowance for aggregate contributions, but exceed the annual limit for personal contributions, in which case only part of the personal contribution will attract relief. The excess over the annual limit is ignored when measuring against the annual allowance in this example.

An individual may be within both allowances in which case relief is available and no tax charge will arise at this stage.

From a practical point of view, any measurement against allowances should start with the annual limit for relief and then progress to the annual allowance, because the annual allowance will only be applied to *relieved* personal contributions (and contributions from other sources, primarily an employer).

Whereas personal contributions paid in tax years are measured against the annual limit for relief, for the purposes of the annual allowance, contributions paid before 9 July 2015 were measured for input periods *ending* in the relevant tax year. So, if an input period ran from 1 August 2013 to 31 July 2014 (they will usually have been 12-month periods), all contributions paid in that input period will have been measured against the annual allowance for the tax year 2014-15. A personal contribution paid immediately before 6 April 2015 would have been measured against the annual limit for the tax year 2014-15.

In his 2015 summer Budget, the Chancellor of the Exchequer proposed a number of measures designed to align input periods with tax years. These measures appeared in the *Finance (No. 2) Act* 2015 and are described at **2.7** below.

2.5.4 Flexible drawdown and the annual allowance

The rules introduced in 2011 to allow the member to take flexible drawdown (see **Chapter 4**) required that no contribution may be made (money purchase arrangements) and no benefit accrued (defined benefit or cash balance arrangements) in the tax year in which the flexible drawdown started. In subsequent years, contributions could have been made, but they would have been subject to the annual allowance charge on the full payment(s) whether paid by employer or member. In effect this means that contributions would have been stopped once the member had taken flexible drawdown. The restriction applied in respect of any contributions, by any contributor to any scheme (or any accrual to any scheme).

Flexible drawdown was superseded by flexi-access drawdown and the money purchase annual allowance on 6 April 2015.

Law: FA 2004, s. 227A

2.5.5 The money purchase annual allowance

In its response to the Budget 2014 consultation, "Freedom and choice in pensions", the government proposed a number of changes to the annual allowance to reflect proposed flexibilities which subsequently appeared in the *Taxation of Pensions Act* 2014. The measures appeared in the same Act.

Until 5 April 2015, an individual who elected to take his benefits by way of flexible drawdown gave up his entitlement to the annual allowance. Contributions in respect of a member could not be paid in a tax year in which flexible drawdown started, and in subsequent years, contributions, whatever their size, would have been subject to the annual allowance tax charge. This restriction was abandoned on 5 April 2015.

The drawdown regime that existed before 6 April 2015 allowed two types of drawdown: flexible and capped. Capped drawdown did not impose any restrictions on future contributions other than the "recycling rule". The 2014 Act introduced a new regime:

- All flexible drawdown plans in place on 5 April 2015 converted to flexi-access drawdown funds.
- All new drawdown plans became flexi-access drawdown funds.
- Capped drawdown plans remained capped drawdown plans until the cap was breached or the member elected to convert to flexi-access drawdown. The advantage of

remaining in capped drawdown is that the restrictions on contributions do not apply, other than the recycling rule.

- In order to take a lump sum without the full panoply of drawdown, the member could take an uncrystallised funds pension lump sum.

The essence of the money purchase annual allowance rules is that if benefits have been flexibly accessed (only available under a money purchase scheme), the annual allowance for money purchase arrangements is subsequently reduced within the overall annual allowance. The money purchase annual allowance was set at £10,000. It was £20,000 in 2015-16 (see the description of the 2015 summer Budget measures below) and reverted to £10,000 in 2016-17. In 2017-18 it will be reduced for the whole tax year to £4,000. The proposal appears in the draft *Finance Bill (No. 2)* 2017.

If the money purchase annual allowance was exceeded in 2016-17, there might have been two consequences:

- there would have been a liability to the annual allowance charge; and
- the annual allowance to be applied to other arrangements (defined benefit schemes) would usually have reduced to £30,000 (the "alternative annual allowance") plus any unused allowance carried forward from the previous three years.

In the 2017 Budget, the government proposed a reduction in the money purchase annual allowance to £4,000. The proposal was subsequently withdrawn from the *Finance Bill* following the announcement of a general election. It subsequently appeared in the draft *Finance Bill (No. 2)*.

No carry-forward is available in respect of the money purchase annual allowance. Furthermore, under this method, any input measured against the money purchase annual allowance will not be measured against the alternative annual allowance and this prevents the same input being measured twice.

The "alternative chargeable amount" is the money purchase contribution that exceeds £10,000 (see the special rules for 2015-16 below) plus the amount that exceeds the alternative annual allowance (and any allowance carried forward). See also the special circumstances of 2017-18 described above. It can be assumed that the alternative chargeable amount will increase in 2017-18 to £36,000.

The rules also describe a "default chargeable amount" as the amount that exceeds the main annual allowance (plus carry-forward).

The annual allowance charge will apply to the greater of the alternative chargeable amount and the default chargeable amount.

The following example is based on an example provided by HMRC (at PTM 056510), but which assumes the money purchase annual allowance proposed for 2017-18 by the draft *Finance Bill (No. 2) 2017*.

HMRC-based example

Isobel has a money purchase arrangement and a defined benefits arrangement and has flexibly accessed her money purchase arrangement in the tax year, which triggers the money purchase annual allowance test in addition to the annual allowance test for that tax year (and subsequent tax years).

The annual allowance for the tax year is £40,000.

She has no available unused annual allowance to carry forward to the current tax year.

Isobel's total pension input amount for the tax year is £39,000, which includes a pension input amount for her money purchase arrangement of £11,000.

All of Isobel's money purchase pension input amount occurred after the flexible access which means the £4,000 money purchase annual allowance has been exceeded for the tax year by £7,000.

The pension input amount for Isobel's defined benefits arrangement is £28,000, which is less than the alternative annual allowance. The alternative annual allowance in this case being £36,000 (the annual allowance of £40,000 less £4,000).

As Isobel's money purchase pension input amount has exceeded the £4,000 money purchase annual allowance, Isobel must establish whether:

- the 'alternative chargeable amount', which is the total of the excess of Isobel's money purchase pension input amount over the £4,000 allowance plus the excess of the defined benefits pension input amount over the alternative annual allowance of £36,000,

is greater than:

- the 'default chargeable amount', which is the excess of Isobel's total pension input amount (the money purchase pension input amount plus the defined benefits input amount) over the annual allowance of £40,000.

That is if:

- the excess of £11,000 over £4,000 (£7,000) plus the excess of £28,000 over £30,000 (nil) = £7,000 (the 'alternative chargeable amount')

is greater than:

- the excess of £28,000 plus £11,000 over £40,000 = £0 (the 'default chargeable amount').

If so, the 'alternative chargeable amount' applies. Otherwise the 'default chargeable amount' applies.

In Isobel's case, the 'alternative chargeable amount' is greater than the 'default chargeable amount', which means the 'alternative chargeable amount' applies.

Isobel is liable to an annual allowance charge on her 'alternative chargeable amount' of £7,000.

2.5.6 Events triggering the money purchase annual allowance rules

The list of events that triggers the operation of the money purchase annual allowance rules is quite extensive:

- Flexi-access drawdown is designated after 5 April 2015. This may be as a consequence of a transfer of funds to a different arrangement. The trigger is assumed to have occurred immediately before the first drawdown payment from the flexi-access fund or from a short-term annuity purchased with flexi-access drawdown funds. It is not assumed to have occurred at the date the funds are designated for flexi-access drawdown (which may have been some time earlier) or even when the pension commencement lump sum is taken (if no withdrawal is taken at the time).

- A capped drawdown fund that was established before 6 April 2015 converts to flexi-access drawdown on or after that date. Conversion may be a consequence of the cap being exceeded or the member notifying the scheme administrator that he or she wishes to convert. The trigger is assumed to have occurred immediately before the first payment from the plan or the short-term annuity after conversion. The money purchase annual allowance will not apply to funds that represent a disqualifying pension credit that has been awarded on divorce (but will apply where these funds are topped up by funds not subject to the credit).
- A flexible drawdown plan was established before 6 April 2015. This automatically became a flexi-access drawdown plan on 6 April 2015 and the trigger applied on that date.
- The plan pays an uncrystallised fund pension lump sum for the first time. The trigger is immediately before the payment.
- A standalone lump sum is paid from a money purchase scheme where the member enjoys primary protection. The trigger immediately precedes the payment.
- An individual purchases a lifetime annuity where entitlement starts after 5 April 2015 and the terms of the annuity allow it to reduce other than in certain prescribed circumstances (generally where the rate of income reflects the movement in nominated freely marketable assets). The trigger event occurs immediately before the first annuity payment.
- The individual becomes entitled to a money purchase scheme pension after 5 April 2015 where there are no more than 10 existing pensioner members or dependants.

The money purchase annual allowance also applies to any of these benefits paid from an overseas pension scheme.

Inevitably, the more complicated aspects of the money purchase annual allowance relate to the special situations. The first of those situations refers to the trigger that occurs part-way through an input period.

Example

If Joe's input period runs from 6 April 2016 to 5 April 2017, his contributions paid in that period will, for the purposes of the annual allowance, fall into the 2016-17 tax year.

If the trigger (for example, the first payment under a flexi-access drawdown) occurs on 6 July 2016, the contributions to be measured against the money purchase annual allowance for 2016-17 will be those money purchase contributions paid on or after 6 July 2016.

Contributions for the whole input period (6 April 2016 to 5 April 2017) will be measured against the alternative or standard annual allowance (the £40,000 etc.).

If the scheme is a cash balance scheme, the input for the year is apportioned on a time basis (in the example it would be 9/12 of the cash balance input for the year).

The legislation dealing with the money purchase annual allowance and hybrid schemes is especially difficult. Few people will be concerned with it in practice, but the principles should be understood. The legislation distinguishes between "any hybrid arrangements" and "relevant hybrid arrangements".

A hybrid arrangement combines defined benefit and money purchase (other money purchase or cash balance) provision. The scheme will pay out benefits under one type of provision or the other in what is sometimes referred to as an underpin. The reference to a hybrid arrangement is to an arrangement to which the input for defined contribution provision is the same as the input for money purchase provision. In these circumstances, the input is assumed to be in respect of the money purchase provision and if there has been an appropriate trigger, the money purchase annual allowance will apply to the input.

A relevant hybrid arrangement is an arrangement:

- which was made or became a hybrid arrangement after 13 October 2014; and
- where the defined benefit input is greater than the money purchase input; and
- where the pension input in question is for an input period that ended after the trigger date.

Where the arrangement is a relevant hybrid arrangement the pension input amount for the possible defined benefits provision is replaced by the pension input amounts for the possible money purchase or cash balance provision in the money purchase annual allowance test, to determine if that would result in an alternative chargeable amount and if so the greatest possible amount.

The process requires each combination of elements (including those of non-hybrid arrangements) to be ordered and measured appropriately against the money purchase annual allowance. If any combination produces an excess over the money purchase annual allowance, the alternative chargeable amount is calculated for each combination. The highest alternative chargeable amount is then compared with the default chargeable amount and the annual allowance charge will apply to the higher of the two.

The process for hybrid schemes is not only very difficult, but is likely to be very rarely used. Examples of how the relevant hybrid scheme rules work can be found in the *Pensions Tax Manual* at PTM 056580 and 056590.

Law: *Taxation of Pensions Act* 2014, Pt. 4 (adding FA 2004, s. 227B to 227G)
Guidance: PTM 056510 to 056590

2.6 Input and defined benefit schemes

2.6.1 Common fund

Defined benefit schemes present different challenges. The way in which these schemes work is to provide benefits from a common fund for all members. There are no separate "accounts" or policies. It follows that contributions to a defined benefit scheme represent an amount needed to fund a total liability for all members and they cannot be identified by member. Input for the purposes of the annual allowance is therefore derived from the increase in the member's benefit over the accrual period. In calculating the input, some items are ignored because they cannot be attributed to contributions and some must be added back because they have derived from contributions, but have since transferred. Furthermore, increases due to inflation protection will also be ignored.

The increase in pension savings in a defined benefit scheme therefore requires the adjusted value of the arrangement at the start of the input period to be deducted from the adjusted value of the arrangement at the end of the input period.

2.6.2 Opening value

The process of determining the "opening value" is described by HMRC as follows:

> **"Step 1**
>
> Find the amount of the member's annual pension that had built up immediately before the beginning of the pension input period.
>
> (This is the amount of built up pension prior to the pension input period in question that would be paid to the member if the member retired at that time having already reached normal pension age and without any extra benefits for ill health.)
>
> **Step 2**
>
> Multiply the annual amount of that pension by 16.
>
> Note: If it is the first pension input amount for the arrangement (i.e. the member's benefits have started to build up for the first time under the arrangement) the opening value of the member's pension is nil.
>
> **Step 3**
>
> If the member's rights under the arrangement include a separate lump sum in addition to the pension, for example many public sector schemes provide a lump sum without

having to give up pension, add the amount of the lump sum to the amount found after step 2.

Note: If it is the first pension input amount for the arrangement (i.e. the member's benefits have started to build up for the first time under the arrangement) the opening value of the member's separate lump sum is nil.

Step 4

Increase the total after step 3 by the 12 month increase in the CPI to the September before the start of the tax year for which the calculation is being done."

For input periods ending in 2015-16, special rules apply and these are described in paragraph **2.13** below. In summary, input to defined benefit schemes is measured over a "combined period" and the opening value is increased by 2.5% rather than the increase in CPI.

Law: FA 2004, s. 230-232, 234-237ZA
Guidance: PTM 055330, 055331, 058070

2.6.3 Closing value

The process of determining the "closing value" is similarly described by HMRC:

"Step 1

Find the amount of annual pension that had built up by the end of the pension input period.

Step 2

Multiply that amount of pension by 16.

Step 3

If the member's rights under the arrangement include a separate lump sum in addition to the pension, for example many public sector schemes provide a lump sum without having to give up pension, add the amount of the lump sum to amount found after step 2."

Certain adjustments must be made to the closing value to ensure that, as far as is possible, the increase in savings is derived from employer funding over the period:

1. The value of transfers to the scheme during the period must be deducted.
2. The value of a transfer to another registered scheme or a qualifying recognised overseas scheme during the period must be added.
3. The value of a pension credit must be deducted.
4. The value of a pension debit must be added.
5. The value of benefits crystallised must be added.
6. The value of benefits reduced as a consequence of the scheme paying the annual allowance charge in the tax year ("scheme pays") must be added unless benefits were taken from the arrangement in the period (or there was a BCE 5, 5A or 5B).

Law: FA 2004, s. 234-236A
Guidance: PTM 055331

How the rules have developed

There have been some changes since the annual allowance rules were first implemented in 2006. The multiplier of 16 was introduced from 6 April 2011 and replaced a multiplier of 10. Taken with the reduction in the annual allowance, this has severely restricted scope for funding. The facility to uprate the opening balance with the CPI was generally made available on 6 April 2011. Until that date, the facility was only available for deferred members.

Minimum payments made in connection with contracting-out on a money purchase basis were abolished on 6 April 2012, but before that date were required to be deducted.

2.7 Input and input periods

2.7.1 Introduction to input periods

The annual allowance is a contribution allowance that was introduced in the 2006-07 tax year. The allowance applies to tax years, but the value of contributions measured against the allowance was not originally the value of contributions paid in the tax year , rather the value of contributions paid in input periods that ended in the tax year, as this section will describe. The 2015 summer Budget and subsequent *Finance (No. 2) Act* 2015 aligned input periods with tax years without creating a retrospective tax charge. The tax year 2015-16 is therefore a year of transition and subject to special rules of operation, described below.

The problem with all these rules is that they necessitate becoming familiar with more jargon. Although we have talked of "contributions", it is more accurate to talk of input. This is because although contributions are simply identifiable in the case of money purchase schemes and arrangements, input is derived from benefit accrual in the case of a defined benefit scheme and bears no relation to a contribution actually paid.

The original rules

Pension input periods may vary by arrangement and although unlikely in practice may even be specific to arrangements. When input is measured for a particular tax year, input will be the aggregate in respect of all input periods ending in the tax year. The immediate consequences of this are that the relevant allowance will be the allowance for the tax year in which the input period ends and if there is a chargeable excess, the appropriate tax rate will be the rate applying to that same year (not necessarily the year in which the contribution was paid).

Law: FA 2004, s. 238; FA 2011, Sch. 17, para. 27(2)
Guidance: PTM 052100-052700

2.7.2 The first input period

The rules regarding input periods and calculation of input changed with effect from 6 April 2011 although the principles remained the same. For these purposes we have to distinguish between the first input period and subsequent input periods. Under a money purchase arrangement, the first input period starts on payment of the first contribution (whatever its source). Under a defined benefit or cash balance arrangement, the first input period starts when benefit accrual starts. Under a hybrid arrangement (combining more than one of these), the first input period starts on the earlier of a contribution being paid to the money purchase section or benefit accrual starting under the other section(s).

If an arrangement was already in place on 6 April 2006 for an individual, then the first input period in respect of a money purchase scheme started when the next contribution was paid. If the scheme was a defined benefit scheme and benefits accrued uniformly over the year, the input period would have started on 6 April 2006. If benefit accrual was not uniform, the input period would have started when accrual next started.

2.7.3 Later input periods

This section has largely been superseded by the *Finance (No. 2) Act* 2015, but still has some relevance. See the section describing the new rules below.

The first input period will usually have ended on the anniversary of the start of the period. If it started on 1 July 2006, it would have ended on 1 July 2007. However, the scheme administrator or member may have nominated a different input period end in respect of a money purchase scheme. This was permitted as long as no two input period ends in respect of the same arrangement arose in the same tax year as a consequence. If both the administrator and member made nominations, the first nomination prevails.

The second and subsequent input periods will have ended after 12 months unless overridden by a nomination. So if it started on 1 July, a subsequent input period will have ended on 30 June. The input period before 6 April 2011 could never have been more than 12 months.

If the arrangement provided defined benefits or was a cash balance arrangement, the nomination could only have been made by the scheme administrator.

There was no requirement to notify HMRC of a change of input period.

2.7.4 Disregarded input before 2011

Under the rules in place before 6 April 2011, if the member took all benefits from an arrangement, there was regarded as being no pension input for the tax year in respect of that arrangement.

Furthermore, the input period in respect of that arrangement also came to an end, creating the possibility of two input period ends in the same tax year.

Similarly, if a member died during an input period, the input periods in respect of all arrangements for that member came to an end and there would be no pension input for those periods.

Both cases (taking benefits and death), gave at least a theoretical opportunity to pay very substantial contributions that would not be measured against the lifetime allowance.

2.7.5 The annual allowance charge

If the annual allowance was exceeded for a tax year before 6 April 2011, the excess was taxed at 40%. This was the annual allowance charge. It was an income tax and collected through the self-assessment process, but could not be reduced by, for example, allowances or reliefs. It was not applied if the member had successfully applied and retained enhanced protection. Although this may have seemed contradictory, there were circumstances in which the value of a defined benefit could have been increased with inflation rather than by way of benefit accrual.

From 6 April 2011, the annual allowance charge is determined by adding the excess to chargeable income for the tax year and applying the marginal highest rates. The changes in 2011 also included a facility, described below, for the scheme to meet the liability in exchange for a commensurate reduction in benefits.

Law: FA 2004, s. 227(4), (4A)

2.7.6 Changes to input periods from 2011

From 6 April 2011, the annual allowance rules were changed although the principles remained the same. In 2015 they changed again, removing the previous flexibility (see the 2015 Budget changes below).

The first input period after 5 April 2011 started when the first contribution was paid or when benefits started to accrue after that date. However, the first input period ended on the following 5 April (or on the same day if it started on the 5 April). The member could have made a nomination that the period should end on a different day, but the first period could not have been longer than 12 months. In a small change to the pre-2011 rules, the nominated date could not have been earlier than the date of the nomination if the nomination was made on or after 19 July 2011 (date of Royal Assent to FA 2011).

Subsequent input periods ended 12 months after they started (i.e. the day before the anniversary) unless a nomination was made. The member (or administrator) could choose any date in the following tax year even if it would extend the input period beyond 12 months.

2.8 Relationship between annual and special annual allowance

Note that under the special annual allowance (abolished on 6 April 2011) and anti-forestalling rules, the input period was set by legislation to the same period as the tax year. This could have unfortunate consequences. Although the special annual allowance charge (high income charge) could be offset against the annual allowance, it could only be offset for the same tax year. This meant that if both charges applied to a contribution that was deemed to have been paid in respect of two input periods (special annual allowance and annual allowance) ending in different tax years, there would have been no offset.

2.9 Taking all benefits

If the member takes all benefits from an arrangement, the revised rules do not generally stipulate that there should be no input amount so the period continues until the scheduled period-end.

Disregarding input from 2011

The revised rules explain that no input will be measured in the tax year in which the member dies or becomes severely ill. The test here is not that of serious ill health (for the purposes of ill-health commutation and where life expectancy is less than 12 months) and neither is it the test for ill-health retirement (unable to carry on the normal job). It is an inability to do any job. When the member takes benefits under either of these headings, the input period ends.

There is no rule about the form a nomination must take. However, if the member makes a nomination, he or she must inform the scheme administrator and if the scheme administrator makes a nomination, the administrator must inform the member.

Law: FA 2004, s. 229

2.10 Carry-forward of allowance

With the reduction in the annual allowance on 6 April 2011 came a facility to carry forward unused allowance from previous years once the allowance for the current year has been exhausted. The conditions are:

1. Unused allowance may be carried forward to the current tax year from the immediately preceding three tax years, starting with the earliest year.
2. The earliest year in which the facility became available was 2011-12, allowing unused allowance from 2008-09 to be carried forward.
3. In 2015-16, the unused allowance must be absorbed at the earliest opportunity starting with 2012-13 and after the allowance for the current year has been exhausted.
4. For the purposes of this facility only, current rules were used to calculate the available allowance to be carried forward to 2011-12, 2012-13 and 2013-14 from the years before 2011-12. This means that an annual allowance of £50,000 is used in the calculation for the earlier years, that the "opening balance" is increased with the CPI in deriving defined benefit or cash balance input and that in deriving defined benefit or cash balance input, a factor of 16 (not the previous 10) is applied.
5. In 2014-15, the annual allowance reduced to £40,000, but the maximum "carry-forward" for each of the previous three years is £50,000 less any allowance used in respect of the allowance. In 2015-16, the maximum amount of carry-forward from 2014-15 is £40,000.
6. To carry forward unused allowance from the previous year, the individual must have been a member of a registered pension scheme, although not necessarily an active member and not necessarily a member of the scheme to which the contribution is now to be paid.

7. The facility to carry forward unused allowance increases the allowable contribution for the current tax year. The increased contribution is relieved in the tax year to which the contribution is carried forward.
8. The facility is not available in respect of the annual limit for relief.
9. No election need be made to HMRC: carry-forward is automatic.

Most practitioners will wish to use the annual allowance calculator provided on the HMRC website (search for "annual allowance calculator").

If the contribution exceeds the annual allowance after applying the carry-forward facility, the member will be subject to an annual allowance charge whether the excess derived from employer or member contributions. Neither the employer nor the member can request a refund of contributions: such a payment would be an unauthorised payment and subject to a range of unauthorised payment charges.

Law: FA 2004, s. 228A

2.11 Changes to the charge and the "scheme pays" facility

2.11.1 The facility

The changes in 2011 included a change to the annual allowance charge which is set at marginal rates of income tax (i.e. usually 40% or 45% in 2017-18).

The annual allowance charge was originally designed to be collected from the member through the self-assessment process. From 6 April 2011, there is a legislative facility that allows the charge to be paid from accrued pension funds providing the payment is offset by a corresponding reduction in benefits. The payment will not constitute an unauthorised payment. It is known as the "scheme pays" facility.

2.11.2 Scheme pays – the obligation

FA 2004, s. 237 requires registered pension schemes to offer the scheme pays facility when the annual allowance (with carry forward allowance) has been exceeded and the annual allowance charge is more than £2,000 in relation to the scheme. There are a number of unusual circumstances in which the scheme can refuse to apply the facility. They are typically where the conditions have not been met, where the scheme enters the Pension Protection Fund or where HMRC have agreed that payment of the charge could be detrimental to other members, such as if the scheme is underfunded.

2.11.3 Scheme pays – the option

The scheme may provide the facility on a voluntary basis if the annual allowance has been exceeded, the amount of the charge is no more than £2,000 and the payment is allowed by the scheme rules.

2.11.4 Scheme pays – requirements

To take advantage of the scheme pays facility, the member must notify the scheme administrator in writing or electronically. Once made, the request cannot be revoked (although it can be amended). HMRC guidance specifies that the notice must be signed if in writing and dated if electronic. The member must confirm that the notification came from the member if it is electronic. There are a number of other requirements of the notice where the charge exceeds £2,000, essentially covering identification (name, title, address, etc.) and confirmation that the member understands the nature of the transaction and that the notification cannot be withdrawn. The requirements of the notice are less if the charge is no more than £2,000.

There are additional requirements if the member is anticipating taking benefits in the near future.

2.11.5 Deadlines

The notification of scheme pays "must be received by 31 July in the year following the year in which the tax year to which the annual allowance charge relates ended". HMRC give the example of the tax year to which the charge relates being 2013-14 and a deadline of 31 July 2015.

There is also a deadline for paying the charge, which is the second 14 February after the tax year to which it relates. So for tax year 2017-18, the deadline is 14 February 2019.

The corresponding reduction in pension may not apply to a dependants' pension unless the reduction is derived from a reduction in the member's pension such as where the dependants' pension is expressed as a percentage of the member's pension.

2.11.6 *Multiple schemes*

There is a maximum that a scheme can be asked to pay. If the individual is a member of only one scheme, the annual allowance is exceeded and the tax charge exceeds £2,000, then the process is simple: the tax charge may be taken from that one scheme. However, if the individual is a member of more than one scheme, the test is applied to each scheme. The charge may only be taken from each scheme for which the annual allowance is exceeded for that year and in respect of which the tax charge would exceed £2,000. The amount of tax payable may only be based on the excess as it relates to that scheme.

If an individual opts for the "scheme pays" facility, it can be combined with a payment from the member. There is nothing to prevent the tax charge comprising part payment from the member and part scheme pays.

If the scheme pays facility is available as of right (for example when the charge exceeds £2,000) liability is joint and several between administrator and member. If it is voluntary the liability is entirely that of the member.

2.11.7 *Effect on planning*

The scheme pays facility has had an impact on advice and member decision-making. The increase in the multiple and the reduction in the annual allowance might have deterred some individuals from future active membership of a defined benefit scheme if they were high earners. The scheme pays facility means that they continue to enjoy valuable defined benefit accrual funded mainly by the employer and a relatively small reduction in benefits is a small price to pay. The position may have been different under the previous rules that required the member to produce a cash payment to meet the annual allowance charge.

Law: FA 2004, s. 237A and 237B (as amended by FA 2011, Sch. 17, para.15); SI 2011/1793 *(The Registered Pension Schemes (Notice of Joint Liability for the Annual Allowance Charge) Regulations)*

2.12 Input periods and planning

The scope for this area of planning has been significantly reduced by changes in the *Finance (No. 2) Act* 2015. These, amongst other things, aligned input periods with tax years after a transition year of 2015-16. This section therefore mainly describes what was available until 2014-15.

When the annual allowance rules were first introduced in 2006 there was particular interest in how input periods could be arranged to accommodate extraordinarily large contributions. The annual allowance increased to a maximum of £255,000. Under the original rules, the input period end could be changed retrospectively (but not since 6 April 2011).

It was therefore possible in extreme cases to invest contributions to a money purchase scheme of over £700,000 within the space of a week. An example would show:

- first input period: contribution paid 1 April, period ended 2 April;
- second input period: contribution paid 3 April, period ended 6 April in the following tax year;
- third input period: contribution paid 7 April, period ended 6 April in the following tax year.

The rules did not allow a higher contribution to be paid by manipulating input periods, but they did allow large bonuses or other "one-off" payments to be invested in pension quickly and on the basis that early contributions in an exempt fund tend to be more valuable over the longer term than later contributions. Even supposing the member had the resources, the facility had a limited use because of the impact of the lifetime allowance.

Input periods could still have been altered before 9 July 2015 as part of sound planning. However, the attraction was not so obvious since 2011 because:

- there was now a facility to carry forward unused allowance;
- the annual allowance was much lower than it was;
- many of those who might have considered the option had already taken advantage of it, thereby limiting future options.

It is always important to remember that for the purposes of measuring contributions against the annual allowance, total contributions were identified for input periods ending in the relevant tax year. For the purposes of measuring personal contributions against the annual limit, the measurement identifies contributions paid in the tax year.

Example

Jim paid a contribution of £40,000 to an arrangement on 1 May 2014. His previous input period ended on 15 April 2014.

The personal contribution was offset and measured against the 2014-15 tax year for annual limit purposes. For annual allowance purposes, the contribution was measured against the 2015-16 tax year because (generally) no more than one input period could have ended in a tax year (and the previous such period ended on 15 April 2015).

2.13 Changes to the annual allowance: 2015 summer Budget

The 2015 summer Budget proposed a number of radical changes to the operation of the annual allowance. The measures appeared in Sch. 4 of *Finance (No. 2) Act* 2015. The main features of the changes are:

- a scaling back of the amount of the allowance for individuals who have income including pension contributions that exceeds £150,000 and income that excludes pension contributions of at least £110,000 (effective from 6 April 2016);

- a realignment of input periods with tax years (from 5 April 2016) with a view to possible eventual abolition of input periods as a concept;
- a transitional tax year (2015-16) so that nobody was retrospectively taxed as the new basis was implemented.

The measures appeared in the *Finance (No. 2) Act* 2015.

Scaling back the annual allowance

From 2016-17, the annual allowance is reduced by £1 for every £2 that adjusted income including employer pension contributions exceeds £150,000, to a maximum reduction of £30,000. The inclusion of employer contributions is to prevent members avoiding the restriction by means of salary sacrifice. Consistent with this, the member will not be subject to the reduction if income excluding pension contributions does not exceed £110,000 (the income threshold). Anti-avoidance measures ensure that salary sacrificed after 8 July 2015 is included within the definition of the threshold.

Where the money purchase annual allowance applies, the "alternative annual allowance" will be reduced in the same circumstances.

Adjusted income

The "adjusted income" is calculated as follows:

- net income as calculated under steps 1 and 2 of *Income Tax Act* 2007, s. 23; *plus*
- tax relief given under the net pay arrangement or relief on making a claim (the two alternative methods of giving relief to pension relief at source) deducted at source; *plus*
- any amounts deducted from pay under the net pay arrangement; *plus*
- any tax relief claimed by non-domiciled members on contributions to an overseas pension scheme; *plus*
- any employer contributions; *minus*
- any defined benefit lump sum death benefit that accrues to the individual in the tax year and is subject to the special

lump sum death benefit charge, primarily because the member was aged 75 or over at date of death.

The calculation in the *Income Tax Act* 2007 (steps 1 and 2) is simply the basic calculation of taxable income for the individual after deducting reliefs and allowances. The allowable deductions in the calculation include personal allowances and relievable personal pension contributions paid under the net pay arrangement (where the employer operates tax relief through payroll) and pension contributions relieved under the "relief on making" a claim provisions (claimed by the individual from the local tax office).

The value of employer contributions in respect of an arrangement is the pension input amount less total member contributions. For a defined benefit or cash balance scheme this means deriving total input from the increase in accrued benefit over the year (as before), but then subtracting the member contributions.

Threshold income

The taper will never apply if threshold income does not exceed £110,000, whatever the level of adjusted income. Threshold income for these purposes is:

- net income calculated under steps 1 and 2 of *Income Tax Act* 2007, s. 23 (above); *minus*
- lump sum death benefits subject to the special lump sum death benefit charge (above); *plus*
- any employment income sacrificed after 8 July 2015 to pay a pension contribution.

Closing input periods

All pension input periods that were open on 8 July 2015 closed on that date. The next input period ran from 9 July 2015 to 5 April 2016. From 6 April 2016, all input periods are concurrent with tax years. A feature of this measure is that it may have created three input periods (or at least two full and one part-period) in the 2015-16 tax year.

Dividing the 2015-16 tax year

The 2015-16 tax year was notionally sub-divided into a pre-alignment tax year (6 April 2015 to 8 July 2015) and a post-alignment tax year (9 July 2015 to 5 April 2016). The total annual allowance for the whole 2015-16 tax year was £80,000. The allowance for the post-alignment tax year was nil, but up to £40,000 of the unused allowance that had not been used in the pre-alignment tax year could have been carried forward to the post-alignment tax year. If the individual was not a member of a registered pension scheme in the pre-alignment tax year, the allowance for the post-alignment tax year was £40,000. Any remaining carry-forward from the three years prior to 2015-16 could have been added to this figure.

By way of a simple example (which assumes no carry-forward and no money purchase annual allowance), if £20,000 was paid on 1 May 2015, a £40,000 allowance would have been available for the post alignment tax year (£80,000-£20,000, but "capped" at £40,000). If £70,000 had been paid on 1 May 2015, the amount available for the post-alignment period would have been £10,000.

The calculation of input for cash balance and defined benefit schemes is more complicated and the Act required that the input for the input period ending in the 2015-16 tax year was derived from the increase in accrual (as before these changes) and then time-apportioned for the notionally divided tax years.

There are corresponding adjustments to the money purchase annual allowance in 2015-16. The pre-alignment allowance itself was increased to £20,000 (usually £10,000) and the alternative annual allowance (where the money purchase annual allowance was exceeded) was increased to £60,000 (usually £30,000). Up to £10,000 that was unused from the pre-alignment tax year may be carried forward to the post-alignment year and this may be supplemented by unused allowance from the previous three years. The maximum alternative allowance available in the post-alignment year was £30,000.

Defined benefit and cash balance schemes

To this point, the rules are fairly straightforward as they apply to money purchase schemes: the input is represented by contributions.

The application of the transitional provisions to defined benefit and cash balance schemes was more complicated and a consequence of the input being derived from the increase in accrued benefit over the input period. The pension input amount for the pre and post-alignment tax years was a proportion of the pension input amount calculated as if all the pension input amounts for pension input periods ending in the 2015-16 tax year had been made in a single pension input period. This is known as the "combined period".

The pension input amount for the post-alignment tax year was the proportion of the input amount for the period from 9 July 2015 to 5 April 2016 (272 days), i.e.:

> Pension input for the combined period x 272/number of days in combined period.

The input amount for the pre-alignment tax year was the input amount for the combined period less the input amount for the post-alignment year.

The following example is from the HMRC 2015 Budget Technical Note.

HMRC example

Pete is a member of a defined benefits arrangement with a pension input period normally of 1 January to 31 December. His combined period is therefore from 1 January 2015 to 5 April 2016 and his pension input period for the combined period is £45,000.

Pete's pension input amount for the post-alignment tax year is therefore £45,000 x 272/(365+96) = £26,551.

Pete's pension input amount for the pre-alignment tax year is therefore £45,000-£26,551 = £18,449.

For the purposes of the transition, the opening value used to derive input from the accrued benefit was increased by 2.5% rather than the increase in CPI.

There were special rules for deferred members.

Special rules applied to the carry-forward rules in respect of the transition year (2015-16). For the purposes of determining the years from which annual allowance could have been carried forward, the transition year was treated as one year. This means that unused allowance could have been carried forward from 2012-13, 2013-14 and 2014-15 to the pre-alignment tax year and where it had not been used in that period, unused allowance from the same tax years could have been carried forward to the post-alignment tax year (as well as the carry-forward of up to £40,000 from the pre-alignment tax year).

If there was an excess or more than one excess that arises in 2015-16, the charges should have been reported as one.

2.14 Sacrificing remuneration

2.14.1 General requirements

Salary sacrifice has for some time been a feature of retirement planning. Quite simply, the process requires the employee (who may be a director) to give up future entitlement to pay by way of an agreement that effectively alters the contract of employment. Once confined to shareholding directors, the facility has now been extended to employees who are members of group pension schemes. The sacrifice may be applied to salary or bonuses. It may be possible to sacrifice dividends, but this requires specialist advice.

The reason for sacrificing salary is to do with redirecting part of the remuneration package. That may be an informal arrangement or part of a structured framework of "cafeteria" benefits. Those benefits may be anything from childcare vouchers to pension contributions with which this section is concerned.

The reasons for "swapping" pay for employer pension contributions are:

- Both the employee and employer save National Insurance because personal contributions are paid after National Insurance contributions have been deducted from pay. Indeed, the NI saving may be used to increase the contribution.
- The sacrificed remuneration reduces the personal tax liability and, of course, the pension contribution is not a taxable benefit.
- It may be more convenient for the employer to pay the whole contribution as an employer contribution.

- Employer contributions are not subject to the annual limit for relief and this may be important if pay is kept low, perhaps because income is derived mainly from dividends in the case of a shareholding director.

On the other hand, remuneration sacrifice comes with warnings:

- To be effective, the process must meet certain requirements described below.
- If pay is genuinely reduced, it may restrict benefits available under a permanent health insurance policy or even make it more difficult to obtain a mortgage.
- Although unlikely to present a problem in practice, it is unlawful to reduce pay below the minimum wage unless the individual is a director (to whom the minimum wage regulations do not apply).
- The sacrifice will, if effective, modify the employment contract, which may have ramifications outside tax.
- The sacrifice may reduce the definition of pensionable pay. This may affect the contribution paid if it is a percentage of pay or it may determine the benefits payable from a defined benefit scheme, especially a career average scheme.

At the time of the 2015 summer Budget, HMRC reported that it was conducting an informal consultation into uses of unfunded non-registered pension schemes and the avoidance of National Insurance liability.

The government issued a Policy Paper on 5 December 2016 (with the Autumn Statement) which confirmed that it would introduce legislation to restrict the NIC and savings advantages of certain salary sacrifice arrangements (by taxing the greater of the value of remuneration sacrificed and the value of a benefit in kind to which the remuneration was diverted), but that employer-provided pension saving would be unaffected as would employer-provided pensions advice. Pension saving in this context means contributions to registered pension schemes.

2.14.2 Practicalities

There are special considerations to do with automatic enrolment.

The usual way in which a salary sacrifice agreement is made is to exchange letters between the employer and the employee, but there is no reason why the employer should not offer an option with a default position if no reply is received by a deadline. The "implied" decision carries a number of risks in practice.

Although some sacrifices may be ineffective if they can easily be reconverted to cash (the cash value may be taxed), this is not the case for sacrifices that redirect pay to a registered pension scheme. Contributions to such a scheme are always exempt from tax.

One of the conditions of a valid sacrifice is that the remuneration must be sacrificed before the employee is entitled to it. This is likely to mean before it is received. It used to be the case that the sacrifice had to be implemented before the relevant bonus period started. This was difficult to operate for bonus periods which started to accrue at the start of the year to which it related (and the bonus would not ordinarily be determined until sometime after that year).

There is no need to make a formal sacrifice in most cases involving discretionary bonuses. The bonus is simply not paid.

As a general rule, the effectiveness of the sacrifice can be jeopardised if the employee has a right to reinstate remuneration at its original level at any time. HMRC have agreed an exception in the case of automatic enrolment. This is an adaptation of the rule in *Heaton v Bell*. However, it will only be applied if the option to vary the employment contract is for a period of less than 12 months.

HMRC will not comment on the effectiveness of a proposed salary sacrifice arrangement but will comment on the consequences for tax purposes of a sacrifice already made.

2.14.3 Dividend sacrifice

Another option discussed in this context is dividend sacrifice. This is fraught with difficulties and potential liability to inheritance tax, not least because dividends are not remuneration. It should only be considered with the help of a specialist lawyer or tax planner. Dividend sacrifice may only be implemented by deed and the issues include:

- The dividend must be sacrificed before the shareholder becomes entitled to it. This means before payment in the case of an interim dividend and before a final dividend is voted by resolution at an annual general meeting (see IHTM 04220).

- As a general rule, a dividend waiver may be treated as a settlement and subject to income tax on the settlor if it enhances the return to other shareholders. This is, on the face of it, not the case when the sacrifice is intended to make a pension contribution available for the individual who waives the dividend.
- Some commentators suggest that waiver should not be a regular event, but the dangers here are less if the exercise is designed to fund a pension contribution.
- A dividend waiver may be treated as a transfer of value for inheritance tax purposes unless it is made within 12 months before it becomes payable. This applies to each dividend waived (IHTA 1984, s. 15).

Law: IHTA 1984, s. 15; ITTOIA 2005, s. 624, 625

Guidance: IHTM 04220; TSEM 4225

2.15 Recycling

As an anti-avoidance measure, FA 2004, Sch. 29, para. 3A penalises (tax-free) pension commencement lump sums that are used to increase contributions to a money purchase scheme. It is the taxation of the lump sums that is affected, not the relief available for contributions. The rule is therefore described in **Chapter 4** (Taxation of member benefits).

2.16 AVCs and freestanding AVCs

Additional voluntary contributions (AVCs) have long been a facility under occupational schemes to supplement benefits. They are personal contributions and are subject to allowances and restrictions as such. They may provide retirement or death benefits but, for practical purposes, the latter are rare.

AVCs are generally collected by way of the net pay arrangement. Under this method, contributions are deducted from pay and passed to the scheme by the employer. The deduction is made after the application of National Insurance contributions, but before tax.

The principle attractions of AVCs are that they are convenient and generally inexpensive. No matter how the scheme as a whole is funded, AVC arrangements are generally established on a money purchase basis and the bulk of charges are absorbed in the fees paid by the employer for the administration of the scheme (the member continues to pay a fund management charge). However, the choice of investment will usually be limited, very often to a managed fund and a deposit account, occasionally a with-profits fund. The choice is likely to be adequate for most employees.

A defined benefit scheme may offer an "added years" or "additional pension" facility. In this case, predetermined contributions paid on a regular basis (sometimes as a single contribution) will buy a predetermined pension or additional years of service (e.g. extra 1/60ths). The problem with added years or additional service is that although they offer certainty, they are difficult to cost and all "guarantees" are removed if contributions are not maintained or the member leaves service. They are only common in public sector schemes.

Freestanding AVCs are offered by life assurance companies. They were introduced in 1987 when it was not possible to contribute to a personal pension scheme at the same time as contributing to an occupational scheme in respect of the same earnings. Freestanding AVCs offered privacy from the employer and greater choice than "main scheme" AVCs. However, the privacy angle was oversold and the contracts were expensive.

The need for freestanding AVCs has been obviated by the current tax regime that allows concurrent contributions to personal pension schemes and occupational pension schemes.

2.17 *In specie* contributions

2.17.1 General rule

This term is misunderstood and incorrectly used. It refers to contributions that are represented by assets rather than cash.

As a rule, contributions may only be paid in cash if they are to attract tax relief, subject to a small exception in FA 2004, s. 195.

When an individual wishes to achieve the outcome of funding a scheme by a transfer of assets, there is a rather convoluted way of doing so if income tax relief is to be gained. The process is as follows:

Step 1

The scheme creates an obligation on the member to pay a contribution and specifies its amount. This can simply be a letter saying that the contribution is due. However HMRC make it clear that it must be an obligation and some might consider that a mere letter would not be enforceable in the courts (which is the real test). A deed would be adequate, but cumbersome.

Step 2

The member transfers assets to the value of the contribution to the scheme.

The obligation will usually be expressed as a contribution net of basic rate tax and the value of assets will reflect the net value. There is HMRC guidance on how to value volatile assets such as shares.

The transfer of assets will represent a disposal for CGT purposes.

The consequences of the value of assets not being equal to the value of the obligation are:

- if the value of assets is below the required value, there will be a scheme sanction charge on the administrator based on the undervalue;
- if the value of assets exceeds the required value, tax relief will be denied on the excess.

The transaction will create a liability to stamp duty.

Law: FA 2004, s. 188
Guidance: PTM 042100

2.17.2 Permitted in specie contributions

FA 2004, s. 195 allows "genuine" *in specie* contributions in tightly defined circumstances. The assets must be eligible shares and they must be transferred in the permitted period. Again, they will usually represent the net value of the contribution and the scheme will recover basic rate tax from HMRC, leaving the member to claim higher rate relief.

Eligible shares are shares:

"a. which the individual has exercised a right to acquire in accordance with the provisions of an SAYE option scheme, or

b. which have been appropriated to the individual in accordance with the provisions of a share incentive plan."

The permitted period:

"a. in relation to shares which the individual has exercised a right to acquire in accordance with the provisions of an SAYE option scheme, is the period of 90 days following the exercise of that right, and

b. in relation to shares which have been appropriated to the individual in accordance with the provisions of a share incentive plan, is the period of 90 days following the date when the individual directed the trustees of the share incentive plan to transfer the ownership of the shares to the individual."

Market value

The transfer must take place at market value. In the case of shares and unit trusts that is calculated in accordance with TCGA 1992, s. 272 and regulations (which were revised with effect from 6 April 2015). The regulations that apply from 6 April 2015 require that the market value of UK listed shares, securities or strips is the lower of the two closing prices for the day "plus one-half of the difference between those two figures" i.e. a mid-price. On any day that the Stock Exchange is not open, the value is derived from the close of the previous day when it was open.

If the share, security or strip is traded on an overseas stock exchange, the rule differs:

"3(1) The market value at any time of securities or strips which are not included in the official UK list but are listed on a foreign stock exchange is —

a. on any day the exchange is open, the price shown in the foreign exchange list for that day as the closing price for the securities or strips on that day (or if more than one price is shown the lower price plus one-half of the difference between those two figures), and

b. on any day the exchange is closed, that value on the latest previous day on which it was open,

3(2) If securities are quoted in more than one foreign exchange list —

a. any foreign exchange list published for a foreign stock exchange which is regarded as the major exchange for such securities is to be used for those purposes in preference to any other such list, but

b. if no exchange is regarded as the major exchange, any such list published for a foreign stock exchange in the territory in which the issuing company is resident is to be used for the purposes of these Regulations in preference to any other such list.

3(3) If a strip or a security exchanged for strips of that security is quoted in more than one foreign exchange list —

a. any such list published for a foreign stock exchange in the territory of the issuing government is to be used for the purposes of these Regulations in preference to any other such list, and

b. any such list published for a foreign stock exchange which is regarded as the major exchange in that territory for such strips or securities is to be used for those purposes in preference to any other such list.

4 In this regulation —

'foreign exchange list' means any publication which performs in the case of a foreign stock exchange a function equivalent, or broadly similar, to that performed by the Stock Exchange Daily Official List,

> 'foreign stock exchange' means a recognised stock exchange in a territory outside the United Kingdom on which securities or strips are traded."

Other assets (including shares that are not marketable) will be subject to an arm's length valuation.

Law: TCGA 1992, s. 272; FA 2004, s. 195; SI 2015/616 *(The Market Value of Shares, Securities and Strips Regulations* 2015)
Guidance: PTM 042100

2.17.3 Asset-backed contributions

Asset-backed contributions are a particular form of *in specie* contribution. They generally refer to large contributions paid to large schemes. Since 29 November 2011, employers have been unable to claim tax relief at time of payment on some asset-backed contributions.

This section provides a brief summary of the legislation and detail should be sought from HMRC and the legislation (principally FA 2012). The topic is very specialised and would merit a book by itself.

There are various types of asset-backed arrangement. In its simplest form, a contribution is paid to a pension scheme by the employer and the contribution is immediately used to purchase a property from the employer. The property offers a predicitable income stream and the property reverts to the employer at the end of, typically, a 15 year term.

The amount of the pension contribution is equal to the value of the property interest disposed of. This will be equal to the net present value of the income stream the pension scheme expects to receive over the 15 year term. In effect, the pension scheme has immediately lent back the value of the pension contribution it received. This "loan" will be repaid by the income stream payments over the term of the arrangement.

In a more complex arrangement, the property (or other income producing asset) is transferred into a partnership. The employer or connected persons will be members of the partnership. The employer makes a contribution to the pension scheme which the pension scheme then invests in the partnership. The amount of the employer contribution and the capital invested will be determined by the net present value of the anticipated income stream attached to the partnership interest the pension scheme acquires. Typically, the majority of the income stream will flow through to the pension scheme's interest.

The arrangement is often used to avoid the self-investment restrictions under DWP legislation that caps investment in the sponsoring employer. It also guarantees payments to the scheme more effectively than a funding schedule because in the event of default, the scheme will take full ownership of the asset.

The structure of the legislation (FA 2012) deals with arrangements established at different times. This summary only deals with asset-backed contributions paid on or after 22 February 2012. Separate rules deal with contributions paid between 29 November 2011 and 21 Febraury 2012 and with arrangements established before 29 November 2011.

There are essentially two different ways in which "repayments" could have been treated under the legislation for accounting purposes and this would have impacted on the tax treatment. HMRC describe the methods as being rather like the difference between a repayment mortgage and an interest only mortgage. The legislation opts for the first basis which is also the basis of the "structured finance arrangement", guidance on which can be found in HMRC's *Corporate Finance Manual*. A feature of this basis is that as time passes, the capital element of each instalment increases and the amount of interest reduces. It is the interest element that receives the relief and relief on the whole contribution is therefore not available at the start of the arrangement.

Law: FA 2012, Pt. 3, Sch. 13
Guidance: PTM 043320

3. The lifetime allowance

3.1 Introduction

One of the more radical changes to the taxation of pension schemes in the 2004 *Finance Act* was the introduction of the lifetime allowance. The lifetime allowance is one of the pillars of the registered pension scheme regime and would not have been viable without the other changes made by the Act that brought all types of registered scheme within one code.

For tax purposes it matters not whether the scheme is a personal pension scheme or an occupational scheme, or whether it is a defined contribution scheme or a defined benefit scheme; all retirement and all lump sum death benefits from registered schemes are subject to the same control on output that is the lifetime allowance.

Once again, the approach of the legislation is not to prohibit behaviour or limit benefits, rather to impose higher tax charges when output exceeds the allowance. Those tax charges are intended to recover tax relief in respect of the wrongly paid or overpaid output.

A test against the lifetime allowance is triggered by a "benefit crystallisation event" (BCE). If aggregate crystallised amounts in respect of an individual either immediately or over a period of time exceed the lifetime allowance, the lifetime allowance charge is payable.

There are other controls on output that we will examine elsewhere. The main alternative control is the regime dealing with authorised and unauthorised payments and in respect of which there is a range of possible tax charges. The distinguishing feature of the lifetime allowance is that its rules only apply when there is a BCE.

The lifetime allowance was introduced on 6 April 2006. It replaced a disparate set of rules:

- Occupational schemes (whatever their design) were, in effect, limited to providing benefits measured as a proportion of final remuneration. Most widely understood was the headline maximum pension of two-thirds of final remuneration after the member had completed at least 20 years' service by normal retirement date.

- In respect of personal pension schemes, relievable contributions were limited, but the pension was not otherwise limited.

Life became complicated for the individual who accrued benefits typically under a range of schemes, some of which were limited by output and some by input, especially as benefit "limits" under the occupational scheme had to take "retained" and "aggregable" benefits into account. So, for example, the apparently simple two-thirds pension limit had to include benefits from all previous schemes and from all schemes in respect of the same employment.

Radical change therefore came with a sigh of relief. However, by setting a new "limit" in the form of the lifetime allowance, there would inevitably be a group of individuals who would be exposed to a tax charge that would not have applied under the rules on which they based their retirement planning. The introduction of the lifetime allowance was therefore accompanied by a detailed set of relieving transitional provisions which also extended to the pension commencement lump sum. These are described in detail in **Chapter 11**.

Law: FA 2004, s. 214

3.2 What the lifetime allowance is and how it works

The lifetime allowance is expressed as a capital value. In its first tax year of implementation (2006-07) it was set at £1.5 million. Over a period of five years, the allowance increased in stages to £1.8 million in 2010-11.

Benefits paid within the allowance are subject to the usual range of taxes described elsewhere in this book. So, for example, the pension is taxed as non-savings income and generous tax-free lump sums are payable on death and retirement.

If the lifetime allowance is exceeded, the excess will be subject to a lifetime allowance tax charge which is 55% if the excess is withdrawn from the scheme as a lump sum or 25% if it is retained in the scheme, transferred to a qualifying recognised overseas pension scheme or paid as an income. The member and the scheme administrator are joint and severally liable for the charge except in circumstances where a charge arises after the death of the member or when the benefit payable is a death benefit lump sum. In those circumstances, the recipient of the lump sum is liable for the charge and the personal representatives (rather than the scheme administrator) are responsible for determining if a charge is due.

On the other hand, if the payment falls into an unusual category of lump sum payable after death, and includes certain arrears of instalments, liability will be shared between the personal representatives and the scheme administrator.

If the administrator is liable, he or she will usually deduct the charge from benefits before they are paid. However, there may be circumstances when the charge will be waived if the administrator acted in good faith. The member may then be charged directly.

If a consequence of the benefit crystallisation event is that "excess" funds are retained or paid as income, that excess is likely to be taxed in addition to the lifetime allowance charge. By way of example, an excess pension would be taxed at 25% before being subject to the usual income tax charges of 40% and/or 45%. The combined tax rate would therefore be 55% or 58.75% in 2016-17.

In measuring the value of benefits crystallised against the allowance, the value of crystallised benefits is accumulated during the member's lifetime. The following is a simple example:

Example

Joe crystallised a money purchase fund of £750,000 in 2006-07 when the lifetime allowance was £1.5 million.

This represented 50% of his lifetime allowance.

In 2010-11 he wished to crystallise further benefits, but the lifetime allowance had increased to £1.8 million. He wanted to know how much he could crystallise without incurring the lifetime allowance charge.

The remaining allowance was (100% available – 50% used) x the current lifetime allowance = £900,000.

The history of the lifetime allowance and its proposed future are:

Tax year	Lifetime allowance
2006-07	£1.5 million
2007-08	£1.6 million
2008-09	£1.65 million
2009-10	£1.75 million
2010-11	£1.8 million
2011-12	£1.8 million
2012-13	£1.5 million*
2013-14	£1.5 million*
2014-15	£1.25 million**
2015-16	£1.25 million
2016-17	£1 million***
2017-18	£1 million***

From 2018-19 the figure increases with the CPI rounded up to the nearest £100. The increase in CPI is measured to the previous September (as with DWP benefit increases).

*those members who had already accumulated large funds were able to protect themselves from the lifetime allowance charge that might otherwise have been prompted by the reduction in the allowance (fixed protection).

**this reduction appeared in FA 2013, s. 48, and again there are protections proposed for those who might otherwise be adversely affected, fixed protection (Sch. 22) and individual protection (FA 2014, s. 44 and Sch. 6).

***this reduction appeared in FA 2016, Part 1. The member may claim fixed or individual protection under FA 2016, Sch. 4.

Law: FA 2004, s. 214-219

3.3 Benefit crystallisation events

3.3.1 Table of amounts crystallised

Measurement against the lifetime allowance (or that amount that has not been exhausted) is prompted by a benefit crystallisation event or BCE. The list of BCEs has been extended since FA 2004. They do not all refer to taking benefits.

Benefit crystallisation events and amounts crystallised, as described in FA 2004, s. 216, are as follows.

Benefit crystallisation events	Amount crystallised (edited)
1. The designation of sums or assets held for the purposes of a money purchase arrangement under any of the relevant pension schemes as available for the payment of drawdown pension to the individual.	The aggregate of the amount of the sums and the market value of the assets designated. Effective date is the date of designation.
2. The individual becoming entitled to a scheme pension under any of the relevant pension schemes.	RVF x P, where: RVF is the relevant valuation factor (described below); and P is the rate of pension paid in the first year from crystallisation. Effective date is the date the entitlement is acquired.
3. The individual, having become so entitled, becoming entitled to payment of the scheme pension, otherwise than in excepted circumstances, at an increased annual rate which: a. exceeds the threshold annual rate, and b. exceeds by more than the permitted margin the rate at which it was payable on the day on which the individual became entitled to it.	RVF x XP, where: RVF is the relevant valuation factor (described below) XP is generally the amount by which (a) the increased annual rate of the pension, exceeds (b) the rate at which it was payable on the day on which the individual became entitled to it, as increased by the permitted margin. Effective date is the date the entitlement is acquired. (This will be described later.)
4. The individual becoming entitled to a lifetime annuity purchased under a money purchase arrangement under any of the relevant pension schemes.	The aggregate of the amount of such of the sums, and the market value of such of the assets, representing the individual's rights under the arrangement as are applied to purchase the lifetime annuity and any related dependants' annuity. Effective date is the date the entitlement is acquired.

Benefit crystallisation events	Amount crystallised (edited)
5. The individual reaching the age of 75 when prospectively entitled to a scheme pension or a lump sum (or both) under a defined benefits arrangement under any of the relevant pension schemes.	(RVF x DP) + DSLS, where: RVF is the relevant valuation factor (described below). DP is the annual rate of the scheme to which the member would be entitled if, on reaching age 75, he acquired an actual right to receive the pension. DSLS is so much of any lump sum to which the individual would be entitled (otherwise than by way of commutation of pension) as would be paid to the individual if, on that date, the individual acquired an actual (rather than a prospective) right to receive it.
5A. The individual reaching the age of 75 having designated sums or assets held for the purposes of a money purchase arrangement under any of the relevant pension schemes as available for the payment of drawdown pension to the individual.	The aggregate of the amount of the sums and the market value of the assets representing the individual's drawdown pension fund under the arrangement, less the aggregate of amounts crystallised by benefit crystallisation event 1 in relation to the arrangement and the individual.
5B. The individual reaching the age of 75 when there is a money purchase arrangement relating to the individual under any of the relevant pension schemes.	The amount of any remaining unused funds.

Benefit crystallisation events	Amount crystallised (edited)
5C. The designation, on or after 6 April 2015 but before the end of the relevant two-year period, of relevant unused uncrystallised funds as available for the payment, to a dependant or nominee of the individual, of (as the case may be) dependants' flexi-access drawdown pension or nominees' flexi-access drawdown pension.	The aggregate of the amount of the sums and the market value of the assets designated.
5D. A person becoming entitled, on or after 6 April 2015 but before the end of the relevant two-year period, to a dependants' annuity or nominees' annuity in respect of the individual if: (a) the annuity is purchased using (whether or not exclusively) relevant unused uncrystallised funds, and (b) the individual died on or after 3 December 2014.	The aggregate of: (a) the amount of such of the sums, and (b) the market value of such of the assets, applied to purchase the annuity, as are relevant unused uncrystallised funds.
6. The individual becoming entitled to a relevant lump sum under any of the relevant pension schemes.	The amount of the lump sum paid to the individual. Usually the date of entitlement. However, if the actual payment is not made until after age 75 is attained, there is no BCE (because the funds will have been measured under BCE 5B). Note that the lump sum is not confined to the pension commencement lump sum and from 6 April 2015 includes an uncrystallised funds pension lump sum to the extent of both taxed and untaxed portions.

Benefit crystallisation events	Amount crystallised (edited)
7. A person being paid a relevant lump sum death benefit in respect of the individual under any of the relevant pension schemes.	The amount of the lump sum death benefit.
8. The transfer of sums or assets held for the purposes of, or representing accrued rights under, any of the relevant pension schemes so as to become held for the purposes of or to represent rights under a qualifying recognised overseas pension scheme in connection with the individual's membership of that pension scheme.	The aggregate of the amount of any sums transferred and the market value of any assets transferred.
9. If regulations under FA 2004, s. 164(1)(f) so provide, the happening of an event prescribed in the regulations in relation to a payment prescribed in the regulations.	An amount determined in accordance with the regulations. This may include a lump sum overpaid in error (to the extent of the overpayment). It may also include certain lump sums paid after death.

Law: FA 2004, s. 164(1)(f), 216
Guidance: PTM 088100

The relevant valuation factor (RVF) is used to convert a benefit expressed as an income to a capital sum for the purposes of measuring its value against the lifetime allowance. It will usually be 20, but rarely may be higher by agreement with HMRC (when the rate of pension increase in the scheme rules is set at more than 5% a year).

Law: FA 2004, s. 276

3.3.2 Timing of simultaneous BCEs

If two or more events take place at the same time in fact, there are rules about their timing for the purposes of applying the lifetime allowance:

- When the pension commencement lump sum is taken with a pension, the lump sum is always assumed to have been paid immediately before the related pension entitlement arose (and before any other simultaneous event). This is even though the lump sum may be paid up to one year after the pension entitlement arises or six months before the entitlement to pension entitlement arises. Note, however, that for the purposes of calculating the amount of available lump sum, the pension and lump sum are valued at the same time when measuring against the lifetime allowance. It would not be possible to exhaust the lifetime allowance with the pension commencement lump sum and apply the related pension to the excess over the lifetime allowance.
- If there are two BCE 7s (lump sum death benefits), they are assumed to be simultaneous for BCE purposes.
- If two or more other events take place simultaneously (or in respect of different arrangements), the member must determine the order in which they are assumed to have arisen for these purposes.

Having an entitlement refers to having an actual right to the payment. An "actual right" (rather than a prospective right) is when a member has the right to a benefit without having to meet any further conditions or take any further actions. Further conditions may otherwise be:

- having to agree to or authorise the payment of a benefit; or
- having to obtain an employer's or scheme trustee/scheme administrator's agreement or co-operation to benefit payment.

An entitlement does not necessarily mean immediate payment. If a member selects the drawdown option and crystallises a pension commencement lump sum, there is an immediate entitlement to pension, but the member may elect for zero withdrawals until sometime in the future.

The timing of BCEs can be quite important if the member is in danger of breaching the lifetime allowance. The lifetime allowance charge will usually require a total tax charge of 55% to be deducted from benefits. This is 55% more than payable in respect of the pension commencement lump sum (which is tax-free in normal circumstances) and 15% more than the higher rate tax payable on income.

There are three aspects of the calculation to be borne in mind here:

- entitlement to the pension commencement lump sum is always assumed immediately to have preceded entitlement to the related pension;
- the maximum lump sum is generally limited to a proportion of the total value of benefits being crystallised (typically 25%); and
- the pension commencement lump sum may only represent a proportion of benefits falling within the lifetime allowance (the lifetime allowance is £1 million in 2016-17).

A lump sum that is paid in respect of funds that exceed the lifetime allowance is not a pension commencement lump sum (it is a lifetime allowance lump sum) and cannot enjoy its tax-free status.

Example

Mary has benefits valued at £800,000 under a personal pension plan (PPP). She also has a money purchase scheme (MPS) valued at £400,000. The lifetime allowance is £1 million.

If she takes benefits from the PPP first, she may allocate £600,000 to providing a pension and £200,000 to the lump sum, if she has no 2006 transitional protection.

If she takes the MPS benefits subsequently, the remaining fund within the lifetime allowance is limited to £200,000 (not £400,000). The lump sum will then be restricted to 25% of funds within the available lifetime allowance, i.e. £50,000 (25% x £200,000).

This example rather oversimplifies the position because it assumes no change in the standard lifetime allowance and recent history shows this to be unduly optimistic. The formula for calculating the available portion is in fact:

(CSLA – AAC)/4

where:

CSLA is the current standard lifetime allowance and

AAC is (broadly speaking) the adjusted value of previous crystallisations.

The adjustment to AAC is a factor expressed as:

CSLA/PSLA

where:

PSLA is the standard lifetime allowance at the time of the earlier BCE(s)

The result in this case would be the same whatever the order of crystallisation.

However, suppose that transitional protection (see **Chapter 11**) allows a lump sum to be paid under the MPS of £100,000, but subject to the lifetime allowance.

In these circumstances, it would be better to take the MPS benefits first (or elect that it was taken first if taken simultaneously with the PP).

The advantage would be that the whole of the enhanced lump sum would be within the lifetime allowance and tax-free and there would have been no additional detriment to the PP lump sum because the value of funds in total has not changed. If the crystallisations had taken place in the original order, only £200,000 of the MPS would fall within the lifetime allowance and the lump sum would be restricted to £50,000.

Law: FA 2004, s. 166(2), 216, 219(6)
Guidance: PTM 088200

3.4 The value of scheme pensions

A pension arrangement may express pension benefits in one of two ways:

- It may express the benefit as a fund that can be used to purchase a lifetime annuity or a drawdown pension. The contribution is defined when it is paid and the amount of the pension fund will be determined by net investment returns and the level of contributions paid. The amount of income will then be determined by the rate of income purchased by the fund (the annuity rate) or may be chosen by the member within the drawdown parameters. The member may choose from a range of additional benefits when purchasing an annuity such as rate of pension increases and death benefits. The benefit is sometimes described as "open-ended".
- It may express the benefit as a lifetime pension (rather than a fund). In this case, the rate of income and additional benefits are determined by the scheme rules and applied by the administrator. Typically this would be a defined benefit scheme offering, for example, 1/60 of final pensionable pay for each year of service. This is a scheme pension and is the only type of pension payable from a defined benefit scheme. Unusually, a money purchase scheme may offer a scheme pension. The main feature of the scheme pension is that it is for the scheme trustees or managers to make available whatever resources are needed to provide the required scheme pension (the value of which is determined by the trustees at the time the pension is taken). The funding commitment is sometimes described as "open-ended".

In order to derive a capital value from a scheme pension for the purposes of measuring benefits against the lifetime allowance, the initial income must be applied to a "relevant valuation factor" (RVF). The RVF is usually 20, but in a very few cases where pension increases may be unusually steep under the scheme rules, a higher figure may be agreed with HMRC by the scheme.

By way of example, a scheme pension of £12,500 would usually equate to a capital value of £250,000 (20 x £12,500) and this would represent 20% of a lifetime allowance of £1.25 million.

This produces some interesting consequences when scheme pensions are compared with other arrangements.

Example

Assume one scheme and a lifetime allowance of £1 million. The annuitant is in good health.

The lifetime annuity option would allow a fund of £1 million (2016-17). If this sum was used to purchase an annuity at age 60, the rate of annuity would reduce as each additional benefit was added. Without any additional benefits, the best rate to be found on *Money Advice Service* on 24 June 2016 was £3,900 a month.

If the pension was linked to the RPI and included a 50% spouse's pension (spouse of the same age), the pension would fall to £2,140.

The allowance would always remain at £1 million as would the value of the crystallised benefit. So, the addition of annuity options would, in effect, reduce the initial pension that fell within the lifetime allowance.

If we assume that the scheme pension is £50,000, then the revaluation factor would require a capital value of £1 million (20 x £50,000) to be measured against the lifetime allowance. However, a range of additional benefits could be added to the basic pension by the scheme rules without exceeding the lifetime allowance because the income is not increased (or reduced).

All this means that a scheme pension of £50,000 (£4,167 a month) offering a 50% widow's pension and pension increases would require an equivalent fund of somewhere in the region of £2.48 million for the 60 year-old if it were to be provided by a lifetime annuity. The problem is that this would exceed the lifetime allowance!

Law: FA 2004, s. 276

3.5 Separate lump sums

For most schemes providing a scheme pension, the pension commencement lump sum is derived from an option to commute part of the available pension. Where a registered pension scheme only provides the member with a pension commencement lump sum if he gives up a proportion of his scheme pension in return, i.e. by commutation, then the pension used in the calculation is the level of pension payable after any lump sum commutation. The payment of the lump sum will be a separate benefit crystallisation event (BCE 6), and the cash value of that lump sum will therefore be valued separately for lifetime allowance purposes.

3.6 Cumulative use of the allowance

In order that the member who has crystallised a pension can keep track of the lifetime allowance used over a period of time, each scheme administrator must make available to the member the value (as a percentage) of each crystallisation under the scheme every time there is a crystallisation, and the cumulative value of crystallisations under the scheme annually (until age 75) for six years or until transfer from the scheme if earlier (the receiving scheme inherits the obligation). If the crystallisation did not involve payment of a pension, only one certificate need be provided. The percentage is taken to two decimal places and rounded down in all circumstances.

Law: FA 2004, s. 219

3.7 Retaining funds

The application of the lifetime allowance changed significantly on 6 April 2011 as a consequence of an amendment in FA 2011. In the Act, the requirement to crystallise benefits by age 75 was removed and there were a number of consequential amendments that are discussed elsewhere in this book. One of those consequential amendments was to supplement the list of BCEs by adding BCE 5B (see **3.3** above). This BCE attempts to account for all uncrystallised money purchase benefits in one go. So, although benefits may not actually be taken, there will be a measurement against the lifetime allowance on reaching 75. Later crystallisations will not prompt a BCE except where there may unusually be an exposure to BCE 3 (beyond inflation increase in scheme pension).

BCE 5A had already paved the way for BCE 5B by requiring a lifetime allowance test at 75 for funds held in a drawdown fund.

Again, if there is a subsequent transaction such as the purchase of an annuity, there will be no BCE although there would be if the transaction took place before age 75.

There are other transactions that do not involve the member taking benefits, but nevertheless prompt a BCE. An obvious example is BCE 8 (transfer to a qualifying recognised overseas pension scheme) where the BCE is applied because the funds are leaving the UK regime.

Other examples are:

- the member reaching age 75 without taking benefits;
- certain above inflation increases to scheme pensions already in payment;
- certain corrective payments made after the member has died
    - o certain payments made after the death of the member, because entitlement to those benefits could not be established before death, are tested as well, and
    - o certain amounts of lump sum, which when paid were believed to have been part of the pension commencement lump sum, but were in fact paid in error as it later transpires there was no entitlement under the tax rules to that level of benefit and such error-payment is not recovered, are also tested.

The scheme administrator has three basic informational responsibilities before, at and after a BCE occurs in the member's lifetime:

- establishing whether a chargeable amount arises at the BCE;
- accounting to HMRC for the lifetime allowance charge due on any chargeable amount that arises at the BCE (on a quarterly basis); and
- providing the member after the BCE with a statement confirming the total level of the member's lifetime allowance that has been used up under the scheme, and if a chargeable amount arose at the BCE, a notice confirming:

- the level of chargeable amount that arose at the BCE;
- the lifetime allowance charge due; and
- whether or not they have accounted for the due charge, or intend to do so in due course.

How a scheme administrator establishes whether a member has enough available lifetime allowance to cover the amount crystallising at a BCE is not prescribed by legislation. It is for schemes to establish the best way for them to do this, based on their own particular circumstances and administrative systems. The administrator may feel able to rely on a declaration or may require something more robust.

Law: FA 2004, s. 215, 216; FA 2011, Sch. 16 para. 43

3.8 Pre-6 April 2006 crystallisations

If an individual crystallised benefits before the current regime was implemented on 6 April 2006, no BCE would have applied to the relevant arrangements. If benefits crystallised before that date and the same funds were subject to a second crystallisation after 5 April 2006, there will be no BCE and no test against the lifetime allowance.

Example

Lorna converts her money purchase fund to a drawdown arrangement in 2004. In 2008 she uses the funds in the same drawdown arrangement to purchase an annuity.

In this case, there is no BCE (and no test against the lifetime allowance) either when Lorna went into drawdown or when she subsequently elected for annuity purchase.

However, at the time of the first BCE after 5 April 2006 in respect of another arrangement, then the value of any pre-2006 crystallised funds must be taken into account when testing the value of crystallised benefits against the lifetime allowance. For these purposes, any pension commencement lump sum taken before 6 April 2006 is ignored, but the value of the pension in payment is measured at the time of the first BCE after 5 April 2006 and then multiplied by 25. The factor is constant and applies whatever the type of pension in payment. In the case of a capped drawdown pension, the income is taken to be the maximum allowable pension after applying the rates published by the Government Actuary's Department (i.e. the basis amount) on a capped drawdown basis.

If an individual commenced capped drawdown (the only drawdown option) before 6 April 2006 and subsequently converted to flexi-access drawdown after 5 April 2015, then if the first BCE arises after 5 April 2015, the value of the drawdown in payment for lifetime allowance purposes will be 80% of the maximum withdrawal at the time of conversion to flexi-access drawdown.

Example

Catherine commenced capped drawdown on 21 November 2005. She converted her plan to flexi-access drawdown on 1 June 2015.

She took no benefits from any other schemes until 1 August 2015 when she crystallised defined benefit scheme benefits. This was therefore her first BCE (BCEs were only introduced on 6 April 2006).

In measuring crystallised benefits against the lifetime allowance:

- The value of the drawdown plan must be taken into account because it is the first BCE after 5 April 2006.
- The value will be 80% of 150% of the basis amount (see **Chapter 4**) multiplied by 25, because the plan converted after 5 April 2015.

3.9 Overlap

3.9.1 Introduction

As we have seen, there will be occasions when a second BCE may arise in respect of the same arrangement. To take a simple example, the member may have designated funds for capped drawdown in 2007 (BCE 1) and may subsequently (but before age 75) apply the remaining fund to the purchase of an annuity in 2015.

The legislation brings some relief in these circumstances to ensure that the same fund is not measured against the lifetime allowance twice (although, of course, the first crystallisation will have reduced the available allowance).

In effect, the required calculation applies the increase in the funds designated for drawdown against the current lifetime allowance.

Example

James designates his personal pension fund as a lump sum (of 25% of the fund – BCE 6) and a drawdown pension (BCE 1) in January 2007 when the lifetime allowance was £1.5 million. The total, value of funds at the time was £1 million.

In January 2017, when the lifetime allowance had reduced to £1 million, James purchased an annuity with his remaining drawdown funds. They were valued at £700,000 at the time.

Calculation 1 (January 2007)

The value of the BCE 6 crystallisation was £250,000/£1.5 million = 16.66%

The value of the BCE 1 crystallisation was £750,000/£1.5 million = 50%

Total benefits crystallised = 66.66%.

Remaining lifetime allowance = 33.34%.

Calculation 2 (January 2017)

The value of benefits crystallised is:

Value of fund – (value of fund at January 2007 – value of BCE 6)

£700,000 – (£1 million-£250,000) = 0 (the result cannot be negative).

If the value of the fund in January 2017 had increased to £1.2 million, the calculation would be:

£1.2 million – (£1 million-£250,000) = £450,000

£450,000/£1 million = 45%

As it happens, 33.34% of the lifetime allowance remains and an amount equal to (45%-33.34% = 11.66% or £116,600) is subject to the lifetime allowance charge.

The rules encourage tax relievable savings to provide a pension in later life rather than estate accumulation (although the flexible pension measures in the *Taxation of Pensions Act* 2014 and the *Finance Act* 2015 make the policy intention more confused because they offer greater relief to death benefits). The overlap rules will only become a serious problem if withdrawals are low and/or investment returns are good and the cumulative value of crystallisations approaches the (significant) value of the lifetime allowance.

The overlap rules (or what the legislation describes as "prevention of overlap") may apply on a second crystallisation in respect of the same arrangement in the following circumstances:

- reaching age 75 when in drawdown (BCE 5A);
- purchasing an annuity with drawdown funds (BCE 4);
- converting a drawdown fund to a scheme pension (BCE 2).

They do not apply:

- on converting from capped drawdown to flexi-access drawdown;
- on converting from flexible drawdown to capped drawdown (this is unauthorised);
- on converting from scheme pension to flexi-access drawdown (this is unauthorised);
- in calculating death benefits.

Law: FA 2004, Sch. 32, para. 3, 4

3.9.2 Planning for overlap

For the financial planner, the real objective is how to reduce overlap and a lifetime allowance charge in respect of increased values under a money purchase scheme after the first BCE. This is not easy. The purpose of legislation dealing with funds later in life is to encourage benefits to be taken as retirement pension rather than accumulated in a tax-advantaged environment to swell the member's estate. To summarise the relevant rules:

- overlap rules may require a second lifetime allowance tax charge in respect of the same arrangement(s);

- the pension commencement lump sum remains tax-free from age 75, but is only available in respect of uncrystallised funds;
- the lump sum paid on death or serious ill-health is taxed at marginal rates of the recipient from age 75 (before age 75 it is generally tax-free, but triggers a BCE);
- dependants' pensions are taxed, but did not trigger measurement against the lifetime allowance until 5 April 2015. From the following day, BCE 5C and 5D were added to the list (see above).

The choices open to the member and adviser are to purchase an annuity or convert to a scheme pension at first crystallisation. This will prevent a subsequent BCE in respect of the arrangement. However, with annuity rates so low at present (2017), this is not an appealing prospect, especially for the younger retiree who will be locked into a guaranteed rate. Scheme pensions are rather cumbersome for achieving this result. There are many factors to take into account, but planning might include:

- Take significant withdrawals to suppress net fund growth (which may mean having a plan for the withdrawals which may be subject to income tax and may fall into the estate for inheritance tax purposes).
- Switch funds to a lower yielding, but less volatile environment. This is not to recommend accepting a lower return for the sake of it but rather to trade growth potential for security. Security will usually be accompanied by lower performing investments and so, in short, the strategy "swaps" quantity for quality.
- Continue uninhibited and pay the tax.
- A combination of any of these.

The problem may be acute for some members, but should not be overestimated: few members will have funds that will prompt a lifetime allowance charge (although the reduction in lifetime allowance makes this observation less valid).

Law: FA 2004, Sch. 32 para. 3 and 4

3.10 Enhancing the lifetime allowance

3.10.1 Introduction

For most people, their registered pension scheme output will be controlled by the standard lifetime allowance (£1 million in 2017-18).

There are some individuals who may claim an enhancement to their lifetime allowance and, in these circumstances, the modified allowance is sometimes referred to as the "personal lifetime allowance" (although this term is not used by the legislation).

Notifications for other enhancements should be submitted no later than five years after 31 January following the tax year in which the relevant event giving rise to the right to claim an enhancement occurred.

Once the enhancement is notified HMRC will provide the individual with a certificate confirming the level of lifetime allowance enhancement factor to which they are entitled.

The member must inform the scheme administrator before a BCE where they intend to rely on an enhanced lifetime allowance at that BCE.

Enhancement may be a consequence of one or more lifetime allowance enhancement factors defined in the legislation. These are as follows:

- the pension credit factor;
- the pre-commencement pension credit factor;
- the cash balance arrangement non-residence factor;
- the other money purchase arrangement non-residence factor;
- the defined benefits arrangement non-residence factor;
- the hybrid arrangement non-residence factor;
- the recognised overseas scheme transfer factor;
- the primary protection factor.

An individual who is entitled to a primary protection factor cannot also have an entitlement to a pre-commencement pension credit factor as those pension credit rights are already factored into the primary protection factor.

The lifetime allowance enhancement factor is expressed as a formula: multiple of the standard lifetime allowance minus one. So if the member claimed primary protection on funds that were valued at £2.25 million (1.5 times the standard lifetime allowance) on 5 April 2006, the factor would be 0.5 (i.e. 1.5 minus 1).

Law: FA 2004, s. 218(5)

3.10.2 Pension credits on dissolution of marriage or civil partnership

In the event of a dissolution of marriage or civil partnership, there are three main options open to the court in respect of the pension rights. The appropriate option is usually determined by the parties and the agreed solution is endorsed by the court. The options are:

- To offset the value of benefits against the value of other assets in determining the overall division of assets.
- To earmark emerging benefits for the benefit of the ex-spouse. This is not popular. The member remains liable for income tax on the whole pension, including the pension earmarked for the ex-spouse. The earmarking order comes to an end on the death of either party or the remarriage of the ex-spouse.
- To share pension rights. The ex-spouse effectively becomes a member of the scheme unless the manager or trustees exercise a right to transfer the ex-spouse out of the scheme by buying out their liability within four months of the date of the order. Alternatively, the ex-spouse may exercise a right to transfer to another arrangement.

Pension sharing may have an impact on the operation of the lifetime allowance.

Where all of the following conditions are met:

- the ex-spouse or former civil partner has acquired a pension credit which is now held in a registered pension scheme;

- he or she acquired the pension credit on or after 6 April 2006;
- it is derived from a pension benefit that was already in payment to the original member at the time of the pension sharing order; and
- the original member became entitled to that pension in payment on or after 6 April 2006 (described as a post-commencement pension in payment),

the lifetime allowance of the ex-spouse or former civil partner may be enhanced to reflect the fact that those pension benefits/rights have already been tested for lifetime allowance purposes when the original member originally drew that pension.

The lifetime allowance enhancement factor is called the pension credit factor.

There is no entitlement to a lifetime allowance enhancement factor if pension credit rights are acquired on or after 6 April 2006 from a registered pension scheme at a time when a pension is not in payment.

The individual against whom the order is made suffers a pension debit. If that individual was entitled to primary protection (see **Chapter 11**) and the order was made on or after 6 April 2006, the personal lifetime allowance would be reduced by the amount of the debit. If the recalculation takes a lifetime allowance enhanced by primary protection below £1.5 million, the primary protection is lost.

If the member enjoys enhanced protection, there will be no opportunity to rebuild rights under a money purchase scheme without losing enhanced protection. It may be possible to reinstate rights under a defined benefit scheme providing the appropriate limit is not exceeded.

Law: FA 2004, s. 220

3.10.3 Pre-commencement pension credit factor

A lifetime allowance enhancement factor is given where the ex-spouse or former civil partner acquired a pension credit before 6 April 2006. Here the lifetime allowance enhancement factor is called the pre-commencement pension credit factor. The deadline for submitting notification of a pre-commencement pension credit was 5 April 2009.

An individual who is entitled to primary protection cannot become entitled to a pre-commencement pension credit factor as those pension credit rights are already factored in to the primary protection factor.

The pension credit factor is calculated by reference to the actual value of the pension credit rights derived from the pension in payment. The factor is the fraction of the standard lifetime allowance the relevant pension credit rights represented at the time the ex-spouse or former civil partner acquired those rights.

For example, if the pension credit rights are £150,000 at the time they are acquired by the ex-spouse or former civil partner, and the standard lifetime allowance at that time is £1 million, the pension credit factor is 0.15.

This factor is then applied to the standard lifetime allowance at any future BCE to provide the uplift to the individual's lifetime allowance for the purpose of that BCE, unless the pension credit factor was generated before 6 April 2012, in which case the uplift for BCEs occurring on or after 6 April 2012 is provided by applying the factor to the figure of £1.8 million if this is more than the standard allowance. The uplift is then added to the standard lifetime allowance at the date of the BCE to arrive at the individual's lifetime allowance.

Law: FA 2004, s. 220, Sch. 36, para. 18
Guidance: PTM 095200

3.10.4 Non-residence overseas enhancement factors

A lifetime allowance enhancement factor may apply where after 5 April 2006, whilst contributing or accruing benefits under a registered pension scheme, an individual is what the legislation calls a "relevant overseas individual". An enhancement is sometimes permitted here where there has been a period when UK tax reliefs have not been available to the individual.

Entitlement to a lifetime allowance enhancement factor may arise where a member transfers benefits into a registered pension scheme from a recognised overseas pension scheme after 5 April 2006. In these circumstances an uplift is sometimes given to reflect the fact that those transferred funds (now held in a registered pension scheme) will not previously have benefited from UK tax relief.

The lifetime allowance enhancement factor given in this circumstance is called the "recognised overseas scheme transfer factor".

Law: FA 2004, s. 221-226

3.10.5 Primary protection factor

The primary protection factor is based on the value of the member's benefits at 5 April 2006, but in the case of retirement benefit schemes can never be more than the HMRC maximum benefit for the individual in the scheme at that time.

When an event arises that gives the member an entitlement to an enhancement factor, the member has up to five years to notify HMRC. The member will be given a reference number which he or she will have to quote when there is a BCE involving the enhanced allowance. In particular, HMRC will have to be informed as part of its compliance process.

In order to "account" for crystallisations, the value of benefits crystallised and expressed as a percentage of the standard lifetime allowance may be set off against the enhanced allowance, also expressed as a percentage.

Example 1

By way of example, if the factor is 0.5, the lifetime allowance for the individual is (1.5 x the lifetime allowance). If the member crystallised £180,000 when the standard lifetime allowance was £1.8 million, the remaining allowance would be (150%-10%) x the standard lifetime allowance.

The process has been complicated by the reduction in the lifetime allowance on 6 April 2012 and the question of how to account for a crystallisation where the enhancement was applied before that date (except in the case of primary protection which has its own rules). In these circumstances, the enhancement is calculated by reference to the greater of the standard lifetime allowance and £1.8 million and the enhancement is then added to the (reduced) lifetime allowance.

Example 2

Enhancement factor added in 2008. Benefits crystallised in 2016-17.

The enhancement is 0.5.

The enhancement is 50% of £1.8 million = £900,000.

The personal lifetime allowance is (£900,000 + £1 million) = £1.9 million.

The remaining available lifetime allowance is also indexed and this can be best illustrated by an example from PTM 092300:

HMRC example

Jacob had £3 million of pension rights protected under primary protection on 5 April 2006, giving an additional lifetime allowance factor of 1.

He took benefits worth £1.8 million in 2011 when the standard lifetime allowance was £1.8 million. At that time, Jacob's primary protection was worth £3.6 million (standard lifetime allowance of £1.8 million plus additional lifetime allowance factor of £1.8 million). So Jacob used up 50% of his personal lifetime allowance.

On 31 March 2014 Jacob took the rest of his benefits that were worth £2 million. The standard lifetime allowance (SLA) in 2013-2014 was £1.5 million. Jacob's primary protection was then worth £3.6 million (£1.8 million plus a factor of 1).

The amount of lifetime allowance used up by Jacob's previous benefit crystallisation is found by multiplying the amount of that BCE (£1.8 million) by the formula

SLA at time of current (2014) BCE/SLA at time of previous (2011) BCE

Where SLA is the standard lifetime allowance. So,

£1.8 million x (£1.5 million/£1.8 million) = £1.5 million.

The SLA has, of course, since reduced further to £1 million.

Both of the above examples assume that the value of benefits was within HMRC limits on 5 April 2006.

In the unusual circumstances of a member enjoying more than one enhancement factor, those factors are aggregated. So if one factor, perhaps for primary protection, was 0.4 and another was 0.3, then the total factor would be 0.7 and the personal lifetime allowance would be 1.7 x the standard lifetime allowance.

Law: FA 2004, Sch. 36, para. 7-11
Guidance: PTM 092300

3.11 Special occupations and the reduced lifetime allowance

There are circumstances where the benefits accrued before 6 April 2006 in a "special occupation" (where HMRC recognised that it was customary to retire before the normal range of pension ages) may still be taken earlier than normal minimum pension age subject to transitional provisions.

In the case of private sector schemes, the lifetime allowance is reduced by 2.5% for each *complete* year that the date of crystallisation precedes normal minimum pension age (now 55). So, if an individual takes benefits one day after their 35th birthday, the reduction will be 47.5% ((55-36) x 2.5) of the lifetime allowance.

In order to account for lifetime allowance used when the reduction applied, the amount crystallised is determined and increased to the same extent as the lifetime allowance. If a benefit was crystallised in 2006-07 and before normal minimum pension age on account of the individual being employed in a special occupation and enjoying transitional rights, that benefit would have been increased by 20% (with the lifetime allowance) to 2011-12 to identify how much lifetime allowance had been used.

If the individual takes benefits from different schemes over a period, then the reduction will reduce (and the lifetime allowance will increase) over that period.

It would not be possible to "stagger" benefits from the same scheme without losing the early pension age transitional protection (which would raise the prospect of unauthorised payment charges).

Law: FA 2004, Sch. 36, para. 19

3.12 Fixed and individual protection

3.12.1 The reduced lifetime allowance

The lifetime allowance reduced to £1 million on 6 April 2016, but members of pension schemes are able to protect already accumulated funds and benefits by claiming fixed or individual protection from the lifetime allowance. These protections replicate the protections available when the lifetime allowance reduced in 2014. A significant difference from earlier options is that the deadline for claiming the 2016 protections will be any date before benefits are taken and after an HMRC reference number has been allocated.

With effect from 6 April 2012, the lifetime allowance reduced from £1.8 million to £1.5 million. For individuals who had planned their affairs on the assumption of the higher lifetime allowance, there was an opportunity to claim fixed protection from the lifetime allowance if the appropriate form was submitted to HMRC by 5 April 2012 (although some latitude on this deadline was allowed at the last minute). The claim could not have been made if the member was sustaining a successful claim for primary or enhanced protection.

The effect of a successful claim for fixed protection was to preserve the lifetime allowance of £1.8 million subject to certain conditions, the most important of which was that there should be no further benefit accrual after 5 April 2012. Technically, the member's lifetime allowance becomes the greater of the current lifetime allowance and £1.8 million and this is known as the underpinned lifetime allowance. The conditions were very similar to those attending a claim for enhanced protection, but not quite the same: whereas under enhanced protection, further benefit accrual to a defined benefit scheme may not be identified until benefits are crystallised or transferred, in respect of fixed protection, the protection is lost immediately there is any increased accrual beyond normal indexation.

Enhanced protection is described at **Chapter 11**.

There are other conditions for retaining fixed protection. They are a restriction on certain types of transfer and a prohibition on establishing a new registered pension arrangement other than to accept a transfer from another registered pension scheme.

If a member has fixed protection, he or she must tell the scheme administrator (and the value of benefits will be calculated by reference to the higher lifetime allowance if there is a BCE). If fixed protection is lost, the member must inform HMRC. Loss of fixed protection can only be prospective and will not affect transactions prior to the loss.

Law: FA 2004, s. 218; FA 2011, Sch. 18, para 13-14

3.12.2 Losing fixed protection

If an individual loses fixed protection:

- he must inform HMRC in writing within 90 days;
- the loss is not retrospective;
- the lifetime allowance will revert to £1.5 million or the current allowance if greater.

The triggers for losing fixed protection are:

- there is benefit accrual in respect of the member under a registered pension scheme;
- there is an impermissible transfer from the member's arrangement;
- there has been a transfer of sums and assets that is not a permitted transfer; or
- the member has made a new arrangement other than in permitted circumstances.

3.12.3 Transfers

A transfer of rights from one arrangement to another will not jeopardise a claim for fixed protection if the transfer is:

- a permitted transfer;
- part of a retirement benefits compliance exercise; or
- part of an age equality exercise.

A transfer is not permitted if:

- it is made to a scheme that is not a registered pension scheme or a recognised overseas pension scheme;

- it is made from an other money purchase arrangement to a cash balance or a defined benefit arrangement; or
- it is made from a defined benefit or cash balance arrangement to another defined benefit or cash balance arrangement.

An impermissible transfer (that will jeopardise fixed protection) includes:

- a transfer of assets from a scheme that does not relate to the individual (although a transfer resulting from the award of a pension credit on divorce will not cause a loss of protection);
- a transfer of assets not relating to a registered pension scheme;
- a transfer of assets to a hybrid arrangement that becomes an other money purchase scheme (not a cash balance scheme);
- a defined benefit or cash balance arrangement becomes an other money purchase scheme;

3.12.4 Automatic enrolment and fixed protection

If an employer is subject to the automatic enrolment duty and automatically enrols an employee into a new pension scheme under the provisions of PA 2008, the employee will have one month from the enrolment date to opt out of the new scheme. Regulations introduced in 2015 convert the employer's obligation to enrol to a discretion if the member enjoys enhanced or fixed protection, so if the employer is warned, enrolment may be avoided altogether. An individual who opts out within that one month period is then treated as never having been a member of the pension scheme. So if an employee is subject to automatic enrolment under the PA 2008 provisions and opts out within one month he will keep his fixed protection. If he does not opt out in time then he will lose his fixed protection. Every three years, the employer will usually have a duty to enrol automatically those who have opted out, so the employee will need to opt out within one month each time this happens. However, under the 2015 amending regulations, the obligation to re-enrol is also changed to an employer discretion in certain circumstances, including where the member enjoys fixed or enhanced protection.

The obligation arises when an employee joins a new employer and the same right to opt out applies.

There is a similar provision where the employer offers automatic enrolment, but not under PA 2008. In that case, the condition is that the opt-out relates back to the date enrolment started (or 6 April 2012 if later) if fixed protection is not to be lost.

The legislation is quite specific about what types of arrangement may permit a transfer of rights.

A transfer from a money purchase arrangement that is not a cash balance arrangement may only be to another such money purchase arrangement. This may be a UK or recognised overseas scheme;

A transfer from a defined benefit or cash balance arrangement may be made to:

- a money purchase arrangement under a registered pension scheme or recognised overseas scheme, in which case the value transferred must be an actuarial equivalent to benefits accrued;
- another defined benefit or cash balance scheme, but only if the transferring scheme is being wound up (a question of fact) and the receiving scheme relates to the same employment;
- another defined benefit scheme or cash balance scheme in the case of a "relevant business transfer" (where all or part of the business is being sold in defined circumstances); or
- another defined benefit or cash balance scheme where the transfer is part of a retirement benefits compliance exercise.

To make the position absolutely clear, fixed protection will be lost if:

- the transfer is to a scheme that is not a registered or recognised overseas pension scheme;
- the transfer is from a money purchase scheme that is not a cash balance scheme to a cash balance scheme or defined benefit scheme;

- the transfer is from a defined benefit or cash balance scheme to another defined benefit or cash balance scheme other than in the circumstances described above.

Law: *The Occupational and Personal Pension Schemes (Automatic Enrolment) (Amendment) Regulations* 2015 (SI 2015/501)

3.12.5 What is benefit accrual?

Fixed protection will be lost if there is benefit accrual and unlike relevant benefit accrual in relation to the loss of enhanced protection, the test is ongoing and immediate (rather than when benefits are taken).

If the scheme is a money purchase scheme other than a cash balance scheme, there is benefit accrual if a contribution is paid (by anybody).

If the scheme is a defined benefit scheme, benefit accrual arises when there is an increase in benefits that exceeds the "relevant percentage" after applying a relevant valuation factor and after making an allowance for inflation-proofing. The value is derived from the following:

(P x RVF) + LS where:

P = the pension under the valuation assumptions before commutation.

RVF = the relevant valuation factor (usually 20).

LS = the lump sum where this accrues separately from the pension (i.e. it is not a commutation). This mainly applies to public sector schemes.

In determining if there has been accrual, the "opening balance" is increased by:

a. the increase that appears in scheme rules and which has applied since 9 December 2010 (often the increase in the Retail Prices Index for deferred members); or
b. the increase in the Consumer Prices Index to September in the previous tax year.

Any actuarial reduction (which would usually reduce as the member became older) that would otherwise apply on taking benefits earlier than normal pension age must be ignored in the calculation (and a subsequent actuarial reduction on taking benefits after there has been benefit accrual cannot reinstate fixed protection). It must also be assumed that the member is in good health.

PTM 093500 to PTM 093800 provide detailed guidance on the application of the relevant percentage.

The test for a cash balance scheme is in essence the same as for a defined benefit scheme: has the "relevant percentage" been exceeded?

Under a hybrid arrangement comprising money purchase and defined benefits, there is benefit accrual when a contribution is paid that is specific to the member or there is an increase in benefits above the relevant percentage in respect of the defined benefit or cash balance arrangement.

If the employer continues to provide an insured defined benefit (e.g. 4 x salary) lump sum death benefit, that will not itself invalidate fixed protection. However, if the death benefit is a money purchase lump sum and the arrangement for the member was established after 5 April 2006, then any contributions paid to the arrangement after 5 April 2012 will constitute benefit accrual and will jeopardise the claim for fixed protection. There are a number of similar circumstances that produce different results and these are described at PTM 093800.

Note that if a pension credit is transferred to a defined benefit or cash balance arrangement, fixed protection will be lost if pension rights are increased by more than the relevant percentage (which they usually will be).

The restriction on benefit accrual will also usually prevent rights being reinstated after a pension debit unless funding took place in the year of the debit and the relevant percentage was not exceeded.

Law: FA 2011, Sch. 18, para. 14(4)
Guidance: PTM 093500-093800

Whether to claim fixed protection

The decision whether to claim fixed protection (and opt out of future accrual) is a difficult one. The starting point is that it can rarely be in a member's interest to opt out of a scheme sponsored and primarily funded by an employer:

- the employer contribution and the tax relief allowed to the member is a valuable part of the member's remuneration;
- the value of defined benefit accrual as measured by the cost of providing the same level of benefit by other means is substantial and far more than the "average" contribution for older scheme members;
- the member may have to forego valuable disability and death benefits on leaving the retirement section of the scheme. These benefits may be expensive to replace and, worse, underwriting considerations may make them impossible to replace.

The introduction of a lower standard lifetime allowance and fixed protection has disturbed these "self-evident truths". To take a simple example, let us suppose that at 5 April 2014, the member had aggregate benefits of £1.5 million (equal to the lifetime allowance on that date) and had no protection of the lifetime allowance other than fixed protection. If he or she paid £1 to a scheme the next day, this would have triggered a loss of fixed protection and would have imported the lower lifetime allowance of £1.25 million.

Assuming no changes in these values when there was a BCE, the "cost" of losing fixed protection was 55% of (£1.5 million-£1.25 million) = £137,500.

Any increase above £1.5 million would also have been subject to tax at 55%.

It may be argued that the impact of the lifetime allowance charge (in effect being applied retrospectively) is "cushioned" by the employer contribution, but this is less valid the older the member.

If a money purchase plan is being funded solely by the member, the considerations are different. There is little point in funding benefits that will be taxed at 55% even if the tax merely represents a recovery of tax reliefs.

3.12.6 Fixed and individual protection 2014

The lifetime allowance fell to £1.25 million on 6 April 2014, but individuals who were in danger of breaching the reduced allowance were given the opportunity to claim protection from the lifetime allowance charge. There were two protection options introduced in FA 2013 and FA 2014:

- fixed protection (FP 2014) – this works in the same way as the 2012 version by providing an underpinned lifetime allowance of the greater of £1.5 million and the current standard allowance; and
- individual protection (IP 2014) – the legislation appears in FA 2014 and was implemented with retrospective effect to 6 April 2014 on the Bill receiving Royal Assent.

There was a three-year period during which a claim for individual protection (2014) could have been registered (to 5 April 2017). It protected the value of benefits at 5 April 2014 (capped by the then lifetime allowance of £1.5 million), but allowed further benefit accrual without jeopardising protection from the underpinned lifetime allowance. The significance of this option is that it is possible to continue benefit accrual in a valuable defined benefit scheme (for instance) without incurring a charge on the additional accrual and up to £250,000 (£1.5 million minus £1.25 million).

3.12.7 Fixed and individual protection 2016

The standard lifetime allowance reduced to £1 million with effect from 6 April 2016. At the same time, some transitional relief was given by the introduction of fixed protection (FP 2016) and individual protection (IP 2016). The protections from the lifetime allowance charge are broadly the same as for previous versions of FP and IP and this section will concentrate on the main features and differences.

Fixed protection 2016

The lifetime allowance is fixed at £1.25 million until 5 April 2018 for those who successfully claim FP 2016. After that date, the allowance will increase each year in line with the CPI measured to the previous September, in parallel with the standard lifetime allowance.

FP 2016 is available to anyone who on 6 April 2016:

- was a member of a registered pension scheme or a relieved member of a non-UK pension scheme;
- did not have primary protection;
- did not have enhanced protection;
- did not have FP or FP 2014;
- did not have IP 2014.

There is, in effect, no deadline for claiming FP 2016 which can only be done online. The only requirement is that FP 2016 must be claimed before benefits are taken. Applications could not have been made before 6 April 2016. No minimum benefit value is required.

HMRC guidance states that if the application is completed correctly, HMRC will not reject it. If the application is rejected, the member will be notified and will have a right of appeal. If the application is accepted by HMRC as valid, the member will be issued a reference number (which can be withdrawn if HMRC subsequently discover that the application was incorrect).

Individual protection 2016

This protection was available from 6 April 2016. The amount of protection from the lifetime allowance (the "relevant amount") is fixed at the value of pension rights on 5 April 2016, provided these exceeded £1 million (up to which the standard lifetime allowance would apply). The maximum value that can be protected is £1.25 million. So, for example, if the value of pension rights at 5 April 2016 is £1.4 million, IP 2016 will only protect £1.25 million.

There is, in effect, no deadline for claiming IP 2016 other than the date that benefits are taken. However, as HMRC point out in their guidance, the statutory obligation which requires administrators to provide values for pension savings at 5 April 2016 only applies for four years and, from 6 April 2020, adminstrators may be reluctant to provide the service.

An application for IP 2016 may be made subject to certain conditions:

- the member has one or more "relevant arrangements" which means that he or she is a member of a registered pension scheme or a "relieved member" of a non-UK pension scheme;

- the "relevant amount" exceeds £1 million;
- the member does not have primary protection;
- the member does not have IP 2014.

Applications must be made online and none will have been accepted before 6 April 2016.

A member may apply notwithstanding that he already has enhanced or fixed protection. The IP 2016 will remain "dormant" unless and until the other form of protection fails (because IP 2016 will be protecting a smaller amount).

Again, the application cannot be refused if it is correct, and there is a facility to appeal against rejection.

3.13 Pension credits (dissolution of marriage)

3.13.1 The options

There are three main options available to the court in respect of pension rights when a marriage or registered civil partnership is dissolved. In fact, the courts are rarely called upon to determine how pension rights should be allocated; rather the arrangements are made by the parties and the court will formalise them by way of a "consent order".

The options are:

1. To take the pension rights into account when determining how other assets and income should be awarded.
2. To share the rights accrued under a pension arrangement. The entitlement of the claimant is immediate and he or she enjoys virtually the same rights as an "ordinary" member. The claimant becomes a "pension credit member".
3. To earmark retirement benefits when they become payable. In this case, the order will "lapse" if the original member or the claimant dies or if the claimant remarries. This is a rarely used option having been superseded by the pension sharing facility in 2000 which allowed a "clean break". The tax position of earmarking is also

unsatisfactory: the scheme member is responsible for tax on the total benefit including the amount earmarked for the claimant (although, of course, the split will reflect this). The earmarked rights are personal and cannot be transmitted to beneficiaries on the claimant's death.

3.13.2 Money purchase schemes

Provided the pension credit is transferred to the member's existing money purchase (other than cash balance) arrangement, the member will not lose fixed protection. The pension credit is not a tax relievable contribution so its payment will not cause loss of the fixed protection.

However, if the pension credit is received from a non-registered pension scheme it is tax relievable. Fixed protection will be lost if it is paid into a registered pension scheme.

Likewise, if the pension credit is transferred into a new arrangement for the member, fixed protection will be lost. This is because setting up of a new arrangement will trigger loss of fixed protection.

3.13.3 Defined benefit and cash balance schemes

If the pension credit is transferred into a new arrangement for a member, fixed protection will be lost due to the setting up of the new arrangement.

If the pension credit is transferred into an existing defined benefits or cash balance arrangement then fixed protection will be lost if at the end of the tax year in which the pension credit is transferred into the arrangement benefit accrual occurs. It is very likely that there will be benefit accrual in such cases.

3.14 Drawdown pensions

Designation of drawdown funds is a BCE 1 (see, generally, **3.3.1**) and prompts measurement against the lifetime allowance. This is so even if no withdrawals are taken and the immediate objective is to take the pension commencement lump sum(s). The lump sum entitlement is a BCE 6 and is assumed to have arisen immediately before the pension entitlement under BCE 1.

The value of the drawdown pension being crystallised for these purposes is the value of the funds being crystallised under this BCE. If drawdown pensions already crystallised before 6 April 2006 are to be taken into account (because this is the first BCE after 5 April 2006), then their value is derived from the maximum allowable drawdown at the time of the BCE multiplied by 25.

Where the first benefit crystallisation event (BCE) in respect of the member that occurs on or after 6 April 2006 is also on or after 6 April 2015, and before that date the arrangement was a capped drawdown pension, the valuation for the purposes of the lifetime allowance is 80% of the maximum annual drawdown amount that could have been paid at the time the funds converted to flexi-access drawdown (so the value is 80% x 25 x maximum capped drawdown pension).

Where the member's first BCE is on or after 6 April 2015, and either the individual was receiving 'capped drawdown' or had opted to receive 'flexible drawdown' in a pension year that began on or after 27 March 2014, the amount of the lifetime allowance available is reduced by 80% of 25 times the maximum amount that could have been paid as a capped drawdown pension.

If the drawdown is phased, then each time new funds are crystallised, there will be a BCE 1 in respect of those funds.

The lifetime allowance tax charge is payable from scheme funds by the scheme administrator.

For technical reasons, the lifetime allowance charge is based on the basic amount of the chargeable amount. The basic amount is the amount that the administrator allocated to the benefit and is generally three times the available lump sum (so the lump sum is 25% of the total fund). So if £75,000 is the basic amount and the lifetime allowance has already been exhausted, the tax will be calculated as (basic amount plus lifetime allowance charge) x lifetime allowance charge or (£75,000 plus £25,000) x 25% = £25,000. The lifetime allowance tax charge of 25% applies when funds are retained by a scheme in spite of the BCE or the benefit is paid as an income.

Law: FA 2004, s. 166 and 216

3.15 Transitional protection

3.15.1 Primary protection

Transitional protection is a term that applies specifically to the protection of pension rights that exceed the standard lifetime allowance from the lifetime allowance charge because those benefits (or the bulk of them) accrued under the tax regime that applied before 6 April 2006. That date is often designated as "A-Day".

The protection falls into two categories and members were invited to claim either or both before 6 April 2011.

Under *primary protection*, the member's standard lifetime allowance (£1.5 million on 6 April 2006) is modified to reflect the value of rights under tax-approved schemes at 5 April 2006 and this figure is then increased to the same extent as the standard lifetime allowance. However, it does not reduce with it. The protection was only available if the member's aggregate pension rights exceeded £1.5 million at 5 April 2006.

If we examine the history of a "modified" lifetime allowance since 6 April 2006 until 5 April 2014, it increased in stages by 20% until 2011-12 (as the standard lifetime allowance increased from £1.5 million to £1.8 million), but then remained at that level: it did not reduce by 16.66% on 6 April 2012 when the standard lifetime allowance reduced.

A member who had claimed primary protection cannot (and probably would not have wanted to) claim fixed protection.

Primary protection cannot be lost unless a pension debit awarded against the member takes the value of benefits below the original protected amount (£1.5 million). It could have been claimed with enhanced protection, described below, and in those circumstances could only have applied if the claim for enhanced protection was lost.

A claim for primary protection will also have consequences for the pension commencement lump sum calculation.

3.15.2 Enhanced protection

A claim for enhanced protection may be made whatever the value of pension rights at 5 April 2006. A successful claim would have removed the lifetime allowance altogether. However, broadly speaking, the protection will be lost if there is future benefit accrual that exceeds inflation or if the member establishes a new registered pension arrangement other than solely for the purposes of transferring accrued rights from one registered scheme to another.

Again, a successful and sustained claim for enhanced protection will have consequences for the calculation of the pension commencement lump sum.

There are two other forms of protection available for those members who had accrued rights prior to 6 April 2006. They do not directly impact on the lifetime allowance:

Scheme specific lump sum protection

The pension commencement lump sum allowance after 5 April 2006 is 25% of the value of benefits being crystallised at the time (i.e. pension and lump sum). Ordinarily, any excess is taxed as an unauthorised payment. However, where the pre-A-Day lump sum rights exceeded 25%, the allowable lump sum (indexed) is protected from unauthorised payment charges.

This form of lump sum protection is available when the member has not claimed primary or enhanced protection and/or the pension commencement lump sum does not exceed £375,000. The protection is scheme specific, unlike lump sum protection consequent to claiming primary or enhanced protection where the protection covers aggregate schemes: it is member specific.

Special occupations

Retirement benefits may only be paid, as a rule, when the member has reached normal minimum pension age, currently 55 (having been 50 until 5 April 2010). There is no maximum.

Any payment made before normal minimum pension age is unauthorised. However, there are exceptions for individuals whose earnings derived from a "special occupation" before 6 April 2006 and whose scheme rules allowed benefits to be taken exceptionally early. There are also exceptions for certain members of public sector schemes where it would be normal to retire early.

3.15.3 Whether to exceed the lifetime allowance

The individual may be faced with an unappetising dilemma of whether to exceed the standard lifetime allowance or the modified lifetime allowance (when the member has primary protection). At least as difficult is the consideration of whether to invalidate a prior claim for enhanced protection.

There will rarely be a definitive answer to cover all situations and much will come down to the individual's circumstances, but a number of observations may be made:

Circumstances	Observations
No transitional protection – further contributions will breach the standard lifetime allowance	If the member is paying the whole contribution, there is little to justify paying further contributions. Tax relief will probably be against an income tax rate of 40% or 45%, but the pension will be taxed in total at 55% or more. The lump sum (otherwise tax-free) will be taxed at 55%. If the employer pays the contribution (or at least a significant part of it), the decision is less clear cut. Tax on the benefit is at a rate of 55%, but the employer contribution still offers an employee benefit which is especially valuable if it is a defined benefit. The employer may offer a benefit or remuneration instead of the contribution and this should be considered on its merits.
Primary protection	The protected funds will probably not be adequate to cover the growth in the funds, especially if further contributions are paid. The effect will be the same as for breaching the lifetime allowance (above).

Circumstances	Observations
Enhanced protection	Further accrual or payment of further contributions is likely to lead to the loss of enhanced protection. The consequence will be one of two outcomes: • either the member will revert to having no transitional protection; or • the type of protection will change to primary protection (if this was claimed as the "default"). The problem here is that if the protection is lost altogether and the funds substantially exceed the lifetime allowance, a 55% charge (at least) will apply to the excess over the lifetime allowance (which could be substantial). The problem is not alleviated to any real extent if the employer pays the contribution because the charge applies to funds already accrued.
Fixed protection	This is not regarded as transitional protection, but follows a similar logic. Fixed protection is similar to enhanced protection except that the protection is lost immediately there is further accrual. In an extreme case (after 6 April 2014), £1 paid to a money purchase scheme could "cost" the member an immediate tax charge of 55% of (£1.5m-1.25m) because the standard lifetime allowance was reduced (rather than frozen).
Individual protection	Individual protection appeared in FA 2014, but is retrospective to 6 April 2014. There is a three year period (to 5 April 2017) during which a claim may be registered. It allows accrued funds to be protected subject to a cap of £1.5 million. It differs from fixed protection in that it allows further benefit accrual. The significance of this option is that it allows further accrual in a valuable defined benefit scheme, for instance, without incurring a tax charge on past accrual between £1.25 million and £1.5 million.

4. Taxation of member benefits

4.1 Pensions and lump sums as authorised payments

4.1.1 Introduction

As we have seen, the pension tax regime is built on a framework of allowances and taxes rather than prohibitions and penalties. As a general rule, payments made from a registered scheme will be unauthorised (and subject to unauthorised payment charges) unless they fall into a category of authorised member or employer payments.

Two of the categories of authorised member payments are member benefits in the form of pensions and lump sums. However, even then, the payment is heavily regulated as to the maximum amount paid, when it can be paid and how it is paid. The law is described in the "pension rules" and the "lump sum rule", each of which has been amended since its introduction in FA 2004.

4.1.2 The pension rules

In summary, the pension rules are (with explanations throughout this chapter):

Pension rule 1: This rule only allows benefits to be taken from normal minimum pension age (usually 55), or earlier if the ill-health condition is met.

Pension rule 2: The rule originally limited a guarantee period under an annuity or scheme pension to 10 years. If a member became entitled to an annuity after 5 April 2015, the 10 year limit need not apply.

Pension rule 3: A defined benefit pension may only be a scheme pension.

Pension rule 4: A money purchase scheme may only pay pension benefits by way of a lifetime annuity, drawdown (including flexi-access drawdown) or scheme pension. A member must be offered the option of selecting a lifetime annuity before being paid a scheme pension.

Pension rule 5: The total amount of (capped) drawdown pension paid in each drawdown pension year from, or under a short-term annuity purchased using sums or assets out of, the member's drawdown pension fund must not exceed 150% of the basis amount for the drawdown pension year.

Law: FA 2004, s. 165, 166 and Sch. 28, 29; ToPA 2014, Sch. 1, para. 79 (inserting FA 2004, s. 273B)

4.1.3 The lump sum rule

There is one lump sum rule which describes the types of lump sums that can be authorised benefit payments to the member:

(a) a pension commencement lump sum;
(b) a serious ill-health lump sum;
(c) an uncrystallised funds pension lump sum;
(d) a short service refund lump sum;
(e) a refund of excess contributions lump sum;
(f) a trivial commutation lump sum;
(g) a winding-up lump sum;
(h) a lifetime allowance excess lump sum; or
(i) a transitional 2013-14 lump sum.

(The 2013-14 lump sum was a temporary measure introduced to deal with the transition to the new pension flexibilities. As such it would only have been paid on or after 19 September 2013 and before 27 March 2014. See **4.2** below.)

There are parallel rules for death benefits.

The benefits available from a scheme will usually be determined by the scheme rules which themselves are subject to the overriding authority of statute and the general law.

Law: FA 2004, s. 165, 166 and Sch. 28, 29; ToPA 2014, Sch. 1, para. 79 (inserting FA 2004, s. 273B)

4.1.4 Exceptions

Occasionally, legislation will be introduced that allows greater flexibility than the scheme rules. The most obvious example (described in **Chapter 1**) was in 2006. This was a temporary override to allow trustees and managers time to make the substantial changes consequent to FA 2004. Where some transactions were disallowed by the scheme rules, trustees and managers could allow them under the overriding authority of the Act.

More recently the ToPA 2014 allows a range of payments to be made from a money purchase scheme that would not be allowed under the scheme rules drawn up under the legislative regime before 6 April 2015. Those payments are:

(a) a payment of drawdown pension;
(b) payment to purchase a short-term annuity;
(c) a payment of dependants' drawdown pension;
(d) payment to purchase a dependants' short-term annuity;
(e) a payment of nominees' drawdown pension;
(f) payment to purchase a nominees' short-term annuity;
(g) a payment of successors' drawdown pension;
(h) payment to purchase a successors' short-term annuity;
(i) an uncrystallised funds pension lump sum;
(j) a flexi-access drawdown fund lump sum death benefit;
(k) a pension commencement lump sum where the person becomes entitled to it in connection with becoming entitled to income withdrawal (or where the person dies after becoming entitled to it but before becoming entitled to the income withdrawal in connection with which it was expected that the person would become entitled to the lump sum); or
(l) a trivial commutation lump sum death benefit where condition B in paragraph 20(1B) of Sch. 29 is met.

Law: FA 2004, s. 165, 166 and Sch. 28, 29; ToPA 2014, Sch. 1, para. 79 (inserting FA 2004, s. 273B)

4.2 When can benefits be paid?

The "headline" benefit is the pension. Tax relief is allowed on input to encourage individuals and their employers to provide them with a sustainable income in retirement. Employer sponsored pensions are sometimes referred to as "deferred pay". With the implication of deferred pay also comes the reality of a deferred liability to tax.

As a general rule, the pension is payable from "normal minimum pension age". This is currently 55, but was 50 between 6 April 2006 and 5 April 2010. The normal minimum pension age applies to members and pension credit members who have been allocated a pension credit on dissolution of marriage.

The pension commencement lump sum must usually be paid within an 18-month period starting 6 months before and ending 12 months after the member becomes entitled to the lump sum. Entitlement to the pension commencement lump sum arises on the day that actual entitlement (as opposed to prospective entitlement) to the linked relevant pension arises. Entitlement does not mean actual payment, but recognises that part of the arrangement has crystallised to provide the pension.

The time limit was overridden where the lump sum was paid between 19 September 2013 and 27 March 2014 (where the related pension was paid between 6 July 2014 and 6 April 2015) in order to allow individuals who had been told of the new pension flexibilities by the government, to await their statutory availability. There was also a facility to exchange some annuities that had been purchased for a more flexible substitute.

With the 2014 Budget Statement the government issued a consultation document and fact sheet entitled "Freedom and choice in pensions". One of the document's proposals was to link the normal minimum pension age to increases in the state pension age. The initial review of normal minimum pension age would be in 2028, by which time the state pension age would have increased to 67 and, by implication, normal minimum pension age would be set at 57.

In its response to the consultation, the government confirmed that for private pension schemes (new and existing), normal minimum pension age would increase to 57 in 2028 and would remain 10 years lower than state pension age thereafter. Exceptions would be certain public service schemes that have special early pension ages (firefighters, police, armed services). Although normal minimum pension age is set to increase in future, the government confirms that it will still retain lower pension ages for "special occupations".

There is now no maximum age from which a pension may start, but there are fiscal disadvantages (albeit reduced in 2015) to drawing pensions after age 74. This is consistent with the legislators' intention to encourage retirement rather than estate planning.

There are now no links between employment status and taking benefits, which is why it is rather misleading to talk of "retirement" or "retirement benefits" (a sign of the times is that the legislation has now dropped the description of "an income in old age" that appeared in ICTA 1970). In any case, a reference to retirement would inevitably have led to difficulties with EU and domestic age equality legislation as it developed.

Benefit commencement may be staged either within a collection of schemes, within a single scheme or within an arrangement.

There are exceptions to the general rule that member benefits will be regarded as unauthorised payments if they are taken before age 55. They are:

- benefits may be taken at any age if the member is required to retire from the normal job on grounds of incapacity and does so (see **4.3.1**);
- benefits may be taken at any age if the member is able to take all benefits as a serious ill-health lump sum (see **4.3.2**);
- some individuals may have a protected early pension age allowed prior to 6 April 2006 because their earnings derived from an occupation from which it was customary to retire early, perhaps because of physical demands (see **4.4**);
- some individuals are members of public sector schemes that allow a special, statutory normal minimum pension age (such as fire fighters).

Law: FA 2004 s. 165, pension rule 1; *The Registered Pension Schemes (Authorised Payments) Regulations* 2009 (SI 2009/1171)

Taxation

Pensions are taxed in a similar way to earned income (non-savings income) and, subject to personal allowances, are generally subject to PAYE procedures on the whole of each payment. They are not subject to a National Insurance liability.

As a general rule, the pension commencement lump sum is available as an option: the member may take benefits as a full pension or as a reduced pension and pension commencement lump sum. There are a few schemes, mainly in the public sector, that accrue the lump sum independently from the pension.

Most members will take the lump sum option even if they require income in retirement. This is because the lump sum can be applied to an alternative income producing asset which may offer better value than the taxed pension. Examples are investment bonds, from which withdrawals may be taken; unit trusts, from which a dividend may be available; or a purchased life annuity (PLA).

Annuity rates have generally been poor since interest rates were maintained at record low levels, but PLAs have tax advantages. For tax purposes, each instalment paid under a PLA is treated partly as a return of the purchase price (tax-free capital content) and partly as savings income (taxed interest element). This is known formally as the "partial exemption scheme". The capital content increases as a proportion of the total payment, the shorter the term and therefore the older the investor. An investor in his or her 80s will find that the whole of each payment is tax-free.

The option to take the lump sum and reinvest is not entirely self-selecting. Under a defined benefit scheme, the lump sum is calculated by reference to a scheme-specific commutation rate which is unlikely to favour the benefits being crystallised. Furthermore, it may be possible to take the lump sum from money purchase benefits provided by a fund accrued under the scheme such as from an additional voluntary contribution, in which case there is no reference to a commutation rate. It is unlikely that the commutation rate would be so poor as to neutralise the advantage of the PLA option, but a comparison of options should be made.

Law: ITTOIA 2005, Pt. 4, Ch. 7 (charge to tax) and Pt. 6, Ch. 7 (partial exemption scheme)
Guidance: IPTM 4300

4.3 Early retirement due to incapacity

4.3.1 Early pension

Both of the following conditions must be met for this facility to apply:

1. The member must be permanently unable to carry on the normal job because of injury, sickness, disease or disability. Although incapacity is permanent, the legislation does envisage that some may recover. The disability must have been certified by a registered medical practitioner (registered under the *Medical Act* 1983) or an overseas equivalent if the member is resident overseas. The requirement is not that the member cannot carry on any job, rather he (or she) cannot continue with the job for which he is suited by reason of education, training or experience. This definition differs from other definitions of disability that arise elsewhere in the pensions tax legislation.
2. The member must actually have retired from the job.

If a member recovers sufficient to return to work, the pension may be reduced or suspended. However, this may be an exception to the general rule that scheme pensions (described elsewhere) may not reduce in payment without tax consequences and certification of a registered medical practitioner will again be required, applying the same rigour as when the member was originally "signed off".

Law: FA 2004 s. 165, pension rule 1

4.3.2 Serious ill-health lump sum

The serious ill-health lump sum allows the whole of the member's rights to be commuted to a tax-free lump sum (before age 75 and within the available lifetime allowance) in the event of illness reducing life expectancy to less than 12 months (again, in the opinion of a registered medical practitioner). It is a BCE 6 if the facility is used before age75. One of the changes introduced by the 2006 regime (and applying to new and existing schemes), is that contracted-out rights are tax-free (as well as other rights commuted in this way).

If the serious ill-health lump sum is paid at or after age 75, there is no test against the lifetime allowance and the lump sum is taxed at marginal rates as if pension income.

The scheme administrator is liable for the charge and will deduct the tax from the ill-health payment.

The commutation rate will be decided by the scheme and will be consistent with other commutation calculations. Alternatively, the scheme may provide the serious ill-health lump sum by way of a term life assurance policy (similar to a critical illness policy).

There are four conditions that must have been met in order for a payment to be treated as a serious ill-health lump sum. These are as follows

1. Before making the payment the scheme administrator must have received written evidence from a registered medical practitioner confirming that the member is expected to live for less than one year.
2. The member must not have used up all of his lifetime allowance at the point the payment is made. Solely for these purposes, BCE 5A and 5B are assumed not to have taken place at age 75. On the other hand if there has been a crystallisation on or after age 75 which would have been treated as a BCE below that age, it is assumed that the crystallisation was a BCE and did use lifetime allowance.
3. The payment must extinguish the member's entitlement to benefits under the arrangement (so all of the benefits under the arrangement must be commuted and paid as a serious ill-health lump sum).
4. The payment must be made in respect of what the legislation refers to as an uncrystallised arrangement (or arrangements). The *Finance Act* 2016 removed the restriction on paying the serious ill-health lump sum from an arrangement that has been accessed in a drawdown or flexi-access drawdown plan.

DWP rules (that always prevail when there is an inconsistency with HMRC rules of the same status) require widows' and widowers' benefits to be retained as dependants' pensions where rights are contracted-out under a defined benefit scheme.

Law: ITEPA 2003, s. 636A; FA 2004, s. 166 and Sch. 29, para. 4; FA 2004, s. 205A and Sch. 31, para. 11; FA 2016, s. 22 and Sch. 5

4.3.3 Reporting the serious ill-health lump sum

There are two circumstances where the scheme administrator must report the payment of a serious ill-health lump sum to HMRC.

The first set of circumstances is where the recipient of the payment:

- is a director of the sponsoring employer of the scheme in the year of payment (or has been in the previous six years);
- is connected to such a director in the same period;
- alone or with others, represented the sponsoring employer in that time;
- is connected to that employer.

The second set of circumstances is where the member is relying on either an enhanced lifetime allowance entitlement, or an entitlement to enhanced protection, to reduce or avoid a liability to a lifetime allowance charge on the payment of the serious ill-health lump sum.

4.3.4 Using the serious ill-health lump sum

Serious ill-health commutation is not used as much as might be expected. Although it is a means of providing an immediate cash injection to discharge liabilities and care costs, it does inflate the estate with funds that would otherwise be protected from estate taxes by a trust. Furthermore, if the serious ill-health lump sum is paid after the member has attained age 75, it will lose its tax-free status and be subject to tax at marginal rates of income tax (perhaps in addition to taxes on the estate).

Law: FA 2004, s. 251(1)(a), (4)(a), as amended by ToPA 2014, s. 2(4); SI 2006/567, reg. 3

4.4 Special occupations

4.4.1 Pre-2006 rules

Before the current tax regime was introduced on 6 April 2006, legislation allowed individuals who derived earnings from certain occupations where it was customary to retire early, to take benefits earlier than the normal statutory minimum age. The "list" of such occupations ranged from ITN newscasters to sportsmen and sportswomen to brass instrumentalists and well beyond.

As part of the simplification of pensions, these rules were scrapped. They are probably not missed because early retirement does not imply a shorter life expectancy. The combination of a short funding term and poor annuity rates at the earlier ages meant that such schemes had little attraction other than as a means of securing early access to a tax free lump sum and this stretched the use of tax advantaged pensions beyond their fundamental objectives.

4.4.2 Transitional protection

With A-Day came the need to protect the benefits of:

- those who had funded pensions on the basis that they would be able to access them earlier than the new normal minimum pension age; and
- those who had already drawn pensions early.

The 2004 Act therefore allows individuals to retain a pension age of less than 50 if the scheme rules allowed the early age on 10 December 2003 (the date of the White Paper proposing the changes that appeared in the 2004 Act) and if the individual was a member of a scheme that allowed the early pension age on 5 April 2006. In respect of occupational schemes only, there are similar provisions that allow an early retirement age of 50 to be retained.

4.4.3 Amount of benefit

There is no restriction on the amount of benefit that may be taken beyond the reduction in the standard lifetime allowance that will apply if benefits are taken before normal minimum pension age (although even this reduction does not apply if the individual enjoys a statutory pension age under a public sector scheme).

There are certain qualifications and clarifications to this transitional provision:

1. The provision does not protect a pension age of 50 or more unless the member had a right to take benefits under an unqualified right in an occupational scheme on 5 April 2006 by virtue of a scheme rule that was in place at 10 December 2003. This is an unusual set of circumstances and also a rare example of different rules applying to occupational schemes from personal pension schemes.
2. The lifetime allowance for the member is reduced by 2.5% for each *complete* year earlier than the current normal minimum pension age the relevant benefit crystallisation event (BCE) arises. So if the event was one day after the member's 35th birthday, the reduction would be (19 x 2.5%) rather than (20 x 2.5%). If the event took place before 6 April 2010 (when normal minimum pension age was 50), the reduction in the lifetime allowance in this example would have been (14 x 2.5%). No reduction is needed if the protected pension age under an occupational scheme is 50 or more because the member had previously enjoyed a right to take benefits from that earlier age under the scheme rules.
3. To retain the protection (which did not have to be claimed from HMRC), all benefits from a scheme with a special pension age must be taken simultaneously. This means that benefits cannot be "phased" unless taken from separate schemes.
4. As a general rule, if rights are transferred to another scheme, the protection is lost, but there are significant exceptions for "block transfers". (See **5.6.2**, **6.6.4** and especially **11.11.3**).

If the member has taken benefits earlier than normal minimum pension age and has been subject to a reduction in the lifetime allowance, a later crystallisation in respect of a different scheme will require that:

- the current lifetime allowance will be used;
- the lifetime allowance will be reduced by 2.5% for each complete year that the crystallisation date falls short of the normal minimum pension age;
- the previously crystallised amount expressed as a proportion of the then lifetime allowance must be deducted from the current adjusted lifetime allowance;
- the remaining amount represents the available lifetime allowance.

The process also applies where the lifetime allowance has been enhanced, for instance by primary protection.

Law: FA 2004 Sch. 36, para. 19-23A

4.5 Taxation of pension

4.5.1 State pension

The state pension is taxable, but is paid without deduction of tax and for taxation purposes is the lowest category of income to be taxed when all sources of income are aggregated for tax purposes. This means:

- if the state pension does not exceed the personal allowance, it will be paid without deduction of tax. If it does exceed the personal allowance, the excess will be subject to income tax at a rate of 20 per cent in 2017-18. The tax will be taken from other sources of income and reflected in coding;
- any excess over the personal allowance will reduce the amount of savings income that may otherwise qualify for the 0 per cent savings rate;
- the pension is taxable which means that it may expose other sources of income to higher rates of tax (such as earnings or private pensions at 40% or 45%, and dividends at 32.5% or 38.1%).

Law: ITEPA 2003, s. 577-579

4.5.2 *Private pensions*

A private pension is taxed in the same way as earned (non-savings) income. It does not therefore qualify for the savings rate. It is not subject to National Insurance if it is derived from a registered pension scheme. The significance of being taxed in this way is that it is included in the lowest layer of private income to be taxed, immediately above the state pension. One practical effect is that if the member has income in the form of savings interest, significant pension income will deny exposure to the 0% tax band that applies to savings income.

Although pensions are taxed in the same way as earned income, they do not represent relevant earnings for the purposes of determining and relieving pension contributions.

4.5.3 *Pensions as authorised payments*

For pension payments to be regarded as authorised payments, they must be paid under the authority of a pension rule that appears in FA 2004, s. 165 and Sch. 28. The pension rules describe the types of pension payable. There is a parallel set of dependants' pension rules.

The rules describe three types of pension:

Scheme pension

A scheme pension (BCE 2) is the only type of pension available in respect of a defined benefit arrangement, and is a statutory option for money purchase schemes. A scheme pension is regarded as a "secure" pension by the legislation.

Lifetime annuity

A lifetime annuity (BCE 4) is an insurance policy issued in exchange for an accrued lump sum which provides a stream of income for the life of the member (and possibly beyond depending on death benefit options included). What makes an annuity in this context different from that of its literal meaning (an annual income) is that it may only be issued by a life assurance company and its rate will be partly dependent on mortality factors. Some religious views preclude investment in annuities which they regard as "gambling" on human life (because investment returns and mortality experience are pooled) and this was a reason for the legislation extending the drawdown option in 2004 and 2011. A lifetime annuity is a "secure" pension.

Drawdown pension

A drawdown pension (BCE 1) is only available in respect of money purchase arrangements and allows regular or irregular payments to be made directly from scheme assets or from a short-term annuity purchased by the scheme in the member's name. Drawdown pensions are derived from an earmarked fund and mortality is not pooled. The practical impact is that the rate of income cannot be enhanced by the mortality of other members and death benefits will be based on the value of the fund at death. A drawdown pension is not a "secure" pension.

Pension guarantee

A pension guarantee is a pension that continues to be paid to the estate of the member or to beneficiaries for the balance of a limited period even though the member may not survive that limited period. It is available in respect of a scheme pension or lifetime annuity and, where the member's entitlement started before 6 April 2015, the maximum gurantee period ("term certain") was 10 years.

The guarantee period under a lifetime annuity may be for any term where the member's entitlement started after 5 April 2015. By way of example, if the member dies just seven years into a ten year guarantee period, the pension will continue to be paid for the remaining three years. Guarantee periods may be established with an annuity protection lump sum which then becomes payable when the guarantee period has expired. Furthermore, an addition to the list of trivial lump sum payments in ToPA 2014, and the increase in maximum trivial and small lump sums in FA 2014 (up to £30,000), allow much greater scope for commuting remaining instalments of the guarantee.

A trivial commutation lump sum death benefit may be paid to an individual in respect of any entitlement he had to receive any guaranteed pension payments of a lifetime annuity or scheme pension payable after the member's death. The lump sum must extinguish the individual's rights to receive the guaranteed pension payments. The measure applies to payments made on or after 6 April 2015.

Pension guarantees are unavailable in respect of dependants' pensions.

Law: ITEPA 2003, s. 579A-579D; FA 2004, Sch. 29, para. 20 (as amended by ToPA 2014, Sch. 1, para. 74(1) to (4))

4.6 Scheme pensions

4.6.1 Scheme pensions: defined benefit and money purchase schemes

A scheme pension is the only type of pension that can be provided by a defined benefit arrangement. It is an option for a money purchase arrangement (and relatively unusual). Rather than accrue a fund with which to buy a compulsory purchase annuity or provide a drawdown pension, the scheme rules express the member's benefit as an income (and usually a pension commencement lump sum).

Under a defined benefit scheme, the benefit will be defined by the rules, usually based on a definition of pensionable pay, years of pensionable service and a rate of accrual.

Under a money purchase scheme, the scheme pension will be determined by the trustees in accordance with the rules and usually based on the size of fund accrued to the member at pension age and the rate at which it can be converted to income.

It is the responsibility of the scheme trustees or manager to provide the appropriate income in accordance with the scheme rules. They may do this by purchasing an annuity as an asset of the scheme, but this is not comparable to providing the member with funds to purchase an annuity on the open market. Rather it is simply a means of "swapping" the mortality and investment risk. The liability for the member's pension remains with the scheme. In practice, the annuity is chosen by the scheme administrator and the better the rate the less will be the strain on other scheme resources.

4.6.2 Requirements of a scheme pension

The scheme pension must meet certain requirements:

- it must be payable at intervals of 12 months or less;
- it must be payable for at least the lifetime of the member;
- it must not reduce in payment (there are exceptions).

If the pension increases beyond the general increase in prices (as defined in the legislation and described below), BCE 3 is triggered. This will rarely result in a tax charge because most members' benefits fall within the lifetime allowance, so the main disincentives are the administration and reporting requirements. There is nothing to prevent a phased introduction of scheme pensions. BCE 3 is the only BCE that can be triggered beyond the member's 75th birthday.

4.6.3 Payments of scheme pension under a guarantee

A scheme pension may be "guaranteed". This simply means that the income will continue for a "term certain" in the event of the member's early death. By way of example, if the pension includes a ten year guarantee and the member dies after seven years, payments will continue for a further three years (see elsewhere).

The scheme rules may require the term certain (payments under the guarantee) to end before the expiry of the term when the recipient:

- marries;
- reaches age 18; or
- ceases full-time education.

Before 6 April 2006, outstanding payments under a guarantee not exceeding five years could have been commuted and there were transitional provisions in respect of payments already being made at that date. The option was withdrawn with effect from 6 April 2006 although the legislation introduced another option (differently taxed) described as a pension protection lump sum (see **Chapter 5**). Furthermore, after the triviality and small fund commutation limits were increased by FA 2014 (maximum £30,000), and a new triviality lump sum death benefit was introduced (see **4.5.3** above), there is more scope for commuting remaining instalments of a guarantee.

A scheme pension is taxable as pension income on the recipient through PAYE.

The taxable pension income for a tax year is the full amount of the scheme pension under the registered pension scheme that accrues in that year irrespective of when any amount is actually paid.

Where the member is entitled to a scheme pension from a defined benefits arrangement, but fails to draw entitlements by age 75, those entitlements are tested for lifetime allowance purposes at that point (BCE 2) even though benefits do not have to come into payment at that date. Other than any lifetime allowance charge due, tax will only become due when that pension entitlement is actually taken.

Law: ITEPA 2003, Pt. 9, Ch. 5A (s. 579A to 579D), Sch. 31, para. 6; FA 2004, s. 165, pension rule 3

4.6.4 Scheme pension increases

There are no significant restrictions on increasing the rate of scheme pension. Most scheme members who are entitled to a scheme pension are unlikely to be able to benefit from such a significant increase under what will probably be a defined benefit scheme.

Should the rate of increase in a particular year exceed the rate of inflation, then there may be a benefit crystallisation event (BCE3), but few members will then be subject to the lifetime allowance. However, BCE3 is the only BCE that can arise when the member has reached age 75.

BCE3 will apply if the rate of increase exceeds the *threshold annual rate and the permitted margin.*

The threshold rate is the greatest of 5%, RPI and £250.

The permitted margin is a notional ongoing cost of living increase since the scheme pension came into payment, and is measured as an annual rate of increase of the greater of 5% or RPI (although there are circumstances when the 5% figure will be set at a different level for particular schemes). Where the 5% figure is increased by agreement with HMRC, the "relevant valuation factor" that converts the pension to a capital sum for the purposes of measuring against the lifetime allowance may be increased beyond 20.

BCE 3 will not apply if there are at least 50 pensioner members and the increase is applied to at least 20 members of a class in the same way (as a percentage or fixed amount). The class may change from year to year and is not a formal classification although there are anti-avoidance provisions. *Pensions Newsletter* 52, published on 8 March 2012, described the circumstances when a Pension Increase Exchange (PIE) exercise will fall within this exception and when it will not. A PIE exercise occurs when an employer offers a "one-off" lump sum in exchange for the employee surrendering entitlement to non-statutory pension increases.

Much of the uncertainty surrounding this rule centres on the definition of "class" and what is meant by the requirement that increases within the class must be at the same rate.

There is no definition of class in the legislation. HMRC offer the following:

> "A class of pensioner member can be determined at the time of each increase and can be interpreted flexibly and within its natural meaning. It can include some, or all, pensioner members of the scheme. It need not be confined to a particular category of membership under the scheme rules. It is possible for a member to be in a different class at the time different increases are applied, but this must be subject to the anti-avoidance rule in RPSM 11104321."

The anti-avoidance rule now appears in PTM 088630.

The scheme may choose to define a class as those members accepting a particular percentage increase.

The requirements will be met if the percentage rate of increase is the same for all members even though DWP rules may in fact restrict the increase more for some members than others.

The offer may apply to only part of the pension (perhaps relating to accrual before a certain date).

The excepted circumstances will not usually apply where the scheme provides a pension commencement lump sum by way of commutation and the PIE offer refers to the pre-commutation benefit. It could only apply in these circumstances if all members commuted at the same rate.

4.6.5 Scheme pension reductions

The rate of pension in a particular year should not be less than the rate in the previous year ("12-month period"). If the pension reduces, the pension payments thereafter will be regarded as unauthorised payments and taxed accordingly. If the pension reduces by a significant amount (if the pension falls below 80 per cent of the initial entitlement – FA 2004, Sch. 28, para. 2A), the lump sum will be treated as an unauthorised payment (although possibly paid many years before). This could lead to a 40 per cent charge on the value of the lump sum. The background to this rule is prevention of avoidance whereby the lump sum was determined by reference to an "artificially" inflated pension. There are a number of exceptions to the requirement for the pension not to reduce:

(1) If the member ceases to qualify for the ill health pension because of recovery from the medical condition. The process for judging whether the member is fit to return to work and take a reduced pension must be at least as rigorous as the process for determining ill health. The example given by HMRC is that if the scheme rules require that the member should not be capable of doing any job on early retirement, then the member should not be able to reduce the pension on returning to any job (rather than the specific job from which he or she retired). FA 2007, Sch. 20, para. 7 introduces the partial reduction in pension to cater for the individual who is unable to return to full earning work, but may nevertheless have made a partial recovery.

(2) If pensions are reduced for all pensioners under the scheme.

(3) If the pension is reduced to reflect entitlement to the state pension and providing that the reduction is no more than the amount of state pension and the bridging is restricted to the period between 60 and the individual's state pension age (the upper age was changed in FA 2013, s. 51 from 6 April 2013 and consequent regulations to reflect the increase in state pension age). The reduction may be between 125 per cent (where the member has been contracted out of the additional state pension) and 250 per cent of the basic

state pension. The formula is 125 + (125 × A/B) where A is the period of employment that is not contracted out and B is total years of employment to which the pension scheme relates *(The Registered Pension Schemes (Bridging Pensions) Regulations* 2007 (SI 2007/826)).

Transitional provisions were introduced to allow bridging pensions to reduce in line with scheme rules where they started on or before 3 July 2007 without the reductions having to comply with these conditions.

The *Finance Act* 2016 introduced enabling regulations which apply the new state single-tier pension to the calculation (to replace the basic state pension and the additional pension) and remove any reference to contracting-out.

(4) If the pension is reduced by a court order or forfeiture.

(5) FA 2005, Sch. 10, para. 11–12 extend the circumstances in which a scheme pension may reduce to include where an individual is re-employed in the public sector and the public sector pension is abated and where there is a pension share on divorce.

(6) The *Taxation of Pension Schemes (Transitional Provisions) (Amendment) Order* 2008 (SI 2008/2990) adds a transitional provision allowing a reduction in scheme pension. This is where the pension was in payment before 3 July 2007 to a member who was a member of the scheme on 5 April 2006 and the scheme rules allowed the reduction on that date.

(7) The *Pension Schemes (Reduction in Pension Rates) (Amendment) Regulations* 2009 (SI 2009/1311) introduce a further category in circumstances where the scheme is being wound up and the assets are insufficient to pay the pension at its full rate. The provision does not apply if it is part of an avoidance arrangement. An avoidance arrangement is described as an arrangement to increase the member's entitlement to a tax-free lump sum. The measure is effective from 6 April 2006.

(8) *The Registered Pension Schemes (Reduction in Pension Rates, Accounting and Assessment) (Amendment) Regulations* 2013 (SI 2013/1111) allow for a reduction in scheme pension as a consequence of the annual allowance charge being met by the scheme under the "scheme pays" facility or on a voluntary basis.

Note that a lien or debt enforced against the pension - because, for instance, of a debt imposed after a criminal act or fraud - is not a reduction.

The reduction is to the legal entitlement. There will be no unauthorised payment if the amount paid is due to the original payment being too high due to administrative error.

The pension is taxed under the PAYE rules on income due, rather than paid in the tax year.

Law: FA 2004, Sch. 28, para. 2(4); FA 2005, Sch. 10, para. 7-10, 11(6); FA 2016, s. 20; *The Pension Schemes (Reduction in Pension Rates) Regulations* 2006 (SI 2006/138); *The Registered Pension Schemes (Bridging Pensions) Regulations* 2007 (SI 2007/826); *The Registered Pension Schemes (Reduction in Pension Rates, Accounting and Assessment) (Amendment) Regulations* 2013 (SI 2013/1111); *The Registered Pension Schemes (Bridging Pensions) and Appointed Day Regulations* 2016 (SI 2016/1005)

4.7 Pension annuities

4.7.1 Definition

An annuity is, in its literal sense, simply a series of payments made at least once every year. In the context of financial services the annuity purchase price is allocated to an annuity fund and the rate of income payable to the annuitant is determined by:

- the yield on assets within the fund;
    - the assets are likely to be government bonds (gilts), corporate bonds and other fixed interest instruments. The rate is therefore strongly determined by interest rates;
- less expenses;

- plus any mortality gain derived from assumptions about the proportions of annuitants who will not survive normal life expectancy;
    - the older the annuitant, the greater the mortality gain. Until recently, rates differed between men and women, but this is now unlawful (since 21 December 2012) as a consequence of the European Court case of Test Achats which removed the UK's derogation from the *EU Gender Directive* in respect of the supply of goods and services.

Annuities are therefore partly dependent on human life and can only be issued by a life assurance company that is chosen by the prospective annuitant.

Short-term annuities are annuities that may be purchased by drawdown funds in the name of the member for a period of up to five years. They should not be confused with the terms "third-way" or "limited period" annuities that offer income or capital protection through structured products for longer periods through the gateway of a drawdown product. These are investment arrangements and include no mortality gain.

The flexible pensions legislation (mainly ToPA 2014) removed some of the requirements of a pension annuity.

Member's lifetime annuity

A member's lifetime annuity under the new rules provides entitlement on or after 6 April 2015. The following conditions apply:

- it must be provided by an insurance company;
- it must be payable until the member's death or if later to the end of a term certain (guarantee);
- there is no requirement that the annuity should not reduce or increase above a certain rate and this makes annuity payment more flexible.

Short-term annuity

A short-term annuity is purchased by a capped or flexi-access drawdown fund in the member's name to provide an income for up to five years. It is taxed on the member under PAYE. The following conditions apply:

- it must be provided by an insurance company;
- it must be payable until the member's death or to the end of a term certain which must not exceed five years;
- entitlement must have vested after 5 April 2015.

Dependant's annuity

A dependant's annuity (post 5 April 2015) must be:

- purchased with the member's annuity (joint-life annuity) or after the member's death;
- provided by an insurance company;
- payable, if the dependant is not the member's child, until death or until the earlier of the dependant's marriage or civil partnership and death of the dependant;
- payable, where the dependant is the member's child, until the earlier of the dependant's ceasing to be a dependant or dying, or until the earliest of the dependant's marrying, entering into a civil partnership, ceasing to be a dependant or dying.

The dependant's short-term annuity is payable for five years or until immediately before the dependant's death. Again it must be provided by an insurance company after 5 April 2015.

Note that no term certain/guarantee is available for dependants' annuities.

Law: EU Gender Directive 2004/113/EC
Case: *Belgian Annuities (Test Achats)* ECJ 2011

4.7.2 Other features of annuities

Pension annuities (other than short-term annuities) are payable for life. They are non-assignable and may not be surrendered. Short-term annuities are purchased by drawdown funds to provide an income for a period of up to five years within any drawdown limits.

Annuities may be subject to a court order requiring payments to be "attached" in the event of a member's bankruptcy (i.e. redirected to another recipient under the *Insolvency Act* 1986, s. 310). They may be subject to a "lien" which in effect reduces the payment if the annuitant has caused loss to the employer through fraudulent or negligent activity. Finally, part of the annuity may be the subject of a pension earmarking order on dissolution of marriage or reduced by a pension sharing order.

4.7.3 Annuity reductions

In respect of annuity entitlement that started *before* 6 April 2015, and subject to exceptions, the pension annuity must not reduce in payment if the purchase price is not to be treated as an unauthorised payment charge. The exceptions allow the annuity to reduce if the level of payments is linked each year to a recognised factor. The factor may be:

Method 1

- RPI;
- the market value of any "freely marketable assets"; or
- an index reflecting the value of "freely marketable assets".

"Freely marketable assets" means assets which are sold on the open market at a price not determined by the member.

Method 2

The variation in the annual amount from year to year reflecting variable bonuses added when the annuity contract is linked to an insurance company's with profits fund. Such bonuses must be in accordance with an *insurance company's* published "Principles and Practices of Financial Management" in relation to with-profits business.

Method 3

A combination of methods 1 and 2.

Method 4

Using this method, the variation in the annual amount paid from year to year is dependent on the factors used in methods 1, 2 or 3 but the member selects the starting level of the annuity based on an assumed annual level of growth of between 0% and 5% in the relevant factor to which their annuity is linked. For example, if increases above the starting level are dependent on bonuses being added by an insurance company's with profits fund, if the with profits fund suffers losses, the amount paid could fall below the level payable in the previous year.

Method 5

This method relates to flexible withdrawals. Variations in the annual amount paid from year to year must be determined in accordance with the following conditions:

> The first condition is where the amount of the annuity payable is linked to any of the factors specified in methods 1, 2 or 3 (or any combination of those factors).
>
> The second condition is that a review must be conducted, by the insurance company by whom the annuity is provided, at least once every three years of the value of the sums and assets which are applied towards the provision of the annuity.
>
> The third condition is that at the time of the review, the maximum and minimum amount of income that may be drawn in each year until the next review must be determined.

The maximum amount of income which the annuitant may draw is 120% of the annual rate of a level annuity which could be purchased with the sums and assets that are applied to its provision for the member, for the term for which the annuity is provided.

In this context the expression "level annuity" means a single life level annuity if a single life annuity has been purchased. If a joint life annuity has been purchased, then it means a joint life level annuity with the same profile between the joint lives as that actually purchased. Likewise if the annuity being purchased is not an impaired life annuity then one should not compare it with an impaired life level annuity.

The minimum amount of income which the annuitant may draw is half of the annual rate of a level annuity which could be paid upon the assumptions in the preceding paragraph of this condition.

For the purposes of this method, the annual rate of an annuity which could be purchased with the sums and assets applied to its provision shall be assumed to be:

a. the freely marketable level annuity rate (if any) applicable in the case of the insurance company in question which could be purchased with those sums and assets; or

b. if the insurance company in question does not offer level annuities, the average of three current market annuity rates for a level annuity.

4.7.4 Annuity options

Pension annuities come in a number of forms. They may include any of the following options:

- Joint-life, typically but not essentially with a spouse or civil partner.
- A guarantee (also known as a "term certain"). This ensures that the annuity will be paid for the period of the guarantee notwithstanding the earlier death of the annuitant (the option is unavailable on dependants' pensions by virtue of FA 2004, Sch. 28, pension rule 2). The conditions of the annuity may require the guarantee payments to come to an end on the dependant's marriage, reaching 18 or ceasing full-time education. Until 5 April 2015 new annuities could not offer a guarantee that exceeded ten years. The more relaxed provisions of the *Taxation of Pensions Act* 2014 remove this maximum.
- An annuity protection lump sum may be payable on death of the annuitant. It will represent the purchase price less instalments paid and is generally taxed at marginal rates applicable to the recipient if death is at age 75 or later and is tax-free if death is before that age (see **5.2** for more detail and other circumstances.
- The pension may include a requirement to increase annually in payment either at a fixed rate or in line with prices.
- The pension may have included a guaranteed rate. This was a feature of with-profits policies that offered a

guaranteed rate when funds were converted to an annuity with the same insurer.

- There are various payment options. Instalments may be paid at any regular frequency that is at least annual, but payments may also be made with or without proportion. If paid with proportion (available on annual instalments), then on the death of the annuitant, a proportionate payment is made for the part-year of survival.
- The payments may be made in advance or in arrears. If paid in arrears, an annual annuity may include an option to pay part of an instalment on death part-way through a year.

All options affect the rate to a greater or lesser extent. No options are right or wrong, but some may be more suitable for some annuitants than others. For example, a pension that increases at 3% a year will only "catch up" with a level annuity after 12 years. Whilst inflation protection is a good thing, the annuitant may prefer to take the higher payments "up-front" if only because they are at their most valuable then and because mortality is a more significant factor at these ages.

The rate of income may also be affected by other factors. As we have seen, it is no longer lawful to discriminate on grounds of gender (although a joint-life annuity is likely to pay for longer than a single-life annuity regardless of gender). However, with more technology and more data, it is now possible to differentiate rates on grounds of:

- health;
- lifestyle (e.g. smoking);
- postcode;
- size of fund.

The annuity market is very competitive and competition has bred innovation. The individual must be given the opportunity to choose the annuity provider under the open market option. If the individual does not exercise the option, the choice is left with the scheme administrator or insurance company.

4.7.5 Phased retirement

This is an automated facility that is made available to members of registered pension schemes who have accrued relatively large funds under a money purchase scheme. The "mechanics" of the product are that the scheme or arrangement is segmented and each year, a number of segments is crystallised. The progressive crystallisation of segments means that income from the scheme will gradually increase and also that a proportion of income each year is free of tax. This is because each segment comprises a tax-free pension commencement lump sum and a taxable annuity.

The option is suitable for higher rate taxpayers who have no need for a capital sum at pension age (the lump sum is included in the income). The option is not as flexible as phased drawdown because the income cannot reduce.

As a product of choice, phased retirement may seem less flexible than repeated payments of the uncrystallised funds pension lump sum (available from 6 April 2015). However, phased retirement does allow for progressive encashments of lump sums without having to draw pension (unlike the uncrystallised funds pension lump sum). This objection is met by the option to take phased drawdown which allows the member to take the lump sum and defer pension altogether.

It remains to be seen how the market for these two products will develop after the introduction of the uncrystallised funds pension lump sum. Early indications are that the simplicity, flexibility and charging structures of the uncrystallised funds pension lump sum appeal to both providers and members.

4.8 Drawdown pensions

4.8.1 Terminology and background

Drawdown pensions have been available in respect of money purchase and cash balance schemes since 1995, but have undergone some changes in terminology. When the 2004 reforms were implemented in 2006, they became known as unsecured pensions and alternatively secured pensions (after age 75).

They were then described as drawdown pensions or, where payments are made directly from the fund rather than a short-term annuity, income withdrawal.

The rules for drawdown pensions seem to have changed annually since A-Day. Indeed, changes were implemented in December 2012 in order to reflect the gender equality requirements of annuities (implemented on 21 December 2012) following the European Court of Justice ruling in the case of *Test Achats* and on 26 March 2013 when higher maximum withdrawals (120% of the "basis amount") were reinstated. From 27 March 2014, the maximum withdrawal increased to 150% of the basis amount and was unlimited from 6 April 2015 under the terms of flexi-access drawdown.

The most radical changes appeared in the *Taxation of Pensions Act* 2014 which was implemented on 6 April 2015. The two main changes to drawdown were firstly to introduce one regime for all drawdown arrangments, subject to transitional provisions, and a fundamental change in the way death benefits were taxed (**Chapter 5**).

Law: FA 2004, s. 165, pension rules 4 and 5

4.8.2 Drawdown types

Drawdown pensions are not secure pensions. They are payable from money purchase arrangements. From 6 April 2015, newly designated drawdown arrangements may only be treated as flexi-access drawdown funds. Rather confusingly, HMRC and the legislation refer to capped drawdown as simply "drawdown". This book uses the term as a generic term for capped and flexi-access drawdown.

Immediately before 6 Apri 2011, there were two types of drawdown pension:

1. Capped drawdown allowed variable payments to be made directly from the arrangement and its assets, subject to a cap on the withdrawal made in a year which was reviewed at regular intervals. The income could have been provided from a short-term annuity purchased by the scheme in the member's name. By implication, new capped drawdown arrangements ceased to be recognised by legislation on 6 April 2015 although it may be so by providers. However,

existing capped drawdown arrangements will be recognised from that date until the cap is breached or the member informs the scheme administrator that he or she wishes to convert to flexi-access drawdown. No new designations of capped drawdown are recognised after 5 April 2015 unless the designation is merely a further designation under an existing capped drawdown scheme.

2. Flexible drawdown allowed unlimited withdrawals to be made directly from the arrangement and its assets providing that the member was able to demonstrate that he or she had a source of secure income that met the "minimum income requirement" in the tax year in which the flexible drawdown started. All flexible drawdown arrangements became flexi-access drawdown pension funds on 6 April 2015 and one of the consequences is that the member is not required to demonstrate a separate source of secure income.

Flexi-access drawdown funds allow unrestricted withdrawals from normal minimum pension age or earlier if the member has to retire early on grounds of ill health.

The member may take a pension commencement lump sum of up to one-third of funds designated for drawdown or 25% of total designated funds (subject to the lifetime allowance and any modification of this percentage by transitional protection) and this will be tax-free. The remaining fund (75%) need not provide an income and is regarded as crystallised (designated) immediately after the pension commencement lump sum is taken.

If the larger portion of the fund is withdrawn, there is no limit other than the size of the fund. This means that the whole fund could be withdrawn in one transaction: 25% would be tax-free and the balance of the fund would be added to the member's income for the year and taxed at marginal rates of income tax. The same result could be achieved by taking an uncrystallised funds pension lump sum (probably at less cost).

Although many have been attracted to the idea of withdrawing the whole fund, there are significant concerns about this strategy:

- a relatively modest fund could expose the member to higher and additional rates of tax on all or a significant part of the fund;
- the fund will now form part of the member's estate for inheritance tax purposes;
- there are few alternative investments that offer the convenience and tax efficiency of the pension fund, particularly on death before age 75.

The designation of flexi-access drawdown funds, or the conversion of capped drawdown to flexi-access drawdown, triggers the application of the money purchase annual allowance (**Chapter 2**). For this reason, some individuals may wish to retain capped drawdown arrangements if they wish to make further contributions because this will not trigger the application of the money purchase annual allowance (although the recycling rule may apply).

The introduction of drawdown may be phased. Designation of flexi-access drawdown before age 75 requires funds to be designated under BCE 1. It may be accompanied by a related pension commencement lump sum under BCE 6. In each case, the funds being designated/crystallised are measured against remaining lifetime allowance.

Law: FA 2004, s. 165(1), pension rules 4, 5, and s. 165(3A) (as amended)

4.8.3 Taxation and BCEs

Neither drawdown option (flexi-access or capped) requires a minimum annual withdrawal to be made in a year. This means that the lump sum may be taken without any pension. Indeed, a combination of phased crystallisations of lump sums, but initially zero withdrawals, can provide a tax-free "income" for a temporary period.

The advantages may be described simply. If an "income" of £10,000 is tax-free, it equates to a gross income (i.e. before tax) of £16,667 for a higher rate taxpayer and £18,182 for an additional rate taxpayer. The chances are that tax exposure will fall with age (and when the pension becomes payable) having already reduced when earnings were replaced by pension.

When a member in receipt of drawdown or phased drawdown reaches age 75, there may be two BCEs:

- BCE 5A will require funds already designated for drawdown to be measured immediately against the lifetime allowance. However, to prevent "overlap" (taxation of the same funds twice) the funds are reduced by any funds previously designated to provide a drawdown pension under BCE 1.

  Example

  Joe crystallises his personal pension plan at the age of 65 when the value of his funds is £1.2 million and the lifetime allowance is £1.5 million. He takes the maximum available pension commencement lump sum of £300,000, and £900,000 is applied to providing a capped drawdown income.

  At the age of 75 he is subject to BCE 5A when the value of his fund is £1,000,000 and the lifetime allowance is £1.5 million.

  Joe's first crystallisation events (BCEs 1 and 6) at the age of 65 used 80% of his lifetime allowance. His BCE at 75 uses (£1 million-£900,000)/£1.5 million x 100% = 6.66%

  He has used 86.66% of his lifetime allowance.

- BCE 5B will require funds that have not yet been designated to be measured immediately against the lifetime allowance, but since 6 April 2011 there has been no need to convert uncrystallised funds to benefits at that stage.

BCE 5A and 5B are "tidying up" exercises. No BCEs will arise after the member's 75th birthday except BCE 3 (which is not relevant to drawdown pensions) even if the member decides to start taking benefits after that date.

Income tax is due on any payments paid in a tax year. If the drawdown pension is being paid using a short-term annuity the taxable amount is the amount due to be paid in the tax year under the terms of the contract, even if the payment is not received in the tax year.

The pension scheme (or the insurer paying the short-term annuity) should deduct the tax due using the PAYE system before making the payment. If the member is not able to produce a statement of income for the tax year (e.g. P45), the member will initially be allocated an emergency code. This means that an annual payment will be taxed as if a monthly instalment and the member will have to reclaim overpaid tax from his tax office. The following is an extract from *Pension Schemes Newsletter* 68 published by HMRC in April 2015:

> "The pension provider might hold a current P45 form for the person making the withdrawal, and therefore know the tax code to be applied for the year. This could be because the person has just stopped working or is no longer claiming Job Seekers Allowance. Where a current P45 is held, the pension provider can deduct the correct amount of tax from payments as they are made.
>
> However, where a current P45 is not held, the pension provider will have to deduct tax from the payment at a temporary rate (called emergency rate). In most cases, this will mean that the person making the withdrawal may be due a tax refund.
>
> The method for claiming the tax back will depend on the person's circumstances – for instance, on what other income they have in that tax year and whether they have emptied their pension fund."

Law: ITEPA 2003, s. 579A-579D, 683(3)

4.8.4 Converting to and from drawdown

There is no reason why a drawdown pension fund should not be converted to a scheme pension or used to purchase a lifetime annuity for the member. Each conversion before age 75 is a BCE.

The scheme pension and annuity may not be converted to drawdown.

A capped drawdown may be converted to flexi-access drawdown (this is not a BCE), but flexi-access drawdown may not be converted to capped drawdown.

Contributions may continue to be made to a scheme providing drawdown, but the first withdrawal from a flexi-access drawdown plan will trigger the operation of the money purchase annual allowance (in effect reducing annual input to money purchase arrangements to £10,000). Furthermore, if contributions are deemed to have derived from recycled pension commencement lump sums, the lump sum may be taxed as an unauthorised payment (see "Recycling" at **4.15**).

4.9 Capped drawdown

4.9.1 The cap

The main distinguishing feature of capped drawdown is that whilst the withdrawal in a year is variable as to frequency and amount, it is limited to 150% of a "basis amount". The basis amount is derived from applying a recently published 15-year gilt yield to tables published by the Government Actuary's Department (GAD) on the HMRC website. In effect, it mirrors a good annuity rate for a single life with no increase options.

The limit was 100% of the basis amount for reviews between 6 April 2011 and 25 March 2013 and 120% for reviews between 26 March 2013 and 26 March 2014. From 27 March 2014, the maximum increased to 150% of the basis amount for any pension year under FA 2014, s. 41(1).

As a practical point, reference to the "GAD rate" is unhelpful and misleading although the term is often used. It can be taken to mean the basis amount or 150% of the basis amount.

4.9.2 The reference period and review – sources

The basis amount must be reviewed at least every three years (the "reference period") and on an anniversary before age 75 and annually on an anniversary after that date. Before age 75, the member may require the administrator to shorten the reference period, but only if the reference date continues to be the same day of the year and it may only be brought forward to the day following the end of the current pension year. The member may wish to bring forward the reference date to take advantage of an increase, possibly temporary, in gilt yields.

The calculation of the basis amount requires a gilt yield for 15 year UK gilts from the FTSE UK Gilt Indices. This figure needs to be for the 15th day of the month before the calculation date. If the 15th is a non-working day the scheme administrator must go back to the nearest working day before the 15th. The gilt yield to be used for dependants who are less than 23 years old is for a short-dated gilt (five year).

As a point of detail, the GAD tables provide rates at gilt yield intervals of 0.25%. If a yield falls between two yields, it is always rounded down (so 2.70% would round down to 2.50% and so on).

In its 2013 Budget Statement, the government announced a review of the GAD calculation and in particular whether the 15-year gilt yield was appropriate to the calculation. It decided that it would not be appropriate to change the basis.

From 21 December 2012, the GAD rates have not distinguished between men and women. This is a consequence of the European Court case of *Test Achats* (2011) that determined that the UK could not derogate from the EU Gender Directive which deals with the provision of goods and services (rather than employee benefits). Directly affected were insurance policies and annuities and the logic was then extended by the UK government to drawdown rates.

4.9.3 Short-term annuities

The scheme may use its funds to purchase a short-term annuity in the name of the member in order to provide a temporary income. The maximum term of a short-term annuity is five years. Care has to be taken with the purchase of a short-term annuity under a capped drawdown arrangement because the maximum income continues to be limited by the current drawdown maximum. Any payments in excess of the maximum withdrawal are taxed as unauthorised payments. Regard will also be had to any imminent review dates that could see the maximum income reduce.

A short-term annuity may only be established on a "single-life" basis, but may be written subject to a guarantee period of up to five years (so that in the event of the member's death before the annuity term has expired, payments will continue for the balance of the annuity term).

4.9.4 Limited period "annuities"

Short-term annuities should not be confused with so-called "limited period annuities" or "fixed term annuities". Limited period annuities are in fact fund options that make use of structured products and derivatives and offer protected returns of income, capital or both. Limited period annuities do not benefit from the mortality gain associated with life assurance annuities: they are not annuities in the financial services sense, but a drawdown investment option. Limited period annuities are occasionally called "third-way annuities".

4.9.5 Undertaking the review: timings

After the initial calculation, the actual review of the maximum withdrawal may take place on a "nominated date". This is any day chosen by the scheme administrator within the 60 days ending on the reference date. The figures used in the calculation are those relevant to the nominated date, i.e.

- the value of the fund on the nominated date;
- the age of the member on the nominated date;
- the gilt yield for the 15th day of the month preceding the nominated date.

4.9.6 Reaching age 75

When the member reaches his or her 75th birthday, reviews are required to be annual, but there is no change to the rules regarding minimum and maximum withdrawals.

When the member switches to yearly reviews of the maximum drawdown pension there is a choice of dates that can be used to work out the new maximum drawdown pension.

If both the member and the scheme administrator agree the administrator can use the value of the drawdown pension fund immediately before age 75.

Alternatively the scheme administrator can choose any day in a period of 60 days ending on the first day of the pension year starting after the member's 75th birthday.

This choice of valuation dates only applies for the first annual review of the maximum drawdown pension after the 75th birthday. For following recalculations of the maximum drawdown pension from the arrangement the scheme administrator can only use a valuation date within the 60 day period ending with the first day of the new pension year.

The valuation is conducted on the same basis as pre-age 75 valuations.

If the member is 75 or over the member and scheme administrator may be able to change the pension year under an arrangement so that it matches the drawdown pension year of another arrangement under the scheme.

The administrator may only change the pension year for an arrangement once.

The pension year for an arrangement may be changed by bringing the current pension year to an end either early or late, but the maximum drawdown pension will remain the same for the pension "year".

4.9.7 Additional reviews

There are circumstances when an additional review must be undertaken. In most circumstances, the review is carried out immediately, but is applied from the next pension year. The additional review does not relieve the administrator of the obligation to carry out the normal review at the end of the reference period. Events that require an additional review are:

- all or part of the fund is used to purchase a lifetime annuity (BCE 4 if under 75);
- all or part of the fund is converted to a scheme pension (BCE 2 if under 75);
- the fund is reduced under a pension sharing order on dissolution of marriage;
- more funds under the same arrangement are designated for drawdown (a BCE 1 if under 75). This is the exception to the general rule: the change will apply immediately if the maximum withdrawal increases as a consequence of

the review, but will only apply from the next pension year if it reduces.

The annual reviews required from age 75 obviate the need for these rules although, if there is a further designation that increases the maximum withdrawal, the new maximum will apply immediately.

4.9.8 *Illustration: extraordinary drawdown reviews*

Event	Recalculation	Effective from	Comment
Conversion to annuity or scheme pension	Date of conversion	Following anniversary	Three-year review date stays in place No recalculation if in the last year of a reference period
Designation of additional funds for drawdown	Date of designation	Immediately if figure increases, next anniversary if it reduces	
Pension debit due to a sharing order on divorce/ dissolution	Date order becomes effective	Following anniversary	

4.10 Temporary periods of non-residence

New rules apply when a member is temporarily non-resident to:

- any drawdown pension paid from a flexi-access drawdown fund to a member;
- any drawdown pension paid from a flexi-access drawdown fund to a dependant;
- the taxable part of an uncrystallised funds pension lump sum;
- any withdrawals from a fund where the individual was entitled to flexible drawdown before 6 April 2015.

The pension will only be taxed when the member becomes UK resident again if the total of relevant withdrawals during the period of temporary non-residence was more than £100,000.

The rules will be the same whether payment is made from a registered pension scheme or a relevant non-UK scheme.

If a payment is made other than in sterling, it will be converted to a sterling equivalent by using the average exchange rate for the year ending 31 March for all payments in the tax year containing that 31 March.

Law: ITEPA 2003, s. 579CA (as amended by ToPA 2014, s. 80-84)

4.11 The benefits and drawbacks of drawdown

4.11.1 The need for drawdown

Drawdown pensions are an option available to members of money purchase arrangements, particularly personal pension plans and small company schemes. Members of these arrangements have a number of options available to them subject to what is in the scheme rules and the facility to transfer to another arrangement. However, the main options are to purchase a lifetime annuity with the fund or to designate a drawdown facility with the current scheme or a scheme to which the funds can be transferred.

The key to comparing the two is to define the use to which the option is to be put. Much of any comparison is determined by qualitative rather than quantitative factors. Each option is designed for a different purpose and the fact find is central to any recommendation.

The annuity offers certainty and a rate that is enhanced beyond the yield on underlying investments by mortality gain. Mortality gain is the increase to the rate occasioned by pooling the funds for individual annuitants and assuming that some of those individuals will die earlier than expected. The "surplus" derived from an individual dying earlier than mortality tables might predict is retained in the fund to enhance the rates of other annuitants.

The certainty derives from most annuities providing a guaranteed rate.

A disadvantage of annuities is that in offering certainty, they must be invested in low risk, low return assets, typically gilts. Gilts offer especially poor returns at present (2017). Worse still, they are unresponsive to circumstances, whether those circumstances are related to the annuitant, the family or, indeed, investment conditions. If an individual purchases a joint-life annuity and his or her spouse dies within 12 months, it is not possible to adjust the rate once it has been set at time of purchase.

Annuities are relatively cheap compared with other options, especially where funds are not that large.

Drawdown pensions offer little certainty (although they may offer a short-term annuity option or investment in a protected fund), but they are then free to invest in assets that offer greater long-term potential for growth through active management.

They are likely to be more expensive than the annuity option unless the funds are fairly substantial and the impact of flat-rate fees less significant.

However, drawdown options do not offer access to pooled funds and shared mortality experience. The consequence is that no drawdown member may "benefit" financially from the death of another individual: there can be no mortality gain. In fact, this absence of mortality gain is known as mortality "drag" and is an important factor in making the decision as to which option to choose. Indeed, the older one becomes, the greater the "drag".

The absence of mortality gain, however, is offset by the facility to pay a lump sum death benefit representing the value of funds on the death of the member (in addition to a range of dependant pensions).

There are advantages of drawdown for the individual who is reasonably tolerant to risk and is able to invest substantial funds. ("Substantial" in this context will depend on the product and the circumstances, but will probably start at £100,000 or more).

Drawdown offers a chance to react to circumstances and to benefit from improvements in underlying investment yields. The fund may be used to purchase an annuity at any time.

The advantages of flexi-access drawdown should not be overstated. The option allows unlimited withdrawals. At first sight it may seem attractive to take the whole fund as one withdrawal, but this would mean that much of the fund would be subject to higher rates (including additional rate) income tax because the withdrawal would simply be added to income for the year for tax purposes.

Taking higher withdrawals than capped drawdown would allow runs the risk of depleting the fund prematurely.

The most legitimate use of flexi-access drawdown is therefore likely to be parallel to the use of enhanced annuity rates. If life expectancy might be shortened by lifestyle or health factors, the member should not be restricted by a cap designed by reference to "average" lives.

4.11.2 Phased drawdown

Phased drawdown refers to a progressive and automated crystallisation of funds held in a money purchase scheme to draw down benefits. The scheme may be "segmented" to facilitate the option, or crystallisation may simply be phased over one arrangement. Each crystallisation comprises part pension commencement lump sum and part pension.

Phased drawdown offers more flexibility than phased retirement under which funds are applied to the purchase of annuities because drawdown income may reduce rather than simply increase with each phase.

Phased drawdown is an automated procedure starting with a specified income. This should not be confused with staggered vesting or partial vesting where a decision is made from time to time to encash funds. In these cases, the member has a choice of taking the maximum income from the minimum number of arrangements (and the minimum pension commencement lump sum element) or the minimum income from the maximum number of arrangements (and the maximum lump sum element). The decision will determine the tax-free death lump sum benefit before age 75 derived from uncrystallised funds: the greater the number of arrangements crystallised, the lower the lump sum death benefit, but the higher the tax-free element of member pension.

An attractive variation on these options, especially for higher rate taxpayers, is to take an income over an initial period (such as ten years) in the form of progressive lump sum crystallisations accompanied by zero withdrawals. The value of a lump sum payment to a higher rate taxpayer equates to 166% of a taxed income payment.

Any individual considering phased drawdown will wish to compare its benefits with taking a series of uncrystallised funds pension lump sums (see **Chapter 7.4**).

4.11.3 Drawdown from 6 April 2015

The measures included in the *Taxation of Pensions Act* 2014 and subsequent *Finance Act* 2015 will undoubtedly have an impact on choices made by those who approach retirement. The measures were accompanied by a requirement for the FCA to provide guidance (not advice) and this appeared in the PSA 2005. The guidance (specifically not advice) is provided by the Pensions Advisory Service (telephone) and the Citizens Advice Bureaux (face to face), branded as "Pension Wise".

The *Finance Bill (No. 2)* 2017 and supporting regulations propose to introduce the Pensions Advice Allowance from 6 April 2017. This allows the member of a registered pension scheme to make a written request to withdraw as much as £500 from his or her scheme(s) on three separate occasions without incurring any tax liability in order to pay for pensions and retirement advice. Features are:

- only one such withdrawal may be made in a tax year;
- the withdrawal may be made at any age;
- the withdrawal may be set against the cost of regulated advice;
- the allowance is available to individuals who have defined contribution or hybrid arrangements; and
- the advice must be provided by a financial adviser who is regulated and authorised to provide the advice (by the FCA).

The request for payment of the allowance must be made in writing and HMRC have confirmed that this may include e-mail.

The flexibility offered by the drawdown changes ironically makes it much more difficult to offer advice and make informed decisions. The following are some of the factors that need to be considered:

- Some people will be tempted to take their whole fund in a single withdrawal, but perhaps without realising that the withdrawal will be added to their income in calculating exposure to income tax in the year of withdrawal. This could easily lead to a substantial liability to additional rate tax.
- Funds that are withdrawn and then continue to be saved are unlikely to be held in an environment that is as tax-efficient, convenient and legitimate.
- Annuity design will become more innovative and targeted as demand falls. Although the annuity market is competitive, a thematic review by the FCA revealed that 80% of annuitants did not take advantage of better rates elsewhere when they converted money purchase funds to benefits.

Law: PSA 2015, s. 47 and Sch. 3; *The Registered Pension Schemes (Authorised Payments) (Amendment) Regulations* 2017 (SI 2017/397)
Guidance: *Pension Schemes Newsletter* 87

4.12 Lump sum benefits

4.12.1 BCE 6

The legislation imposes significantly higher tax charges on payments from registered pension schemes unless they are authorised payments. Authorised payments are not necessarily, or even usually, tax-free but unauthorised payments are subject to taxes designed primarily to recover tax relief already allowed. Typical examples of authorised payments are retirement pensions (under the "pension rules") and the pension commencement lump sum (taken under the "lump sum rule").

BCE 6 records the member taking a relevant lump sum from the scheme. The lump sum in this case is "relevant" if it is one of the following:

- a pension commencement lump sum;
- a serious ill-health lump sum;
- a lifetime allowance excess lump sum; or
- an uncrystallised funds pension lump sum.

In each case, the payment will be measured against available lifetime allowance and will only constitute an unauthorised payment to the extent that it exceeds the applicable amount (below).

4.12.2 Lifetime allowance lump sum

The lifetime allowance excess lump sum is only payable to an individual under the age of 75 if the lifetime allowance has been exceeded and is an alternative to taking the excess benefit as an income (most individuals will opt for taking the lump sum "up front"). Its legislative authority prevents it being taxed as a surrender of benefits and therefore an unauthorised payment.

Law: FA 2004, Sch. 29, para. 11

4.12.3 Serious ill-health lump sum

In order for the serious ill-health lump sum to be payable, there must be some remaining lifetime allowance, but assuming there is, no further measurement is made against the lifetime allowance and no lifetime allowance charge will apply. Before age 75, the lump sum will therefore be tax-free. Beyond age 74, the serious ill-health lump sum is taxed at marginal rates in all cases.

Law: FA 2004, Sch. 29, para. 4

4.12.4 Pension commencement lump sum

The most important of the authorised lump sum payments is the pension commencement lump sum. The pension commencement lump sum must be taken in the period that:

- begins six months before the related pension entitlement starts; and
- ends twelve months after the related pension entitlement starts.

There is a small exception to these limits where the amount of available lifetime allowance has been underestimated and lifetime allowance charge is subsequently refunded to the scheme which is then able to pay a further pension commencement lump sum (within 12 months of receiving the refund).

The 2014 Budget introduced a number of relaxations to the rules for taking pension and lump sum benefits from money purchase schemes. Many of the measures were to date from 27 March 2014, but would strictly speaking not become law until the Finance Bill was enacted in July 2014. HMRC therefore published guidance to deal with the transition (all of which would appear in FA 2014).

- the requirement that the lump sum be paid within 6 months before or after the entitlement to an associated pension arises was suspended if the lump sum was paid on or after 19 September 2013 and before 6 April 2015;
- if:
    - the lump sum was paid before the member would otherwise be entitled and before 6 October 2015;
    - the scheme was a money purchase scheme; and
    - the related pension was provided by an annuity,

  the payment would not be unauthorised. This enabled the member to cancel an annuity purchase within the FCA cancellation rules in order to take advantage of the new flexibility;
- similarly, if the annuity was cancelled and the lump sum was also repaid to the scheme, there would be no unauthorised payment;
- if the lump sum was paid back to the scheme in these circumstances, then the value of any subsequent payment of the lump sum remains at the value initially calculated (before repayment);
- if the lump sum or annuity options were reversed in this context, the BCEs would also have been reversed.

Whenever the lump sum is taken, it is normally assumed for BCE purposes that it started immediately before the actual entitlement to the related pension (on the same day). If the member dies between taking the pension commencement lump sum and becoming entitled to the pension, the lump sum entitlement is deemed to have arisen immediately before death.

If the entitlement to the lump sum arose before the member's 75th birthday, but was not paid until after that date, no BCE 6 will arise (contrary to the usual rule) because there would have been a test of uncrystallised funds at age 75.

If the pension commencement lump sum is taken when the member has already reached age 75, then it is assumed for these purposes only that there is a BCE and a lifetime allowance to determine if there is an "available portion" (below). BCE 5B is ignored. In all other circumstances, there would be no BCE 6 and no lifetime allowance after age 75 and no lump sum would be payable without incurring unauthorised payment charges.

The pension commencement lump sum is generally payable tax-free. If it does not meet the requirements of a pension commencement lump sum, then it will not be treated as such but will be an unauthorised payment. If it exceeds the required lump sum allowance, the excess will be an unauthorised payment unless the lump sum represents an excess over the lifetime allowance (when it becomes subject to the lifetime allowance charge rather than unauthorised payment charges).

There are circumstances when the pension commencement lump sum may be an authorised payment and may fall within the lifetime allowance, but may subsequently be chargeable to tax:

- when the member is adjudged to have recycled all or part of the lump sum to a relievable pension contribution under a money purchase scheme;
- when a member significantly reduces a scheme pension (by at least 20%). This may suggest that an artificially high pension was taken in order to inflate the related lump sum. The "excess" is known as an "excluded lump sum".

The legislation tells us that if the pension commencement lump sum exceeds the "permitted maximum", then the excess is not a pension commencement lump sum. This means that the excess will not be an authorised payment.

Note however that guaranteed minimum pensions from pre-1997 contracted-out accrual may not be commuted although they may be used in the calculation. Section 9(2B) rights that accrued under a post 1997 contracted-out defined benefit scheme may be commuted.

Law: ITEPA 2003, s. 636A(5); FA 2004, Sch. 29, para. 1; FA 2014, s. 43 and Sch. 5

4.13 Pension commencement lump sum: permitted maximum

Legislation describes the "permitted maximum" as the lower of:

a. the *available portion* of the member's lump sum allowance; and
b. the *applicable amount.*

There are two significant qualifications:

- no pension commencement lump sum can be an authorised payment in respect of a "disqualifying pension credit" (i.e. the permitted maximum is nil). These represent funds allocated to a pension credit member on dissolution of marriage or civil partnership from which the corresponding pension debit member has already taken retirement benefits. In other words the pension credit was awarded in respect of funds that had already crystallised;
- the maximum lump sum amount is subject to modification (to the member's advantage) under the transitional provisions discussed elsewhere.

Available portion

The available portion of the member's lump sum allowance is:

CSLA – AAC/4

where:

CSLA is the current standard lifetime allowance; and

AAC is the aggregate of the relevant amount in the case of each benefit crystallisation event which has occurred in relation to the member before the member becomes entitled to the lump sum, as adjusted (and if no such benefit crystallisation event has occurred, is nil).

The adjustment of the relevant amount in the case of a previous benefit crystallisation event referred to in the definition of AAC is the multiplication of the amount by:

CSLA/PSLA

where:

CSLA is the current standard lifetime allowance; and

PSLA is the standard lifetime allowance at the time of the previous benefit crystallisation event.

Under a money purchase scheme, this will simply mean 25% of the fund. Under a defined benefit scheme, the maximum lump sum is again intended to represent 25% of total benefits being crystallised, but the value of the related pension in this case derives from the scheme commutation rate. There is an anti-avoidance provision that will render a payment of lump sum as unauthorised if it is derived from a transfer from a money purchase arrangement to a defined benefit arrangement solely undertaken to improve the available pension commencement lump sum (to the extent of the "artificial" increase in lump sum).

Applicable amount

This is simply described as being one-third of the value of funds crystallised to provide pension benefits under a money purchase scheme or one-quarter of total benefits being crystallised under a defined benefit scheme. In effect it is 25% of total benefits crystallised at any one time.

Law: FA 2004, Sch. 29, para. 2, 3

4.14 Protected lump sums

4.14.1 Transition

This is fairly straightforward subject to mastering the implications of commutation rates. However, once again, the difficulty derives from the transitional provisions included in the 2004 Act which were designed to protect lump sum rights accrued until A-Day.

The maximum lump sum available to a personal pension arrangement (issued after 31 May 1987) was 25% of the fund providing the lump sum and related pension. No protection is necessary in these cases.

The maximum lump sum available in respect of a retirement annuity contract (issued before 1 June 1987) was three times the residual pension. This would rarely produce a lump sum of 25% of total benefits being taken and in any case would vary according to age and annuity rate. From 6 April 2006, the maximum lump sum available from these arrangements is 25% of the funds providing the lump sum and related pension. (It may be worth pointing out that the minimum pension age for these arrangements was 60, but the 2004 Act reduced this initially to 50 and then 55 from 2010).

The maximum lump sum available in respect of an occupational scheme (and section 32 buy-out policy) varied according to when the original scheme was approved and any further restrictions imposed by the scheme rules. Broadly speaking, the maximum was either based on an accrual to "normal retirement date" of 3/80 of final pensionable remuneration for each year of service (as defined) to a maximum 120/80 or an accelerated rate of accrual that provided up to 120/80 after, initially, ten years' service and subsequently twenty years' service.

The complications set in when an individual was entitled to benefits from more than one scheme (including personal pension schemes and retirement annuity contracts) that have accrued benefits other than in concurrent employments. The guiding principle was that the benefit limits were in respect of aggregated benefits and not "freestanding". These rules gave rise to the term "retained benefits" which referred to benefits from a previous scheme that had to be taken into account in calculating the maximum benefit from a subsequent scheme.

The legislators therefore sought to combine simplification of a rather dense set of rules with fairness for those who expected a level of benefit that would be jeopardised by the new rules without alleviating provisions.

4.14.2 Two types of lump sum protection

There are two forms of lump sum protection.

Member specific lump sum protection applies to aggregate lump sum entitlement of a member where the lump sum rights exceeded £375,000 at 5 April 2006 and the member had claimed primary or enhanced protection.

Scheme specific lump sum protection applies to lump sums that exceed 25% of rights under a scheme and where member specific protection is unavailable. This protection did not have to be claimed.

If the member does not qualify for protection under either heading, the lump sum will be limited to the lesser of 25% of benefits being crystallised and 25% of the current lifetime allowance.

Example

Jo has benefits which were valued at £1.7 million at 5 April 2006. She claimed primary protection.

The total lump sum benefit was valued at £300,000 at the same time.

None of the available lump sums under each arrangement exceeded 25% of the value of an arrangement.

In this case, the first test is for member-specific protection. Jo claimed primary protection, but the lump sum rights did not exceed £375,000 at 5 April 2006. Member-specific lump sum protection is therefore not available.

Jo then considers scheme specific lump sum protection. However, the lump sum did not exceed 25% of the value of any arrangements so this option is not available to her.

Jo's maximum lump sum is limited to 25% of the lifetime allowance or 25% of the value of total benefits if less. In this case the maximum lump sum is 25% of the lifetime allowance: £250,000 in 2017-18.

In each case, the lump sum allowance is described as being "modified". The modifications are again fairly straightforward, but what causes difficulty is the calculation of the lump sum at 5 April 2006. The calculations of member specific lump sums

The protected lump sum is based on the accrued lump sum rights if the member had left service to retire at 5 April 2006 assuming that the member had reached the minimum age at which no deductions would have applied to the benefit.

Law: FA 2004, Sch. 36, para. 24

4.14.3 Member specific lump sum protection

The member specific lump sum at 5 April 2006 should be easy to identify in these circumstances: it was required to be disclosed when the claim for primary and/or enhanced protection was made (on form APSS 200). If the member claimed primary protection, and the lump sum rights exceeded £375,000, the certified amount is increased to the same extent as the standard lifetime allowance, but not reduced.

If the member had claimed enhanced protection, and the lump sum rights exceeded £375,000, the pension commencement lump sum remains the same proportion of total benefits whenever they are taken.

There is no direct risk to the lump sum protected under this heading if the member transfers benefits because the protection is member specific. However, as discussed elsewhere (in particular, in Chapter 11) there are circumstances when enhanced protection may be lost on transfer and by implication this would lose the related lump sum protection.

The member may choose which scheme to commute if he or she enjoys primary protection. This may encourage a member to take the whole (or bulk) of the lump sum from a money purchase arrangement if commutation rates are less than generous under a defined benefit scheme. This option is unavailable in the case of enhanced protection although the member may choose from which arrangements under the same scheme benefits should be taken. Typically, therefore, the lump sum would be taken from a money purchase additional voluntary contribution arrangement thereby minimising the exposure of a defined benefit to commutation factors determined by the trustees.

Law: FA 2004, Sch. 36, para. 24

4.14.4 Scheme specific lump sum protection

Scheme specific lump sums at 5 April 2006 are more difficult to identify in many cases and, as no claim was required, there will often be no contemporaneous record. The principle adopted in calculating the lump sum to be protected is similar to that for member specific protection.

An example shows how the lump sum is valued when benefits have accrued concurrently in the same employment.

Based on an HMRC example

Fred has total pension rights on 5 April 2006 of £100,000, split equally between two schemes. Fred has total lump sum rights of £50,000, again split equally between the two schemes.

He takes all his benefits from both schemes in 2016 when the standard lifetime allowance was £1 million. So the value of Fred's pre-6 April 2006 lump sum rights is increased by 20% (in line with the increase in the lifetime allowance in 2011-12). In 2016, Fred had pension rights of £80,000 in Scheme 1 and £170,000 in Scheme 2. Fred was not an active member of Scheme 1 after 5 April 2006, but continued to accrue benefits in Scheme 2. He takes drawdown pension from both schemes.

Fred can receive lump sum benefits of £97,500 made up of

Scheme 1 – £37,500

Scheme 2 – £60,000

The Scheme 1 lump sum benefit is made up of

- £30,000 for the pre 6 April 2006 benefits (£25,000 lump sum right at 5 April 2006 increased by 20%), plus
- £7,500 for the increase in the value of benefits after 5 April 2006 (being 25% of the increase in the benefits value after 5 April 2006). The increase in the value of benefits after 5 April 2006 is calculated as

£80,000 – [£50,000] = £30,000

The Scheme 2 lump sum benefit is made up of

- £30,000 for the pre 6 April 2006 benefits (£25,000 lump sum right at 5 April 2006 increased by 20%), plus
- £30,000 for the increase in the value of benefits after 5 April 2006 (being 25% of the benefit increase after 5 April 2006) calculated as

  £170,000 – [£50,000] = £120,000.

This example is equally valid if Fred had purchased a lifetime annuity or had a scheme pension provided instead of taking drawdown pension from his money purchase arrangement.

However, the valuation of pre-2006 benefits may have been problematic when the available lump sum would exceed HMRC limits without adjustment. Again, HMRC provided an example (at PTM 063140):

Further HMRC example

Asif has pension and lump sum rights for a single employment on 5 April 2006. His total pension rights are £210,000 and total lump sum rights are £60,000. These rights are held in three schemes. His rights are held in a single arrangement under each scheme.

Asif's maximum permitted lump sum for the employment under HMRC limits was calculated as £54,000. So his lump sum rights exceed HMRC limits by £6000. His maximum permitted pension under HMRC limits was greater than £210,000.

Therefore VULSR must be adjusted whilst VUR remains the same.

The position before adjustment was as follows

- Scheme 1 – pension rights of £60,000; lump sum £15,000; lump sum percentage 25%
- Scheme 2 – pension rights of £60,000 ; lump sum £20,000; lump sum percentage 33.33%
- Scheme 3 – pension rights of £90,000; lump sum £25,000; lump sum percentage 27.78%

The reduction in Asif's lump sum rights from £60,000 to £54,000 must be apportioned amongst the three schemes. The legislation specifies that the apportionment is as follows.

Scheme lump sum – (excess lump sum x scheme lump sum/total lump sums)

So for scheme 1 the apportionment would be

£15,000 – (£6000 x £15,000/£60,000) = £13,500

After adjustment, Asif's lump sum percentage from each of the three schemes becomes

- Scheme 1 – pension rights of £60,000; lump sum £13,500; scheme percentage 22.5%
- Scheme 2 – pension rights of £60,000; lump sum £18,000; scheme percentage 30%
- Scheme 3 – pension rights of £90,000; lump sum £22,500; scheme percentage 25%

So after the required adjustment, only the rights in Scheme 2 qualify for protection as the lump percentage exceeds 25% of the uncrystallised pension rights in that scheme.

Rights in schemes 1 and 3 may be taken at 25% because the normal rules for pension commencement lump sums in Sch. 29 FA 2004 apply to the rights under those two schemes.

The adjustment is in effect a deduction from the value of the lump sum rights under an arrangement of a proportion of the excessive lump sum found by applying the formula:

V/AV

where:

V is the value of the uncrystallised lump sum rights under the arrangement; and

AV is the total value of the uncrystallised lump sum rights under all the arrangements in respect of the employment being pensioned.

It is worth noting here that if a personal pension arrangement receives a transfer of protected lump sum, the available lump sum at crystallisation may be more than 25% of total benefits. The "new" rules removed the 25% cap that would have applied to transferred lump sums before 6 April 2006.

Law: FA 2004, Sch. 36, para. 32-34

4.14.5 Increases with the lifetime allowance

The protected scheme specific lump sum may be increased to the same extent as the standard lifetime allowance, but will not reduce with it (so in 2016-17, it is 20% higher than it was in 2006-07, reflecting the increase in the lifetime allowance from £1.5 million to £1.8 million between 2006-07 and 2011-12).

The protection can, of course, only apply to the lump sum accrued to 5 April 2006. If there is subsequent accrual, the pre-A-Day protected accrual may reduce the accrual that would otherwise have been available after that date. Where there has been pre and post A-Day accrual (which may simply mean investment returns in the case of a "paid-up" money purchase scheme), the permitted maximum lump sum is:

(VULSR x ULA/FSLA) + ALSA

where:

VULSR is the value of uncrystallised lump sum rights;

ULA is the underpinned lifetime allowance;

FSLA = £1.5 million; and

ALSA is the greater of the additional lump sum and nil.

The additional lump sum amount is one quarter of:

LS + AC – (VUR x CSLA/FSLA),

where:

LS is the lump sum paid;

AC is:

(a) in a case where the member becomes entitled to the pension in connection with which the lump sum is paid before reaching the age of 75, the amount crystallised by reason of the member becoming entitled to the pension, and

(b) in a case where the member becomes entitled to that pension after reaching that age, the amount that would have been so crystallised but for Sch. 32, para. 2

VUR is the value of the individual's uncrystallised rights under the pension scheme on 5 April 2006;

CSLA is the current standard lifetime allowance (or the underpinned allowance if the member has successfully claimed fixed protection 2012 (£1.8 million), 2014 (£1.5 million) or 2016 (£1.25 million)); and

FSLA = £1.5 million.

It would always be possible to take a lump sum based on the new rules (25% of total crystallised benefits etc.) if that yielded a better result.

What the calculation shows is that the greater the pre-A-Day protected lump sum, the smaller the post A-Day lump sum.

As an historical note to this, when the 2004 Act was implemented, the calculation only applied if a contribution was paid to the same scheme after 5 April 2006. This led to the unintended (but perhaps foreseeable) consequence that members would pay a nominal contribution to the scheme after that date in order that accrual would continue. Common sense eventually prevailed.

Law: FA 2004, Sch. 36, para. 34

4.15 Recycling

4.15.1 Background to recycling

Recycling refers to a process where the member takes a retirement lump sum from a registered pension scheme and either in anticipation of taking the lump sum or taking it subsequently, contributions to the scheme are increased. It is only relevant to money purchase arrangements.

The problem that HMRC are trying to address is that the lump sum is generally tax-free and is being reinvested in an arrangement for which tax relief at marginal rates is also available. Of course, only 25% of benefits being crystallised may be reinvested and the scheme may then only provide a further lump sum of 25% of total benefits so the opportunities for taking lump sums as capital payments are restricted.

For the recycling rule to apply, the increase in contributions must be significant and the local tax office must refer the case to Pension Schemes Services in Nottingham. It is unusual for the rule to be applied in practice.

4.15.2 Conditions for the recycling rule to apply

The recycling rule applies when all of the following conditions are met:

- the individual receives a pension commencement lump sum;
- because of the lump sum, the amount of contributions paid into a registered pension scheme in respect of the individual is significantly greater than it otherwise would be;
- the additional contributions are made by the individual or by someone else, such as an employer;
- the recycling was pre-planned;
- the amount of the pension commencement lump sum, taken together with any other such lump sums taken in the previous 12 month period, exceeds £7,500; and
- the cumulative amount of the additional contributions exceeds 30% of the pension commencement lump sum.

Some of these terms (such as "pre-planned") are defined below, but HMRC have considerable scope for interpretation and offer guidance on how they will exercise their discretion in PTM 133840 to 133860. In summary, HMRC will be looking to see if contributions increased (not just replaced) because the member took the pension commencement lump sum. HMRC recognise that there are many ways in which contributions may be increased (e.g. sale of investments, remuneration sacrifice, increases due to a predetermined basis) and these transactions may be contemporaneous with taking the lump sum, but that will not be enough for the rule to apply: the key is to identify that the contribution increased because the lump sum was taken. On the other hand, HMRC will be on the look-out for artificial schemes.

Similarly, however, there will be no recycling if there was no intention of using the lump sum to fund the increased contributions.

Law: FA 2004, Sch. 36, para. 3A
Guidance: PTM 133840-133860

4.15.3 Pre-planning

Pre-planning requires the member to have formed the intention to increase contributions either before or at the time the lump sum is paid (not after). This is the "relevant time". In effect, the member may receive the lump sum and increase contributions or increase the contributions and receive the lump sum.

The guidance points out that it is for HMRC to show that pre-planning was present, not for the member to prove absence of intention. This is rather a "double-edged" sword because it could preclude the member from putting his or her case.

HMRC accept that a significant increase in this context means in practice that the contribution increases by more than 30% of contributions that might otherwise have been paid. Note that this is an increase not maintenance of a contribution before benefits were taken.

The increase in contribution will be measured cumulatively over a period of time which is:

- the tax year in which an individual takes a pension commencement lump sum with the intention of using it to make significantly increased contributions to a registered pension scheme;
- the two tax years immediately preceding the tax year in which the individual took the lump sum; and
- the two tax years immediately following the tax year in which the individual took the lump sum.

This is to avoid the member increasing contributions piecemeal and avoiding the rule, but is not especially onerous.

4.15.4 The "cost" of recycling

When all the conditions for the recycling rule to apply are in place the lump sum used to increase contributions becomes an unauthorised payment and subject to unauthorised payment charges. If the lifetime allowance charge applies to the lump sum, that takes precedence and the unauthorised payment charges will not apply to that portion of lump sum.

4.15.5 Disclosure

There are requirements on the member to disclose to the scheme administrator if the lump sum is to be used for recycling purposes and applications will therefore include a standard declaration to be signed by the member. If the member does not disclose the intention and there is recycling, the administrator is able to apply for a discharge from the scheme sanction charge.

Note that the recycling rules apply to overseas schemes and to individuals who qualify for migrant member relief if those rules would have applied should the scheme have been a registered pension scheme.

4.16 Retirement guidance

In his 2014 Budget Statement, the Chancellor of the Exchequer committed the government to introducing a framework to deliver impartial guidance for anyone reaching retirement. The objective was described in the consultation document "Freedom and choice in pensions", which laid a great deal of emphasis on the need for impartiality and avoiding conflicts of interest. "Pension Wise: Your Money, Your Choice" is described as a "free and impartial government service about your defined contribution pension options".

The Financial Conduct Authority is responsible for setting the high level standards but overall responsibility "until maturity" of the facility remains with the Treasury in consultation with the Pensions Regulator and the Money Advice Service. The "face to face" guidance is delivered by the Citizens' Advice Bureaux and telephone guidance is delivered by the Pensions Advisory Service. The facility does not offer advice or specific recommendations.

The cost of the service is funded by a "levy on financial services firms".

Note also that the *Finance Bill (No. 2)* 2017 and supporting regulations effective from 6 April 2017 propose to introduce the Pensions Advice Allowance (see **4.11.3**).

Law: PSA 2015, s. 47 and Sch. 3; *The Registered Pension Schemes (Authorised Payments) (Amendment) Regulations* 2017 (SI 2017/397)

Guidance: *Pension Schemes Newsletter* 87

5. Death benefits

5.1 Background – authorised payments

Under the pension tax regime introduced by FA 2004 and implemented on 6 April 2006 (A-Day), many types of payment may be made from a UK registered pension scheme, but so-called "unauthorised" payments incur substantially higher income tax charges than authorised payments. In effect, unauthorised payments are tax-inefficient.

Payments made consequent to the death of a member may be authorised payments if they adhere to fairly specific conditions. They may take the form of lump sums and/or pensions and are governed by the lump sum death benefit rule and the pension death benefit rule respectively.

Tax rules are not the only regulator of death benefits. They will also be determined by:

- the scheme rules; and
- DWP legislation that deals with the protection of members and their dependants and contracting-out.

The death benefit may be provided by funds that have accrued to the member before death and/or life assurance. The cost of life assurance may be covered by the member or a sponsoring employer. Premiums for life assurance do not enjoy the tax reliefs that were available before A-Day.

The importance of observing the pension death benefit or lump sum death benefit rule is demonstrated by FA 2004, s. 172B. This section explains that if, as a result of the death of a relevant member, the pension rights of another member who immediately before the death was "connected" to the relevant member are increased, the increase is to be taxed as an unauthorised payment. There is nothing to stop the beneficiary member receiving a death benefit under the pension or lump sum death benefit rules just like anyone else, but a reallocation of funds, for example, will be an unauthorised payment. There are exceptions. The unauthorised payment rules will not apply if (per FA 2004, s. 172B):

> "7(b) the benefits to which each of at least 20 members of the pension scheme has an actual or prospective entitlement under the pension scheme are increased at the same rate in consequence of the death.
>
> (7A) ... if:
>
> (a) the increase ... is an increase in the rate of a dependants' annuity, nominees' annuity, successors' annuity or dependants' scheme pension or in rights representing a nominee's flexi-access drawdown fund, successor's flexi-access drawdown fund, dependant's drawdown pension fund or dependant's flexi-access drawdown fund, and
>
> (b) the increase is attributable to rights of the dead member to payments under a dependants' annuity, nominees' annuity, successors' annuity or dependants' scheme pension or rights representing a nominee's flexi-access drawdown fund, successor's flexi-access drawdown fund, dependant's drawdown pension fund or dependant's flexi-access drawdown fund ."

Payments falling within these rules include annuities purchased from insurance companies with funds accrued under a registered pension scheme.

Payments may be made in the form of cash or *in specie* by means of assigning assets.

The inheritance tax implications of pension planning are examined in **Chapter 10**.

Law: FA 2004, s. 164, 172B

5.2 Death benefits and the lifetime allowance

The death benefits recognised by the registered pension scheme legislation appear in the pension death benefit rules and the lump sum death benefit rule. Schemes are usually established in such a way as to give discretion to the trustees, manager or administrator as to how to distribute death benefits. (Under an occupational scheme this is achieved by way of a discretionary trust.)

The pension death benefit rules (dealing with income benefits) are:

Pension death benefit rule 1: the pension death benefit is payable to a dependant, nominee or successor of the member and nobody else. However, this is subject to rule 2.

Pension death benefit rule 2: in a defined benefit arrangement, the only pension death benefit payable is a dependants' scheme pension.

Pension death benefit rule 3: the pension payable under a money purchase scheme to a dependant is:

(a) a dependants' scheme pension (but only if the dependant had an opportunity to select a dependant's annuity), or

(b) a dependants' annuity, or

(c) a dependants' drawdown pension.

Pension death benefit rule 3A: in respect of a money purchase arrangement, the only pension death benefit payable to a nominee of the member is a nominee's annuity or nominee's drawdown pension

Pension death benefit rule 3B: no payment of pension death benefit, other than a successors' annuity or successors' drawdown pension in respect of a money purchase arrangement, may be made to a successor of the member.

Pension death benefit rule 4: the total amount of dependant's capped drawdown pension paid to a dependant in each drawdown pension year from – or under a dependants' short-term annuity purchased using sums or assets out of – the dependant's drawdown pension fund in respect of a money purchase arrangement must not exceed 150% of the basis amount for the drawdown pension year. This refers to dependant's capped drawdown to which entitlement started before 6 April 2015 and which has not converted to newly-designated flexi-access drawdown.

Whilst the discretion is unfettered in relation to distibution of the lump sum (although subject to scheme rules), legislation intervenes in respect of income benefits. FA 2004, amended mainly by ToPA 2014 and FA 2015, restricts income beneficiaries to dependants, nominees and nominated successors under money purchase schemes and dependants under defined benefit schemes as this chapter will describe. In practice, this means that income benefits may only be paid to a dependant or nominated beneficiary (and the administrator may override a nomination providing payment is to another nominated beneficiary), but the lump sum may be paid to anyone who falls within the class of beneficiaries mentioned in the scheme rules and any expression of wish completed by the member. The beneficiary actually designates how the benefit should be taken, but may only take an income benefit if he or she has been nominated. (So, for example, if nominated, the beneficiary could designate funds for an income or lump sum, but if not nominated, the funds could only be taken as a lump sum.)

Where the trustee, manager or administrator has discretion, that discretion will be limited by the rules of the scheme as well as legislation. So, for example, the rules may be drawn widely to include anyone mentioned in the will, any dependants and anyone specified in an "expression of wish" completed by the member (this is only an example).

The trustees, manager or adminstrator need not fear that the courts will challenge their decision although the the courts may challenge the process and whether the discretion has been exercised diligently.

Trustees are already required to act in the best financial interests of members and beneficiaries, but the PSA 2015 extends this obligation to administrators of non-trust-based schemes that provide collective benefits or shared risk schemes.

The normal exposure to inheritance tax does not apply and this is explained in **Chapter 10**.

The lump sum death benefit rule simply lists the authorised lump sums payable on death of the member:

- (a) a defined benefits lump sum death benefit;
- (b) a pension protection lump sum death benefit;
- (c) an uncrystallised funds lump sum death benefit;
- (d) an annuity protection lump sum death benefit;
- (e) a drawdown pension fund lump sum death benefit;
- (ea) a flexi-access drawdown fund lump sum death benefit;
- (f) a charity lump sum death benefit;

(h) a trivial commutation lump sum death benefit; or

(i) a winding-up lump sum death benefit.

The lump sum death benefit payable before retirement benefits have been taken will generally either be a defined benefit lump sum death benefit (where the benefit is predetermined according to a formula, such as a multiple of pay) or an uncrystallised funds lump sum death benefit (such as a "return of fund" under a money purchase scheme) and paid before age 75 if it is to be measured against the lifetime allowance under BCE 7. In these circumstances, the crystallisation is measured against the deceased member's lifetime allowance, not that of the beneficiary.

However, the beneficiary (not the scheme administrator) is liable for the lifetime allowance tax charge which will be at a rate of 55% and will be deducted from the benefit.

Generally speaking, lump sum death benefits where death occurs before the age of 75, are tax-free if they fall within the member's lifetime allowance. If the member dies after reaching the age of 75, the lifetime allowance will not apply, but the lump sum will be liable to tax. The question then is whether the liability is to the special lump sum death benefit charge or to income tax as if the payment was of income.

Member dies after reaching the age of 75

The "special lump sum death benefits charge" will apply where the member had reached the age of 75 at death and certain lump sums are paid to a "non-qualifying person". Those lump sums are:

- a pension protection lump sum death benefit;
- an annuity protection lump sum death benefit;
- a drawdown pension fund lump sum death benefit;
- a flexi-access drawdown fund lump sum death benefit.

The charge also applies on the death of a member who has reached the age of 75 if payment is to a non-qualifying person in respect of a defined benefit lump sum death benefit or an uncrystallised funds lump sum death benefit.

Member has not reached age 75

The charge applies on the death of a member who had not reached age 75 at date of death where the lump sum is paid outside a two-year "window" (described below) and is:

- a drawdown pension fund lump sum death benefit;
- a flexi-access drawdown fund lump sum death benefit;
- an defined benefit lump sum death benefit; or
- an uncrystallised funds lump sum death benefit.

The special lump sum death benefits charge will also apply where the lump sum is paid to a non-qualifying person on the death of a dependant, nominee or successor of a deceased member where: the dependant, nominee or successor had not reached the age of 75 at the date of his or her death, and the death benefit is a drawdown or flexi-access drawdown lump sum death benefit and is paid outside the two-year "window".

The charge falls on the scheme administrator.

The "window" is "two years beginning with the earlier of the day on which the scheme administrator of the scheme first knew of the member's death and the day on which the scheme administrator could first reasonably have been expected to have known of it".

A non-qualifying person is any of the following acting in the capacity of trustee:

- a trustee or personal representative, acting in that capacity, providing the trust is not a bare trust;
- a director of a company;
- a partner in a partnership firm;
- a member of a limited liability partnership.

The general application of the charge to payments outside the two years was withdrawn by the wording of the Act, effective from 6 April 2016.

When the charge is applied because payment was outside the two-year window (but the member was under 75 at death), it is the special lump sum death benefit charge at a fixed rate of 45% and the liability falls on the scheme administrator.

If the payment is to a non-qualifying person, the liability is also to the special lump sum death benefit charge. This is charged on the scheme administrator (so no refund is available to the administrator or beneficiaries).

When the trustees subsequently make a payment to the beneficiary of the trust, the gross amount of the payment is treated as income and taxed at the marginal rates of the recipient, but the charge may be set off against the amount paid by the scheme administrator. (The *Pensions Tax Manual* explains that the individual beneficiary must account for the gross amount on his or her self assessment return or on repayment form R40). The effect of this convoluted process is that tax is paid at the individual's marginal rates as if he or she had received the payment directly.

The process also requires the scheme administrator and trustees of the recipient trust to meet certain disclosure obligations.

Within 30 days of the payment (or the regulations coming into force on 6 February 2017), the administrator must disclose to the trustees:

- the amount on which tax has been charged;
- the amount of that charge;
- the name and reference number of the scheme making the payment;
- the name, date of birth and date of death of the individual in respect of whom the payment is made.

On receipt of this information, the trustees of the trust must disclose the same information to the beneficiary within 30 days of receipt or of the rules coming into force.

If the liability arises simply because the member had reached the age of 75 at date of death, the liability is to marginal rates of income tax and falls on the recipient.

There will be no liability to inheritance tax in respect of the member's estate where payment is made under the special lump sum death benefit provisions.

The taxation of lump sums paid to so-called "by-pass" trusts is described in **Chapter 10**.

Pensions payable to dependants or other beneficiaries from uncrystallised money purchase funds, following the death of a member before age 75, will be subject to a BCE 5C (applied to flexi-access drawdown) or 5D (applied to the purchase of a lifetime annuity) and may therefore be subject to the lifetime allowance tax charge. These pensions will otherwise be free of income tax. If death is at age 75 or over, they will be taxed at marginal rates of income tax.

Law: FA 2004, s. 165-168, 206, 216, and Sch. 28, 29; ToPA 2014, s. 3 and Sch. 2; PSA 2015, s. 37; F(No. 2)A 2015, Pt. 4; *The Registered Pension Schemes (Provision of Information) (Amendment) Regulations* 2017 (SI 2017/11)

5.3 Available death benefits

5.3.1 Money purchase schemes

Dependants' and nominees' pensions

In the event of the member's death (and subject to the scheme rules), a money purchase scheme may provide the following benefits:

- a dependant's or nominee's pension by way of an annuity;
- a dependants' scheme pension;
- a dependant's or nominee's drawdown pension.

In the event of the death of a dependant or nominee who has "inherited" a pension in this way, any of their pension may be paid to a nominated successor. Similarly, on the death of a successor, the pension may be paid to another nominated successor.

The nomination may be made by the member, the nominee or a previous successor (if the benefit is now passing to a successor).

The definition of dependant is described below (**5.4**)

A nominee may not be a dependant and correspondence with HMRC has suggested that a dependant may not become a nominee when he ceases to be dependent.

A scheme administrator may nominate an individual to receive a beneficiary's pension if there are no surviving dependants of the member and the member has not nominated a charity.

The use of the term "nomination" in the 2014-15 legislation is confusing because it is inconsistent with what has gone before. However, to summarise:

- The lump sum death benefit may be paid to any beneficiary whether or not he has been nominated. (This is consistent with the operation of discretionary disposal that has applied before and still does for defined benefit schemes.) In effect, the scheme administrator or trustees may override an expression of wish.
- The income death benefit may only be paid to an individual who has been nominated (see above).
- The nomination may be overridden by the scheme administrator in order to pay a lump sum to another beneficiary (not necessarily nominated).

The exercise of a nomination does not immediately prompt the application of a charge to inheritance tax.

There are two possible BCEs that are relevant:

> **BCE 5C**: The designation, on or after 6 April 2015 but before the end of the relevant two-year period, of relevant unused uncrystallised funds as available for the payment, to a dependant or nominee of the individual, of (as the case may be) dependants' flexi-access drawdown pension or nominees' flexi-access drawdown pension.
>
> **BCE 5D**: A person becoming entitled, on or after 6 April 2015 but before the end of the relevant two-year period, to a dependant's annuity or nominee's annuity in respect of the individual if:
>
> (a) the annuity is purchased using (whether or not exclusively) relevant unused uncrystallised funds, and
>
> (b) the individual died on or after 3 December 2014.

The scheme may also pay a lump sum to any beneficiaries (i.e. not just dependants or nominated beneficiaries), but this may be subject to tax.

A charge to tax may therefore arise on payment of a beneficiary's pension or a lump sum if:

- death is at age 75 or over (charged as income and tax is at marginal rates of income tax); or
- payment is to a non-qualifying person or not within the two-year rule (charged at 45%); or
- death is before the age of 75, but the lifetime allowance is exceeded (subject to the lifetime allowance charge at 55%).

The "two-year" rule requires the payment to be made within two years of the scheme administrator first learning of the individual's death or within two years of when it would have been reasonable for him or her to haved learned of the death, if earlier. If the payment is not made within this period, the lump sum will be taxed as a special lump sum death benefit at 45%. This is explained in more detail in **section 5.2** above.

Law: FA 2004, Sch. 28, para. 15-24G
Guidance: PTM 071000

Lifetime annuity

The only benefits a lifetime annuity contract secured from a money purchase arrangement can provide on the death of the annuitant are as follows:

- the provision of a further annuity for any dependants or nominees of the member. A nominee's annuity may have been purchased with a member's lifetime annuity (a joint-life annuity) on or after 6 April 2015 or may have been purchased after a member's death on or after 3 December 2014 where entitlement to the annuity started on or after 6 April 2015;
- the continuation of any member's lifetime annuity for the term of any remaining guarantee period; and
- the payment of an annuity protection lump sum death benefit.

The nominee's annuity must be payable by an insurance company and is payable until death of the nominee or until the earliest of the nominee's marriage, civil partnership or death. A dependant's annuity is payable until the dependant ceases to be dependent.

On the death of a dependant, nominee or successor on or after 3 December 2014 and in capped or flexi-access drawdown, undrawn funds may be applied to the purchase of a lifetime annuity for a successor. A successor will have been nominated by the previous beneficiary.

A successor will have become entitled to an annuity on or after 6 April 2015. It must be payable by an insurance company and payable until the death of the successor or the earliest of marriage, civil partnership or death.

Undrawn funds are funds that have crystallised but that have not yet been drawn down to provide a benefit.

This will prompt a BCE 5D if death is before age 75.

Regulations allow funds representing a beneficiary's annuity to be transferred to another annuity where it will represent the original annuity or to the original "relevant" pension scheme.

Law: FA 2004, Sch. 28, 29

Scheme pension

The only benefits a money purchase arrangement is authorised to provide on the death of a (pensioner) member in receipt of a scheme pension entitlement are as follows:

- the provision of a dependants' scheme pension, dependants' or nominee's annuity, or dependants' or nominee's drawdown pension to any dependant or nominee of the member;
- the continuation of any member's scheme pension for the term of any term-certain period or guarantee that remains;
- the payment of an annuity protection lump sum death benefit.

A successor's drawdown or annuity is also available, as for the lifetime annuity.

There are parallel rules for short-term annuities purchased as part of a flexi-access or capped drawdown scheme.

Law: FA 2004, Sch. 28, 29

Drawdown pension

The only benefits a money purchase arrangement is authorised to provide from any drawdown pension fund left on the death of the member are:

- the allocation of funds to provide any dependant or nominee of the member with a dependant's or nominee's flexi-drawdown pension. The process is that the individual is nominated and that beneficiary then designates how the fund should be applied (e.g. flexi-access drawdown or annuity);
- the payment of drawdown pension fund lump sum death benefit; and
- where there is no surviving dependant of the member, the payment of a charity lump sum death benefit to a charity nominated by the member.

Taxation of money purchase death benefits

In certain circumstances the death benefit is tax-free:

- the payment is an authorised payment within the pension death benefit rules or the lump sum death benefit rule;
- the benefit is an income or lump sum;
- the member, nominee, dependant or successor died on or after 3 December 2014;
- the member was not yet aged 75 at death;
- entitlement to the death benefit arose on or after 6 April 2015;
- the payment of the benefit met the requirements of the two-year rule (above); and
- the payment is within the member's lifetime allowance.

If the payment is not authorised, it will be taxed as an unauthorised payment.

If the individual died on or after age 75, the payment will usually be taxed at marginal rates. See **5.2** above for more detail.

Law: FA 2004, Sch. 28, 29; F(No. 2)A 2015, Pt. 4

Taxation of foreign pensions for nominees and dependants

The *Taxation of Pensions Act* 2014 is primarily concerned with benefits from UK registered pension schemes. However, the Act harmonises the treatment of recognised overseas pensions with UK pensions: pensions payable to nominees and dependants are exempt from UK tax if the member died before the age of 75.

5.3.2 Defined benefit schemes

Scheme pension

The only benefits a registered pension scheme is authorised to provide on the death of a (pensioner) member in receipt of a defined benefit scheme pension are as follows:

- the provision of a dependants' scheme pension to any dependants of the member;
- the continuation of any member's scheme pension for the term of any term-certain period of guarantee that remains; and
- the payment of a defined benefits lump sum death benefit or a pension protection lump sum death benefit.

Uncrystallised rights

The only benefits a defined benefits arrangement is authorised to provide in respect of any uncrystallised rights remaining under the arrangement where the member dies are as follows:

- the provision of a dependants' scheme pension to any surviving dependant of the member; and/or
- the payment of a defined benefits lump sum death benefit.

In practice, the benefits will be insured. Under a defined benefit scheme, uncrystallised rights are not identified by member and it would be impractical and financially unsustainable to pay benefits from the fund. The lump sum death benefit and dependants' pensions are therefore provided by way of a group life assurance policy. PA 2004, s. 255 requires that the member of such an arrangement should accrue retirement benefits under a related arrangement in order for the life cover to be registered. In the event of a claim, any rights under the funded scheme are extinguished.

Law: FA 2004, Sch. 28, 29; PA 2004, s. 255

5.3.3 Hybrid schemes

When a member draws entitlements under a hybrid arrangement there are two possible outcomes:

- the arrangement is treated as a money purchase arrangement (which also covers a cash balance arrangement) or a defined benefits arrangement at that time, depending on the form benefits that are being provided; or
- where differing forms of benefits are provided under the arrangement, the arrangement will be split, with each constituent part being treated as the appropriate type of arrangement.

If the member dies after this crystallising of retirement benefits, those benefits may be provided under those arrangements (or the arrangement) as any other money purchase arrangement or defined benefits arrangement.

Where a member dies before drawing his or her entitlement (or all of his or her entitlements) death benefits may be provided in respect of those uncrystallised rights on the same basis as under a money purchase arrangement or defined benefits arrangement, depending on the scheme rules.

Law: FA 2004, Sch. 28, 29

5.4 Dependants

We have seen that following the death of a member, lump sums and pensions may constitute authorised payments. This does not mean that they will be tax-free, but they will not incur unauthorised payment charges on the member or scheme administrator.

The lump sum is generally payable to any beneficiary, usually under the "discretionary disposal" rules.

The pension death benefit, on the other hand, will only be an authorised payment if it is paid to dependants.

The statutory definition of a dependant for these purposes is:

> "1. A person who was married to or a civil partner of, the member at the date of the member's death is a dependant of the member.
>
> 1A. If the rules of the pension scheme so provide, a person who was married to, or a civil partner of, the member when the member first became entitled to a pension under the pension scheme is a dependant of the member.
>
> 2. A child of the member is a dependant of the member if the child:
>
>   a. has not reached the age of 23 [but see below], or
>
>   b. has reached that age and, in the opinion of the scheme administrator, was at the date of the member's death dependent on the member because of physical or mental impairment.
>
> 3. A person who was not married to or a civil partner of, the member at the date of the member's death and is not a child of the member is a dependant of the member if, in the opinion of the scheme administrator, at the date of the member's death:
>
>   a. the person was financially dependent on the member,
>
>   b. the person's financial relationship with the member was one of mutual dependence, or
>
>   c. the person was dependent on the member because of physical or mental impairment."

Law: FA 2004, Sch. 28, para. 15 (as amended); FA 2016, Sch. 5, para. 6

There are some points to note about this definition:

- the ages of 18 and 21 have no significance;
- a child over the age of 23 can only be classed as dependent if at the date of death he or she was dependent because of physical or mental impairment (not, for example, because of an extended university education) or if he or she

designated a drawdown (or flexi-access drawdown) pension before the age of 23, but reached that age after 16 September 2016;

- although the determination of dependence is a matter for the scheme administrator, no such determination has to be made for spouses, registered civil partners or children (natural or adopted) under the age of 23 (subject to the partial withdrawal of the age 23 restriction above). These individuals are automatically regarded as dependent;
- an individual may only receive a tax-authorised dependants' pension death benefit following the member's death if he or she was a dependant of the member when the member died, or in the case where scheme rules recognise someone who was married to, or who was the civil partner of, the member when that member's pension entitlement first arose, was within that category. Aside from the latter qualification (spouse or civil partner), being dependent on the member when the member retires or draws benefits is not enough to be classed as a dependant. To be paid an authorised pension death benefit, the recipient must otherwise have been dependent on the member when the member died;
- "married" includes married under the *Marriage (Same Sex Couples) Act* 2013.

A dependants' scheme pension need not be payable for the life of the dependant, need not be paid annually and need not be maintained at its initial level (or above). Indeed, some schemes, mostly in the public sector, require the dependants' pension to stop on the remarriage of the dependant or even if the dependant lives with another individual "as man and wife".

However, no dependants' pension may include a guaranteed term or capital protection.

A dependants' annuity must be payable at least annually and may only be varied according to the same rules as a member's pension. The annuity must stay level or increase or vary in accordance with an inflation index. If the dependant is a child, the annuity must end when the child is 23 unless he or she remains dependent because of physical or mental disability. If the dependant is an adult, the scheme rules may determine that it should end on the remarriage or civil partnership of the dependant.

Guidance: PTM 071000 and 000001 (Glossary)

5.5 Dependants' drawdown pensions

A drawdown dependants' pension (flexi-access or capped) may be payable to a dependant (see **section 5.4**) from a registered money purchase pension scheme or cash balance scheme on the death of a member. The income may be paid as a drawdown pension from a short-term annuity or income withdrawal/drawdown directly from the fund. It is taxed under the PAYE procedures.

Capped drawdown is only available to a dependant where the dependant's pension started before 6 April 2015. Capped drawdown may convert to flexi-access drawdown at the request of the dependant or when the maximum withdrawal (150% of the basis amount) is exceeded.

When a dependant's pension is designated or converted to a flexi-access pension, it is known as a "newly designated" flexi-access pension.

The definition of dependant will require a child to be under the age of 23 to be eligible. However the *Finance Act* 2016, (para. 6 and Sch. 5, effective 17 September 2016) allows payment to continue beyond age 23 in the case of flexi-access and capped dependant's drawdown.

Designating a dependant's pension will be a BCE 5C if death was before age 75 and there could be a lifetime allowance tax charge on such an event.

The income is taxed as pension income under the PAYE process. If it is paid directly from the fund the charge is on payments actually made in the tax year, but if it is paid from a short-term annuity it is taxed on payments due.

However, no pension commencement lump sum is available with a dependants' drawdown pension and any payments made under a pension guarantee would also be unauthorised. The beneficiary could withdraw the whole fund under flexi-access drawdown, but no part of the withdrawal would be free of income tax.

The pension may have been established under a capped drawdown (before 6 April 2015) or flexi-access drawdown option (from that date).

Capped drawdown is paid over a succession of "pension years" starting with the date funds are designated for drawdown (not, for example, date of death of the member). Those years (i.e. start and end dates of the 12 month period) cannot be changed until the member has reached age 75 and then it may only be changed by the administrator who wishes to harmonise review dates of arrangements within the same scheme, although the review date may be brought forward by 12 months. When the dependant reaches age 75, a review will be triggered for the first anniversary (of designation) after the 75th birthday.

The maximum capped annual drawdown is calculated in the same circumstances and in the same way as the member's drawdown, but using the personal details of the dependant. There is no maximum withdrawal if the dependant has designated funds for flexi-access drawdown.

This means (among other things) that the maximum withdrawal must be calculated every three years before age 75 and every year from that date. The 60-day window leading to the pension review date is available for calculation of the maximum withdrawal although the revised maximum will be effective from the pension review date.

A beneficiary may, subject to the rules of the scheme, use a (flexi-access) drawdown fund to purchase a pension annuity.

Law: FA 2004, Sch. 36, para. 21-24G; FA 2016, Sch. 5

5.6 Drawdown for children: transitional protection

5.6.1 When the pension may be paid

Special note should be made of pensions payable from a registered pension scheme to children of the member and which started before 6 April 2006. There are two sets of circumstances where a dependants' pension may be payable although it would not usually be allowed under the new rules.

The first set of circumstances provides that pensions may continue:

- if the child is still in full-time education or undertaking vocational training; or
- where at the point of reaching the age of 23, or at the time of ceasing full-time education / vocational training, the child was suffering from a physical or mental deterioration that was either serious enough to prevent him from following a normal employment, or which would seriously impair his earning capacity.

A particular requirement to qualify under the first category is as follows:

- *either* the member died before 6 April 2006, and the child's pension was:
    - in payment before this date, or
    - was due to be paid,
- *or* the member's pension was in payment on 5 April 2006, and the child was born before 5 April 2007.

Also, whether either of the above applies, the "first scheme rules condition" must have been satisfied. The condition is that on 5 April 2006, the rules of the pension scheme allowed a pension to be paid to a child of the member following the member's death, until a time no later than when the child eventually ceased full-time education or vocational training (or earlier).

To qualify for continued payment of a child's pension after reaching age 23 under this provision, the circumstances of any given case must fully meet the requirements of at least one of the above circumstances.

The second set of circumstances provides that a pension may be paid to an adult child dependant if both of the following conditions are satisfied:

- the first condition is that:
    - the member's pension was in payment before 2 July 2008;
    - the child's pension (death benefit) was in payment on 1 July 2008;

    - the child's entitlement to the pension death benefit arose before 1 July 2008 (on or after the member's death); or
    - the entitlement to the pension death benefit was subject to the discretion of the trustees of the scheme, and the discretion was capable of being exercised following the member's death (in favour of the child) so that the entitlement could have arisen before 1 July 2008.
- the second condition, the "the scheme rules condition", is that on 5 April 2006, the rules of the pension scheme allowed a pension to be paid to a child of the member (following the member's death) if, at the date of the member's death, the child was financially dependent on the member (or their financial relationship was one of mutual dependence).

Law: FA 2004, Pt. 4; FB 2016, cl. 22 and Sch. 5
Guidance: PTM 071000

5.6.2 Transfers and continued protection

Should the member transfer rights that include these transitional protections, the protections will generally be lost unless they are part of a block transfer. In brief, a block transfer refers to a transfer of all rights in respect of two or more members from the same scheme to the scheme as part of the same transaction. The normal requirements of a block transfer are supplemented in these circumstances.

To be a "relevant block transfer" both of the following further conditions must be met:

- The transfer value being received must have come either:
    - directly from the original pension scheme where the above protected rights originate, or
    - indirectly from the original pension scheme where the protected rights originate, having passed through one or more intermediate schemes before reaching the latest one, having enjoyed this same protection along the way, thanks to the earlier application of

this or the preceding bullet, as appropriate, together with having met the following conditions along every part of the journey, including in the final receiving scheme.

- Following the transfer, the receiving scheme (which would include each intermediate scheme in a series of sequential transfers) must:
  - provide the child with an entitlement to the payment of pension (i.e. make them a pensioner member); or
  - in the event that it was the parent who transferred into the receiving scheme before their death, that parent must have been admitted as a member of the receiving scheme; or
  - in the event that it was the parent who transferred into the receiving scheme before his death, and that parent made an irrevocable election designating part of the sums or assets representing his rights for the payment of a pension to the child, the child is then entitled to such payment from the receiving pension scheme following the parent's death.

5.7 Dependants' and other beneficiaries' pensions: restrictions

5.7.1 General

The dependant's, nominee's or successor's pension may not be commuted to a pension commencement lump sum, it may not be guaranteed and it may not be allowed pension protection.

It is taxed as pension income.

As a general rule, there is no limit on the level of a beneficiary's pension. However, there will be a limit on the allowable dependants' scheme pension under a registered pension scheme where the scheme member died after 5 April 2006 and had reached the age of 75 before his or her death, and at the time of that death was actually receiving one or more scheme pensions under the scheme, or was prospectively entitled to receive them.

5.7.2 Restriction of aggregate dependants' pensions

If the member has reached the age of 75 at date of death, the aggregate dependants' scheme pensions payable from a registered pension scheme must not exceed the amount of the member's scheme pension (the initial member pension limit) at the date of death of the member (although certain adjustments are permitted to the member's benefits for this purpose). If there is more than one dependant, the "limit" is apportioned. The rules are tortuous for such a rare set of circumstances, but are designed to prevent tax abuse.

The initial pension limit is made up of three elements:

1. either
    a. if the member has died within 12 months of starting to receive a scheme pension, the amount of pension that would have been paid to the member in the 12 months from the date the member first became entitled to the pension had the member not died; or
    b. if the member lived for more than 12 months from starting to receive a scheme pension, the aggregate of the scheme pension(s) paid to the member from the registered pension scheme (or by an insurance company) in the 12 month period immediately preceding the date of death (referred to in the legislation as "the pre-death year"); plus
2. the amount of scheme pension that would have been paid in that period if the member had drawn the scheme pension(s) to which he or she had a prospective entitlement under the registered pension scheme or associated contract with an insurance company; plus
3. where a tax-free lump sum had been paid in connection with the member's scheme pension, 5% of the amount of the lump sum paid.

5.7.3 Restrictions in later years

In the years following the 12 months after death of the member, the dependants' pension is also limited (the current pension limit). The rule provides that if in any of these 12 month periods, other than in excepted circumstances, the amount of dependants' scheme pension payable exceeds the "current member pension limit" then the excess will not be treated as a dependants' scheme pension and will be an unauthorised member payment.

The excepted circumstances are:

- there are 50 or more pensioner members in the scheme at the start of the 12 month period in which the dependants' scheme pension was increased; and
- the circumstances satisfy one of the tests set out below.

Whether or not the amount of increase in the dependants' scheme pension is within excepted circumstances depends whether certain tests are satisfied. If the increase satisfies one of these tests, even if the dependants' scheme pension exceeds the "current member pension limit" the increase will be an authorised member payment.

The increase will be within excepted circumstances if the 50 pensioner member rule is satisfied, and the increase in pension falls within one of the following:

1. The dependants' scheme pension payable by the scheme has increased by the same amount as all other dependants' scheme pensions payable by the same scheme. For this purpose, it is necessary to compare the amount of each such pension payable in the 12 month period in which the increase in question occurs with the same pensions paid in the previous 12 month period. This test would, for example, be satisfied if all dependants' scheme pensions were increased by £1,000 on the same date.
2. The dependants' scheme pension payable by the scheme has increased by the same percentage as all other dependants' scheme pensions payable by the same scheme. This is determined by comparing the change in each such pension from the previous 12 month period to the 12 month period in which the increase takes place, as a percentage of the pension payable in that previous 12 month period. This test would be satisfied, for example, if a scheme awarded a 10% increase in all dependants' scheme pensions; or

3. Both a percentage increase and a flat rate increase have been applied to the dependants' scheme pension and the total increase in the dependants' scheme pension payable by the scheme is made up of the same percentage increase and the same amount as all dependants' scheme pensions payable by the scheme in a 12 month period.

The current member pension limit is the "initial member pension limit" plus the total of:

- the "permitted margin"; and
- the "excepted circumstances amount".

The permitted margin

This is described in the *Pensions Tax Manual* as follows:

> "The permitted margin is the amount of the initial member pension limit ... increased by the greater of two measures – calculation A and calculation B.
>
> Calculation A
>
> > Increase the initial member pension limit by the relevant annual percentage for the period from the beginning of the 12 month period after the end of the post-death year (that is, the rate in the 13th month after the member's death) to the first month of the 12 month period in question.
> >
> > The relevant annual percentage is either
> >
> > - the annual rate agreed in respect of the member's **scheme pension** (that is, if a relevant valuation factor of greater than 20 had been agreed in respect of that pension) or
> > - 5% per annum.
>
> Calculation B
>
> > Increase the initial member pension limit by the percentage increase in *RPI* from the beginning of the 12 month period after the end of the post-death year (that is, the rate in the 13th month after the member's death) to the first month of the 12 month period in question. But if RPI has remained level or has decreased over this period, then

no increase is permitted under calculation B for this period.

This means that increases in the dependants' scheme pension are permitted on a cumulative basis, or as a one-off large increase, or as smaller annual increases.

The excepted circumstances amount

This is the amount by which a dependants' scheme pension has been increased in any year since the post-death year, where the excepted circumstances apply in respect of that increase.

The amount of the increase will be the difference between the pension in the year of the increase as compared with the pension in the previous 12 month period.

This amount, the initial member pension limit and the permitted margin are added together to calculate the current member pension limit."

Payments that exceed this limit will be taxed as unauthorised payments.

Guidance: PTM 072120

5.8 Pension guarantees (terms certain)

A pension guarantee may be applied to a member's scheme pension, a member's lifetime annuity or a member's short-term annuity. It is not available in respect of dependants' pensions. It will be available as an option for the member (rather than the scheme) in respect of lifetime and short-term annuities. The benefit of a pension guarantee is that it will continue to pay instalments of pension until the end of the term certain regardless of the earlier death of the member. The maximum allowable term of ten years was removed in respect of new annuities implemented on or after 6 April 2015. The maximum allowable term is ten years for scheme pensions (including defined benefit pensions).

By way of example, if the pension is subject to a ten year guarantee and the member dies after pension payments have been made for seven years, the pension will continue for a further three years.

The guaranteed payments can be commuted within the authorised payment rules in certain quite restricted circumstances by virtue of a provision in ToPA 2014. In any case, the annuity or pension protection lump sum may be included to be paid when the guarantee has expired.

A lump sum death benefit is a trivial commutation lump sum death benefit if one of two conditions is met and the lump sum does not exceed £30,000:

The first condition is that the lump sum:

(a) is paid to a dependant entitled under the pension scheme to pension death benefit in respect of the member; and

(b) extinguishes the dependant's entitlement under the pension scheme to pension death benefit and lump sum death benefit in respect of the member.

The second condition is that:

(a) the lump sum is paid after the member's death to an individual entitled to be paid a pension under the scheme:

  (i) which the member was entitled to be paid immediately before the member's death, and

  (ii) which is payable to the individual under pension rule 2 (which describes guarantee periods);

(b) if the pension is an annuity or scheme pension payable by an insurance company, the lump sum must extinguish all entitlements in respect of the member under the contract concerned; and

(c) if the pension is a scheme pension payable by the scheme administrator, the lump sum extinguishes all entitlements to receive a scheme pension in respect of the member from the scheme administrator under pension rule 2.

The rules of the scheme may stipulate that the payments under the guarantee following the death of the member should come to an end on the remarriage of the beneficiary (or living together "as man and wife"), when the beneficiary reaches 18 or when the beneficiary's full-time education comes to an end.

The guaranteed payments are taxed on the recipient under PAYE. Tax is calculated by reference to payments due, not necessarily paid in the tax year. Payments will also fall into the estate for inheritance tax purposes if they are paid via the member's personal representatives. It is possible to write these payments under a trust in order to by-pass the estate.

A flexi-drawdown pension may not be guaranteed unless it is funded by a short-term annuity.

Law: FA 2004, s. 165, pension rule 2

5.9 Lump sum death benefits

The death benefits described here are:

- the defined benefit lump sum;
- the uncrystallised fund lump sum;
- the pension protection lump sum;
- the annuity protection lump sum;
- the drawdown lump sum;
- the charity lump sum.

The *Taxation of Pensions Act* 2014 (amended by the *Finance (No. 2) Act* 2015) radically changed the taxation of death benefit lump sums and attitudes to pension funds as part of the estate. The relevance of inheritance tax is described in **Chapter 10**.

Law: ToPA 2014, s. 3, Sch. 2; F(No. 2)A 2015, Pt. 4

5.9.1 Types of lump sum death benefit

Lump sum death benefits are payable to any beneficiaries who are described within the scheme rules, so there is no need to prove the recipient's dependency or identify a nomination (although trustees may wish to take note of an expression of wish). They may be paid in addition to dependants' pensions.

There are a number of different types of lump sum death benefit, but there is no consistent tax treatment. However, the broad rule is that the benefit will be free of tax if it is neither a winding-up lump sum death benefit nor a triviality lump sum death benefit:

- the payment is an authorised payment;
- the individual died before age 75;
- payment is within the available lifetime allowance; and
- it is paid within the two-year "window" described below.

If it is not an authorised payment, it will be taxed accordingly. If it does not meet either of the other two conditions, it will be subject to income tax at marginal rates of income tax. This charge is described in more detail at **5.2** above.

5.9.2 Defined benefit lump sum

A defined benefit lump sum:

- is payable from a defined benefit arrangement on the death of the member,
- but cannot be a pension protection death benefit lump sum, a triviality death benefit lump sum or a winding-up death benefit lump sum.

If the member was below the age of 75 on death, there will be a BCE and the recipient may be liable for a lifetime allowance tax charge if the member's lifetime allowance has been exceeded. The rate is currently 55%. There is no test against the lifetime allowance once the member has reached age 75, but from that age, there will be a charge at the marginal rates applicable to the recipient on the whole amount paid as a lump sum. The member is liable for the tax and it will usually be deducted from the death benefit lump sum under PAYE and the RTI process. See also **5.2** above. Where the lump sum is paid to a trustee, personal representative, company director or business partner, the special lump sum death benefit charge may apply instead of the charge to income tax (as described in **5.2** above, and see **5.9.3** below).

A defined benefit lump sum is one that is calculated by reference to a proportion or multiple of pay (for example, four times basic salary) rather than simply as an amount of money.

Law: FA 2004, Sch. 29, para. 13; F(No. 2)A 2015, Pt. 4

5.9.3 Uncrystallised lump sum benefit

The uncrystallised lump sum death benefit is payable from a money purchase scheme (including a cash balance scheme) before the member has taken benefits from the arrangement.

If the member was below the age of 75 on death, there will be a BCE 7 and the recipient may be liable for a lifetime allowance tax charge if the member's lifetime allowance has been exceeded. The rate is currently 55%. There is no test against the lifetime allowance once the member has reached age 75 but, from that age, there will usually be a charge at marginal rates unless paid to a trust that is not a bare trust, in which case the charge will be at a flat-rate 45%. This is the special lump sum death benefit charge (see **5.2**). The member is liable for the tax and it will be deducted from the death benefit lump sum under PAYE (the scheme administrator is liable for the special lump sum death benefit charge). See also **5.9.2** above.

Law: FA 2004, Sch. 29, para. 13

5.9.4 Pension protection lump sum

A pension protection lump sum is payable from a defined benefit scheme if the option is included in the scheme rules and if the member dies while the pension is in payment. It guarantees a lump sum representing as much as the balance of pension not paid. When the pension crystallises, the application of the revaluation factor places a capital value (AC) on the pension of P x 20 where P is the initial pension. If the pension was in payment on 6 April 2006, the value is derived from multiplying the pension by 25.

The value of the pension protection lump sum at any time is AC – (value of instalments paid) – (any lump sum paid under an annuity purchased to secure the pension).

The lump sum is usually tax-free within the available lifetime allowance if the member died before age 75, but is otherwise taxed at marginal rates. See **5.2** for more detail, and see **5.9.2** and **5.9.3** where payment is to a trustee, etc.

Law: FA 2004, Sch. 29, para. 14

5.9.5 Annuity protection lump sum (includes scheme pensions)

An annuity protection lump sum is available when the member purchases a lifetime annuity or commences a scheme pension with funds accrued under a money purchase scheme (including a cash balance scheme). The value of the benefit can be as much as the amount that crystallises to provide the member's pension less any instalments of the annuity already paid. If the annuity was in payment at 6 April 2006, the amount crystallised is assumed to have been the level of income multiplied by 25.

The lump sum is tax-free if the member died before age 75, but is otherwise usually subject to the special lump sum death benefit charge at marginal rates of income tax. It is payable by the scheme administrator (who will deduct it from the benefit under PAYE) or the insurance company in the case of an annuity. See **5.2** for a deeper explanation, and see **5.9.2** and **5.9.3** where payment is to a trustee, etc.

Law: FA 2004, Sch. 29, para. 16

5.9.6 Drawdown lump sum (and flexi-access drawdown lump sum)

The drawdown lump sum death benefit is a lump sum that is not a charity lump sum that is payable on the death of a member whilst in receipt of a drawdown pension. It is also payable on the death of a dependant or nominee who has inherited a drawdown pension from a member or on the death of a successor. Its value should not, in effect, exceed the value of the fund.

The drawdown pension fund death benefit allows as much as the value of the undrawn, but crystallised, fund to be paid as a lump sum. It is tax-free if the individual was under 75 at date of death, but otherwise is subject to income tax at marginal rates of the recipient, which the scheme administrator will deduct under PAYE. See **5.2**, and see **5.9.2** and **5.9.3** where payment is to a trustee, etc.

The lump sum cannot include any payment from a short-term annuity which can only be represented by an annuity guarantee following the member's death.

5.9.7 *Charity lump sum*

A lump sum death benefit is payable to a charity if:

- there are no surviving dependants of a member;
- it is paid from the member's drawdown fund; and
- it is paid to a charity nominated by the member.

A charity lump sum death benefit can also be paid if all the following apply:

- the member was 75 or older when he or she died (the *Finance Act* 2016 withdrew this restriction if payment is made on or after 16 September 2016);
- the member had uncrystallised rights (benefits that have not started to be put into payment) under any type of arrangement at the time of death;
- there are no dependants of the member; and
- the charity has been nominated by the member.

A charity lump sum death benefit may also be paid on the death of a dependant of the member. There must again be no other surviving dependants of the member. The lump sum is payable in respect of a drawdown fund.

The lump sum must be paid to either:

- a charity nominated by the *member*; or
- if the member had not chosen a charity, a charity selected by the dependant.

A lump sum is also payable to a charity on the death of a nominee or successor if there are no surviving dependants of the member. The lump sum must be paid to a charity nominated by the member, but in the absence of succh a nomination, to a charity nominated by the nominee or successor.

The legislative requirement of the charity is simply that it is a *bona fide* charity and not necessarily registered (it could be overseas). Nevertheless, HMRC guidance states the following:

> "All charities registered with the Commission of England & Wales are listed on a Register – this Register can be searched on-line at www.charity-commission.gov.uk. This website also

> gives information as to the requirements imposed on such charities and how a charity can register.
>
> The Scottish counterpart is the Office of the Scottish Charity Regulator (www.oscr.org.uk).
>
> The Northern Irish counterpart is, from 1 May 2010, the Charity Commission Northern Ireland (www.dsdni.gov.uk/ccni).
>
> If the charity does not use the payment for charitable purposes the payment will not have been a charity lump sum death benefit. It will be treated as an unauthorised member payment."

There is no tax charge on the scheme administrator of the pension scheme making the payment of a charity lump sum death benefit. There is no tax charge on the charity receiving the payment as long as it is used for charitable purposes.

Law: FA 2004, Sch. 29, para. 17
Guidance: PTM 079300

5.9.8 Trivial commutation lump sum death benefit

A lump sum death benefit is a trivial commutation lump sum death benefit if it is no more than £30,000 and:

- it is paid to a dependant entitled under the pension scheme to pension death benefit in respect of the member or under a guarantee; and
- it extinguishes the dependant's entitlement under the pension scheme to pension death benefit and lump sum death benefit in respect of the member.

There is no minimum age for this to be payable and unlike the similar lump sum payable to a member, the monetary cap relates to each scheme rather than the aggregate value of schemes.

This facility has obviated the need for a winding-up lump sum death benefit which has been removed from the statute books.

5.9.9 Life cover lump sum

A life cover lump sum can only be paid where the member is age 75 or over at the time of death. It is a lump sum that could have been paid under a scheme approved under ICTA 1988, Pt. 14, Ch. 1 before 6 April 2006.

This provision allows certain lump sums, e.g. small lump sums known as funeral expenses or funeral grants, which were paid from occupational pension schemes, to continue to be paid after 5 April 2006.

A registered pension scheme may only pay a life cover lump sum where all the following conditions are met:

- the scheme was a retirement benefits scheme approved for the purposes of ICTA 1988, Pt. 14, Ch. 1 immediately before 6 April 2006;
- the member was in receipt of benefits from the scheme on or before 5 April 2006 or was entitled to one or more life cover lump sums which in aggregate amount to £2,500 or less;
- the member had a right under the scheme to a life cover lump sum on 5 April 2006;
- on 10 December 2003 the rules of the scheme contained a provision that:
    - gave the member the right to a life cover lump sum at that point, or
    - would have given the individual the right to a life cover lump sum if he or she had been a member of the scheme at that point; and
- the rules of the scheme in relation to life cover lump sums have not changed since 10 December 2003.

A life cover lump sum can only be paid after age 75 so its payment is not a benefit crystallisation event and does not count for the purposes of the lifetime allowance. There is no income tax charge on a life cover lump sum.

5.10 Transitional protection issues

5.10.1 Introduction

Chapter 11 describes various measures that were put in place to ease the transition from the pre-2006 regime to its successor whilst retaining subsisting rights. The most significant areas concern primary and enhanced protection and the protection of lump sums calculated by reference to each scheme and which exceed the new allowances.

The transitional measures also have an impact on death benefits.

The principle is that where a "personal" lifetime allowance has been modified by, for instance, primary protection, then it is modified for the purposes of death benefits as well as retirement benefits.

5.10.2 Primary protection

However, there is a "twist". The value of the primary protection factor will have been calculated by reference to retirement benefits. If the value of death benefits at date of death exceeds the "personal" lifetime allowance, the beneficiary of the lump sum may notify HMRC that the value of protection should be increased to the value of the death benefit.

The death benefit so protected is known as the "pre-commencement rights to death benefits". The modification will not apply to:

- lump sum death benefits paid in respect of income drawdown; or
- lump sum death benefits paid in other circumstances where the member is drawing benefits.

5.10.3 Value of pre-commencement rights

The value of pre-commencement rights to death benefits is the value of lump sum death benefits that would have been payable if the member had died on 5 April 2006, but with certain exclusions:

- any amount that if paid would have given HMRC grounds for withdrawing scheme approval under the pre-2006 rules;
- the dependants' pension proportion amount (if any). This arises when part of the lump sum is used to provide dependants' pensions;
- the amount of any lump sum death benefit payable under a policy of life assurance on 5 April 2006 by any scheme

(other than an occupational pension scheme with at least 20 members on 5 April 2006) where:

  - the policy does not pay out a lump sum after 5 April 2006, or
  - the terms of the policy are varied significantly in the period 5 April 2006 to the date of the individual's death.

  A variation made in order to comply with the *Employment Equality (Age) Regulations* 2006 or the *Employment Equality (Age) Regulations (Northern Ireland)* 2006 – or any regulations replacing or amending them – will be ignored for this purpose.

- the amount of any lump sum death benefit payable from an occupational pension scheme on 5 April 2006 where:
  - the individual was not continuously employed in the period from 5 April 2006 to the date of his death by either the same employer as had employed him on 5 April 2006 or by a person connected with that employer, or
  - the individual was already entitled to benefits under the occupational pension scheme before his death.

Where a policy held on 5 April 2006 for the purposes of an occupational pension scheme is surrendered, and a new one taken out, the new policy will be treated as a pre-6 April 2006 existing policy where the reason for the surrender and taking out of the new policy is either:

- to comply with the *Employment Equality (Age) Regulations* 2006 – or any regulations replacing or amending them, or
- as part of a transaction to ensure that the activities of an occupational pension scheme (as defined PSA 1993, s. 1) comply with either PA 2004, s. 255 or the *Pensions (Northern Ireland) Order* 2005, art. 232, and the rights under the old and new policy are not significantly different.

Law: FA 2004, Sch. 36, para. 11A-11D

5.10.4 *Enhanced protection*

If we are considering an individual who enjoys enhanced protection, we must determine whether:

a. further contributions for life assurance or benefit accrual; or

b. payment of a death benefit

may result in the loss of the protection.

Premiums to pay for life assurance will not jeopardise enhanced protection under a money purchase scheme if:

1. the life assurance contract was made before 6 April 2006;
2. there is no surrender value (i.e. it is a term assurance);
3. the policy only pays a benefit on death; and
4. the policy is not varied to increase the term or sum assured.

Premiums to pay for life assurance under a hybrid scheme will not jeopardise enhanced protection if:

1. they are paid by the sponsoring employer; and
2. they only provide a defined benefit lump sum or an uncrystallised lump sum death benefit that is a cash balance benefit (described in **Chapter 1**).

Life assurance under a defined benefit scheme or cash balance scheme will not jeopardise enhanced protection if any increases in benefit remain within the "appropriate limit". The value of the appropriate limit is increased if:

1. a recipient of the lump sum notified HMRC; and
2. the value of the deceased member's right to lump sum death benefits on 5 April 2006 in respect of the pensionable employment to which the arrangement relates as re-calculated by:
   - an indexation increase, or
   - a re-calculation of the right on 5 April 2006 using the individual's earnings immediately before their death

   is greater than the previously calculated appropriate limit.

The *appropriate limit* is the greater of the indexed amount and the earnings recalculation amount.

The *indexed amount* is the greatest of:

- the value from increasing the benefit by 5% per annum from 5 April 2006;
- the value from increasing the benefit in line with GMP revaluation factors; and
- the value obtained from increasing the benefit in line with RPI from 5 April 2006.

For a defined benefit scheme the *earnings recalculation* amount allows the pension calculation (pensionable service x pensionable earnings x rate of accrual) to be modified to assume that benefits were taken at 5 April 2006, but using current (i.e. later) pensionable earnings and using the actual age when benefits commenced (so, if appropriate, applying early retirement factors).

The *post commencement earnings limit* for capped members is the lower of:

- 7.5% of the standard lifetime allowance (or, from 6 April 2012, £1.8 million where this is greater than the standard lifetime allowance) when the "first relevant event" occurs; and
- the individual's highest earnings from the employment being pensioned in any consecutive 12 months in the three year period ending with the earliest of:
    - the "first relevant event",
    - the individual leaving the pensionable employment to which the defined benefits or cash balance arrangement relates, and
    - the individual's death.

The *first relevant event* is the earlier of the first benefit crystallisation event or the first permitted transfer to an other money purchase arrangement.

Where the individual died or left pensionable employment before the first relevant event the amount of earnings can be increased from the date of death or leaving the pensionable employment (as appropriate) until the date of the first relevant event. The increase is the greatest of:

- an annualised increase of 5%;
- for contracted-out rights, right subject to revaluation, or preserved rights an annualised increase at the percentage rate; and
- the percentage increase in the Retail Price Index.

The *post commencement earnings limit* for non-capped member is the individual's highest earnings from the employment being pensioned in any consecutive 12 months in the three year period ending with the earliest of:

- the first relevant event;
- the individual leaving the pensionable employment to which the defined benefits or cash balance arrangement relates; and
- the individual's death,

as long as this amount is not more than 7.5% of the standard lifetime allowance (or, from 6 April 2012, £1.8 million where this is greater than the standard lifetime allowance) at the first relevant event.

Where this amount is more than 7.5% of the standard lifetime allowance (or, from 6 April 2012, £1.8 million where this is greater than the standard lifetime allowance) the *post commencement earnings limit* for non-capped members is the greater of:

- 7.5% of the standard lifetime allowance (or, from 6 April 2012, £1.8 million where this is greater than the standard lifetime allowance) at the first relevant event, and
- total earnings from the pensionable employment for the three year period ending with the earliest of the three dates shown above, divided by three.

The *first relevant event* is the earlier of the first benefit crystallisation event or the first permitted transfer to an "other" money purchase arrangement.

Where the individual died or left pensionable employment before the first relevant event the amount of earnings can be increased from the date of death or leaving the pensionable employment (as appropriate) until the date of the first relevant event.

Law: FA 2004, Sch. 36, para. 15A

6. Transfers and refunds

6.1 Overview

6.1.1 Transfers and opt-outs

One of the recurring themes of pensions reform over the last 30 years has been what used to be called "portability", that is the facility to move pension rights from one scheme to another and, by implication, from one employer to another. Although the original objective of the facility may have been simply to allow an individual to move pension rights as he or she moved jobs, the whole issue has been clouded by complications and competing claims over entry and exit charges (money purchase schemes), the value of a defined benefit compared with a projection (defined benefit and defined contribution schemes) and latterly the safety of a defined benefit scheme itself and an individual member's benefits (especially if he or she has accrued a substantial pension benefit).

This chapter will make passing references to a number of these issues, mainly to highlight the inherent dangers of transfers, but will primarily concentrate on the tax issues.

Before going any further, however, we must distinguish "transfers" from "opt-outs". Transfers refer to the movement of accrued pension rights from one pension scheme to another. This may be a consequence of an opt-out, but usually follows an individual leaving the service of the employer or pension scheme. As a general rule, a member is ill-advised to opt out of a scheme that continues to accrue benefits:

- The employer is making contributions which are akin to remuneration. Opting out is a way of waiving remuneration which most employees would not countenance if, for example, they were being asked towaive current pay.
- Opting out may be even more foolhardy for a member of one of the diminishing number of defined benefit schemes because the cost of providing an equivalent benefit in any other way is so large. It is no coincidence that few employers are now providing this benefit other than for

past service. Opting out may mean not just opting out of retirement benefits, but valuable life cover and dependants' benefits. Some members may not be able to apply for cover on an individual basis.

The opt-out decision became less straightforward when the lifetime allowance was reduced in 2011 and in 2014. The problem is that £1 of contribution after 5 April 2014, for instance, could trigger a lifetime allowance charge on as much as £250,000 of already accrued benefit if fixed protection is invalidated.

If an individual opts out, there is no obligation to accept him or her back in the scheme on the same terms. The automatic enrolment rules require "opt-outs" to be reinstated, but not necessarily on anything like the original terms.

There have been three developments that could have influenced the opt-out or transfer decision:

- The 2013 Budget confirmed that the government was considering the introduction of "individual" protection and the measure duly appeared as FA 2014, s. 44 and Sch. 6. If this protection is claimed, the lesser of the value of benefits and £1.5 million is protected from the lifetime allowance charge after its reduction to £1.25 million on 6 April 2014. The measure was followed by FA 2016, s. 19 and Sch. 4, which introduced a corresponding provision when the lifetime allowance reduced from £1.25 million to £1 million. The member is able to enjoy further benefit accrual without jeopardising the protection, unlike fixed protection (also available) that will be lost on future accrual. The problem with losing fixed protection is that not only is future accrual not protected, but also any benefits falling between £1.25 million and £1.5 million that have already accrued (£1 million and £1.25 million for Individual Protection 2016). Individual protection may be claimed at any time before 6 April 2017 using an HMRC electronic application.
- The *Pensions Act* 2014, s. 34 made it unlawful for anyone to offer a non-pension inducement to transfer benefits from a defined benefit scheme (such as a commission rebate or a remuneration increase). This supplements legislation that

already makes it unlawful to induce an eligible employee to opt out of an automatic enrolment scheme.

The introduction of flexible pensions (flexi-access drawdown, uncrystallised funds pension lump sum, etc.) against a background of low fixed interest returns has aroused an interest in greater access to pension funds.

In April 2013, the DWP announced that it intended to legislate for the introduction of automatic transfers. The primary legislation (enabling regulations to be made) appears in PA 2014, s. 33 and Sch. 17. The measure requires that when an individual moves from one job to another, the accrued pension will automatically transfer to the scheme provided by the new employer. It is proposed that the measure will only apply to transfer values up to £10,000 (having accrued from a certain date) and that employees should be able to opt out of the system or be required to consent to the transfer as the circumstances dictate. This proposal, which will be introduced by regulation, raises many issues, not least of which is that the DWP will wish to avoid the possibility of benefits accrued under a "good" scheme being automatically transferred to a "not so good" scheme. The DWP announced in July 2015 that the measure was being postponed until 2017 and there were some doubts about whether it would go ahead given its complexity. It has since been postponed indefinitely (by announcement).

In its Budget 2014 consultation document "Freedom and choice in pensions", the government proposed:

- to remove the option to transfer rights from an unfunded public service defined benefit scheme except in exceptional circumstances;
- to consider removing the option to transfer from a funded public service defined benefit scheme except in exceptional circumstances;
- to consider removing the option to transfer from private sector defined benefit schemes except in exceptional circumstances;
- to consider other options in relation to private sector defined benefit schemes as the more relaxed regime for defined contribution schemes is implemented.

The *Pension Schemes Act* 2015 included a measure to prevent transfers from unfunded public service defined benefit schemes to other schemes that are capable of giving effect to flexible benefits (primarily money purchase schemes).

The Act also enables the establishment of collective benefits.

Where, in all circumstances, the rate or amount of the benefit payable to or in respect of a member depends entirely on:

(a) the amount available to pay that member's and other members' benefits; and

(b) factors used to determine what proportion of that amount is available for the provision of the particular benefit,

these benefits are defined as "collective" in the Act. The definition also provides that a benefit which is a money purchase benefit is not a collective benefit.

The Act proposes that regulations may require that trustees or managers of pension schemes offering collective benefits set targets in relation to the rate or amount of those benefits. In particular, regulations can be made about, amongst other things, the way that targets are expressed, recorded and published. The intention is that members of a scheme with collective benefits should be provided with a reasonable estimate of the benefits that they can expect to receive from the scheme; in the absence of a well defined pot over which the individual has clear ownership, the target is a way of illustrating for the member what they might receive. The Act allows regulations to require trustees or managers of a scheme to obtain an actuarial certificate confirming that the actuary is of the opinion that the probability of the assets being sufficient to meet the initial targets is in line with the level set out in the regulations.

Regulations may, in particular, make provision for matters to which the actuary should have regard, and may require trustees or managers to provide the actuarial certificate to a specified person. Regulations may also make provision about the content of the actuarial certificate and require the trustees or managers to obtain the certificate from an actuary who has certain qualifications or attributes.

None of these proposals has a direct impact on the tax treatment of registered pension schemes although the schemes will be registered. Legislation is being sponsored by the DWP.

6.1.2 Pension flexibility and advice

The introduction of a much more liberal regime for taking pension benefits from 6 April 2015 does not only impact on money purchase schemes. It is true that few of the measures apply to defined benefit schemes, but the option, for example, to take unrestricted withdrawals from a money purchase scheme will inevitably attract the attention of members of defined benefit schemes.

The Pensions Advice Allowance payment became available on 6 April 2017 and allows authorised payments from registered pension schemes and within the scheme rules to be made to "persons" to fund the cost of retirement advice or the implementation of that advice. "Persons" is likely to cover members and beneficiaries of members such as dependants. The conditions of the advice are:

- the payment is requested in writing and an appropriate declaration is signed;
- no more than two requests for the allowance have been made in respect of the person;
- no allowance has already been successfully claimed in the tax year;
- the advice is regulated by the Financial Conduct Authority;
- the payment is made directly to the adviser; and
- the payment does not exceed £500 (which suggests that if it does, the whole payment is unauthorised rather than just the excess).

The payment is tax-free to the recipient and the member or survivor although the adviser must charge VAT if applicable.

The measure complements the "employer-arranged pensions advice exemption" that allows employers to provide each employee with £150 to be allocated to pensions advice. The payment is deductible for the employer and tax-free for the employee. The government had proposed increasing the award to £500, but the measure was a casualty of the shortened 2017 *Finance Bill*.

The government has already established a means of providing "guidance" (through Citizens Advice and the Pensions Advisory Service) under the brand of "Pension Wise". However, the ramifications of transferring from a defined benefit scheme to a money purchase scheme offering flexibility require a more serious and individually tailored approach.

The *Pension Schemes Act* 2015 requires the trustees or managers of a pension scheme to check that a member or survivor has received appropriate independent (of the scheme) advice before converting "safeguarded benefits" (benefits that are not money purchase benefits) to a scheme in which the member will acquire flexible benefits (such as flexi-access drawdown). There is an exception from this requirement where the transfer value does not exceed £30,000.

The person to whom the member or survivor refers must be authorised under the FSMA 2000 to carry on the appropriate regulated activity. The detail will appear in regulations.

There will also be regulations that specify in what circumstances the employer will be required to pay for a member or survivor to take independent advice. The provision of advice under this heading will be exempt from income tax unless it is part of a salary sacrifice arrangement.

Further protection is proposed after the government completed a consultation on barriers to transferring. As a consequence, it intends giving the FCA power to impose a "charge cap" on transfer values (charge cap does not include market value adjustments or loss of terminal bonus).

The Pensions Regulator will also introduce guidance for trustees to ensure that they are processed promptly and accurately. Trust-based schemes will be required to be more accountable and transparent on transfers through a new reporting regime.

Meanwhile, Pension Wise will be required to offer more guidance to help individuals through the transfer process.

Law: *Income Tax (Earnings and Pension) Act* 2015, Pt. 4; *Pensions Schemes Act* 2015, s. 48; SI 2002/205 *(The Income Tax (Exemption of Minor Benefits) Regulations* 2002); SI 2015/742 *(The Pension Schemes Act* 2015 *(Transitional Provisions and Appropriate Independent Advice) Regulations* 2015); SI 2017/397 *(The Registered Pension Schemes (Authorised Payments) (Amendment) Regulations* 2017)

6.1.3 Where to transfer

It would be unusual, in view of the adverse tax consequences, for an individual to wish to transfer accrued rights to anything other than a registered pension scheme or qualifying recognised overseas pension scheme.

The main options available under the registered pension scheme category are:

- An occupational pension scheme (i.e. established and at least part funded by an employer).
- A personal pension scheme (i.e. established by a pension provider and possibly funded wholly or partially by an employer). The arrangement may be established solely to accept a transfer.
- A stakeholder pension scheme (i.e. usually established by a pension provider and possibly funded wholly or partially by an employer). There are a few stakeholder schemes that have been established as trust arrangements and cover industries or, at least, groups of employers. They may also be established by an employer as a type of occupational scheme. The arrangement may be established solely to accept a transfer.
- A deferred annuity (i.e. established by a life assurance company solely for the purpose of accepting a transfer from a registered pension scheme). Deferred annuities are also known as "buy-out" policies or "section 32" policies.

The contrasting and common features of each are:

- An occupational scheme can refuse to accept a transfer. If it accepts the transfer, it must calculate benefits in respect of the transferred amount on the same basis as transfers from the scheme.

- A personal pension scheme may refuse to accept a transfer, but may be constrained by its rules (many were established under "model rules" or a variation on them). The transfer request must be authorised by the member. The scheme cannot provide a guaranteed minimum pension in respect of contracted-out rights accrued before 6 April 1997.
- A stakeholder pension plan may not refuse to accept a transfer of accrued rights from a registered pension scheme. The transfer request must be authorised by the member. The scheme may not provide a guaranteed minimum pension.
- A deferred annuity is primarily designed to allow trustees of an occupational pension scheme to "buy out" their liability to provide accrued benefits. Although the member of a scheme might direct that accrued rights be transferred to the policy, the trustees may unilaterally transfer rights, most commonly in respect of a pension credit member after a dissolution of marriage (and within four months of the court order) and in the event of a scheme being wound up (and after the member has been given the option of transferring elsewhere).

The deferred annuity is able to preserve a guaranteed minimum pension. Having left service under the occupational pension scheme the guaranteed minimum pension will re-value at a fixed rate determined at date of leaving rather than in line with national average earnings as would have been the case during active membership of the occupational scheme.

Deferred annuities may also be used to buy out the rights of members in the event that the scheme is wound up. Notice of wind-up would be given to members who would have an opportunity within a given time-frame (up to three months statutory minimum) to transfer to an alternative vehicle such as a personal pension plan of their choice. The important feature of the deferred annuity is that transfer may be prompted by the member, but does not require member consent.

The new flexibility afforded to annuities brings with it the option for a nominee to transfer to another annuity or to the original scheme. If funds representing rights in an annuity are transferred to another annuity, the second annuity is assumed to be the original annuity, so must be established on the same terms. This option was always available to member and dependant annuities.

6.2 What transfers are allowed?

The short answer is that consistent with the pension tax legislation generally, any type of transfer is allowed, but there may be unfortunate tax consequences in the case of some transfers. Allowable transfers between registered schemes are authorised payments and "recognised transfers".

As a general rule, an individual may transfer accrued rights between any registered pension schemes or between a registered pension scheme and a qualifying recognised overseas pension scheme without the payment from the ceding scheme to the accepting scheme being regarded as an unauthorised payment (described elsewhere). Even in the case of authorised payments there may be disadvantageous tax consequences if the rights (or a proportion of them) accrued before 6 April 2006 and are protecting a pension commencement lump sum that exceeds the normal maximum. The position may be summarised in a simple table:

Transaction	Consequences
Registered scheme to registered scheme	No disadvantageous tax consequences unless there is transitional protection. This requires planning.
Registered scheme to QROPS	There is a BCE 8 and measurement against the lifetime allowance. Otherwise no problem.
Registered scheme to scheme that is not registered or QROPS	Very serious: the whole transfer is taxed as an unauthorised payment. The scheme could be subject to a de-registration tax charge.

Transaction	Consequences
Non-registered scheme or other overseas scheme to registered scheme	The transfer is not a recognised transfer and is not a contribution, so no tax relief is available. The transfer is not included in the definition of input for annual allowance purposes. It may be invested in tax-advantaged funds. Transfer is not a BCE, but the fund will be included in the eventual BCE for the arrangement and measured against the standard lifetime allowance (i.e. no enhancement).

Law: FA 2004, s. 188(5)

This table only examines the tax consequences. There may be other deleterious consequences of transferring, especially from defined benefit schemes.

The PSA 2015 has stopped transfers from unfunded public sector schemes. The concern is that the flexibility rules could put a strain on public finances as members (particularly low paid) transferred accrued rights to money purchase schemes in order to access funds.

Transfers are allowed from funded public sector defined benefit schemes and private sector defined benefit schemes subject to appropriate regulated advice.

6.3 Transfer of contracted-out rights and safeguards

The facility to contract out of the additional (earnings-related) state pension on a money purchase basis was withdrawn for new and existing accrual on 6 April 2012. This had consequences for individuals who wished to transfer contracted-out defined benefit rights to a money purchase scheme or personal pension scheme that was not a "buy-out" policy.

From 6 April 2012, pension rights that are transferred from a contracted-out defined benefit scheme to a money purchase scheme will be treated in the same way as other money purchase rights under the receiving arrangement, but to protect the member the following conditions must be met:

- he or she must consent in writing to the transfer;
- the transfer payment must be at least equal to the cash equivalent transfer value;

- the member must confirm in writing to the transferring scheme that:
    - he or she has received a statement from the receiving scheme showing the benefits to be provided by the transfer payment,
    - he or she accepts that those benefits may be different in amount and form from those provided by the transferring scheme, and
    - the receiving scheme is not required to pay a survivor's pension from the transferred amount.

In the 2013 Budget Statement, the Chancellor of the Exchequer announced that contracting out on a defined benefit basis would be withdrawn when the single-tier pension was introduced in 2016-17. The abolition of contracting-out on a salary-related basis appears in *Pensions Act* 2014, s. 24 (but was effective from 6 April 2016). Guaranteed minimum pensions were not abolished with contracting-out.

Law: FA 2004, s. 164(c), 169

6.4 Calculation of the transfer value

The basis of calculating a transfer value is relatively straightforward. DWP "preservation" legislation requires that if the member has completed two years' scheme service, the accrued benefit cannot be reduced and that the basis of calculating benefits for "early leavers" should be consistent with the calculation of benefits for "stayers".

For practical purposes, the preserved benefit under money purchase arrangements is the value of the fund less any charges. The transfer value under a defined benefit scheme is more complicated to determine. This section will concentrate on defined benefit schemes.

If the member has completed less than two years' service, then he or she is entitled to a refund of personal contributions (and no preserved pension). If he or she has completed three months' service, a transfer value representing all contributions is also available. The government removed this option to take a refund after completing 30 days of qualifying membership in any scheme that does not provide salary-related benefits under PA 2014, s. 36 and PSA 2015 (see also **2.3.10**). This measure is effective from 1 October 2015.

The transfer value must represent the "cash equivalent" of the preserved pension after two years' service and as a matter of practice will be calculated on the same basis for shorter periods of service.

The process takes the preserved pension at date of leaving and increases it with an assumed rate of price increases, or 2.5% if more appropriate, and then converts the re-valued pension to a required fund at normal pension age assuming an appropriate rate on gilts. The "fund" is then discounted using a suitable investment discount rate to the present day.

There is, since October 2008, a statutory underpinning of the transfer value calculation:

- Transfer values are determined by reference to a scheme specific basis and by reference to the expected cost of providing a pension. They should take into account the member's accrued benefits, available options and discretionary benefits.
- Trustees will be responsible for determining the assumptions used (as they are in relation to scheme funding). They will have to strike a balance between the interests of members and those who wish to transfer and there is no regulatory guidance on this. Trustees are under an obligation to consult an actuary about assumptions and other aspects.
- Trustees will be required to determine assumptions on a "best estimate" basis.
- Trustees will be required to use a discount rate which reflects a "best estimate" of future returns having regard to the asset mix of the scheme.
- Transfer values may be reduced if the scheme is underfunded. Indeed, the trustees may feel that they have little alternative to reduce transfer values in pursuing their obligation to all members.

- Reasonable administrative costs may be deducted from the transfer value.

If the scheme is a money purchase scheme, the transfer value simply represents the value of the member's account, policy or "pot". In a few cases (small self-administered schemes) the scheme rules will determine how to identify a member's share of a single fund.

Transfer values in respect of defined benefit schemes vary with market conditions and especially the yield on gilts. As a general rule, as interest rates fall and the gilt yield also falls, the transfer value will increase. This is because gilts will form an important part of the portfolio and the lower the return the higher the capital required to meet the defined benefit which must be reflected (not replicated) by the transfer value.

6.5 Member has enhanced or primary protection

If the member has enhanced protection from the lifetime allowance, the transfer may be an authorised payment, but enhanced protection will be lost unless the transfer is a permitted transfer. A permitted transfer requires the transfer value to be the same value before and after transfer. Only certain transfers are permitted:

- transfers to a money purchase scheme that is not a cash balance scheme, but is a recognised scheme;
- if the transfer is from a defined benefit or cash balance arrangement to another recognised cash balance or defined benefit arrangement relating to the same employment as part of a winding-up process;
- where the arrangement is a cash balance arrangement or a defined benefits arrangement relating to a present or former employment, rights are transferred in connection with a relevant business transfer so as to become held for the purposes of, or to represent rights under, a cash balance arrangement or defined benefits arrangement made under a registered pension scheme or recognised overseas pension scheme; or
- where the transferring arrangement is a cash balance arrangement or a defined benefits arrangement, rights are transferred as part of a retirement-benefit activities

compliance exercise so as to become held for the purposes of, or to represent rights under, a cash balance arrangement or defined benefits arrangement relating to the same employment and made under a registered pension scheme or recognised overseas pension scheme.

A "relevant business transfer" means a transfer of an undertaking or a business from one person to another:

- which involves the transfer of at least 20 employees; and
- in the case of which, if the transferor and the transferee are bodies corporate, they would not be treated as members of the same group.

If the member has primary protection, a transfer will have no impact on the claim for primary protection.

Law: FA 2004, Sch. 36, para. 12(2)

6.6 Lump sum protection

6.6.1 Transitional protection in 2006

There are circumstances when an individual is entitled to a pension commencement lump that exceeds the normal maximum because protection is given to rights accrued prior to 6 April 2006. In some circumstances, the protection will be lost if rights are transferred.

6.6.2 Enhanced protection

If the member has enhanced protection (member-specific) and the total pension commencement lump sum from all schemes exceeded £375,000 at 5 April 2006, the lump sum will be protected. The protected value will be the greater of the proportion of benefits that was represented by the lump sum at 5 April 2006 (so, if it was 35% of benefits in 2006, it may be 35% of total benefits in 2016) and 25% of the standard lifetime allowance.

The lump sum will remain protected if the transfer is a permitted transfer.

6.6.3 Primary protection

If the member has primary protection (member-specific) and the lump sum exceeded £375,000 at 5 April 2006, the protected lump sum is the total lump sum at that date increased to the same extent as the standard lifetime allowance (but not reduced with it). In 2013, the lump sum will be 20% higher than it was on 6 April 2006 because the standard lifetime allowance increased from £1.5 million to £1.8 million between 2006-07 and 2010-11.

A transfer of benefits in this case will have no impact on the lump sum.

Law: FA 2004, Sch. 36, para. 12(2A), 17A

6.6.4 Scheme specific lump sum protection

This protection is available when lump sum protection under either of the above headings is unavailable because the member does not have enhanced or primary protection or because the aggregate lump sum at 5 April 2006 was no more than £375,000.

Protection is only available if benefits from the scheme start at the same time (i.e. are not phased or staggered).

As a general rule, scheme specific protection is lost on transfer from one scheme to another except in certain specific circumstances. The main set of circumstances is when the transfer is part of a "block transfer". A block transfer is a transfer of rights in respect of two or more members from the same scheme to the same scheme as part of the same transaction. Partial transfers do not meet the requirement although the amount not transferred will retain its protection.

The individual must not have been a member of the receiving scheme for more than 12 months if protection is to be retained and there must not already have been a transfer to the same scheme.

In unusual circumstances, a transfer will be regarded as a block transfer even though only one individual is involved. In this context it may be worth noting that retirement annuity contracts and section 32 policies may only ever be single member schemes.

The transfer of all the benefit rights in respect of a member after 5 April 2006 to a deferred annuity contract will be treated as if it were a block transfer where:

- the winding up scheme condition (see **6.6.5**); and
- the annuity condition (see **6.6.6**)

are met.

Where these conditions are met the deferred annuity contract is treated as having become a registered pension scheme on:

- the date the contract was made (for a purchased annuity policy); or
- the date the policy was assigned (for an assigned policy).

The transfer is treated as if it were a block transfer and so, subject to the payment conditions being met, the member will continue to be able to have a lump sum of more than 25 per cent.

Transfers to a registered pension scheme that is not a deferred annuity contract made on the winding up of a pension scheme may be a block transfer under the normal block transfer provisions.

Law: FA 2004, Sch. 36, para. 31

6.6.5 The winding-up scheme condition

The winding up scheme condition refers to a transfer that is made from a registered pension scheme that is winding up.

Before the start of the scheme wind-up the member had the right to a lump sum of more than 25 per cent.

Where the scheme started to wind up before 6 April 2006 and the scheme was either:

- a retirement benefits scheme, or
- an annuity contract which is used to secure benefits provided by a retirement benefits scheme but which does not provide for the immediate payment of benefits (a section 32 policy)

this condition will be met if the member would have had a right to a lump sum of more than 25 per cent if the scheme had started to wind up on or after 6 April 2006.

A deferred annuity contract (section 32 policy) set up before 6 April 2006 would automatically become a registered pension scheme on 6 April 2006 and so will be covered by these provisions. For the avoidance of doubt any retirement benefits scheme or deferred annuity contract that has only one member is covered by these provisions. How and when a scheme (including single member schemes) winds up is a question of fact.

A scheme may have several participating employers. Subject to certain requirements being met, a partial winding-up of the scheme will constitute a scheme winding-up for the purposes of these provisions.

6.6.6 The annuity condition

This condition is met where the member's rights under the scheme have been extinguished by either:

- the purchase of one annuity policy that does not provide for the immediate payment of benefits (i.e. a deferred annuity, also known as a "buy-out" policy) and does not authorise the making of any payment that would be an unauthorised payment; or
- the assignment to the member of one annuity policy.

6.7 Protected pension ages

There is a parallel set of rules designed to protect abnormally low pension ages. The conditions for qualifying for a low pension age are described in **Chapter 4**. Again, the payment from the low age will only be authorised if all benefits from the scheme are taken simultaneously.

The further condition that must be added to accommodate a transfer is that the transfer is part of a block transfer. The block transfer must again be a transfer of two or more members of the same scheme to the same scheme as part of the same transaction.

6.8 Classification of registered pension schemes

Registered pension schemes may include:

- personal pension plans that will have been registered by the administrator of the personal pension scheme;
- personal pension schemes that started before 6 April 2006 and were automatically registered on that date;
- retirement annuity contracts that were automatically registered on 6 April 2006;

- occupational pension schemes that will have been registered by the administrator of the occupational pension scheme;
- occupational pension schemes that started before 6 April 2006 and were exempt approved before that date;
- section 32 policies (deferred annuity policies) that do not have to be individually registered and are automatically registered when they are established;
- freestanding additional voluntary contribution schemes set up before 6 April 2006 that will have been automatically registered on 6 April 2006.

Law: FA 2004, Sch. 36, Pt. 3

6.9 Transfers to QROPS

6.9.1 Recognised transfer: BCE 8

A transfer to an overseas scheme will only be a recognised transfer (and therefore an authorised payment) if the receiving scheme is a qualifying recognised overseas pension scheme (QROPS).

The rules on what could meet the requirements of a QROPS were fairly relaxed on 6 April 2006. Since then, HMRC and the government have embarked on a process of tightening those requirements.

The easiest way to avoid difficulties with HMRC is to follow the letter of the legislation, but that may be to stifle creative planning. Indeed, the *Registered Pension Schemes Manual* included a statement published by HMRC on 6 December 2011 that was designed to outline the purpose of QROPS. The requirements described here are those relating to QROPS from 6 April 2012.

A transfer to a QROPS is unusual in that it is treated as a BCE 8. This is because the money is leaving the UK system so the BCE is akin to a settlement of account. However, the money is being retained by a scheme, albeit an overseas scheme, and the lifetime allowance tax charge, if applicable, will be at a rate of 25 per cent.

Law: FA 2004, s. 216

Guidance: PTM 102000

6.9.2 The four main conditions of a QROPS

These are considered in depth at **9.4.1** below.

Law: FA 2004, s. 150, 169

6.9.3 ROPS to QROPS

In order for a ROPS to be a QROPS, certain steps must be taken and further conditions met.

The scheme manager is the person (or the persons) administering or responsible for the management of the ROPS. The scheme manager of the ROPS must:

- notify HMRC that the scheme is a ROPS, and state in which country or territory the scheme is established;
- provide such evidence as HMRC may require to show that the scheme is indeed a ROPS (which may include supplying a copy of the scheme rules); and
- undertake to:
    - inform HMRC if the scheme ever ceases to be a ROPS, and
    - comply with any prescribed information requirements that fall on the scheme manager, including:
        - answering information notices, and
        - providing HMRC with certain information on payments made in respect of certain scheme members.

The initial requirements are set out in the APSS251 form, which collects information and undertakings as well as providing information on when supporting details need to be supplied. If further evidence or information is required on receipt of the APSS251, HMRC will write to the scheme manager.

Law: FA 2004, s. 169

6.9.4 The effect of QROPS status and loss of status

QROPS status does not confer an overseas pension scheme with the same combination of UK tax exemptions that a registered pension scheme enjoys. In particular, it does not affect the pension scheme's liability to UK tax on any income it has from UK property.

If a QROPS invests in an unauthorised unit trust any gains accruing to that unit trust remain chargeable if the overseas scheme is exempt from capital gains tax or corporation tax on such gains only by reason of its residence.

QROPS status does not directly affect every aspect of the pension scheme and is principally of relevance to the transfer of UK tax-relieved pension savings and to the treatment of payments from such schemes. For example, there is no change to the UK tax treatment of any pension income from a QROPS – this is treated in the same way as a pension from any other pension scheme outside of the UK.

If a scheme that is a QROPS stops being a QROPS, whether voluntarily or otherwise, it can no longer receive a recognised transfer under FA 2004, s. 169.

Existing members of such a pension scheme at the time of loss of status, are not prevented by the tax rules from continuing as members of the ongoing scheme. They may receive benefits that were due under the QROPS from the sums that had transferred in from the originating RPS when the scheme was a QROPS, in the same way as they would if QROPS status had continued. The loss of status will not of itself incur member payment charges.

6.9.5 Overseas pension scheme

To be an overseas pension scheme, the scheme must be established outside the UK (and not a registered pension scheme). It may be a scheme established by an international organisation. An international organisation is defined by legislation and includes, for example the UN and the EU. We will consider it no further here.

Of more relevance, it may be a personal pension scheme or an occupational pension scheme that meets two main conditions: the "regulation requirements test" and the "tax recognition test". These tests are considered in depth at **9.4.2** below.

Law: FA 2004, s. 150(1), (7); *The Pension Schemes (Categories of Country and Requirements for Overseas Pension Schemes and Recognised Overseas Pension Schemes) Regulations* 2006 (SI 2006/206) as amended by *The Registered Pension Schemes and Overseas Pension Schemes (Miscellaneous Amendments) Regulations* 2012 (SI 2012/884)

Guidance: RPSM 13104060

6.9.6 Recognised overseas scheme

A recognised overseas pension scheme is an overseas pension scheme that meets the benefits tax relief test and one or more other requirements. These tests are considered in depth at **9.4.3** below.

6.9.7 Qualifying recognised overseas pension scheme

(See also Chapter 9.)

In order to be a *recognised transfer*, and therefore an authorised payment, the scheme must also be *qualifying* to accept a transfer value from a UK registered pension scheme. To be qualifying, the receiving scheme must undertake to provide specified information to HMRC (and any further information HMRC may request).

A list of QROPS is maintained and published by HMRC. However, the member and scheme administrator have a general obligation to check if a scheme is recognised as being a QROPS by HMRC. The list only reflects that the administrator has declared that the scheme meets the requirements of a QROPS and HMRC may subsequently override this. Alternatively, some schemes may request that they do not appear on the list and HMRC must respect the confidentiality of the scheme. If the transferring administrator has acted diligently and in good faith, but turns out not to have met the requirements, HMRC may waive the scheme sanction charge.

It may be that HMRC will withdraw QROPS status because of failure to provide information. In those circumstances, any future transfers to the scheme from registered pension schemes will be unauthorised payments, but the scheme may continue as an overseas or recognised overseas pension scheme and benefits accrued may be paid in the normal way. There are no unauthorised payment charges for losing "qualifying" status.

The 2013 *Finance Act* and supporting regulations included more measures. Section 53 of the Act enables HMRC to make regulations requiring accurate information to be provided to HMRC in certain circumstances, which are widely drawn. It includes sanctions for non-compliance (essentially loss of QROPS status) if non-compliance is significant (i.e. described in the legislation) and prejudices the collection of tax. QROPS status may also be withdrawn if there is no scheme manager.

Section 54 harmonises the reporting forms and inspection powers for QROPS with those for registered schemes. It includes a power to request documents that are 10 years old (before the notice). The provisions relate to new and existing QROPS and schemes that have ceased to be QROPS.

The consequent regulations provide much of the detail:

- Basic details of the QROPS must be re-notified to HMRC every five years, as must changes to information already provided. This measure is effective from 1 April 2015. Basic details include address and contact details of the scheme manager.
- Basic information must be provided to HMRC when the scheme makes a payment in respect of a member. This includes the scheme details and details of the relevant member including National Insurance number. This measure is part of an attempt to track transfer values that are transferred on to another scheme that is not as restricted as the QROPS.
- The scheme manager of a QROPS that receives a transfer from another overseas pension scheme must check whether or not the transferring member has a UK tax-relieved fund or a relevant transfer fund included in the transfer. This is in order to establish if the receiving QROPS may have to provide information to HMRC about payments that may yet be made out of the receiving QROPS. The scheme manager should ask the individual to declare whether or not the transferred funds include any amounts that have received UK tax relief or have originated in a UK registered pension scheme. If so, more detailed information will need to be obtained by the QROPS scheme

manager to establish if the individual will have a relevant transfer fund in his or her receiving scheme. The important point here is that a further onward transfer does not "shake off" HMRC interest.

Law: FA 2004, s. 150(1), (7); FA 2013, s. 53, 54; *The Pension Schemes (Categories of Country and Requirements for Overseas Pension Schemes and Recognised Overseas Pension Schemes) Regulations* 2006 (SI 2006/206) as amended by *The Registered Pension Schemes and Overseas Pension Schemes (Miscellaneous Amendments) Regulations* 2012 (SI 2012/884); *The Registered Pensions Schemes and Overseas Pension Schemes (Miscellaneous Amendments) Regulations* 2013 (SI 2013/2259)

Guidance: RPSM 13104070

6.10 Assignment of a policy

Some money purchase schemes are established as a trust which holds policies in the names of members. This will often allow the member the option of having the policy assigned to him or her. The assignment of a policy in this way is, in effect, a transfer of rights between registered pension schemes in respect of the same member. The policy is treated as registered in the same way as a deferred annuity policy.

Note that an assignment of the policy or its benefits to anything other than a registered pension scheme would be an unauthorised payment.

6.11 Pension Protection Fund

In the event of a scheme entering the Pension Protection Fund (PPF) (because the employer has become insolvent and the defined benefit scheme is underfunded), the assets and liabilities of the scheme are transferred to the PPF which pays compensation to the members. The transfer is an authorised payment, but the transfer to PPF is not subject to the tax rules that usually apply to transfers.

6.12 The nature of a transfer

The subject matter of a transfer is the accrued rights of a member rather than the assets. The transfer may be voluntary or it may be enforced by the winding-up of a scheme or following the award of a pension credit on dissolution of a marriage.

The value of rights being transferred is usually represented by cash, but there is nothing to prevent the transfer of an asset to represent the same value. If an asset is transferred between money purchase schemes, there will be no liability to stamp duty (in contrast to *in specie* contributions that require the scheme to purchase the asset).

The transfer is not regarded as a contribution by the tax legislation and is not measured against the input controls (annual allowance, annual limit).

6.13 Member rights

A member of an occupational scheme has four separate entitlements to transfer:

- if the member has a preserved benefit under an occupational pension scheme, he may transfer accrued rights without the permission of the scheme manager or trustees. The maximum period that could have elapsed before a member had a preserved pension under an occupational scheme was two years although under PA 2014, s. 36 this reduced to 30 days for money purchase schemes from 1 October 2015;
- if the member has completed three months' scheme service, he has a right to a transfer value;
- if the member has rights under a personal pension scheme, he has a right to transfer without the permission of the scheme manager or trustees (but the right does not extend to retirement annuity contracts);
- the same right extends to members of stakeholder pension schemes and the National Employment Savings Trust.

Broadly speaking, a statutory right that is preserved under pension legislation arises when a member has completed two years' pensionable service in a defined benefit (salary related) scheme. The scheme rules, determined by the employer, may specify a shorter period. The preserved rights must be calculated consistent with the rights of those who remain in service until normal pension age. The transfer value which in this case is known as a cash equivalent transfer value (i.e. equivalent to the value of a preserved pension), must be a fair representation of the preserved benefit expressed as a capital value. The valuation assumptions for the transfer value are determined by the trustees on advice from the scheme actuary, in accordance with regulations and consistent with those made when valuing the scheme. The objective of the regulations and actuarial practice is to prevent discrimination against early leavers.

There are circumstances when a transfer value may be reduced and indeed when the trustees or manager would be expected to reduce the transfer value. This is essentially where the scheme is underfunded and the transfer value is expected to be reduced to reflect the underfunding. If the value was not reduced, quite apart from the perceived unfairness of allowing a member (especially a senior employee) to leave with a full value not available to others should the scheme wind up, the transfer value would exacerbate the problem for those remaining in the scheme.

In the case of a money purchase scheme, the right to a preserved pension (and transfer value) arises after 30 days. The value will simply be the value of the individual's fund, or if there is a single fund for a number of members that is not "earmarked", such as a small self-administered scheme, it will be calculated in accordance with the scheme rules.

Law: *Pension Schemes Act* 1993, Pt. IV (as amended)

6.14 Three-month transfer values

A relatively recent option is the transfer value made available to members who have completed three months' scheme membership. Before the option was made available, the member would usually have lost all entitlement and claimed a refund of personal contributions less tax. The scheme may have offered a deferred pension based solely on member contributions (and therefore insignificant).

The option of a three-month transfer is not a cash equivalent transfer value because the member is not entitled to a preserved pension after only three months, but the value will be calculated on the same principles and assumptions as a cash equivalent transfer value.

Generally speaking, the transfer value represents better value than the refund of member contributions because the transfer value is calculated by reference to employer and member contributions.

Under PA 2014, s. 36 (effective from 1 October 2015), pension rights vest after just 30 days' qualifying membership in a money purchase scheme and, by implication, a transfer value becomes immediately available. PSA 2015, s. 39 (not yet implemented) extends this provision to the new collective arrangements envisaged by the legislation. The relevance of the "three month transfer value" is therefore now restricted to schemes that are not money purchase schemes.

Law: PA 2004, s. 264

6.15 Transfer deadlines

Section 95 of PSA 1993 withdraws the right to transfer from an occupational pension scheme (retirement benefits scheme) beyond the later of:

- one year before normal retirement date; and
- six months after the member leaves service.

The scheme may, within its rules, offer an option to transfer after these deadlines, but the member loses the right.

Schedule 4 of PSA 2015 extends the right to transfer to any age if the transferring arrangement is providing flexible benefits, benefits have not crystallised and accrual has stopped. The same schedule gives a statutory right to transfer individual categories of benefit within the same scheme where these is more than one category (e.g. AVC and employer-paid benefits or money purchase and defined benefits).

6.16 The right to a transfer value

Members of retirement benefit schemes who have completed three months' scheme service have a right to transfer accrued benefits to another registered pension scheme (but not a right to a preserved pension if service is less than two years) subject to the deadlines described. Members who have completed two years' scheme service have a right to a preserved pension and consequently a right to a transfer in the form of a "cash equivalent transfer value" of that preserved pension.

These are statutory rights and cannot be modified by scheme rules except in favour of the member.

Members of a stakeholder pension scheme have a right to transfer uncrystallised rights to a registered pension scheme. This is also a statutory right. Stakeholder schemes are also required to accept transfers.

Members of personal pension schemes do not have a statutory right to transfer uncrystallised rights although they do have a right to exercise an open market option when benefits are taken. A right to transfer may (and often will) be written into the scheme rules.

As a general rule, the trustees or managers of a scheme may not transfer rights without the consent of the member. The exceptions are:

- the scheme is wound up, although the member must be given a choice to exercise a voluntary transfer;
- the individual is awarded a pension credit on dissolution of marriage. The option for the trustees or manager is available for up to four months after the court order;
- the pension rights are transferred as a consequence of a corporate and benefit restructure.

A relatively new option has seen whole defined benefit schemes being taken over either by a pension trust or by a life assurance company. In effect, the trustees company buys out the liabilities of the scheme as a whole. This does not represent a transfer of benefits in relation to the individual members.

Law: PSA 1993, Pt. IV, Ch. IV

6.17 Transfers and dissolution of marriage

In the event of a marriage or registered civil partnership being dissolved, one of the options open to the court is a pension sharing order. In practice, the parties to the marriage or civil partnership agree how pensions should be dealt with and the court simply endorses the agreement by means of a "consent order."

One of the most popular options is the "pension sharing order" under which one party suffers an immediate reduction in benefits (a pension debit) and the other party is awarded a pension credit. The pension credit member is treated for nearly all intents and purposes in the same way as any other member for member protection purposes. The tax rules are described elsewhere.

The trustees or managers of an occupational scheme have the option of transferring the pension credit member to a section 32 policy without the consent of either the member or the pension credit member. However, the option expires three months after the credit is implemented.

The "unilateral" transfer requires care by the trustees or managers:

- the only vehicle that can receive the transfer value without the member's consent is the section 32 (deferred annuity) policy;
- there is undoubtedly a duty of care to ensure that the trustees do their best to secure the most appropriate policy.

The duty of care may be a step too far for many trustees and the option is rarely taken up.

However, a pension credit member has the same rights to transfer as a member and the same considerations will apply.

Law: *Welfare Reform and Pensions Act* 1999, Pt. IV

6.18 Crystallised benefits

Transfers are usually discussed in the context of benefits that have not yet crystallised. The tax rules allow transfers on a broadly "like for like" basis after benefits have started although there may be other reasons that make the option unattractive.

Law: FA 2004, s. 169(1B)-(1E); SI 2006/499 *(The Registered Pension Schemes (Transfer of Sums and Assets) Regulations* 2006)

Guidance: PTM 105000, 107000

6.19 Pensions in payment

6.19.1 Basic rules for transferring pensions in payment

The tax rules allow transfers between registered schemes or from a registered pension scheme to a qualifying registered overseas pension scheme of pensions in payment to be regarded as authorised payments subject to fairly tight restrictions. In practice this is an unusual transaction except in the case of drawdown pensions where there is more scope for investment flexibility.

Transfers of pensions in payment refer to member or dependant pensions. The most important condition of the transfer is that it must be on a "like for like basis". However there are other requirements that are specific to the type of pension being transferred. The logic behind the requirement is that the receiving arrangement is treated for tax purposes as simply a continuation of the transferring arrangement.

6.19.2 Scheme pensions

If the pension is a scheme pension (typically in respect of a defined benefit scheme, but occasionally from a money purchase scheme), the pension from the receiving scheme is treated as a continuation of the original pension (and there is no BCE triggered by the transfer). More significantly, in measuring whether there has been an increase that could trigger a BCE 3, the permitted margin (an increase broadly representing an assumed rate of inflation) is measured from the start of the initial pension. The initial pension is also the reference point for reductions in the pension (which could cause the lump sum to be treated as unauthorised) and for calculating the maximum pension protection lump sum. The balance of a pension guarantee period will also move to the receiving scheme.

There will be occasions, typically on winding up, where it is more appropriate that the liability for future payments of scheme pension should be adopted by an insurance company. In those cases, the insurance company annuity must conform to the scheme rules that applied to the original scheme pension. The same goes for dependants' pensions.

Law: FA 2004, s. 169 (1A)
Guidance: PTM 107000

6.19.3 Annuity

The transfer of a lifetime or short-term annuity for a member or dependant presents a logical challenge. The annuity is not part of a registered pension scheme: what distinguishes this type of annuity is that it effectively allows the scheme to "buy out" its liability when it is purchased.

Logic is restored by treating the receiving annuity as a continuation of the original annuity. There are no BCEs at that stage rather like the scheme pension without all the additional restrictions.

Law: FA 2004, Sch. 28, para. 3(2B), 6(1B), 17(3), 20(1B)
Guidance: PTM 105000

6.19.4 Drawdown

If an individual has designated funds for the purpose of drawdown, albeit withdrawals may not yet have started, a transfer of those funds to another arrangement may be an authorised payment. The same option applies to an individual who benefits from a dependants' drawdown fund.

The primary conditions for a successful transfer of drawdown funds are that:

- the whole of the drawdown funds in the scheme must be transferred; and
- they must be transferred to a new arrangement that holds no other funds. In other words it has been established for the purpose of the transfer. (Note that the requirement is that the *arrangement* holds no other funds, not that the *scheme* holds no other funds.)

The transfer must be on a "like for like" basis. A capped drawdown may only be transferred to a capped drawdown (although this may subsequently be changed to flexible drawdown) and a flexible drawdown may only transfer to a flexible drawdown (which cannot be converted to capped drawdown).

The recipient drawdown is regarded as an extension of the original drawdown. This means that:

- there need be no further minimum income requirement declaration in the case of flexible drawdown;
- the original "timetable" of reviews remains in place: pension years and review dates do not change;
- the receiving scheme must adopt the maximum drawdown figure calculated by reference to the original scheme before it is recalculated.

This last point has perhaps unforeseen consequences. It means that an individual cannot take the lump sum and then transfer the balance of rights to pension to another scheme unless it is able to offer drawdown and calculate a drawdown rate. If, for example, an individual is entitled to a defined benefit pension (only), then to convert to drawdown the full value of uncrystallised rights needs to be transferred and benefits crystallised in the receiving scheme.

These rules and conditions apply to member and dependant drawdown plans.

If a drawdown designation took place before 6 April 2006, then there would have been no BCE at that time and there will be no BCE if the drawdown fund subsequently purchases a lifetime annuity or the member reaches age 75. In order to identify these funds when the member has other funds designated for drawdown that crystallised after 5 April 2006, the pre-2006 funds must be ring-fenced if they are subsequently transferred.

Law: FA 2004, s. 169(1D), 1E; SI 2006/499 *(The Registered Pension Schemes (Transfer of Sums and Assets) Regulations* 2006)
Guidance: PTM 104000

6.19.5 Transfer to QROPS

A transfer of pension in payment (or designated drawdown fund) to a qualifying recognised overseas pension scheme may be a recognised transfer and therefore an authorised payment. The main requirement is that the transfer should be on a "like for like" basis.

However, what distinguishes this transfer from transfers between registered pension schemes is that this is a BCE 8, but the "overlap" relieving provisions will apply. This will have the effect that the amount crystallised (or an appropriate proportion) under the original BCE 1, 2 or 5B will be deducted from the amount crystallised under the BCE 8 occurring on transfer.

Law: FA 2004, s. 169(1B)-(1E), Sch. 32, para. 17; SI 2006/499 *(The Registered Pension Schemes (Transfer of Sums and Assets) Regulations* 2006)
Guidance: PTM 102000

6.19.6 Transfer from an overseas scheme

A transfer to a registered pension scheme from a recognised overseas pension scheme is neither a recognised transfer nor an unauthorised payment. Legislation tells us that it is not a contribution, so it does not qualify for tax relief on being received by a registered pension scheme.

Special treatment is therefore given to the lifetime allowance of a member who transfers funds from a recognised overseas pension scheme to a registered pension scheme.

No UK tax relief has been received, so the transferred amount does not reduce the available lifetime allowance. However, any part of an amount transferred that relates to UK tax relieved contributions made after 5 April 2006 will count against the member's lifetime allowance (this could arise where the member is a UK tax resident who is a member of a scheme provided by an overseas employer such as a French bank).

The member's lifetime allowance is increased, or "enhanced", by an appropriate factor (the lifetime allowance enhancement factor or LAEF), from the date of the transfer. The member must claim this enhancement no later than five years after 31 January following the tax year in which the transfer is made, and register the amount with HMRC.

For the member's annual allowance, the treatment of the transfer value depends on the type of scheme receiving the transfer. If the receiving scheme is either a defined benefit scheme or a cash balance scheme, the transfer value may be subtracted from the closing value. If the receiving scheme is any other type of money purchase scheme, the transfer is not included, as only contributions are included for the annual allowance.

Law: FA 2004, s. 188(5), 224-226
Guidance: PTM 095400

6.19.7 Transfer to retirement annuity contracts

Retirement annuity contracts may only receive transfers from other retirement annuity contracts.

Law: *The Personal Pension Schemes (Transfer Values) Regulations* (SI 1987/1112) as amended by *the Taxation of Pension Schemes (Consequential Amendments of Occupational & Personal Pension Schemes legislation) Order* 2006 (SI 2006/744)

6.19.8 Fragmentation of transfer values

As a general rule, transfer values may be "fragmented" and allocated to more than one receiving scheme. (See **Enhanced protection**). Similarly, the rules allow part of a transfer value to remain with the original scheme although in practice this is unusual. Furthermore, it will not be allowed in the case of crystallised rights.

Schedule 4 of PSA 2015 gives a statutory right to transfer individual categories of benefit within the same scheme where there is more than one category (e.g. AVC and employer-paid benefits, or money purchase and defined benefits).

Guidance: PTM 100010

6.20 Direct payment to insurance company

Where the receiving scheme is provided by an insurance company, any payment of transfer value not made to the scheme administrator or insurance company direct can incur a fine of £3,000 on the transferring scheme administrator.

This is to prevent registered schemes being used as a means of releasing funds by way of shared commission that would otherwise have been treated as authorised administration payments.

Law: FA 2004, s. 266
Guidance: PTM 100010

6.21 Cooling off

If a transfer is made to another registered pension scheme and the member is entitled to change their mind under a statutory cooling-off provision, the repayment of the transfer to the original registered pension scheme will not be regarded as an unauthorised payment.

However, under the FCA Conduct of Business rules, there is no requirement to include a "cooling-off" period in the sales and advice process (unlike other personal pension transactions). This is because whatever the tax rules may permit, the transferring scheme will often be unwilling to take back the transfer value (especially to a defined benefit scheme).

Guidance: PTM 100010

7. Pension scheme lump sums and authorised payments

7.1 Lump sums as authorised payments

As we have seen elsewhere in this book (and as summarised in **Chapter 1**), registered pension schemes enjoy a wide range of relatively generous tax reliefs. Tax relief costs the Treasury a great deal of money and the limits on its availability are therefore tightly circumscribed.

As a general rule, any payment (construed in the widest sense) made from a registered pension scheme must be regarded as an authorised payment if it is to avoid unauthorised payment charges that may fall on the member and/or the scheme administrator.

Payments that meet the requirements of the "lump sum rule" are authorised payments (although other authorised payments are available under other rules). The lump sum rule includes at FA 2004, s. 166:

- (a) a pension commencement lump sum;
- (b) a serious ill-health lump sum;
- (ba) an uncrystallised funds pension lump sum;
- (c) a short service refund lump sum;
- (d) a refund of excess contributions lump sum;
- (e) a trivial commutation lump sum;
- (f) a winding-up lump sum;
- (g) a lifetime allowance excess lump sum; or
- (h) a transitional 2013-14 lump sum.

The most obvious authorised payments are pensions and retirement lump sums that comply with legislative requirements, but they extend to death benefits, payments for investments and administration payments. In each case, the "licence" to make the payment comes with conditions. Being "authorised", however, does not mean that the payment will be tax-free: some payments are tax-free, but others are subject to income tax.

Some lump sum payments are measured against the member's lifetime allowance if they are paid before age 75. They are known as "relevant lump sums" and each payment of a relevant lump sum is a BCE 6. Relevant lump sums are:

- the pension commencement lump sum;
- the serious ill-health lump sum;
- the uncrystallised funds pension lump sum; and
- the lifetime allowance lump sum.

The trivial commutation lump sum and winding-up lump sum are not BCEs and not measured against the lifetime allowance, but they are only available if the lifetime allowance has not been exhausted.

The short service refund lump sum and the refund of excess contributions lump sum are payable whether or not the lifetime allowance has been exhausted and are not measured against the lifetime allowance.

If a payment is authorised, but is exceeded, the excess will be subject to unauthorised payment charges. Exceeding the authorised amount does not invalidate the whole payment.

This chapter will describe authorised lump sums that are payable to the member.

7.2 The pension commencement lump sum

7.2.1 The maximum

The pension commencement lump sum is described in **Chapter 4**. It must normally be related to a pension and is therefore available, generally, at any age from 55. Since 6 April 2011, it has been possible to take the pension commencement lump sum beyond age 74.

There are circumstances when an individual has pre-commencement rights (occupational scheme rights accrued prior to 6 April 2006) that enable all benefits from a scheme to be taken as a "stand alone" lump sum. In other words there is no related pension. These lump sums are unusual and are described in **Chapter 11**.

If the pension commencement lump sum is kept within prescribed allowances, it is a BCE 6 and is tax-free. It is measured against the lifetime allowance.

The prescribed allowance is subject to a permitted maximum. The permitted maximum is the lesser of the available portion and the applicable amount.

The available portion is simply described as 25 per cent of the lifetime allowance less any proportion of the lifetime allowance already used.

The applicable amount can be described as 25 per cent of the capital value of related benefits crystallised, comprising pension and pension commencement lump sum, but ignoring any disqualifying pension credit held and, where a money purchase arrangement is involved, ignoring any drawdown pension funds that have already been designated.

These factors may be modified in individual cases by the 2006 transitional provisions.

Law: FA 2004, s. 216 and Sch. 29, para. 1-3A
Guidance: PTM 063000

7.2.2 Allocating lump sum to another arrangement

If a member can identify two or more arrangements in the same scheme, he can, subject to scheme rules, choose to take the lump sum from one arrangement and pension from the other even though this would mean that the applicable amount in respect of one of the arrangements would be excessive. This is an important option for members of defined benefit schemes who have contributed to a money purchase additional voluntary contribution arrangement under the same scheme. It may be that the commutation terms under the defined benefit arrangement are not generous (the trustees will never wish to "make a loss") and taking the lump sum from the money purchase arrangement will provide a greater benefit.

If the member has primary protection from the lifetime allowance (**Chapter 11**), the lump sum may be taken from any scheme in any proportion: the protection is at member level rather than by scheme or arrangement.

Law: FA 2004, Sch. 36, para. 28

7.2.3 Lump sums from age 75

A condition of paying the pension commencement lump sum is that there remains adequate lifetime allowance to "absorb" the payment. This is so even if there can technically be no relevant BCE after age 75. However, if the lump sum is paid at any time from age 75, the whole uncrystallised fund will have been measured against the lifetime allowance under BCE 5 or 5B when the member reached age 75. For these circumstances only, it is assumed that there was no BCE 5 or 5B at age 75 and no lifetime allowance was used at that time. In other words, the BCE 5 or 5B will not of itself prevent there being available lifetime allowance for these purposes.

Law: FA 2004, Sch. 29, para. 1(3)(b)
Guidance: PTM 063220

7.2.4 Artificially high lump sums

The pension commencement lump sum payable in respect of a defined benefit scheme is calculated by reference to the relevant pension (which is a scheme pension). This leaves scope for abuse without anti-avoidance regulation. Simply put, the initial pension could be artificially and temporarily started at an unsustainable high level only to be reduced after the lump sum had been calculated and paid. The main control prevents a scheme pension from being reduced in payment except in prescribed circumstances, as follows.

1. If the member ceases to qualify for the ill health pension because of recovery from the medical condition. The process for judging whether the member is fit to return to work and take a reduced pension must be at least as rigorous as the process for determining ill health.
2. If pensions are reduced for all pensioners under the scheme.
3. If the pension is reduced to reflect entitlement to the state pension, providing that the reduction is no more than the amount of state pension and the bridging is restricted to

the period between 60 and the state pension age for the individual. The reduction may be between 125 per cent (where the member has been contracted out of the additional pension) and 250 per cent of the basic state pension. The formula is 125 + (125 × A/B) where A is the period of employment that is not contracted out and B is total years of employment. If the initial pension is a bridging pension (and is excepted from the general rule against reductions), the pension commencement lump sum must be calculated by reference to the reduced pension not the temporarily "uplifted" amount. The basic state pension, the additional earnings-related pension and the facility to contract-out were abolished on 6 April 2016. The *Finance Act* 2016 therefore amends the bridging legislation to refer to the single-tier pension for those who reach their state pension age after 5 April 2016 and the calculation is redrawn accordingly.

4. If the pension is reduced by a court order or forfeiture. Forfeiture powers must appear in the scheme rules and may be prompted by an attempt to assign benefits or to defraud the employer.
5. The pension may be reduced by a lien where the member has committed a criminal, negligent or fraudulent act or omission that has caused loss to the employer. This is not a reduction because the rate remains the same.
6. Where an individual is re-employed in the public sector and the public sector pension is abated.
7. Where there is a pension share on divorce.
8. Where the pension was in payment before 3 July 2007 to a member who was a member of the scheme on 5 April 2006 and the scheme rules allowed the reduction on that date.
9. Where the scheme is being wound up and the assets are insufficient to pay the pension at its full rate. The provision does not apply if it is part of an avoidance arrangement. An avoidance arrangement is described as an arrangement to increase the member's entitlement to a tax-free lump sum. The measure is effective from 6 April 2006.

The penalties for not observing the rule against reductions in scheme pension are quite severe. All future pension payments will be treated as unauthorised and, if the pension falls to below 80 per cent of its initial value, the pension commencement lump sum is treated (retrospectively) as an unauthorised payment. The latter is especially austere given that the lump sum will otherwise have been tax-free.

The payment of the pension commencement lump sum need only be reported to HMRC in certain circumstances where 2006 transitional provisions apply (although administration is always subject to HMRC audit).

Law: FA 2004, Sch. 28, para. 2-4A (amended by FA 2005, Sch. 10, para. 12); FA 2016, s. 20

Guidance: PTM 062340

7.2.5 Lump sums and defined benefits

The calculation of the lump sum is relatively straightforward where pension is being provided by way of an annuity or drawdown: it is 25 per cent of the fund that is designated for the provision of the pension. Under a defined benefit scheme, the principle is similar, but the calculation is more complicated. This is because in order to determine the 25 per cent figure, we are required to use the scheme commutation rate.

The formula is expressed in the legislation as:

$$(LS + AC/4)$$

where:

LS is the lump sum, and

AC is the amount crystallising for lifetime allowance purposes by reason of the member becoming entitled to the scheme pension.

HMRC example

Stephen has rights under a defined benefits arrangement. He draws benefits on his normal retirement date of 65 when he is entitled under the rules to a scheme pension of £10,000 per annum, and a lump sum of £40,000.

The scheme administrator calculates the amount that crystallises for lifetime allowance purposes before actually paying benefits out (so they can advise Stephen of this fact, and seek confirmation from him that he has available lifetime allowance to cover the amount that will crystallise at the two BCEs).

The amount that will crystallise for lifetime allowance purposes in respect of the scheme pension entitlement is £200,000 (the relevant valuation factor of 20 times £10,000).

So the applicable amount is £40,000 (the lump sum) plus £200,000 (the amount crystallising through BCE 2 in respect of the scheme pension), divided by four, which is £60,000.

The proposed lump sum in this case is £40,000 and therefore within the applicable amount.

Defined benefit schemes do not provide an income derived from designating a fund. The benefit is expressed as an income and the calculation requires us to derive the value for BCE purposes. Most scheme rules provide an option to take a lump sum by commutation of pension. However, some schemes (mostly in the public sector) express the lump sum as a separately accrued benefit.

Where the lump sum is derived from commuting pension, the calculation requires the application of a commutation rate, the amount of pension given up to provide the lump sum. The commutation rate is determined by the scheme trustees on advice from the scheme actuary. It will be influenced by prevailing interest rates. HMRC explain:

> "Where the commutation factor used by the scheme to calculate the level of pension given up in exchange for the lump sum payment is different from the relevant valuation factor used to calculate the crystallised value of the scheme pension, the resulting "AC + LS" figure is not easily identifiable in advance. This is because the lump sum (LS) being generated by the commutation will not be the same as the crystallised value of the scheme pension being given up – therefore the additional "LS" generated will be different to the notional reduction in "AC". So the total of "LS + AC" will vary depending on the actual level of scheme pension being commuted.

> As generally in this circumstance the scheme will simply allow for the payment of the maximum pension commencement lump sum permitted the applicable amount will not be immediately apparent, as in order to calculate that amount you need to know the actual lump sum that is going to be paid. Until you know what the lump sum payment is you cannot ascertain what the actual reduced scheme pension entitlement will be (and so cannot calculate "AC")."

The applicable amount in respect of a defined benefit scheme can be ascertained by using the following equation:

$$P \times CF/(1+(0.15 \times CF))$$

where:

P is the annual pension; and

CF is the commutation factor.

The formula assumes a "relevant valuation factor" of 20 (the factor applied to determining the capital value of the pension for the purposes of the BCE). The factor of 0.15 is derived from 75/100 × relevant valuation factor.

If the member is entitled to a scheme pension from a money purchase scheme, the applicable amount is determined by reference to the fund being applied to providing the pension and is three times that value.

Example

Jane is entitled to a pension of £30,000 before commutation. The commutation factor adopted by the scheme is 12:1.

The applicable amount is:

$$P \times CF/(1 + (0.15 \times CF)) =$$

$$30{,}000 \times 12/(1 + (0.15 \times 12)) =$$

$$360{,}000/(1 + 1.8) = £128{,}571$$

The reduced pension is 30,000-128,571/12 = £19,286.

Law: FA 2004, Sch. 29, para. 2, 3(6)-(8)
Guidance: PTM 063240

7.3 Serious ill-health lump sum

7.3.1 Conditions of payment

There are circumstances when the whole of the member's pension rights may be commuted.

The conditions for payment of the serious ill-health lump sum are that:

- a registered medical practitioner has certified that the member will not survive 12 months;
- it is payable within the lifetime allowance;
- the serious ill-health lump sum will extinguish all rights of the member under the scheme;
- the arrangement(s) to be commuted are uncrystallised. However, if the member has reached his or her 75th birthday, BCEs 5A and 5B (and any lifetime allowance used by virtue of those BCEs) are ignored for these purposes.

The serious ill-health lump sum is payable at any age. Payment of the lump sum is a BCE 6 below the age of 75. Within the lifetime allowance it will be free of tax in these circumstances. If it is paid when the member is 75 or over, it will be subject to the serious ill-health lump sum charge at marginal rates of income tax. Tax will generally be deducted by the administrator from the payment under the PAYE procedures (the member is liable).

The scheme administrator must report a serious ill-health lump sum to HMRC when the recipient of the payment:

- is a director of the sponsoring employer in the year of payment (or has been in the previous six years);
- is connected to such a director in the same period;
- alone or with others, represented the sponsoring employer in that time; or
- is connected to that employer.

The scheme administrator must also report where the member is relying on either an enhanced lifetime allowance entitlement, or an entitlement to enhanced protection, to reduce or eliminate a liability to a lifetime allowance charge on the payment of the serious ill-health lump sum.

The serious ill-health lump sum can be a valuable benefit for a member who finds himself or herself in the unfortunate position of having a poor prognosis and in need of cash, perhaps for medical treatment. Furthermore, the tax-free status of the lump sum is attractive. However, there are reasons to suggest that this should in many cases be the last option to be considered.

The terms of the commutation may not be attractive. However, the balance of the lump sum will form part of the member's estate and, if the member is over the age of 75, could in effect be subject to both the income tax charge and the 40% inheritance tax charge.

Law: FA 2004, Sch. 29, para. 4
Guidance: PTM 063400

7.3.2 Tax charges and reporting

If (when added to other crystallisations) the lump sum exceeds the lifetime allowance the excess will be taxed at 55 per cent.

The 55% charge is chargeable on the scheme administrator and may be deducted from benefits.

The payment of this lump sum is reportable to HMRC and, in the absence of a report, the administrator can be expected to be visited with penalties. There has been abuse in the past. The circumstances when a report is required are:

- the claimant controls the employer or is connected to a controller (at time of claim or in the previous six years);
- the claimant has represented or is connected to the employer; or
- the member is entitled to an enhanced lifetime allowance or enhanced protection (**Chapter 11**).

The serious ill-health lump sum will be taxed at marginal rates of income tax if the member has reached his or her 75th birthday. Otherwise it will usually be tax-free, even to the extent of contracted-out rights.

Guidance: PTM 16400

7.4 The uncrystallised funds pension lump sum

The uncrystallised funds pension lump sum (UFPLS) was introduced by the *Taxation of Pensions Act* as part of the government's policy of flexible money purchase benefits. It allows the member to take lump sums directly from a money purchase fund without the necessity of establishing a flexi-access drawdown plan. The facility has been available since 6 April 2015. Particular features of the option are:

- It is paid in respect of uncrystallised rights and only from a money purchase arrangement.
- It must not represent rights attributable to a disqualifying pension credit (a consequence of divorce where no pension commencement lump sum is available).
- The lump sum is only available from normal minimum pension age or earlier on grounds of permanent incapacity.
- The whole payment is treated as a BCE 6 and recorded against the lifetime allowance.
- The facility is unavailable if the member claims transitional protection of the lump sum. This means that the lump sum exceeds 25% of total benefits under the arrangement or the member has claimed primary or enhanced protection and the value of lump sum rights at 5 April 2006 exceeded £375,000, or the value of the available portion (proportion of the remaining lifetime allowance) is less than 25% of the sum.
- Payment of an uncrystallised funds pension lump sum triggers the application of the money purchase annual allowance.
- The lump sum must not exceed the available lifetime allowance. (In practice, more could be paid, but the excess would not be treated as an uncrystallised funds pension lump sum if the member was not yet aged 75, and would be taxed as a lifetime allowance lump sum at 55%. At 75 or over, the excess is generally taxed as income.)

Within the lifetime allowance, a proportion (25%) of the uncrystallised fund pension lump sum will be free of tax and the remaining 75% will be taxed as pension income.

It is early to assess the importance of this option. It is a less cumbersome way of taking irregular payments from a money purchase fund than flexi-access drawdown and certainly appears a more efficient way of phasing retirement benefits (by way of a series of programmed withdrawals, for instance).

The UFPLS is an alternative means of "drawing down" uncrystallised funds. As such, it is not drawdown. It refers to a facility available from 6 April 2015 that allows the member to encash uncrystallised funds for a lump sum. It is a BCE 6 (on the whole encashment), although it is taxed as if 25% were a tax-free lump sum and the balance of 75% were pension income (i.e. at marginal rates of income tax).

Where it is available, it provides a simpler and potentially cheaper means of taking withdrawals from a drawdown fund without crystallising more than is necessary, and without the complexity of phased retirement or phased drawdown.

So this may be a useful option for "no frills" products such as low-cost or stakeholder plans or, indeed, group money purchase schemes because it does not involve the administration and cost of establishing a drawdown arrangement.

For a 40% or 45% taxpayer who is sensitive to tax and has a substantial pension fund, flexi-access drawdown offers the most appropriate solution if it is structured properly. The decision will be influenced by the projected income profile for the years after partial or full retirement and how it might be affected by changes in circumstances on the way. If it is assumed that there would be other sources of income which would gradually reduce over time, the new rules encourage the member to phase the tax-free pension commencement lump sum.

Example

By way of example, the member might take a tax-free "income" for 10 years before age 75 and then withdraw pension income. The income will obviously be taxed at 20% or, by that time, 40%, but not for 10 years. If he or she dies before age 75, the balance of the fund will be paid tax-free, but on death after 74, it will be taxed at 40% or 45%. Some members will prefer to know that whether they live or die, the same fund will be taxed at 40% or 45% and the tax-free element will remain tax-free.

The problem with the uncrystallised funds pension lump sum is that the member is forced to take three parts of taxed pension fund with every one part of tax-free lump sum. So he or she will inevitably have some residual fund that would potentially be tax-free unless it was all taken into the estate (when it would be taxed at 40%). This means that for the individual who may start a partial or even full retirement on a high income that is expected to reduce, the option to take a series of pension commencement lump sums for an initial period is not available. To a 40% taxpayer, the tax-free element of £10,000 equates to a gross payment of £16,667, but only £12,500 for a basic rate taxpayer.

Finally, there is the issue of the lifetime allowance for those who are about to breach it or are close to doing so. If they wish to take a large withdrawal to put a brake on the size of the fund then far better to maximise the tax-free lump sum withdrawal at this stage than to have to take lump sum and pension.

Law: FA 2004, Sch. 29, para. 4A (inserted by ToPA 2014, s. 53-62)
Guidance: PTM 063300

7.5 Short service lump sum

If a member has not completed two years' scheme service, then DWP rules allow that, subject to scheme rules, there should be no preserved benefit. In practice, this facility only applies to defined benefit schemes.

The options open to the member under DWP rules are:

- to qualify for a preserved benefit in respect of personal contributions;
- to qualify for a preserved benefit in respect of all contributions (unlikely in practice);
- to transfer a sum to another registered pension scheme based on employer and member contributions. This option is only available under DWP rules if the member has completed three months' service;

- to lose all benefit and take a short service lump sum (refund of personal contributions).

None of these options is a BCE.

If the member takes a refund of personal contributions, the refund is subject to income tax (because those contributions will have received tax relief when the contributions were paid).

The conditions of short service lump sum are:

- the scheme is an occupational scheme (not a personal pension plan or work-based personal pension plan);
- service terminated before normal pension age;
- there have been no previous BCEs in respect of the scheme;
- the refund extinguishes all rights under the scheme;
- the payment is made before age 75.

The refund may include investment growth within the limit that applies to the short service lump sum. Any excess may be a scheme administration payment, but HMRC will wish to monitor abuse. The allowable refund is the value of personal contributions paid and interest at a commercial rate. Any excess over the value of contributions paid may be treated as a scheme administration payment and will be taxed as interest under ITTOIA 2005, s. 369 and be paid gross. If the payment exceeds the value of contributions plus interest, the excess will be unauthorised.

The short service lump sum is subject to income tax at the basic rate on the first £20,000 and at a rate of 50 per cent beyond that.

Under PA 2014, s. 36, where benefits provided by a scheme are exclusively money purchase benefits, there will be an entitlement to "short service benefit" immediately after the member has completed 30 days' qualifying membership of the scheme. The obvious effect of this section is that short service refunds, hitherto available within the first two years of service, will now only be available within the initial 30 days. Alternatively, the member has a statutory right to transfer after the 30 days have elapsed. The new measure only applies to individuals who become active members after the section comes into force. The measure will be implemented on 1 October

2015 and will only apply to qualifying service that starts on or after that date.

Law: FA 2004, Sch. 29, para. 5
Guidance: PTM 045000

7.6 Refund of excess contributions lump sum

One of the controls on input is the annual limit for relief. This allowance relates to personal contributions and is applied separately from the annual allowance that refers to aggregate contributions from all sources.

The annual limit is a restriction on contributions that can enjoy income tax relief. If it is exceeded, the member simply does not qualify for tax relief on the contribution (and HMRC will recover any relief given at source).

If the annual limit is exceeded, the provider is not entitled to refund contributions without the member's consent. Rather, the member has a choice of either leaving the contributions invested or, within six years of the end of the tax year in which the excess arose, withdrawing a lump sum representing the value of the excess contribution. HMRC initially took the view that the payment was an authorised payment made under the lump sum rule, but was not a refund of contributions. It merely *represented* the value of the excess. This meant that the payment would not reinstate annual allowance used by payment of the excess. Regulations that came into force on 28 January 2015 have revised the rule which has been described in the *Pensions Tax Manual* (at PTM 053200) as follows:

> "The following is not included in the pension input amount:
>
> - relievable pension contributions that are paid by, or on behalf of, the individual during the pension input period but are subsequently returned to the individual by way of a refund of excess contributions lump sum that is made in a pension input period ending in the tax year 2014-15 or a later tax year ... .
> - Note – for the exclusion from the pension input amount mentioned in the first bullet point above the refund of excess contributions lump sum could occur during the same pension input period in which the

> contributions were paid or in a later pension input period. A refund of excess contributions lump sum that is paid in a pension input period ending in the tax year 2013-14, or an earlier tax year, would not have the effect of reducing the pension input amount for the pension input period during which the contributions were paid."

If a contribution which is not excessive in this sense is refunded, the refund is an unauthorised payment. Similarly, if a contribution that exceeds the annual allowance is exceeded, that will also constitute an unauthorised payment.

The refund of excess contributions lump sum is tax-free and is not a BCE so does not trigger measurement against the lifetime allowance.

The refund may be accompanied by a reasonable rate of interest which may be specified as part of the refund amounts in the scheme rules or may be a "one-off". If it is the latter, the interest will be taxed as a scheme administration payment.

Law: FA 2004, s. 188(2), 190 and Sch. 29, para. 6; SI 2015/80 (the *Finance Act* 2004 *(Registered Pension Schemes and Annual Allowance Charge) (Amendment) Order* 2015)

Guidance: RPSM 09104800

7.7 Trivial commutation lump sum

The rules regarding this lump sum have been subject to a number of adjustments since it appeared first in FA 2004. This has been primarily because of what HMRC regarded as abuse. The consequence is that there are few, if any, opportunities for planning and the rules are disproportionately complicated. The original provisions have now been supplemented by rules regarding the administration of small lump sum payments ("small pots") described at **7.10** below. Indeed, the increase in the "small pots" limits (2014) and the uncrystallised funds pension lump sum have allowed the government to confine the trivial commutation rules to defined benefit schemes. Trivial commutation is no longer an option in respect of money purchase arrangements (although it remains in amended form to allow the balance of an annuity or pension guarantee to be commuted if the lump sum is less than £30,000).

The trivial commutation lump sum rules allow a member to commute small benefit rights from one or more schemes within a 12-month window which must fall after the member reaches age 60. Small lump sums are generally associated with lump sums that derive from administrative issues, such as the adjustment to a previous payment that is realistically too small to purchase further benefits.

For a trivial lump sum to be payable, there must be some remaining lifetime allowance. For this purpose, BCEs 5A and 5B (drawdown or uncrystallised funds at age 75) are disregarded. If there have been events since age 75 that would have been treated as BCEs before that age, then the value of those crystallisations must be offset against the lifetime allowance.

The maximum commutation amount from 27 March 2014 is £30,000 (having previously been £18,000).

The conditions for paying the trivial lump sum are:

- the member must have reached normal minimum pension age, currently 55, or must have retired earlier because of ill-health (i.e. meets the "ill-health condition");
- there must be remaining lifetime allowance, but payment is not a BCE. As HMRC point out this must be the case given that total benefits (not just those being commuted) must include crystallised rights and not exceed £30,000;
- the total trivial lump sum must not exceed the trivial commutation limit;
- the total of lump sums payable under this heading must be paid within a 12-month window which starts with payment of the first lump sum;
- there must have been no previous payments of triviality lump sums except within the 12-month period (other than payments before 6 April 2006 which are ignored);
- the payment(s) must extinguish all rights under the scheme(s) from which they are paid.

Both crystallised and uncrystallised benefits may be commuted on these grounds.

When the lump sum is paid, 75 per cent of the amount will be subject to tax as if it had been paid as pension. The remaining 25 per cent is tax-free and reflects the tax-free status of the pension commencement lump sum.

Law: FA 2004, Sch. 29, para. 7
Guidance: PTM 063500

7.8 Winding-up lump sum

The winding-up lump sum is a commutation of small pension rights that is payable subject to conditions when an occupational scheme is wound up. Although similar to a triviality lump sum, a significant difference is that there is no minimum age requirement.

The conditions of commutation are:

- no contributions are being paid by the sponsoring employer to any other scheme (and none will be paid in the next 12 months);
- there is remaining lifetime allowance. For these purposes, BCEs 5A and 5B (reaching age 75) are ignored, but any transactions that occur from age 75 and would otherwise be treated as BCEs are assumed to have been BCEs and trigger a measurement against the lifetime allowance;
- the payment will extinguish all rights under the scheme from which it is paid;
- the benefit to be commuted is trivial. The triviality limit is £18,000.

Payment of the winding-up lump sum is not a BCE. Like a triviality lump sum, 75 per cent of the lump sum is taxed as if it had been paid as pension and the balance of 25 per cent is payable tax-free.

Note that winding-up must be reported to HMRC. Also that if HMRC believes that the wind-up is being undertaken purely to facilitate payment of a winding-up lump sum, the scheme administrator will be fined up to £3,000 in respect of each member paid the lump sum. This is likely to affect very small schemes and the potential fine is intended to be significant in relation to the "benefit".

Law: FA 2004, Sch. 29, para. 10
Guidance: PTM 063600

7.9 Lifetime allowance excess lump sum

If the lifetime allowance is exceeded, the excess is subject to the lifetime allowance charge. The charge is 25 per cent if the excess is retained by the scheme or paid as an income benefit. If the excess is paid as a lump sum, that lump sum is a lifetime allowance lump sum and is subject to a lifetime allowance tax charge of 55 per cent for which the member and scheme administrator are jointly and severally liable.

The scheme is not required to offer the lump sum option and, particularly in the case of a defined benefit scheme, may not do so.

The three main conditions for payment of the lifetime allowance lump sum are:

- the lump sum is not a short service lump sum or refund of excess contributions lump sum. These are each taxed more favourably than the lifetime allowance lump sum and are not BCEs;
- the member has reached normal minimum pension age or has retired on grounds of ill health;
- the member has not reached the age of 75.

For technical reasons, the lifetime allowance excess lump sum triggers a BCE 6 (although it is only payable when it is subsequently calculated that the lifetime allowance had been exceeded).

Law: FA 2004, Sch. 29, para. 11
Guidance: PTM 084000

7.10 Other small lump sums ("small pots")

7.10.1 Conditions for payment

These rules cover situations where for one of a variety of reasons, generally administrative, the member is left with small amounts of pension rights that cannot usefully be applied to providing pension benefits. Typical would be "relevant accretions" to a scheme in respect of a member who has previously transferred rights to another registered pension scheme. The conditions for a small lump sum payment in this instance are described in the *Pensions Tax Manual* (at PTM 063700) as follows:

"The conditions are:

- there has been a recognised transfer out of a registered pension scheme (the originating scheme) in respect of a member (the transferred member), and
- the recognised transfer was to another registered pension scheme or to a **qualifying recognised overseas pension scheme**, and
- after that transfer, there was a "relevant accretion" in the scheme for the member (whether still living or dead), meaning:
    - a payment is made into the originating scheme in respect of the member for whom the transfer-out was made (this will typically apply to **money purchase benefit** rights), and/or
    - there is a further allocation of value to the "member's arrangement" above the value which the **administrator** had expected the sums and assets held for the purposes of that arrangement to be worth when the transfer-out was made – as might occur for example, with a corrective revaluation of sums and assets (again, this will typically apply to money purchase benefit rights), and/or
    - the scheme administrator becomes aware for the first time, of the member's entitlement to a further benefit, in circumstances where they could not reasonably have been expected to be aware of it at the time of the transfer out – for example following a court judgment relating to a **defined benefits arrangement**, or as might occur when implementing revised legal conclusions on the application of overriding sex equalisation legislation where the retrospective effect may lead to small additions to original benefit entitlements,

- and a payment is then made from the originating scheme to the transferred member (or in respect of the transferred member if that person has since died) (the payment out), and
- the payment extinguishes the transferred member's entitlement to benefits under the originating scheme, and
- the payment does not exceed £10,000 – and the payment does not exceed the value of the "relevant accretion", where the value is:
  - the amount of the payment in, or
  - the amount of the increase in the value of the of the sums and assets held for the purposes of the arrangement receiving the further allocation of value, or
  - the value of the further benefit to which the administrator becomes aware the member is entitled,

as appropriate, and

- the payment is made within 6 months after the relevant accretion occurred

However, a payment made in these circumstances will only be an authorised member payment if the "relevant accretion", was:

- not a contribution into the scheme ... , and
- not a recognised transfer-in, nor any other transfer into the pension scheme of any sums or assets held for the purposes of, or representing accrued rights under another pension scheme (including from a scheme that is not a registered pension scheme)."

Law: FA 2004, s. 169(1)(f); SI 2009/1171 (*The Registered Pension Schemes (Authorised Payments) Regulations* 2009)
Guidance: PTM 063700

7.10.2 Administrative error

A similar set of rules applies where as a result of an administrative error, a money purchase scheme holds small funds after the main accrual has been applied to the purchase of a lifetime annuity. The conditions for payment of the small lump sum are again reproduced from the *Pensions Tax Manual* (at PTM 063700):

> "The conditions are:
>
> - a pension has been purchased for the member by the scheme, with an insurance company in one of the ways bulleted at the top of this page, and
> - if that pension was purchased on or after 6 April 2006, then all or part of the member's lifetime allowance must have been available at the time of the purchase, and
> - after that pension was purchased, there was a 'relevant accretion' in the scheme for the member (whether still living or dead), meaning:
>   - a payment is made into the scheme in respect of the member for whom the pension was purchased (this will typically apply to money purchase benefit rights), and/or
>   - there is a further allocation of value to the "member's arrangement" above the value which the administrator had expected the sums and assets held for the purposes of that arrangement to be worth when the pension was purchased – as might occur for example, with a corrective revaluation of sums and assets (again, this will typically apply to money purchase benefit rights), and/or
>   - the scheme administrator becomes aware for the first time, of the member's entitlement to a further benefit, in circumstances where they could not reasonably have been expected to be aware of it at the time of the pension was purchased – for example following a court

judgment relating to a defined benefits arrangement, or as might occur when implementing revised legal conclusions on the application of overriding sex equalisation legislation where the retrospective effect may lead to small additions to original benefit entitlements,

- and a payment is then made from the scheme to the member (or in respect of the member if that person has since died) (the payment out), and
- the payment extinguishes the member's entitlement to benefits under the scheme, and
- the payment does not exceed £10,000 [author note: under reg. 10 a larger lump sum of £30,000 can be paid where, were it not for the fact that the lump sum would not extinguish all of the rights under the scheme because of an annuity in payment the lump sum could have been paid as a lump sum. Rights under the scheme will have been extinguished unless the annuity is purchased by the scheme as an asset rather than applied by the member to purchase of an income under the open market option] – and
- the payment does not exceed the value of the 'relevant accretion', where the value is:
  - o the amount of the payment in, or
  - o the amount of the increase in the value of the of the sums and assets held for the purposes of the arrangement receiving the further allocation of value, or
  - o the value of the further benefit to which the administrator becomes aware the member is entitled,

as appropriate."

The payment must be made within six months after the "relevant accretion" has occurred.

However, the payment made in these circumstances will be an authorised member payment only on the proviso that the "relevant accretion" was not a recognised transfer-in, nor any other transfer into the pension scheme of any sums or assets held for the purposes of, or representing accrued rights under another pension scheme (including from a scheme that is not a registered pension scheme).

Law: *The Registered Pension Schemes (Authorised Payments) Regulations* 2009 (SI 2009/1171)
Guidance: PTM 063700

7.10.3 Other payments

There are facilities to pay small lump sums from the Financial Services Compensation Scheme (FSCS) and in narrow circumstances where a small annuity or scheme pension was being paid to a member. In each case, the payment must not exceed £10,000, but must extinguish the member's rights under the scheme.

Small lump sums are not trivial commutation lump sums, but are taxed in the same way: 75 per cent of the fund is subject to income tax and 25 per cent is tax-free.

From 1 December 2009 it has been possible to pay small lump sums from occupational schemes without complying with the narrow constraints of the triviality rules. The conditions are:

- the payment is made to a member who has reached the age of 60;
- the member is at "arm's length" from any sponsoring employer of:
    - the scheme paying the small lump sum, and
    - any other scheme that is both an occupational pension scheme and a registered pension scheme, which relates to the same employment as the paying scheme;
- the "small lump sum" payment does not exceed £30,000;
- the member's benefit rights, under the scheme paying the small lump sum and any related scheme, have a combined commutation value that does not exceed £30,000;

- the payment extinguishes the member's entitlement to benefits under the paying scheme; and
- in the three years before the day the small lump sum is to be paid out, there have been no recognised transfers out relating to the member, from either:
    - the scheme paying the small lump sum, or
    - any "related scheme".

A member is at "arm's length" from a sponsoring employer if that individual is:

- not a 20 per cent "controlling director" of a sponsoring employer (in relation to either the paying scheme or any related scheme); or
- not "connected" with a person who is a controlling director of a sponsoring employer (in relation to either the paying scheme or any related scheme).

A measure to deal with personal pension schemes and stakeholder schemes appeared in regulations in 2012 and applies only to personal pension schemes (including manager stakeholder schemes). It allows a payment to a member that will not be an unauthorised payment if:

- the member is at least 60;
- the payment does not exceed £30,000;
- the payment extinguishes entitlement under the arrangement; and
- the member has not previously received more than two payments under this regulation.

The DWP has acknowledged that the number of "small pension pots" will increase significantly with the introduction of automatic enrolment. Under PA 2014, s. 33 and Sch. 17 (not yet implemented), the Secretary of State for Work and Pensions must introduce a system that provides for money purchase benefits to be transferred automatically from a previous employer's scheme to a new employer money purchase scheme of which the individual is an active member. The transfer value must be less than £10,000 and the member must be able to opt out of the system or in other circumstances be required to provide consent. There are disclosure requirements of the scheme. The signs are that the implementation of this measure will not be progressed.

Furthermore, s. 36 of the Act provides that the member will become entitled to a benefit after completing just 30 days' qualifying scheme service and short-service refunds of personal contributions after this period will become unauthorised payments.

Law: *The Registered Pension Schemes (Authorised Payments) Regulations* 2009 (SI 2009/1171)

Guidance: PTM 063700

7.11 Scheme administration payments

7.11.1 Member payments

Payments made in respect of a member for the purposes of the administration of the scheme may be scheme administration member payments and authorised payments. The payments may cover salaries and fees, but also the purchase price of investments of the scheme. It is the job of the scheme trustees or managers to deliver benefits, and investments are an important means of delivering those benefits.

The amount of the payments must be reasonable and determined at arm's length. If the reasonable amount is exceeded, the excess will be taxed as an unauthorised payment.

Scheme administration member payments are subject to income tax (the heading depends on the application of the payment).

Guidance: PTM 142000

7.11.2 Authorised employer payments

Some payments from a registered pension scheme are classed as authorised employer payments.

Authorised surplus payments

DWP rules allow a surplus to be refunded to a sponsoring employer in certain circumstances. Those circumstances will only arise in relation to defined benefit occupational schemes when the accrued fund exceeds the liability it is intended to meet. There are anti-avoidance provisions, particularly in relation to death benefits where the member was connected with the sponsoring employer.

There are specific circumstances in which a surplus payment can be made. *Pensions Act* 1995, s. 37 states:

> "The power .... may only be exercised if:
>
> a. the trustees have obtained a written valuation of the scheme's assets and liabilities prepared and signed by a prescribed person;
> b. there is a certificate in force:
>   i. stating that in the opinion of that person the prescribed requirements are met as at the date by reference to which the assets are valued and the liabilities are calculated, and
>   ii. specifying what in the opinion of that person is the maximum amount of payment that may be made to the employer;
> c. the payment does not exceed the maximum amount specified in the certificate;
> d. the trustees are satisfied that it is in the interests of the members that the power is exercised in the manner proposed;
> e. where the power is conferred by the scheme on the employer, the employer has asked for the power to be exercised, or consented to its being exercised, in the manner proposed;
> f. there is no freezing order in force in relation to the scheme under section 23 of the PA 2004; and
> g. notice of the proposal to exercise the power has been given, in accordance with prescribed requirements, to the members of the scheme."

This set of circumstances relates to an ongoing scheme that is not being wound up. Surpluses that arise on winding up are covered by s. 76 of the same Act:

> "1. This section applies to a trust scheme in any circumstances if:

a. it is a registered pension scheme under section 153 of the FA 2004,

b. the scheme is being wound up, and

c. in those circumstances power is conferred on the employer or the trustees to distribute assets to the employer on a winding up.

2. The power referred to in subsection (1)(c) cannot be exercised unless the requirements of subsections (3) and (in prescribed circumstances) (4), and any prescribed requirements, are satisfied.

3. The requirements of this subsection are that:

    a. the liabilities of the scheme have been fully discharged,

    b. where there is any power under the scheme, after the discharge of those liabilities, to distribute assets to any person other than the employer, the power has been exercised or a decision has been made not to exercise it, and

    c. notice has been given in accordance with prescribed requirements to the members of the scheme of the proposal to exercise the power…".

There are circumstances when surplus payments may be made to the employer although they do not fall within s. 37 or 76. If the scheme is not winding up, the payment must be allowed within the scheme rules and those rules must limit the amount of surplus that can be refunded.

If the surplus arises on the death of a member, any surplus payment to a sponsoring employer will be subject to additional conditions. The main condition is that the member must not be connected to the sponsoring employer.

For this purpose a member is "connected" to a sponsoring employer at the date of death where:

- if the sponsoring employer is a partnership, the member is "connected" with:

  - a partner in the partnership, or
  - a person who was a partner in the partnership at any time during the year preceding the member's death;

or

- if the sponsoring employer is a company:
  - the member is, at the date of death, a "controlling director" of the company,
  - the member was a "controlling director" of the company at any time in the year preceding the member's death,
  - the member is "connected" with a person who is a "controlling director" of the company at the date of the member's death, or who was a "controlling director" of the company at any time during the year preceding the member's death.

If there is no employer to which a surplus is payable, the surplus is *bona vacantia* (which is neither taxed as an authorised surplus payment nor as an unauthorised payment).

Tax is generally payable on surplus payments at a rate of 35 per cent. If the employer would not be liable to tax the payment may be exempt. The charge does not apply if:

- apart from the authorised surplus payments charge, the sponsoring employer receiving the payment would have been exempt, or entitled to claim exemption, from income tax or corporation tax in respect of the payment;
- the sponsoring employer receiving the payment is a charity; or
- the authorised surplus payment is being made in relation to a scheme that is winding up and that winding up started before 19 March 1986.

The person liable for the charge is the scheme administrator of the scheme making the payment and the charge will be deducted from the fund.

Note, however, that under FA 2014, the payment is not subject to the authorised surplus payment charge if the surplus derives from an unauthorised payment under FA 2004, s. 172A (surrender – see **7.12.2** below).

Law: PA 1995, s. 37; FA 2004, s. 207 (as amended by FA 2014, Sch. 5, para. 11)
Guidance: PTM 144000, 145000

7.11.3 Scheme administration payments

These are payments made by a registered pension scheme in respect of a member in order to facilitate the administration of the scheme. The term has a very wide meaning: it covers anything from payments of salaries and fees to investment in scheme assets. The overriding principle is that transactions should take place at a commercial value.

Guidance: PTM 143000, 144000

7.11.4 Shares in the sponsor

Payments made to acquire shares in a sponsoring employer are not scheme administration employer payments (and are therefore unauthorised) if either:

- the market value of the shares in the sponsoring employer held by the pension scheme is five per cent or more of the total value of the funds held by the pension scheme; or
- the total market value of the shares held by the pension scheme in any and all of the sponsoring employers under the pension scheme is 20 per cent or more of the total value of the funds held by the pension scheme.

Payments in either of these circumstances will be unauthorised employer payments and taxed accordingly. Note that this is one of the few instances when the tax rules for occupational schemes differ from those for personal pension plans. Personal pension plans do not have "sponsoring employers" although the employer may make a contribution. A sponsoring employer not only pays contributions, but establishes the terms of the scheme through the trust deed and rules.

Guidance: PTM 122000

7.11.5 Extent of investment tax reliefs

As a general rule, investments of a registered pension scheme are exempt from UK tax on income and capital gains. They cannot be exempt from overseas taxes and neither are they exempt from other taxes such as VAT and stamp duty.

This means that there is a large element of pension benefit that is tax-free on input (contributions), tax exempt on UK income and capital growth and tax-free on retirement and death benefit lump sums.

There are some investments that do not enjoy the exemptions associated with the fund.

Property investment LLPs

There is an exception to the normal rule (allowing exemption) in relation to income derived from investments or deposits held by a registered pension scheme as a member of a property investment LLP.

A property investment LLP is "a limited liability partnership whose business consists wholly or mainly in the making of investments in land, and the principal part of whose income is derived from investments in land".

Law: ITA 2007, s. 1004

On the other hand, s. 2(1)(a) of the *Limited Liability Partnerships Act* 2000 requires of the LLP that "two or more persons associated for carrying on a lawful business with a view to profit must have subscribed their names to an incorporation document".

There is a contradiction here between the requirement for trading (see below) and investment so caution is needed.

Where a registered pension scheme receives income, including stock lending fees, as a member of a property investment LLP, then that income will not be exempt from tax. Similarly, any gain arising to the scheme as a member of a property investment LLP will not be exempt from capital gains tax.

Trading

The pension fund may be chargeable if its activities constitute "trading". Income from a trading activity undertaken by a registered pension scheme is not investment income and so does not qualify for this tax exemption.

Guidance: PTM 121000

Stock lending fees, futures and options

Stock lending fees and income derived from futures and option contracts might normally be considered trading income.

However, subject to special rules, such income in relation to registered pension schemes can generally qualify for tax relief.

Law: ICTA 1988, s. 659A

Underwriting commissions

Underwriting commissions, to the extent that they are applied for the purposes of the scheme and would otherwise be chargeable are also exempt from income tax. Case law established that sub-underwriting could be regarded as trading and was subject to tax at the rate for discretionary trusts. However, in *BT Pension Scheme Trustees v Clark* [2000], the Court of Appeal, taking into account the size of the scheme involved, held that sub-underwriting was an integral part of the scheme's investment activities and income deriving from those activities was not trading income. The court refused to treat the case as a "test case", so future cases will continue to turn on the facts.

Life assurance company funds

Where a registered pension scheme invests in funds provided by a life assurance company, they enjoy the same exemptions as those applying to direct investment.

7.12 Specific unauthorised payments

We have seen that the legislation is tightly drawn to define where payments (as widely defined) will be authorised, for example to pay benefits within certain parameters, to pay for scheme administration, or to invest in scheme assets.

FA 2004 specifies certain specific unauthorised payments.

7.12.1 Assignment

The fundamental rule is that benefits to which the member has an actual or prospective right cannot be assigned without incurring unauthorised payment charges. There are exceptions:

- on the death of a member who is receiving a pension that is subject to a guarantee, the pension is assigned to a beneficiary;
- a court order can require pension rights to be shared or earmarked on the dissolution of a marriage or civil partnership;
- the pension may be, in effect, assigned if made subject to an attachment order if the member becomes bankrupt.

The rule extends beyond pensions to pension commencement lump sums, which is why a lender cannot take a charge on the pension commencement lump sum. The value of the benefit assigned for these purposes is the greater of the market value (which may be an actuarial calculation of income) and what was actually paid for it, although these circumstances are difficult to imagine.

7.12.2 Surrender

The surrender of benefits to which the member has an actual or prospective right will usually incur unauthorised payment charges. The surrender refers to the scheme or annuities purchased with scheme proceeds.

There are a number of exceptions (that is, where surrender is not unauthorised):

- pension sharing orders on dissolution of marriage;
- a surrender of benefits by a member to provide a pension for a dependant after the member's death;
- a provision in FA 2014, Sch. 7, para. 10 provides that a surrender of benefits in favour of a dependant will be treated as an unauthorised payment unless allocated to the same scheme as that under which the surrendered rights were held;

- a transfer to another arrangement of the member or dependant;
- where payments under one annuity are replaced by payments from another annuity;
- a surrender of rights to fund an authorised surplus payment. This exception is repealed by FA 2014, Sch. 7, para. 10, and where unauthorised payment charges apply, there is no liability to the authorised surplus payment charge;
- a surrender as part of a retirement-benefit activities compliance exercise; or
- a surrender of benefits to comply with equality legislation.

The provision does not apply to defined benefit or cash balance schemes unless the surrender reduces one member's (or dependant's) benefits and there is a corresponding increase in the benefits of another member (dependant) and the two members are or have been connected.

7.12.3 Increase in benefits on death

Should a member's benefits increase as a result of the death of another member who is connected with him, then the increase will be regarded by the legislation as an unauthorised payment. The legislation refers to the increase being "attributable" to the death of the member. The scope of the restriction extends to annuities purchased by the scheme administrator.

Until 5 April 2007, on the death of a member who was in receipt of an alternatively secured pension (similar to a drawdown pension over the age of 75), it was possible to reallocate funds. This option was withdrawn as was the alternatively secured pension.

The amount of the unauthorised payment is the increase in the "second" member's benefit less any authorised death benefits. There are circumstances when the increase will not be treated as an unauthorised payment under this heading:

- if the payment is regarded as an assignment (because that is already covered – see above);
- if at least 20 members receive the same rate of increase; or

- if the increase in the second member's rights comprises an increase in the member's rights under an existing dependants' scheme pension, dependants' annuity, or dependants' drawdown pension fund that the second member already had in respect of the deceased member.

7.12.4 Unallocated contributions

A scheme is treated as making an unauthorised payment where

- an employer pays contributions into the scheme;
- those contributions are not allocated to any individual;
- the contributions are subsequently allocated to a member's other money purchase arrangement or hybrid arrangement that includes the provision of other money purchase benefits in a tax year;
- the amount of the allocated contributions exceeds the "permitted maximum"; and
- in the tax year in question, the member and the employer are connected or the member is connected with a person who is connected with the employer.

In this context the "permitted maximum" is the annual limit for relief (the allowance for personal contributions) available to the member in the tax year in which the allocation of contributions takes place (regardless of the amount of contributions actually paid by or on behalf of the member in that year) less any contributions paid by the employer in respect of the member in that same tax year.

The "permitted maximum" is further reduced if the member is a member of one or more other registered pension schemes by dividing the figure found in the paragraph immediately above by the number of schemes of which the person is a member.

The amount of the deemed unauthorised payment is the amount by which the allocated contributions exceed the "permitted maximum".

7.12.5 Increases in benefits

When a pension input amount for a member who is connected with the sponsoring employer exceeds the notional unconnected person input amount, the excess may be an unauthorised payment for the relevant arrangement in the particular input period. This restriction applies only to defined benefit schemes and cash balance schemes (or hybrid schemes that include one of those elements).

The notional unconnected person input amount is what the input would have been had the member not been connected with the employer at any time in the input period. The input in respect of defined benefit and cash balance schemes is primarily derived from the increase in accrual that can be attributed to contributions.

7.13 Unauthorised payments – tax

7.13.1 The charges

If a registered pension scheme makes an unauthorised payment, it may generate three tax charges and, in extreme circumstances, scheme discontinuance which itself would trigger a discontinuance charge.

The tax charges are:

- the unauthorised payment charge (40 per cent of the payment);
- the unauthorised payment surcharge (if the payment exceeds a threshold, 15 per cent of the payment); and
- the scheme sanction charge (in addition to the other charges, this will be at a rate of 15 per cent. There are circumstances when it is payable by itself at a rate of 40 per cent).

Guidance: PTM 134000, 135000

7.13.2 Scope of "payment"

Unauthorised payments may be member payments or employer payments. Payments may be:

- transfers of cash;
- transfers of assets;
- transfer of money's worth; or
- "value shifting".

Any payment made (or benefit provided) from, or in connection with, an investment acquired with registered pension scheme funds is treated as a payment or benefit from that registered pension scheme. This is the case even if the pension scheme has wound up and/or if the investment was acquired after the scheme has wound up.

In this context an investment includes insurance and annuity contracts.

So a payment could include the following:

- giving a pension scheme asset, e.g. shares, to an individual or other person;
- selling a pension scheme asset for less than it is worth (this is a transfer of value or money's worth to the recipient); or
- the pension scheme buying an asset for more than its market value (this is a transfer of money's worth to the seller).

Once again, to avoid abuse, there are special restrictions for payments to members, former members and anyone connected with a member, including sponsoring employers and former sponsoring employers.

The definition is so wide that it covers anyone connected with the above.

Guidance: PTM 132000

7.13.3 Who is liable for how much?

Unauthorised payments charge

The person liable to the unauthorised payments charge is the member, or former member, who received the payment or in respect of whom the payment was made if the payment was made when the member, or former member, was alive. If the payment was made after the death of the member or former member, the person who receives the payment is liable.

The person liable to the unauthorised employer payments charge is the sponsoring employer, or former sponsoring employer, who received the payment or in respect of whom the payment was made.

If more than one person is liable then those persons are jointly and severally liable to the charge in respect of the payment. Joint and several liability means that all parties to the charge are equally liable to the whole charge, and that payment by one will discharge the liability of the other(s), to the extent of the amount paid.

Under FA 2014, s. 43 the scheme administrator may claim relief from the scheme sanction charge and the member may claim relief from the unauthorised payment charge to the extent that those charges are in respect of an unauthorised payment in respect of which the court has ordered money or assets to be restored to the scheme. On the other hand, no relief is available on the "contribution" (which would otherwise be able to claim relief twice).

The tax charge is at a rate of 40 per cent, based on the amount of the unauthorised payment.

The charge is a freestanding tax charge, which means, for example, that any losses a taxpayer may have cannot be set against the tax charge.

Guidance: PTM 134000

Unauthorised payment surcharge

An income tax charge called the unauthorised payments surcharge will apply if unauthorised payments made by a registered pension scheme go above a set threshold within a certain time period. Unauthorised payments to which the surcharge applies are known as surchargeable unauthorised payments.

The unauthorised payments surcharge is paid in addition to the unauthorised payments charge. The rate of the unauthorised payments surcharge is 15 per cent, based on the amount of the surchargeable unauthorised payment. So together with the unauthorised payments charge the total tax liability in respect of a surchargeable unauthorised payment is 55 per cent.

The surcharge is a freestanding tax charge, which means any losses a taxpayer may have cannot be set against the tax charge. It is payable by the person responsible for paying the unauthorised payments charge.

The surcharge applies when the amount of the payments over a 12-month period reaches 25 per cent of the value of the scheme relating to the member (both crystallised and uncrystallised). The period starts with a reference date.

A reference period starts with the reference date and ends on the earlier of:

- 12 months following the reference date; and
- the day on which the surcharge threshold is reached.

The reference date is the date of payment of the first unauthorised member payment made to or in respect of the member concerned.

Subsequent reference dates will occur on the payment of an unauthorised member payment in respect of the same member after the end of a reference period.

The second reference date for that same member will be the date of first payment of an unauthorised member payment to or in respect of that member from that registered pension scheme after the first reference period. The second reference period will run from the second reference date until the earlier of 12 months later or the reaching of the surcharge threshold.

The rules for surchargeable employer payments are similar except that in determining the threshold that will trigger the tax charge, reference is made to the value of the whole scheme sponsored by the employer.

There are very rare circumstances in which a successful application may be made for a discharge from the surcharge. The underlying reason is that it would not be just and reasonable for the surcharge to apply. HMRC do not list examples. A trustee or guardian may also make an application on behalf of an individual who is incapacitated. There is a right of appeal.

Guidance: PTM 134000

De-registration charge

In extreme circumstances, HMRC may de-register a scheme in which case, and in addition to the charges already described, there will be a de-registration charge. The de-registration charge is 40 per cent of the value of scheme cash and assets.

De-registration is rare for two reasons:

- the conditions that must exist for there to be a de-registration are unusual; and
- HMRC have a discretion as to whether to exercise their power to de-register a scheme.

The charge was introduced primarily to prevent administrators from "exporting" small schemes or simply breaking the trusts ("pension liberation"). A scheme may be de-registered in the following cases:

- The scheme has made scheme chargeable payments and the total of these in any 12 month period exceeds the "de-registration threshold" (25 per cent of the value of scheme cash and assets). During the 12-month period, if there is more than one payment, the values are expressed as a percentage of value at the time of the payment and the percentages are aggregated.
- The scheme administrator has failed to pay a substantial amount of tax, or interest on tax, that is owing.
- The scheme administrator has failed to provide information required by HMRC, and the failure is significant. (This means that either the amount of information the scheme administrator has failed to provide is substantial, or the failure to provide the information is likely to result in serious prejudice to the assessment or collection of tax).
- The application to register the pension scheme contained information that was materially incorrect.
- Any other information provided to HMRC was materially incorrect.
- A declaration accompanying the application to register the pension scheme was materially false.
- Any other declaration to HMRC in respect of other information given to HMRC was materially false.
- There is no scheme administrator.

In early 2013 there were reports that HMRC had established a special unit to deal with the promotion of schemes that purport to "liberate" pension funds from the constraints of pension legislation. The device used is usually a small self-administered scheme which is not regulated by the FCA. The concern of HMRC is that individuals do not appreciate the potential tax charges involved and the relatively high fees generally associated with the transaction. For scheme administrators, the difficulty is that they may refuse a transfer from a personal pension scheme (other than stakeholder scheme) if, for example, they have doubts about the receiving vehicle, but they have no right to refuse a request to transfer from an occupational scheme (save in very specific circumstances).

Similarly, the Pensions Regulator cannot override the right to transfer. In effect, this means that the trustees and administrator of the receiving scheme may be subject to enforcement action by the Pensions Regulator (and/or the Serious Fraud Office) and the trustees and administrator of the transferring scheme may be subject to enforcement action if they do not meet a request to transfer within a six-month deadline. The Regulator has attempted to solve this conundrum by explaining that it will be sympathetic to delays in transferring if the trustees of the transferring scheme can demonstrate their concerns about the destination of the transfer value and that they have made a serious attempt to determine whether the transaction is legitimate. "Sympathy" will be demonstrated by not taking action against the transferring scheme trustees in respect of the delay.

The Pensions Regulator and HMRC have worked together to prevent the promotion of liberation schemes and this has culminated in a number of measures in FA 2014. The two main new areas of legislation are:

- Registration of schemes is no longer automatic and registration may be refused or withdrawn if the administrator is regarded by HMRC as not being "fit and proper" for the responsibility or if HMRC judge that the purpose of the scheme is not to provide a pension benefit. There is an appeals process.
- There are a number of technical changes to primary legislation concerning surrender of benefits (see **7.12.2** above).

Scheme sanction charge

A scheme sanction charge falls on the scheme administrator if the scheme makes a scheme chargeable payment. As part of the anti-avoidance regime, liability may arise even though the individual is not UK resident. It may be due even if the scheme has been wound up (and will fall on the last administrator).

Scheme chargeable payments are:

- any unauthorised payment by the pension scheme other than a payment that is exempted;
- a payment that the pension scheme is treated as having made and that is classed as a scheme chargeable payment because of unauthorised borrowing;
- a payment that the scheme is treated as having made and that is classed as a scheme chargeable payment (income from taxable property or gains from taxable property).

There are circumstances when the charge may be waived if the administrator has acted in good faith or where there has been restitution on the order of the court of the Pensions Regulator.

The charge is 40 per cent of the total scheme chargeable payments made in the tax year reduced by the lesser of:

- the amount of the unauthorised payments charge that has been paid, and
- 25 per cent of the scheme chargeable payments that are "tax paid".

A scheme chargeable payment is "tax paid" if all or part of the unauthorised payments charge due has been paid. So, by way of example, if an unauthorised payment is made of £100, then this may be subject to an unauthorised payment charge of 40 per cent. If so, the scheme sanction charge would then be applied which would be (40% of £100) less (25% of £100) = £15 (15%).

In practice, the scheme sanction charge will usually be at a rate of 15 per cent, but there are some transactions that do not generate an unauthorised payment charge, such as the receipt of income or capital gains from taxable property and in those cases, the scheme sanction charge applies at a rate of 40 per cent.

Under FA 2014, the scheme administrator may claim relief from the scheme sanction charge to the extent that it is in respect of an unauthorised payment in respect of which the court has ordered money or assets to be restored to the scheme.

Guidance: PTM 135000

8. Investments

8.1 The purpose of investment

Pension funds generally enjoy exemptions from UK tax on income and capital gains.

There are essentially three guiding principles relating to those tax exemptions:

- the purpose of the investment in assets by the scheme trustees or manager is solely to deliver retirement and death benefits within the rules of the scheme;
- the investments should not be capable of allowing personal use or financial advantage to a member or anyone connected to a member other than by way of authorised retirement or death benefit payments; and
- any gain should be derived from the assets as investments, not from trading profits.

The history of tax rules relating to pension investments demonstrates more than any other aspect of pensions, the "cat and mouse" approach that has been adopted by HMRC and the legislators over the years in response to ever new forms of tax planning. By way of example, the proposals for change that found their way into FA 2004 were much more relaxed than their predecessors. In a sense, they could afford to be; gone were the unenforceable bans on certain investments and activities and in their place came tax charges on transactions that the legislators and HMRC wanted to discourage.

The position did not last long and came to an abrupt end with the introduction of "taxable property" into the legislative framework by way of FA 2005. Taxable property has a more sweeping scope than what went before and the tax "penalties" for investing in taxable property are more severe (leading at one stage to talk by some advisers of a challenge under the *Human Rights Act*).

8.2 Main areas for consideration

There are special considerations for:

- transactions with members (and those connected with them);
- loans to individuals and loans to sponsoring employers;
- scheme borrowing;
- "value shifting";
- benefits in kind; and
- taxable property.

The considerations may differ (unusually) according to whether the scheme is an occupational scheme or a personal pension scheme. Furthermore, there may be HMRC and DWP restrictions that may also vary depending on whether it is a "small" or "large" scheme.

A more recent consideration in respect of small schemes is the greater interest and therefore regulation of SIPP providers by HMRC as a consequence of SIPPs becoming regulated in 2007 and the failure of some providers which had or could have had a detrimental impact on members.

8.3 Investment-regulated schemes

Small schemes will often allow the member to choose how his or her pension fund should be invested rather than granting discretion to a fund manager. These types of scheme are known as "investment regulated schemes" and their investments as "member-directed investments". They attract closer scrutiny from HMRC. In the market place, they are known as "self-invested personal pension schemes" (SIPP) and "small self-administered schemes" (SSAS). The distinction is more than cosmetic: the establishment, administration and winding-up of SIPPs are now regulated by the Financial Conduct Authority (previously Financial Services Authority) whilst SSAS are not (although their investments may be).

Directly invested pension plans are almost always subject to the same tax reliefs and controls as any other type of scheme. This brings us to another principle: the choice of pension scheme type can hardly ever be determined by tax treatment. They are treated the same. What may differ is the degree of supervision and who the relevant regulator is. So, for example, SSAS are not regulated by the FCA (although their investments may be), and this has encouraged some small businesses to opt for this type of arrangement rather than SIPP.

The general approach to investment taken by the tax legislation, as in other areas, is to permit anything that is not fraudulent, but to tax some types of transaction more than others. The pension fund may therefore derive income and gains from investments which will be exempt from UK tax or it may derive profit from trading which will not be so exempt. The question of what constitutes trading is a complex one that is described by HMRC in the *Pensions Tax Manual* at PTM 121000 but mainly in the *Business Income Manual* at BIM 20205.

There is no ban on members (and those connected) transacting with their pension scheme, but the transaction must take place at "arm's length" and on commercial terms. This is to prevent a member, for example, extracting value from the scheme other than as an authorised payment by selling at an artificially high price or buying at an artificially low price. Care must be taken in the case of occupational schemes when the sponsoring employer is connected to a member (who may, for example, be a controlling director of a sponsoring company).

Law: FA 2004, Sch. 29A, para. 1-5
Guidance: PTM 121000

8.4 Benefits in kind

Since the introduction of taxable property into the legislation, these rules have had no application to taxable property held by investment-regulated schemes. This is because any personal use of assets by the member or anyone connected will be "caught" by the taxable property restrictions which take precedence.

Where a person who is, or has been, a scheme member, or a member of his or her family or household, enjoys the personal use of scheme assets, the cash equivalent of the benefit in kind will be charged on the member as an unauthorised payment. This also applies where a registered pension scheme has been wound up since the investment was acquired. Use of scheme assets in this way must be reported to HMRC by the scheme administrator.

The cash equivalent is derived from the annual rental value of land and, usually, 20 per cent of the value and the cost of improvements when the asset was originally made available to the beneficiary. Motor vehicles are taxed as if they were provided to the beneficiary by his or her employer.

In all these cases, however, the benefit in kind charge will not apply if the asset is charged as taxable property and this will usually be the case (especially in the case of motor vehicles which would be regarded as tangible moveable property).

Again, the rule only applies if the taxable property rules do not. It exists to prevent avoidance of the benefit in kind rules by providing the benefit through a pension trust.

In addition, the scheme administrator must give details of any benefits provided to the member before 7 July following the end of each tax year to enable the member to declare the unauthorised payments received on their individual self-assessment returns.

Members of a person's family, as determined by ITEPA 2003, s. 721, include that person's:

- spouse or civil partner;
- children and their spouses or civil partners;
- parents; and
- dependants.

And the following are members of a person's household:

- the person's domestic staff; and
- his or her guests.

Where, after the death of a person who is, or has been, a scheme member, an asset held by the registered pension scheme is used to provide a benefit to a person who, at the time of the person's death, was a member of the person's family or household, an unauthorised payments charge will be made on the person receiving the benefit.

However, where a person who is, or has been, a scheme member is provided with a benefit by reason of his or her employment, and has already been taxed on the benefit as an employee, the payment will not be treated as an unauthorised payment on the member as well. This avoids creating a double tax charge.

Where a benefit is provided by reason of an excluded employment an unauthorised payment charge will be made if:

- it is a benefit that would have been chargeable on the member if the employment was not an excluded employment;
- it is an occupational pension scheme that is holding the asset providing the benefit; and
- the member, or member of his family or household, is a director with a "material interest" in the sponsoring employer.

"Material interest" has the meaning given by ITEPA 2003, s. 68 but broadly means owning five per cent of the share capital or having an entitlement to five per cent of the assets.

Law: FA 2004, Sch. 29A, para. 1-5
Guidance: PTM 121000, 133900

8.5 Loans from pension schemes

8.5.1 Types of loan

There are three types of loan to consider in this context:

- loans to sponsoring employers or past sponsoring employers: these are restricted to small occupational schemes by DWP legislation;
- loans to members: these are unauthorised payments under tax legislation; and
- loans to arm's length third parties: these are allowable under both DWP and tax legislation.

The following are not classed as loans for these purposes and are not subject to the restrictions relating to employer loans if they are listed or dealt in on a recognised stock exchange or offered to the public:

- debentures;
- debenture stock;
- loan stock;
- bonds;

- certificates of deposit; and
- other instruments relating to the owing of monies.

If a scheme provides a guarantee for a loan, it is regarded as making the loan.

Loans expose a rare difference between the tax rules for personal pension schemes and occupational schemes. The rules relating to sponsoring employers cannot apply to personal pension schemes because they are never sponsored by an employer (although the employer may make a contribution). "Sponsorship" extends to establishing the rules of the scheme and establishing the scheme trust.

8.5.2 Basic requirements of loanback

Loans to the employer are generally not allowed by DWP legislation. Specifically exempted are such investments where the scheme is restricted to directors and the loan is against earmarked policies of those directors.

Small self-administered schemes are exempted from the restriction on investment subject to:

- all members being trustees; and
- where the rules of the scheme provide that before any investment of resources is made in an employer-related investment, each member must agree in writing to the making of that investment.

A small self-administered scheme is defined in these circumstances as having fewer than 12 members where all the members are trustees or one of the trustees is independent.

Loans to sponsoring employers are tightly regulated by HMRC under five main headings:

- security;
- interest rates;
- term of loan;
- maximum amount of loan; and
- repayment terms.

If the conditions are not met, unauthorised payment tax charges will apply. The sum to be charged will depend on the reason why the condition has not been met. For example, the basis of calculating the charge (the unauthorised payment) will be different between security being inadequate and the interest rate being too low.

Security

The loan must be secured by a first charge on an asset held by the sponsoring employer or another person. The value of the asset must be at least the value of the loan and interest. If taxable property is used as security for a loan from an investment-regulated scheme such as a small self-administered scheme, there may be further tax charges as if the scheme had invested in taxable property.

Interest

All loans made by registered pension schemes to employers must charge a commercial rate of interest at least equivalent to a specified rate. There is therefore no problem with charging more than the specified rate and reasonable interest will usually be deductible for the employer if incurred wholly and exclusively for the business.

The minimum interest rate a scheme may charge is calculated as one per cent above the average of the base lending rates of the following six leading high street banks:

- The Bank of Scotland;
- Barclays Bank plc;
- HSBC plc;
- Lloyds plc;
- National Westminster plc; and
- The Royal Bank of Scotland plc.

The average rate calculated should be rounded up as necessary to the nearest quarter of a per cent.

Interest rates come into force on the operative date of each month, which is on the sixth working day, but they are calculated using the interest rates in force on the reference date, which is the 12th working day before the operative date.

This rate is the same as that charged on unpaid corporation tax self-assessment and will be published on the HMRC website (this includes the one per cent above base rate).

A registered pension scheme may make a loan at a fixed rate of interest as long as that interest rate is at least the rate specified. As long as the terms of the loan remain unchanged there will be no requirement to alter the interest charged on the loan during its life.

Term

The repayment term of the loan must not exceed five years. If the employer has genuine difficulties repaying the loan, the loan may be extended, but only for up to five years. No further roll-over is allowed. There is no need to re-test the 50 per cent amount (see below) unless there is a further advance.

Maximum loan

The maximum amount of the loan is 50 per cent of the value of scheme assets immediately before the loan is made. The proportion does not have to be re-tested again. It is therefore conceivable that a fall in scheme values could mean that the loan subsequently represents more than 50 per cent of total assets (and, of course, the loan remains an asset of the scheme). In theory, there is no reason why a scheme should not borrow in order to lend to the employer.

Repayment terms

The loan must be repaid in equal instalments of interest and capital for each complete loan year, starting on the first day of the loan and ending on the last day of the 12 month period. The rules will not allow a loan to be "back-end loaded" or established on an interest only basis.

8.5.3 Loans to connected persons

Any loan made to a person who is, or has been, a scheme member or person or company connected with the person who is, or has been, a scheme member or sponsoring employer will be an unauthorised payment.

A payment made by a registered pension scheme to a person who:

a. is connected with a member or sponsoring employer (or was connected with a member at the date of the member's death); and
b. is not a member or sponsoring employer,

will be treated as made in respect of the member or sponsoring employer.

8.5.4 "Arm's length" loans to unconnected third parties

These are allowed both from personal and occupational schemes. They are not subject to the rules described above for loans to sponsoring employers. So, for example, however unwise it may otherwise be, the loan need not be restricted to 50 per cent of the value of scheme assets.

Circumstances are occasionally the mother of invention in financial services and this is exemplified by the growth in third-party loans. There is nothing to prevent loans being made from SIPP or SSAS to an unconnected third party. These loans are not being made to a sponsoring or connected employer and they do not suffer the restrictions imposed on loans to employer sponsors (such as the 50 per cent restriction). The administrator and the investor will wish to ensure that the loan is on commercial terms because it is genuinely at arm's length and that it represents an acceptable risk. With lending being tight from the commercial banks, the LIBOR rate in the region of five per cent and an uncertain stock market, these loans and syndicated loans look attractive to both investor and borrower.

The word of warning here is that if the loan is invested in taxable property, directly or indirectly, it will constitute an unauthorised payment.

Law: FA 2004, s. 162, 179, Sch. 30
Guidance: PTM 123100, 123200, 123300

8.5.5 Loans as an investment

Loans are a useful source of capital for the sponsoring business, especially, as we have noted, when credit is generally tight. The 2006 rules have ensured that pension benefits are better protected than was the case prior to their implementation. Not only are they a source of liquidity, but the capital made available has enjoyed tax relief when paid as a contribution. That is not to say that the capital is more generally tax-relievable because the loan must be repaid from after-tax money.

Care should be had for the impact a loan will have on retirement benefits. The loan may be seen as a relatively secure investment of the scheme (although some members would wish their pension rights to be more insulated from the fortunes of the employer), but the rate of return is likely to be unattractive over the longer term and trustees might wish to consider the "opportunity cost" of being denied access to actively managed funds that are invested in "real" assets.

8.6 Borrowing

Registered pension schemes are allowed to borrow for whatever purpose they deem to be suitable under HMRC rules. There are, however, restrictions under DWP legislation and the general requirements of trustees to act solely in the financial interest of members.

From the HMRC perspective, the rules are relaxed and are only restrictive as to the amount that may be borrowed. There are therefore no restrictions on the source of the loan save that if the loan is from a connected person, it must be on commercial terms.

The purpose of the loan is not specified in the tax legislation so it may be to purchase an asset or simply to fund a transfer value or pension commencement lump sum to avoid a forced sale of an asset.

A registered pension scheme is authorised to borrow an aggregate amount up to 50 per cent of the net value of the fund immediately before the borrowing has taken place. Any subsequent fall in the value of assets will not affect the amount of the allowable loan. The requirement to take into account the net value means that any existing borrowing will be taken into account in the calculation.

Under a money purchase scheme, the borrowing limit applies to each arrangement.

HMRC give the following example of maximum borrowing where the scheme already has an outstanding commitment:

HMRC example

PP Ltd Registered Pension Scheme has assets worth £200,000 but has a liability in the form of borrowing of £50,000.

The maximum amount which can be borrowed is £200,000 less £50,000 x 50% = £75,000, i.e. further borrowing allowed of £25,000.

There is no objection to the scheme offering security for the loan. Indeed the true value of the scheme assets will, in effect, be the gross value less borrowing.

Although scheme borrowing is usually associated with money purchase schemes that are not cash balance schemes, there is no reason why the facility should not be available to other types of scheme and subject to the same restrictions.

Law: FA 2004, s. 182-185
Guidance: PTM 124000

8.7 Equities

8.7.1 Principle

The HMRC *Registered Pension Schemes Manual* (which preceded the *Pensions Tax Manual*) made a general statement about investing in equities that was deceptively simple:

> "Registered pension schemes may invest in equities regardless of whether or not they are quoted on a recognised stock exchange and regardless of whether the company is a UK company or an overseas company. A registered pension scheme is restricted however, in the amount that can be invested in the shares of a sponsoring employer company."

The difficulties may be listed:

- On the face of it, it matters not whether the shares are quoted. However, there are significant restrictions on investment-regulated schemes (SIPP or SSAS) that have made investment in unquoted companies problematic to the point of being almost impractical for the "average" investor.
- FCA regulation has made advised sales in the area of unquoted shares difficult.

- FCA supervision has imposed obligations on SIPP providers that require a greater duty of care towards members. Furthermore, the FCA has introduced a capital adequacy formula that increases the cost for the provider of allowing investments that do not appear on a standard list. This is to prevent a "disorderly exit" from the market if things go wrong. The new capital adequacy rules were implemented on 1 September 2016.
- There are DWP restrictions on investing in a sponsoring employer (although these apply to larger schemes of 100 members or more).
- The HMRC restrictions on investing in a sponsor are tight.

8.7.2 Shares in the sponsoring employer – HMRC restrictions

The proportion of the total scheme assets represented by investment in the sponsoring employer must not be as much as five per cent. If the scheme invests in a number of sponsors, the aggregate value must not be as much as 20 per cent of scheme asset value. There is no restriction on the proportion of the company held in a pension scheme so whilst direct investment in an enterprise may lose tax relief on trading activities, the relief will not be lost if trading is through a company. In fact, the five per cent restriction will prevent most abuse.

8.7.3 Investing in the employer – DWP restrictions

"Employer-related investment" is defined as:

- investments held by a collective investment scheme with no more than ten participators and the scheme owns no more than ten per cent that would otherwise have been employer-related;
- any guarantee or security given to secure obligations of the employer or an associate;
- any loan to anyone whose repayment depends on the employer unless the purpose was not to give financial assistance to the employer.

The regulations restrict employer-related investments to no more than five per cent of the value of scheme assets. Loans to the employer are generally not allowed.

Small self-administered schemes are exempted from the restriction on investment subject to:

- all members being trustees; and
- where the rules of the scheme provide that before any investment of resources is made in an employer-related investment, each member must agree in writing to the making of that investment.

A small self-administered scheme is defined in these circumstances as having fewer than 12 members.

8.8 Value shifting

Value shifting refers to "shifting value" from a pension scheme to a member or sponsoring employer. This may be evidenced by an increase in the value of assets held by a scheme member or sponsoring employer or the reduction in liability of a member or sponsoring employer.

Value shifting is treated as if it were a payment and payments that are not made on arm's length terms in this way are unauthorised. They will generate an unauthorised payments charge on the member and a scheme sanction charge on the scheme administrator.

HMRC give an example of value shifting:

HMRC example

Andrew is a member of ABC Ltd Retirement Benefits Scheme.

ABC Ltd RBS owns 100% of the class A shares in ABC Ltd.

Andrew owns 100% of the class B shares in ABC Ltd.

Both the class A shares and the class B shares have similar rights but the class A shares subsequently change their rights so they no longer have the rights to dividends.

The result is that the value from the class A shares has passed to the B shares and therefore to the member without any payment.

Andrew will be subjected to an unauthorised payment charge equivalent to the decrease in value of the shares held by the scheme. The scheme will also suffer a scheme sanction charge.

HMRC also give examples of value shifting in relation to lease transactions and removal of rights or restrictions. HMRC also point out that if value reduces as a consequence of an arm's length transaction (such as a rent review) that will not necessarily constitute value shifting.

Law: FA 2004, s. 174
Guidance: PTM 133700

8.9 Taxable property

8.9.1 Introduction

The individual member or adviser who wishes to engage in tax planning through a small scheme will be attracted by the idea of directing or influencing investments within the definition of an investment-regulated scheme.

The taxable property provisions will only apply if the scheme is an investment-regulated scheme and the asset is regarded as taxable property. Investment may be direct or indirect (through a "vehicle").

The tax rules are quite broad, but the tax charges can be quite severe. Those charges may arise in respect of unauthorised payment charges (including the scheme sanction charge) when payments are made for investments or when rent is received from taxable property or a gain is made on disposal. Where income or capital is derived from the ownership of taxable property, unauthorised payment charges will not apply, but the scheme sanction charge may.

8.9.2 De-registration and pension liberation

It is possible that ill-advised investment could prompt de-registration (where the unauthorised payment reached the threshold of 25 per cent of scheme asset value in a 12-month period). HMRC are unlikely to use their discretion to de-register and incur the de-registration charge unless there has been a flagrant abuse. It would be unusual for a SIPP to cross this threshold because, as we saw in **Chapter 1**, a SIPP provider will usually offer one scheme with many diverse members. Individuals will become members as evidenced by arrangements and plan. By contrast, a SSAS will be specific to an employer (possibly a group of employers) and membership will unusually exceed three or four.

HMRC and the Pensions Regulator are devoting considerable resource to monitoring firms that encourage members of SSAS to "liberate" their funds and in the process incur significant tax charges (including the de-registration and unauthorised payment charges) and adviser fees.

8.9.3 Investment-regulated schemes

Taxable property comprises residential property (with minor exceptions) and tangible moveable property (again with minor exceptions). It may be owned directly or indirectly. Some property that might be classed as taxable if owned directly by the scheme may not be so taxable if owned indirectly through the medium of a "genuine diverse commercial vehicle" (GDCV).

The definition of an investment-regulated scheme necessarily differs according to whether the scheme is a personal pension scheme or occupational scheme (charges and access terms preclude it from being a stakeholder scheme).

If the scheme is a personal pension scheme, an investment regulated pension scheme is one where one or more of its members is or has been able (whether directly or indirectly) to direct, influence or advise on the manner of investments held for the purposes of an arrangement under the scheme relating to the member. It also applies where the condition is satisfied by a person related to the member.

It is worth reminding ourselves here that the normal structure of a personal pension scheme comprises one scheme with members being invited to invest in arrangements. It is unusual for a provider to operate more than a handful of schemes (indeed the provider may offer only access to one scheme) although they may have many members invested in many arrangements.

If the scheme is an occupational pension scheme, an investment regulated pension scheme is one which has at least one member who meets the self-direction condition, and where there are fewer than 50 members.

The self-direction condition is met if the member is or has been able (whether directly or indirectly) to direct, influence or advise on the manner of investments held for the purposes of the scheme. It also applies where the condition is satisfied by a person related to the member.

Law: FA 2004, Sch. 29A, para. 1-5
Guidance: PTM 121000

8.9.4 Linked investments anti-avoidance

A further category of occupational pension scheme can be an investment regulated pension scheme. This is where:

- the scheme is an occupational pension scheme that is not itself an investment regulated pension scheme; and
- one or more of its members (or a person related to a member) is or has been able (whether directly or indirectly) to direct, influence or advise on the manner of investments linked to an arrangement under the scheme relating to the member.

The arrangement is then treated as if it were an investment regulated pension scheme.

HMRC point out that:

> "For the purposes of the above investments are linked to an arrangement relating to the member if
>
> - they are held for the purposes of an arrangement under the pension scheme relating to the member, but
>
> - they are so held other than by virtue of a just and reasonable apportionment of the sums and assets held for the purposes of the scheme."

This is to prevent large occupational schemes setting up separate sections that allow particular classes of members to direct that their funds are invested in taxable assets. So rather than simply being an apportionment of the collective assets held for the whole scheme these are specific assets held just for the member's arrangement.

> "Alternatively this will also include a pool of assets held for a limited number of arrangements where those arrangements effectively form a separate section of the scheme designed to allow investments in residential property.
>
> For each of these categories of scheme, persons are related to the member if
>
> - the person and the member are **connected persons**,
> - the person acts on behalf of the member or a person connected with a member."

The rules are quite difficult and wide-reaching because of HMRC's perception of the way member-directed plans were being marketed by some advisers following FA 2004.

Law: FA 2004, Sch. 29A, para. 1-5
Guidance: PTM 121000

8.9.5 Examples of taxable property

HMRC have reproduced a list of what constitutes taxable property and what does not from FA 2004. The list itself deserves comment.

Residential property

According to HMRC:

> "Residential property can be in the UK or elsewhere and is
>
> - a building or structure that is used or suitable for use as a dwelling;
> - any related land that is wholly or partly the garden for the building or structure;
> - any related land that is wholly or partly grounds for the residential property and which is used or intended for use for a purpose connected with the enjoyment of the building;
> - any building or structure on any such related land;

- in limited situations a hotel, which includes an inn, or similar accommodation, will be counted as taxable property though this will only be where it provides accommodation rights such as timeshare;
- a beach hut;
- any building specified in Regulations as residential property."

Not residential property

Again according to HMRC:

> "Certain buildings that would otherwise be within the definition of residential property are not to be treated as residential. A building used for any of the following purposes is not residential property
>
> - a home or other institution providing residential accommodation for children. This means a dedicated children's home not simply any home that children can live in, for example, a family's house;
> - a hall of residence for students. This does not include normal houses or flats let to, for example, university students;
> - a home or other institution providing residential accommodation with personal care for persons in need of personal care by reason of old age, disability, past or present dependence on alcohol or drugs or past or present mental disorder;
> - a hospital or hospice;
> - a prison or similar establishment;
> - any building specified in Regulations as not to be treated as residential property."

The list of what is residential property should preclude farm land connected with a farmhouse (which will itself be residential property). In other words, they can be regarded separately.

Guidance: PTM 121000

Off-plan

It has been fashionable to buy property "off-plan". This means that the property is developed just short of being habitable and then sold. In that case, it is not residential property until it is recognised by HMRC as habitable and perhaps receives a certificate of habitation.

Guidance: PTM 121000

Halls of residence

In the list of property that is not taxable property, student halls of residence may be privately owned. They must be connected to a college or university and must be reserved exclusively for the students. They should not be self-contained or have separate bedrooms, but have communal living areas to avoid being classed as residential property.

Guidance: PTM 125200

Twin purposes

Buildings that serve the twin purposes of residence and a profession (e.g. dental and medical surgeries) present more of a problem. They will generally be regarded as taxable property. If the residential property such as a flat has a separate entrance from the commercial part of the building and no internal connection then it will not be taxable property even if there is a communal hallway.

Different parts of a building are inter-connected if they share a common entrance and an individual can move from one part to another without moving through common areas.

If a building such as a barn is attached to a residential property and is used for commercial use, but occasionally for personal use (such as parking a car), HMRC will examine the primary use. Some situations may need HMRC guidance.

Guidance: PTM 125200

Timeshare and hotels

Timeshare ownership constitutes residential and therefore taxable property. Hotel ownership is not ownership of residential property and therefore is not ownership of taxable property if, alone or with others, the individual owns the whole hotel. However the legislation tells us:

> "But a person does not hold an interest in residential property consisting of hotel accommodation directly unless:
>
> a. the person holds part only of the hotel accommodation or any estate, interest, right or power in or over such a part and, as a result, any person has a right to use or occupy that or any other part of the hotel accommodation, or
> b. the person has a right to use, or participate in arrangements relating to the use of, part only of the hotel accommodation or a description of property to which that part belongs."

Law: FA 2004, Sch. 29A, para. 14(2)
Guidance: PTM 125200

Job-related residential property

Although the foregoing is about defining residential property for the purposes of determining if property is taxable property when held by an investment-regulated pension scheme, there are unusual circumstances when property which is undoubtedly residential is exempt from the taxable property provisions. Those circumstances concern "job-related" residential property and fall into two categories:

First, the property is (or, if unoccupied, is to be) occupied by an employee who:

- is neither a member of the pension scheme nor connected with such a member;
- is not connected with the employer; and
- is required as a condition of employment to occupy the property.

An example is a caretaker's flat.

Second, the property is (or, if unoccupied, is to be):

- occupied by a person who is neither a member of the pension scheme nor connected with such a member; and

- used in connection with business premises held as an investment of the pension scheme.

An example is a flat above a shop that is leased from the scheme with the shop, where the flat is occupied by the trader in connection with his operating the trade from the shop.

Law: ITA 2007, s. 993 (connected person)
Guidance: PTM 125200 (and see Chapter 1 of this book)

Ground rents

If they are held as an asset of an investment-regulated scheme, ground rents will be regarded as taxable property.

Guidance: PTM 125200

Tangible moveable property

The other main heading of taxable property is "tangible moveable property". This refers to assets that you can touch (unlike financial obligations such as gilts, for example) and move (even with the help of a crane. So, industrial machinery can be moved, but a ventilation system perhaps cannot).

There are a number of practical exceptions to the requirement for tangible moveable property to be treated as taxable. Indirect holding of tangible moveable property that meets the following conditions will not be taxable property:

- the market value of the asset must not be greater than £6,000 (which can be problematic: for example, do a computer server and terminals constitute one asset or a number of assets?);
- the interest in the asset is held indirectly by the investment regulated pension scheme;
- the asset is held solely for the purposes of the administration or management of the vehicle that holds it directly; and
- neither a scheme member, nor anyone connected to a scheme member, personally occupies or has use of the asset.

This provision prevents any taxable property tax charges arising in respect of low value assets that are used in the normal operation of the vehicle's business. Examples of assets included are small items of plant and machinery and office equipment.

Investment grade gold bullion is exempt from the definition of taxable property. The definition of investment grade gold is gold of a purity not less than 995 thousandths that is in a form of a bar or a wafer, of a weight accepted by the bullion markets. These standards distinguish the bullion from, for example, jewellery which is taxable property (if of required value).

Guidance: PTM 121000, 125300, 125400

8.9.6 The tax charges

The taxable property provisions apply when the asset is "acquired" and this term has a very wide meaning which is described in PTM 125300 and 125400. If the property is gifted to the scheme, no unauthorised payment charges will apply because no tax relief on contributions has been claimed.

If an interest in taxable property is acquired directly by an investment-regulated scheme, there will be an immediate unauthorised payment charge (40% of the value) and a scheme sanction charge (15% of the value). There may be an unauthorised payment surcharge (15% of the value) and in rare cases a de-registration charge (40% of the value of scheme assets immediately before de-registration).

Guidance: PTM 125300, 125400

8.9.7 Chargeable value

Where an interest is acquired in taxable property under a lease, the value of the lease is converted to a capital value on the principles used for calculating stamp duty land tax.

The value in these cases is the purchase price plus any incidental costs of purchase where they have come from tax-relieved funds.

If a scheme takes a first charge on employer taxable property as security for a loan, the scheme will have acquired an interest. The only costs likely to have been incurred at this stage are legal and administrative costs and if these derive from tax-relieved contributions, they will be subject to an unauthorised payment charge. However, if the scheme subsequently enforces its charge, unauthorised payment charges will apply to the full value of the property.

Similar rules apply to charging orders imposed by the court.

As an anti-avoidance provision, where an investment-regulated pension scheme acquires a direct interest in taxable property for less than its market value, and immediately before the acquisition the interest was held by a registered pension scheme which was not an investment-regulated pension scheme, the unauthorised payment amount is the market value of the interest at the time it was acquired.

If taxable property is improved, then the cost of improvements is an unauthorised payment to the extent of the cost. If property within an investment-regulated scheme is converted to taxable property, the value of the property becomes the amount of the unauthorised payment. If each member's interest is not clear in a multi-member scheme, the unauthorised payment is apportioned on a "just and reasonable" basis.

The scheme sanction charge will apply (to the scheme administrator) when income is received from taxable property or when a gain is made on disposal of taxable property. In each case, the rate of charge is 40 per cent. Unauthorised payment charges will not otherwise arise in these circumstances.

The scheme sanction charge is applied to income profit each year or, if higher, 10 per cent of the opening value increased each year with the Retail Prices Index. If the property has been improved with the an unauthorised payment, then the opening value is increased in the year the payment is made by the amount of the payment and in addition to the RPI increase. Income is apportioned for part years of ownership.

The formula provided by HMRC is:

$$(MV + UP) \times (1 + RPI)$$

where:

MV is the opening market value, determined as follows:

- in the tax year the first interest in the taxable property is acquired etc., this is the market value immediately after it first becomes taxable property; and
- in any later tax year it is the deemed value of the immediately preceding tax year.

UP is zero unless there has been any improvement to or further acquisition of an interest in the taxable property in the tax year, in which case it is the total of any unauthorised payments treated as made by the pension scheme in respect of the improvements or further interests acquired.

RPI is the percentage increase in the retail prices index (expressed as a decimal) from the first day in the tax year that the scheme held the taxable property interest to the last day of that tax year. If the index falls the figure is 0.

If a pension scheme disposes of taxable property, then a net gain on all disposals of taxable property by the scheme in a tax year may be subject to a scheme sanction charge at a rate of 40 per cent. Broadly speaking, the normal CGT rules apply (although CGT as such does not). This means that the gain for the year is derived from the gain less losses on taxable property for the tax year and the purchase price is increased by acquisition costs and the cost of improvements. Losses cannot be carried back or forward.

If the taxable property is tangible moveable property and is a wasting asset any loss arising on disposal of such assets may only be set against gains arising from other assets of that category in that same tax year.

Where an asset only becomes a taxable property asset after its original acquisition by the scheme it is treated as acquired at the time it became a taxable asset and its cost is the amount of unauthorised payment treated as made by the pension scheme at that time.

If an asset is not a taxable asset throughout the time it is held by the scheme the gain on its disposal is to be reduced on a time basis to the period when it was a taxable asset.

Guidance: PTM 125300

8.9.8 Indirectly owned – chain of owners

The legislation refers to taxable property being directly or indirectly held. If it is held indirectly, it will be held by a vehicle such as a company or retail investment product. The property may or may not be taxable property. There may be a number of owners between the pension scheme and the property and the extent of the scheme's interest will be derived from the whole "chain". For example:

> If the scheme owns an interest in 50% of company A,
>
> that owns an interest in 20% of company B,
>
> that owns an interest in 40% of company C,
>
> that owns the property,
>
> then the scheme indirectly owns 4% (50% of 20% of 40%) of the property.

The property may be taxable property if the scheme is an investment-regulated scheme, but will not be subject to unauthorised payment charges on taxable property if any of the vehicles in the chain of ownership is a genuine diverse commercial vehicle (GDCV).

Guidance: PTM 125400

8.9.9 Genuine diverse commercial vehicles

There were three types of GDCV described in the *Registered Pension Schemes Manual*. References to GDCV have disappeared in the later *Pensions Tax Manual*, but the rules and guidance remain the same:

- UK Real Estate Investment Trusts (REIT);
- "other kinds of vehicle"; and
- trading concerns.

Guidance: PTM 125400

Real Estate Investment Trusts

In order to qualify as a GDCV, the REIT must meet certain conditions. The conditions are similar for all three GDCV types. The objective is to ensure that ownership is diffuse and that the pension scheme does not have a dominant interest, but also that it is not capable of personal use.

According to HMRC the pension scheme's interest in the UK REIT must meet the following conditions.

The pension scheme:

- must not directly or indirectly hold an interest in the UK REIT for the purposes of enabling a member of the pension scheme or a connected person of a member to occupy or use the property, and
- must meet either the condition (a) or (b) below,
  a. where the pension scheme is an occupational pension scheme, the pension scheme – together with any associated persons – must not hold directly or indirectly an interest in the UK REIT that exceeds any one of the limits in the paragraph below, or
  b. where the pension scheme is not an occupational pension scheme, no arrangement under the pension scheme, together with any associated persons, may hold directly or indirectly an interest in the UK REIT that exceeds any one of the limits in the paragraph below.

The limits referred to in conditions (a) and (b) above are:

- 10% or more of the share capital or issued share capital of the UK REIT;
- 10% or more of the voting rights in the UK REIT;
- a right to receive 10% or more of the income of the UK REIT;
- such an interest in the UK REIT as gives an entitlement to 10% or more of the amounts distributed on a distribution in relation to the UK REIT;
- such an interest in the UK REIT as gives an entitlement to 10% or more of the assets of the UK REIT on a winding up or in any other circumstances;
- such an interest in the UK REIT as gives rise to income and gains derived from a specific property.

These limits apply to indirect holdings of a UK REIT as well. So if a pension scheme holds 50 per cent of company A which in turn owns 15 per cent of a UK REIT then the pension schemes interest in the UK REIT will be 7.5 per cent. The indirect holding in the UK REIT will therefore be less than 10 per cent.

A pension scheme which is not an occupational pension scheme may have holdings in a UK REIT through one or more arrangements for members that are not associated persons. In these circumstances the tests of whether 10 per cent or more of the UK REIT is owned will apply separately for each arrangement. Where the same member has more than one arrangement they must be considered jointly.

"Associated person" in relation to a pension scheme means:

- any member of the pension scheme;
- any person connected with such a member;
- any arrangement (under that or another pension scheme) relating to a member of the pension scheme;
- any arrangement (under that or another pension scheme) relating to a person connected to such a member;
- any associated pension scheme, see below.

In the above a pension scheme is associated with another pension scheme if members representing at least 10 per cent by value (see above) of one pension scheme are members of the other pension scheme or connected with such members.

In this page "associated person" in relation to an arrangement means:

- the member of the pension scheme to which that arrangement relates;
- any person connected with such a member;
- any arrangement (under that or another pension scheme) relating to a member of the pension scheme to which that arrangement relates;

- any arrangement (under that or another pension scheme) relating to a person connected to such a member.

Law: FA 2006, Pt. 4; ITA 2007, s. 993, 994; CTA 2010, s. 1122
Guidance: PTM 125400

8.9.10 Other kinds of vehicle

Again we may turn to the *Pensions Tax Manual* which in turn takes its cue from FA 2004, as amended.

If a vehicle meets certain conditions, and if the pension scheme and associates directly or indirectly own 10 per cent or less and there is no right to have private use of any taxable property, they will not be subject to a tax charge. The vehicle must meet three conditions.

Condition 1

1. the total value of the assets held directly by the vehicle is at least £1 million; or
2. the vehicle holds at least three assets directly which are residential property,

and in either of these cases no asset held directly by the vehicle which is taxable property has a value which exceeds 40 per cent of the total value of the assets held directly.

In applying these rules:

- assets must be valued in accordance with generally accepted accounting practice;
- no account is to be taken of liabilities secured against or otherwise relating to assets (whether generally or specifically); and
- where generally accepted accounting practice offers a choice of valuation between cost basis and fair value, fair value must be used.

Condition 2

If the vehicle is a company,

- it is resident in the UK and is not a close company; or
- it is not resident in the UK and would not be a close company if it were.

Condition 3

The vehicle does not have as its main purpose, or one of its main purposes, the direct or indirect holding of one or more animals used for sporting purposes. This is to recognise that many racehorse syndicates have many members and provide them with certain benefits related to the horse ownership such as attendance at race meetings as an owner with access to the owner's enclosure.

The rules regarding the pension scheme's interest in the vehicle (for it to be a GDCV) are the same as those described above under REIT.

Guidance: PTM 125400

8.9.11 Trading concerns

These are vehicles that are arm's length trading vehicles. There are four conditions to be met:

Activity

The vehicle's main activity is the carrying on of a trade, profession or vocation.

Control

The pension scheme, if it is an occupational pension scheme, either alone or together with associated persons does not have control of the vehicle.

Where the pension scheme is not an occupational pension scheme, an arrangement under the scheme either alone or together with associated persons does not have control of the vehicle.

The second part of this condition means that the condition will be met where for example, a personal pension scheme held 51 per cent of the voting shares of a company but in respect of 51 different arrangements under the scheme for unconnected members and one per cent of the shares are held by each arrangement.

Controlling director

Neither a pension scheme member nor a person connected to such a member is a controlling director of the vehicle or any other vehicle which holds an interest in the vehicle directly or indirectly. Where the pension scheme is not an occupational pension scheme as explained above this test applies at arrangement level rather than at scheme level, so if in the example above a member of an arrangement does not meet this condition, tax charges will apply.

But if this condition along with the other thee conditions are met in relation to the other 50 arrangements under the scheme, then the indirect holdings held by those arrangements will not be subject to tax charges.

Interest

The pension scheme does not directly or indirectly hold an interest in the vehicle for the purposes of enabling a pension scheme member or a connected person of such a member to occupy or use the property.

"Control" has the meaning given by CTA 2010, s. 450 and 451. References in those sections to a company are read as references to the vehicle, and references to associates as including associated persons.

The definition of a "connected person" and the meaning of "control" now appear in ITA 2007. Sections 993-995 are reproduced below.

Guidance: PTM 125400

8.9.12 Section 993: Meaning of "connected" persons

1. This section has effect for the purposes of the provisions of the Income Tax Acts which apply this section.
2. An individual ("A") is connected with another individual ("B") if:
    a. A is B's spouse or civil partner;
    b. A is a relative of B;
    c. A is the spouse or civil partner of a relative of B;
    d. A is a relative of B's spouse or civil partner; or

   e. A is the spouse or civil partner of a relative of B's spouse or civil partner.

3. A person, in the capacity as trustee of a settlement, is connected with:
   a. any individual who is a settlor in relation to the settlement;
   b. any person connected with such an individual;
   c. any close company whose participators include the trustees of the settlement;
   d. any non-UK resident company which, if it were UK resident, would be a close company whose participators include the trustees of the settlement;
   e. any body corporate controlled (within the meaning of section 995) by a company within paragraph (c) or (d);
   f. if the settlement is the principal settlement in relation to one or more sub-fund settlements, a person in the capacity as trustee of such a sub-fund settlement; and
   g. if the settlement is a sub-fund settlement in relation to a principal settlement, a person in the capacity as trustee of any other sub-fund settlements in relation to the principal settlement.
4. A person who is a partner in a partnership is connected with:
   a. any partner in the partnership;
   b. the spouse or civil partner of any individual who is a partner in the partnership; and
   c. a relative of any individual who is a partner in the partnership.

   But this subsection does not apply in relation to acquisitions or disposals of assets of the partnership pursuant to genuine commercial arrangements.
5. A company is connected with another company if:
   a. the same person has control of both companies;

b. a person ("A") has control of one company and persons connected with A have control of the other company;

c. A has control of one company and A together with persons connected with A have control of the other company; or

d. a group of two or more persons has control of both companies and the groups either consist of the same persons or could be so regarded if (in one or more cases) a member of either group were replaced by a person with whom the member is connected.

6. A company is connected with another person ("A") if:

a. A has control of the company; or

b. A together with persons connected with A have control of the company.

7. In relation to a company, any two or more persons acting together to secure or exercise control of the company are connected with:

a. one another; and

b. any person acting on the directions of any of them to secure or exercise control of the company.

[Sub-paragraph 7 has always caused difficulty. In its broadest sense, all shareholding directors would always be connected to each other.]

8.9.13 Section 994: Meaning of "connected" persons: supplementary

1. In s. 993 and this section:

"company" includes any body corporate or unincorporated association, but does not include a partnership (and see also subs. (2));

"control" is to be read in accordance with sections 450 and 451 of CTA 2010 (except where otherwise indicated);

"principal settlement" has the meaning given by para. 1 of Sch. 4ZA to TCGA 1992;

"relative" means brother, sister, ancestor or lineal descendant;

"settlement" has the same meaning as in Ch. 5 of Pt. 5 of ITTOIA 2005 (see s. 620 of that Act); and

"sub-fund settlement" has the meaning given by para. 1 of Sch. 4ZA to TCGA 1992.

2. For the purposes of s. 993:
   a. a unit trust scheme is treated as if it were a company; and
   b. the rights of the unit holders are treated as if they were shares in the company.
3. For the purposes of s. 993 "trustee", in the case of a settlement in relation to which there would be no trustees apart from this subsection, means any person:
   a. in whom the property comprised in the settlement is for the time being vested; or
   b. in whom the management of that property is for the time being vested.

   Section 466(4) does not apply for the purposes of this subsection.
4. If any provision of s. 993 provides that a person ("A") is connected with another person ("B"), it also follows that B is connected with A.

8.9.14 Section 995: Meaning of "control"

1. This section has effect for the purposes of the provisions of the Income Tax Acts which apply this section.
2. In relation to a body corporate ("company A"), "control" means the power of a person ("P") to secure:
   a. by means of the holding of shares or the possession of voting power in relation to that or any other body corporate; or
   b. as a result of any powers conferred by the articles of association or other document regulating that or any other body corporate,

that the affairs of company A are conducted in accordance with P's wishes.

3. In relation to a partnership, "control" means the right to a share of more than half the assets, or of more than half the income, of the partnership.

8.9.15 Other definitions

"Controlling director" means a director to whom CTA 2010, s. 452(2)(b), (3) applies, broadly 20 per cent controlling directors. In sub-section (3) read the reference to associates as including associated persons.

The term "associated person" in relation to the pension scheme has the same meaning as for REIT and "other vehicles".

Assets with a market value of no more than £6,000 may be ignored in determining taxable property that is indirectly owned if the assets are used in the administration of the business. This is interpreted in quite a narrow way by HMRC. So, the vehicle may not qualify as a GDCV, but acquisition of the asset will not be subject to unauthorised payment charges.

8.9.16 Specific issues with taxable property

Unlisted companies

From an HMRC point of view, there is no reason why the scheme should not invest in unlisted shares. However, there is less chance that the unlisted company will qualify as a genuine diverse commercial vehicle and this in turn will increase the risk of investments by the vehicle being taxed as, for example, tangible moveable property. Administrators will be concerned that they may have a liability to the scheme sanction charge without knowing how the company is investing its resources.

Tangible moveable property

The *de minimis* exception from the taxable property rules for assets valued at no more than £6,000 is only of significance where purchase is indirect (e.g. through a company) where the vehicle is not a genuine diverse commercial vehicle. The requirement of the asset to be used in the management of the vehicle precludes direct investment.There is no charge if the vehicle is a GDCV.

What constitutes a single item is not clear.

Charging orders

The *Pension Schemes Newsletter* no. 37 (May 2009) explains HMRC's approach to charging orders over taxable property. A charging order is described as a court order placing a charge over the judgment debtor's property in the amount that is owed. The point at issue is whether this unwittingly gives the creditor scheme an interest in taxable property.

HMRC now take the view that putting the charging order in place immediately creates an interest in taxable property. This is an unauthorised payment, but the amount of the payment is defined as the amount of consideration plus fees and costs associated with the acquisition. This figure is likely to be negligible because there will be no consideration.

Intellectual property

Intellectual property ("knowhow") is not tangible moveable property and therefore not taxable property. However, there may be some doubts over whether payments made for it are capital in nature or income, in which case the income may be regarded by HMRC as trading and therefore taxable.

Insurance company funds

Some insurance companies give members of personal pension schemes significant control over how their arrangements are invested. This brings the arrangements within the definition of an investment-regulated scheme. These are contract-based schemes where the assets are owned by the insurance company rather than trustees. However, the funds will also be subject to the "permitted links" rules that appear in the *FSA Handbook* (Glossary).

These rules are in many respects tighter than those relating to investment-regulated schemes. They include a number of requirements including restricting investment to assets available in a properly functioning market and there is a limit on investment in specific assets. The permitted links rules (Conduct of Business Sourcebook 21) were last updated in June 2017 (Release 17).

Investment in National Savings & Investment products

National Savings & Investments has produced a guide to which of its products may be purchased by a self-invested personal pension scheme (SIPP). There is no mention of small self-administered schemes (SSAS), but the guidance does refer to investments held in a SIPP "in the form of corporate trusts". The list of products that will not trigger an unauthorised payment is:

- guaranteed equity bond;
- inflation-beating savings (sic);
- fixed interest savings certificates;
- pensioners guaranteed income bonds;
- income bonds;
- capital bonds; and
- fixed rate savings bonds.

For clarity, a list of products that would trigger an unauthorised payment is also provided. The list is:

- premium bonds;
- ISAs;
- easy access savings account;
- investment account; and
- children's bonus bond.

Investment limits apply to the member not the trustee (which would also make investment by a SSAS problematic). Note also that NS&I's search criteria are determined by the name and details of the member not the trustees.

With-profits reattribution

Regulations specify that where payments are made to with-profits policyholders as part of a scheme approved by the court and which seeks to reattribute inherited estate, those payments will not be regarded as unauthorised payments if they are exchanged for rights over the estate and the payments do not reduce the value of the member's pension arrangements (*Registered Pension Schemes (Authorised Member Payments) Regulations* 2007 (SI 2007/3532)).

8.10 Employer finance

There are two ways in which an investment-regulated scheme can provide financial support for a sponsoring employer. A key principle is that they do not rely on tax relief for their advantage, rather they provide the employer with more independence from commercial lenders.

8.10.1 Loanback

The facility to borrow from the sponsoring employer's scheme provides the employer with valuable independence. Although the loan must be provided on a properly underwritten and commercial basis, it does offer access to money which may from time to time be in short supply in the commercial market.

In the past, an attraction of these loans was that they were not required to be so rigorously underwritten as they are now and security was not required. The consequence on default by the employer was that benefits were lost, the contributions having been granted tax relief on the way. The loan facility remains valuable, but can no longer be regarded as the "last resort" of the ailing company.

There are some aspects worth considering:

- the loan is provided from funds that have enjoyed tax relief, but must be repaid from after-tax funds. They are not tax-efficient in the same way as a pension mortgage, for instance;
- the loan to the employer is also an asset of the scheme, so when interest rates are low, there may be an opportunity cost for the member who is not able to enjoy higher investment returns from other opportunities;
- the first charge on employer assets will inhibit further borrowing from other sources;
- the rate of interest (which is a deductible expense) is competitive;
- the main problem is that the loan would not be available for a term of more than five years (perhaps ten years)

which may not be suitable although if the member is a trustee of the scheme, a new loan is likely to be available when the current loan expires;

- the value of assets in the scheme must be substantial in order to make loans viable.

8.10.2 Property purchased by the pension fund

The alternative means of providing financial assistance to the employer is for the scheme to purchase an asset for or from the employer.

If the asset is to be purchased from the employer, it must be at arm's length and the scheme must charge a commercial rent for use by the employer. The asset will usually be a commercial property. Again the purchase is made from funds that have enjoyed tax relief and again funds must be substantial for the transaction to be viable. The tax relief "advantage" is a bit of a chimera in this context because any contribution to any pension scheme is likely to attract tax relief. In other words, tax relief may assist the purchase of the property, but it does not give an investment-regulated scheme a tax advantage over other pension arrangements. The funds available may be boosted by the scheme borrowing up to 50 per cent of the net asset value.

The attractions of purchasing property are that:

- liquidity is made available to the employer in exchange for long-term assets being transferred to the (long-term) pension fund;
- the employer controls the landlord. Sometimes the employer is offered the option of buying the freehold from a landlord and uses the pension fund for this purpose;
- funds are available that might be difficult to secure on the market, especially if the employer is required to borrow;
- contributions (purchase price) have attracted tax relief;
- rent is deductible and may simply replace contributions (but should not if benefit targets are to be maintained);
- the asset is protected from creditors when in the pension fund (although, of course, the money paid to the employer as part of the transaction is not);

- disposal of the asset in the pension fund is free of capital gains tax although pensions are taxed at the normal rates of income tax (which are generally higher). Of course, 25 per cent of the fund is tax-free;
- tax relievable contributions can be used to repay borrowings;
- interest paid by the scheme is not relievable because the fund is UK tax exempt, but rent may be used to finance the interest payments on borrowings and as we have seen rent is deductible for the employer.

There are some significant words of caution, however:

- it makes no investment sense to invest funds in one asset that represents a large part of the fund and is, by its nature, illiquid (but the employer will have other priorities);
- the maximum borrowing available under HMRC rules (50 per cent of net assets) must include any amounts used for incidental costs such as legal fees and stamp duty;
- borrowing will exacerbate this problem;
- the problem of liquidity becomes more acute if a significant member leaves service for whatever reason, retires or dies;
- property owned by the pension fund is not available as security for future employer borrowings;
- if the property is already being leased, a formal renegotiation of the rent would be needed to reduce the rent;
- by transferring an interest in business property to a pension fund, valuable capital allowances may be lost.

The rules of the SIPP will allow a sum equivalent to the value of their accrued rights to be paid to a beneficiary nominated by trustees in the event of death. Date of death is by its nature unexpected and the planning cannot be accurate. The problem is especially acute when assets are illiquid and even more so when financed by borrowing.

The way in which the fund is normally protected is for life assurance to be taken out by each member on the life of other members and outside the scheme. In the event of the death of a member, the sum assured is paid to the other members who are then able to make a further contribution to the scheme. The sum assured will take into account that a contribution that exceeds the annual allowance will generate a tax charge on the member which will either be paid by the member or paid by the scheme in exchange for a commensurate reduction in benefits.

8.11 Flexibility of investment-regulated schemes (SIPP and SSAS)

The primary attraction of SIPP and SSAS is their investment flexibility. For a wide range of reasons, a much more diverse market place (and the options that it now offers) has persuaded many investors to move away from the convenience of packaged products such as life assurance policies and unit trusts. The life assurance companies have responded with innovations such as platforms and multi-fund offerings, but to some, more sophisticated investors with significant fund values, there is an obvious attraction in a personally designed or bespoke investment portfolio. This is the reason, of course, why many stockbrokers have formed branded alliances with SIPP/SSAS administrators: the product deconstructs what the life assurance companies have done in the past (and will continue to do for many investors).

Another less measurable reason for taking the SIPP/SSAS option is that it can provide a more personal investment service, again reflecting the attractions of a good stockbroker.

The reference to "significant fund values" is important in this context. Traditionally, the bulk of charging in respect of life assurance and collective products has been in the form of percentage charges. As a general rule (not always), SIPP/SSAS administrators charge flat fees by task or time spent. This means that on the SIPP/SSAS, the incidence of charges will be relatively high in respect small funds, but relatively low for the larger funds. This has led to a burgeoning market in switching institutional funds to SIPP/SSAS when they reach a certain size.

The impact of charging is not always straightforward, however. Life assurance and collective investment scheme charges are sometimes difficult to identify and recent publicity has focused on so-called "hidden" charges such as dealing costs. On the other hand, SIPP and

SSAS products may be financed by "trail" fees from investments or interest from money whilst held on deposit.

Then there are those investors who have special knowledge of a particular asset class and whilst some would take this as a reason to diversify, many professional investors would rather use their own skills. For example, why would a property investor wish to invest in a life assurance company property fund when he can invest his fund directly (leaving aside considerations such as liquidity and diversity)?

One of the criticisms of the way SIPP and SSAS were marketed was that some investors were far from sophisticated and funds were not of an appropriate size. One of the outcomes of closer FSA/FCA scrutiny including most notably publication of a thematic review and guidance in late 2012 is that SIPP administrators are now aware of the greater responsibility they have to ensure the appropriateness of investments and the appropriateness of the adviser. The administrator will also wish to ensure that the investor understands the nature of their investment decision and the quality and scale of the risk involved. An administrator will sometimes meet this requirement by simply asking for the "story behind the investment choice" as one administrator has said. The "due diligence" expected of the administrator in this respect will extend to ensuring that proper attention has been paid to the issue of liquidity whether it is to pay benefits or under a common fund, to provide a transfer value. Indeed, there may be some self-interest here: the administrator will wish to be certain that there are sufficient funds to cover any potential liability to the scheme sanction charge and the lifetime allowance (in addition to appropriate avoiding action).

Another area that is vexed for the administrator is that of requests for transfers to other registered pension schemes and the danger of facilitating so-called "pension liberation" exercises. We should remember that although there is a general right to transfer from a stakeholder scheme or an occupational scheme, no such legislative right applies to personal pension schemes and retirement annuity contracts. In other words, the administrator of a SIPP can refuse to allow a transfer if it considers the transfer to be for doubtful purposes. However, if the scheme rules give a right to a transfer, the problem becomes one of disclosure (first to the investor).

8.12 Transitional protection

As a general rule, pre-A-Day investment will be protected from the taxable property rules if it was held legitimately under the "old" rules and there is no improvement to the property. Maintenance is not improvement nor is work done under a statutory obligation.

Off-plan investment before A-Day is protected if it never converts to purchase a residential property within the pension. If the interest is sold as a result of these rules, it will not necessarily be treated as trading.

8.13 SIPPs and the FCA

In November 2012, the FSA consulted on a new regulatory capital framework for SIPP operators. After a period of reflection it amended its original proposals in time for an implementation date of 1 September 2016 and published a policy statement (PS14/12).

In its response to the consultation the FCA explained that it had had experience of operators who had "exited the market" and how expensive it had been, on occasion, to transfer or realise non-standard assets in these circumstances. The result had been that members could find the value of assets in their SIPP contributing to administration costs. The practical consequence was inevitably a significant increase in the levy imposed on SIPP providers and/or a restriction on more risk-laden assets.

The restriction on assets is intended to allow choice, but to offer incentives by way of a reduced capital adequacy requirement for SIPP business that restricts investment to a "standard asset list". This will inevitably affect the range of options made available to members as providers contain capital adequacy requirements, but has nothing to do with HMRC regulatory restrictions.

The main points from the FCA's response are:

- Assets under administration (AUA) will continue to be the "primary metric" for calculating capital requirements despite its drawbacks (because there is no practical alternative). However, the constant used in the Initial Capital Requirement (ICR) calculation will vary according to the size of AUA to reduce the disproportionate impact of the calculation on smaller firms. The FCA would expect the same measure to be used for client valuations as for capital requirements.

- The AUA will be taken to be the average value of personal pension plans at the last four quarter-ends.
- The fixed minimum capital requirement will increase from £5,000 to £20,000.
- A capital surcharge will continue to be central to the new framework. The surcharge reflects the increased risk posed by non-standard assets and FCA has amended its list of non-standard assets as well as making changes to a number of other related areas (particularly to do with property). The result is that the surcharge will generally reduce slightly for small firms compared with the original consultation.
- The FCA does not see additional controls and systems as an adequate substitute for having appropriate capital (including PII) in place to allow an orderly exit from the market. It encourages firms to have a strategy in place.
- The FCA has supplemented the standard assets list with gold bullion, NS&I products, bank account deposits, units in regulated collective investments and UK commercial property (unless the property cannot be registered with the UK Land Registry). To reduce the compliance burden, valuations and asset breakdowns for discretionary fund managers need only be undertaken quarterly. There is an overriding requirement that operators should treat an asset as non-standard if they have reason to believe that disposal would take more than 30 days.
- Assets corresponding to the ICR should be realisable within one year and assets corresponding to the capital surcharge, 30 days. However, this is a backstop and the FCA would expect operators to hold a range of maturities.
- The regulatory capital test will not change from liquid capital to own funds.

The FCA recognises that there will be a significant extra cost to firms (more so if they accept non-standard assets), but believes that the costs are outweighed by the benefits of allowing an orderly exit from the market if a firm fails. Furthermore, the FCA believes that the changes will not have an appreciable impact on competition. It admits that many firms already hold capital well in excess of the requirement.

The most likely consequence of the changes, in addition to the benefits claimed by the FCA, is that more small firms will be viable under the new capital adequacy regime than would have been the case under the original proposals.

8.14 VAT and pension investments

8.14.1 VAT and SIPPs

Personal and stakeholder pension plans are most commonly issued by life assurance companies. Such companies are mainly exempt from VAT, but this means that they are able to reclaim little or no input tax. Funds may therefore be exempt from tax on income and capital gains, but unable to recover tax credits on dividends or VAT.

SIPPs are treated differently because their services are "unbundled" and typically not offered by life assurance companies. However, a succession of cases established that where there is a connection with a life assurance company, perhaps the life assurance company is an administrator, there may be an exemption from VAT.

When the SIPP is invested in property, the scheme administrator or trustees may register voluntarily in order to be able to reclaim input VAT on improvements.

8.14.2 VAT and occupational pension schemes

The standard rate of VAT in 2017-18 is 20 per cent and the registration threshold is £85,000. Most supplies made by pension funds are exempt which means that it is difficult to reclaim input tax. Where supplies are not exempt, they will most likely be subject to the standard rate, but occasionally the zero rate allowing recovery of input tax. The payment of pensions and receipt of contributions are exempt transactions.

The rules of VAT have always been difficult to apply in respect of employer-sponsored schemes which divide the responsibilities for running the scheme between employer and trustees. Guidance appears in *VAT Notice* 700/17 (November 2011) which applies to all funded occupational schemes. The *Notice* describes two activities in running such a scheme: administration is regarded as a business activity of the employer, while investment is a business activity of the pension scheme trustees. The *Notice* provides a list of administration services such as establishment, valuation and preparation of accounts in respect of which the employer may be able to recover input tax. However, VAT on fees in respect of investment activities such as brokerage and advice will not be so recoverable by the employer.

Where it is difficult or impossible to separate the investment activities from other activities and the third party issues a single invoice, the input tax will be apportioned according to an indicative norm: 70 per cent in respect of investment activities and 30 per cent in respect of administration services, though this can be varied by the taxpayer with supporting evidence or by HMRC. If separate invoices are provided, an alternative method and split may be used if it can be justified.

At present, HMRC treat pension funds as carrying on an economic activity so that VAT is recoverable. In the *Wheels Common* case it was argued that as a collective investment scheme, a defined benefit scheme should be exempt from VAT. The argument was rejected by the European Court and reported in March 2013.

The European Court of Justice case of *Fiscale Eenheid PPG Holdings BV cs te Hoogezand* (PPG) concerned an employer's entitlement to deduct VAT paid on services relating to the administration and management of a defined benefit pension scheme.

The Court decided that an employer, like PPG, that has set up a pension fund that is legally and financially separate can deduct the VAT incurred on administration and pension fund management services, provided that there is a direct and immediate link between the services and the employer's own supplies.

The Court did not answer the question of whether the scheme was a "special investment fund", and therefore exempt, as this point had already been addressed by the Court in the case *of Wheels Common Investment Fund Trustees and Others* in 2012, a case that was supported by the National Association of Pension Funds, but whose verdict has been questioned by at least one leading UK pension lawyer. The judgment in that case was that a UK defined benefit scheme could not be regarded as a special investment fund and therefore exempt from VAT.

The Court reiterated in PPG that, in order to deduct the VAT incurred on a cost, a business must establish a direct and immediate link between the supply received and the taxable supplies that the business makes. Whether there is a direct and immediate link will depend on whether the cost of the input services is incorporated in the price of the supplies made by the business.

In respect of specific costs of investment management, these will have a direct and immediate link to the supplies of the investments themselves. For example, the costs of managing a property within a pension fund will have a direct and immediate link to the rental income derived from the property. They cannot therefore be general costs of the employer. A similar analysis can be applied to the financial investments.

However, where the services received go further than the management of the investments, they may be general costs. Therefore, provided that the supply is received by the employer, the VAT incurred will potentially be deductible by the employer. As a result, HMRC have changed their policy on the recovery of input tax in relation to the management of pension funds. This means that there are circumstances where employers may be able to claim input tax in relation to pension funds where they could not previously.

However HMRC will not accept that the VAT incurred in relation to pension fund management/administration is deductible by an employer in the following circumstances where:

- the supplies were not made to the employer (this includes, but is not limited to, consideration of whether the employer has commissioned and paid for the services);
- the supply is limited to investment management services only (that is, it is not a combined supply of both investment management and pension administration services).

Additionally, where the employer receives the supply but the pension fund bears the cost of the services (whether by way of reimbursement or a set off against pension contributions), HMRC will require an equivalent amount of output VAT in respect of the amounts reimbursed to be accounted for. This amount is potentially deductible by the pension fund to the extent that it is engaged in taxable business activities.

HMRC have published further guidance in *R&C Brief* 8 (2015). It accepts the unusual nature of a defined benefit scheme where it could be said there are two recipients of supplies: the scheme and the sponsoring employer. Detailed guidance (and guidance in relation to money purchase schemes) is provided by *R&C Brief* 43 (2014) and this emphasises that the employer must contract and pay for services to be a recipient of supplies (payment of a contribution is insufficient). The guidance states:

> "Given the unique nature of these DB pension arrangements HMRC accepts that tripartite contracts can be used to demonstrate that the employer is the recipient of a supply of DB pension fund management services. An employer may therefore be able to deduct VAT incurred on these services in line with its residual recovery position where, as a minimum, the contract with the service provider evidences that:
>
> - the service provider makes its supplies to the employer (albeit that the contract may recognise that, in the particular regulatory context in which DB schemes operate, the service provider may be appointed by, or on behalf of, the pension scheme trustees)
> - the employer directly pays for the services that are supplied under the contract
> - the service provider will pursue the employer for payment and only in circumstances where the employer is unlikely to pay (for example, because it has gone into administration) will it recover its fees from the scheme's funds or the pension scheme trustees
> - both the employer and the pension scheme trustees are entitled to seek legal redress in the event of breach of contract, albeit that the liability of the service provider need not be any greater than if the contract were with the pension scheme trustees

alone and any restitution, indemnity or settlement payments for which the service provider becomes liable may be payable in whole to the pension scheme trustees for the benefit of the pension scheme (for example in circumstance where the scheme is not fully funded)

- the service provider will provide fund performance reports to the employer on request (subject to the pension scheme trustees being able to stipulate that reports are withheld, for example where there could be a conflict of interest)
- the employer is entitled to terminate the contract, although that may be subject to a condition that they should not do so without the pension scheme trustees prior written consent (this can be in addition to any right that the pension scheme trustees may have to terminate the contract unilaterally)".

On paying and recharging of costs, the 2015 guidance states:

> "For an employer to be able to deduct any VAT, it will be necessary for them to be issued with a valid VAT invoice for the full cost of the supply and to pay the service provider directly for the full cost of the services. HMRC does not accept that an equivalent increase in contributions to the fund or any payment that is made by, or through, the fund constitutes payment by the employer.
>
> If an employer recharges the net cost of those services to the pension scheme, that recharge is consideration for an onward taxable supply and VAT is due accordingly. This amount is potentially deductible by the pension scheme to the extent that the pension scheme is engaged in taxable business activities.
>
> Pension scheme trustees and employers will normally regularly review the level of contributions required by the employer into its pension fund/s to ensure those funds are able to meet the forecast pension benefit commitments. HMRC accept that if adjustments are made to these contributions, to

> take account of the fact that it is the employer rather than the fund that is paying for certain costs, that does not constitute consideration for a supply by the employer to the pension fund. This is provided that there is no specific reduction equal to the actual costs that were incurred in any given period."

Insurance-based schemes will be subject to the arrangement that the life assurance company has with HMRC. As a general rule, life assurance companies are partially exempt and can reclaim very little VAT. The consequence is that while their pension funds enjoy the usual exemptions from tax on income and capital gains, there is no such relief from the standard rate of VAT on inputs.

Some new properties or reconstructions may qualify for zero-rating, but this is only likely to affect large self-administered schemes because it is restricted to certain types of residential property, which is generally disallowed for investment by SSAS.

A corporate trustee could apply for group registration with an employer, but this would achieve little as these trustees are associated with insured executive pension schemes where the VAT liability falls on the insurance company.

Note that in *JP Morgan v HMRC Commissioners* [2007], the ECJ held that management expenses of investment trust funds are exempt from VAT. It is unclear whether the exemption extends to other pooled funds because the issue was not before the court.

The European Commission has proposed exempting pension scheme investment expenses from VAT.

Guidance: *R&C Brief* 43 (2014); *R&C Brief* 8 (2015)

8.15 Stamp duty

Stamp duty is a tax on certain written documents (not the transactions they evidence). It is chargeable at a fixed rate of £5 and payable when a trust deed is literally stamped. This is no longer a requirement and the tax is of no future relevance.

Stamp duty reserve tax is a tax collected by direct assessment and payable in respect of agreements to transfer chargeable securities to a pension fund for money or money's worth at a rate of 0.5 per cent.

There are no specific exemptions for registered pension schemes. Declarations of trust establishing schemes which invest in insurance policies are not exempted from the fixed rate of stamp duty (£5 from 1 October 1999) notwithstanding other exemptions relating to insurance policies, most notably in relation to personal pensions and retirement annuity contracts.

An *ad valorem* stamp duty land tax (SDLT) was introduced in December 2003 and is payable in respect of sale, purchase and leases of land. The rates and thresholds are as follows for non-residential land or property:

Purchase price / lease premium or transfer value (non-residential or mixed use)	SDLT rate
Up to £150,000 (annual rent < £1,000)	Nil
Up to £150,000 (annual rent £1,000+)	1%
Over £150,000 to £250,000	1%
Over £250,001 to £500,000	3%
Over £500,000	4%

Note: for the above purpose, the annual rent is the highest annual rent known to be payable in any year of the lease, not the net present value used to determine any tax payable on the rent as described below.

After 5 April 2006, *in specie* contributions will not attract relief against corporation tax or income tax. If the asset is transferred to meet the debt created by an obligation to pay the contribution, then there will be a liability to stamp duty land tax (but relief will be available against corporation tax or income tax). The same principle applies to the use of assets to pay benefits (e.g. the lump sum). An asset can only be used to satisfy a debt / financial obligation already incurred and this will generate a liability to stamp duty land tax unless paid in order to meet a prior obligation.

There is usually no *ad valorem* charge to SDLT in the case of an *in specie* transfer of accrued rights where the beneficiary (e.g. member or dependant) remains the same. The charge would simply be at a fixed rate of £0.50. However, if there is an attaching mortgage, a transfer is likely to generate a charge at the *ad valorem* rate.

9. International aspects and the lifetime allowance

9.1 Scope of international aspects

There are two circumstances in which the standard lifetime allowance may be enhanced for an individual because of the international aspects of their pension accrual. There are, of course, other international aspects to consider such as how the benefits will be taxed if the member takes benefits from a UK registered pension scheme while tax resident in an overseas jurisdiction.

9.2 Enhancing the lifetime allowance

9.2.1 Making a claim for enhancement: the two circumstances

It is for the member to make a claim to HMRC for an enhancement to the lifetime allowance in the following circumstances:

- during a period of active membership the individual has been a member of a UK registered pension scheme whilst a relevant overseas individual; or
- the member has transferred rights from a recognised overseas pension scheme to a UK registered pension scheme.

The legislative world of enhancing the lifetime allowance is not an easy one to decipher when we consider international aspects. UK tax relief is available on contributions in respect of a relevant UK individual and taxes are "clawed back" on "excessive" benefits, but while no tax relief is available on contributions from a *relevant overseas individual* (see **9.2.2** below), benefits are not restricted by the lifetime allowance. In short, if a member is eligible for UK tax relief on personal contributions, he will not be entitled to a lifetime enhancement factor as a relevant overseas individual.

The basis of allowing the enhancement is that the member has built up benefits in a UK registered scheme without attracting UK tax relief on contributions.

If the individual qualifies for a non-residence lifetime allowance enhancement, his lifetime allowance will be enhanced by a non-residence factor. This is calculated by dividing the amount of contributions to, or accrual under, the individual's pension arrangement during that part-period by the standard lifetime allowance for the tax year in which that part-period ends. As explained at PTM 095330 (and in relation to other money purchase schemes) the non-residence factor for each part of active membership during which the member is a relevant overseas individual is calculated as follows:

> "Establish the total amount of contributions made by or in respect of the individual to the other money purchase arrangement between the dates determined as follows:
>
> - the latest of the following dates:
> - the date when the individual became a relevant overseas individual
> - the date when benefits first began to accrue to or in respect of the individual under the other money purchase arrangement, and
> - 6 April 2006.
> - the earliest of the following dates:
> - immediately before the benefit crystallisation event,
> - the date when the individual ceased to be a relevant overseas individual, and
> - the date when benefits ceased to accrue to or in respect of the individual under the other money purchase arrangement.
>
> Express the resulting amount as a factor of the standard lifetime allowance as at the date under the second set of bullets above.
>
> If there was an earlier part of the active membership period relating to the arrangement during which the individual was a relevant overseas individual the two factors for the two part-periods should be aggregated."

Active membership for this purpose begins on the later of the date accrual starts and 6 April 2006.

HMRC example (at PTM 095330)

Calculating the non-residence factor for an other money purchase arrangement

Marilyn began to accrue benefits under her other money purchase arrangement on 6 January 2006. She was seconded to work overseas on 6 November 2006 and so became a relevant overseas individual on 6 April 2007.

Marilyn returned to work in the UK on 6 May 2010 and so ceased to be a relevant overseas individual on 5 April 2010. That was before a benefit crystallisation event and before she ceased to accrue benefits under the other money purchase arrangement.

The total contributions made by and in respect of Marilyn between 6 April 2007 and 5 April 2010 amounted to £175,000.

The other money purchase arrangement non-residence factor is therefore 0.1. This is calculated by dividing £175,000 by £1.75 million (the standard lifetime allowance for the 2009-2010 tax year).

£175,000/£1.75 million = 0.1

There are examples for cash balance and defined benefit schemes at PTM 095320, 095340 and 095350.

Law: FA 2004, s. 221-226
Guidance: PTM 095310, 921000

9.2.2 Relevant overseas individual

A relevant overseas individual is one who:

- has no UK taxable relevant earnings in the tax year in question;
- is not UK tax resident in the tax year;
- has not been UK tax resident at some time in the previous five tax years and when joining the scheme;
- with his spouse or civil partner has not received UK taxable general earnings from Crown employment.

This description is a mirror image of the definition of the eligibility conditions for an individual (a relevant UK individual) to be able to contribute to a UK registered scheme and qualify for tax relief.

Tax relief will be available for up to five years on contributions of the UK non-resident if the scheme operates relief at source, but relievable contributions will be limited to £3,600 and will only be relieved at UK basic rates.

Law: FA 2004, s. 221(3)
Guidance: PTM 095310

9.2.3 Secondments

An individual may be seconded overseas to work for another employer while retaining a legal contract of employment with an employer in the UK. HMRC state that they are likely to accept that the individual is "not employed by a person resident in the UK" (and so does not have relevant UK earnings) if the arrangements are such that all the employment costs of the individual (particularly pension costs) are being borne overseas. This would be the case if the costs were paid by the UK person but then recharged to the overseas employer and is because the enhancement factor is intended to determine periods of active membership of the scheme that have not benefited from UK tax relief. In this context, tax relief is both that available to the member (ignoring the £3,600) and that available to the employer.

The circumstances described above are to be distinguished from the situation where an individual is sent overseas by the UK employer to perform duties for the UK employer. Any recharge here will be a charge for work done by the UK employer for the overseas entity. The individual will be considered to be employed by a person resident in the UK so an enhancement factor will not be appropriate.

Guidance: PTM 114000

9.2.4 Deadlines for claims

The claim for enhancement must be made no later than five years after the 31 January following the end of the accrual period. The end of the accrual period is the earliest of:

- immediately before a benefit crystallisation event in relation to the individual's arrangement;
- the individual ceases to be a relevant overseas individual; and
- benefits cease to accrue to or in respect of the individual under the arrangement.

Points to note here are:

- the rule refers to accrual in respect of an arrangement, not a scheme; and
- it may be too late to wait for benefits to crystallise.

Separate notification is required for each arrangement and each period of active service overseas. After each notification, HMRC will provide a certificate showing the enhancement factor.

PTM 095320 to 095360 illustrate how the enhancement factor is calculated for each type of arrangement: cash balance, defined benefit, other money purchase and hybrid.

Law: *The Registered Pension Schemes (Enhanced Lifetime Allowance) Regulations* 2006 (SI 2006/131), reg. 7
Guidance: PTM 095300 to PTM 095600

9.2.5 Section 615 schemes

These are occupational pension schemes established in the UK under 615(6) of ICTA 1988. They must be established under trust by an employer operating wholly or partly outside the UK. Such schemes provide retirement benefits for employees working wholly outside the UK.

A section 615 scheme is exempt from many, but not all, of the regulatory provisions that apply to pension schemes in the UK. For tax purposes, it counts as neither a registered pension scheme nor an employer-financed retirement benefits scheme. Contributions are deductible for the employer.

The government proposed the abolition of new schemes in the 2016 Autumn Statement, and the closure of existing schemes to new savings. The measure was enacted as FA 2017, s. 3, effective from 6 April 2017.

9.2.6 *Taxation of non-UK registered pension schemes*

FA 2017 inserts a new Chapter 5A in FA 2004. It deals with registered pension schemes that are based outside the UK. The 2004 Act already allowed for registered schemes to be based outside the UK, requiring that the scheme administrator should be based in the European Economic Area. Until 5 April 2017, advice on these schemes was non-statutory and could be found most recently in the *Pensions Tax Manual*.

Guidance that preceded the legislation was published by HMRC on 3 January 2017. The guidance explains that with the exception of the annual allowance and taxable property provisions, the general rule is that Part 4 of FA 2004 only applies to non-UK registered pension schemes to the extent of UK-relieved funds. If the member has no relieved funds, there will be no exposure to the lifetime allowance charge and no need to provide BCE statements.

UK relieved funds include the following:

- funds that have at some stage have been held by a UK-based registered scheme; these would represent transferred rights;
- funds held at some stage for a relieved member of a relevant non-UK scheme (see **9.3.6**);
- funds that relate to accrued rights in respect of which the member has benefited from UK tax relief.

The funds will include any investment returns that can be attributed to UK relieved pension funds.

The lifetime allowance provisions (including enhancement factors) will only apply to UK-relieved funds. Non-residence factors in respect of rights held under a non-UK registered scheme are not available.

Total pension input to a non-UK registered pension scheme will be measured against the annual allowance and this will be subject to regulation.

The taxable property provisions (see **Chapter 7**) apply in full to non-UK registered pension schemes. They are not restricted to funds that are UK-relieved. This will be subject to regulation.

Law: FA 2004, s. 242A–E (as added by FA 2017, s. 9 and Sch. 3)
Guidance: *Pension Tax for Overseas Pensions* (HMRC – 3 January 2017)

9.3 Migrant member relief

9.3.1 When it applies

Migrant member relief (previously known as "corresponding relief" although the rules have changed) applies where an overseas resident takes up residence in the UK as an existing member of an overseas scheme. So, for example, the individual may work for a bank based in Paris and is a member of the bank's (French) pension scheme, but is required to work from a UK branch.

Individuals can receive UK tax relief on contributions made by them, and on contributions made in respect of them by their employer, as if the contributions to the overseas pension scheme were made to a UK registered pension scheme. Employers may claim a deduction for contributions made to an overseas pension scheme in respect of employees who are eligible for migrant member relief.

Law: FA 2004, s. 188; ITEPA 2003, s. 307, 308A
Guidance: PTM 111200

9.3.2 Annual and lifetime allowances

Lifetime allowance and annual allowance provisions will apply in respect of contributions to overseas pension schemes that have received migrant member relief.

In order for an individual to qualify for migrant member relief, a number of conditions must be met:

a. the individual must be a *relevant migrant member* (see **9.3.4** below);
b. the individual must have UK taxable relevant earnings;
c. the individual must be UK tax resident when the contributions are paid;
d. the individual must have notified the scheme administrator that he or she intends to claim migrant member relief;

e. the scheme must be a qualifying overseas scheme (as defined – see **9.3.7** below) when the contribution is paid.

Under section FA 2004, s. 189(2) the earnings referred to in condition (a) include income from self-employment. They do not include earnings that are not taxable in the UK under a double taxation agreement.

Generally speaking, an individual will be treated as UK tax resident from his date of arrival until his date of departure. So, for example, someone who works in the UK from 19 July 2011 to 16 October 2015 will receive relief on contributions made throughout that period.

The relief provisions dovetail with those applying in respect of a member of a UK registered scheme. There is no reason why an individual should not be an active member of both, but the maximum personal contribution that is relievable comprises the maximum payable to each (e.g. 100 per cent of UK taxable relevant earnings). Tax relief on a relief at source basis is unavailable to overseas schemes so tax relief must be claimed by the relevant migrant member in respect of contributions to the qualifying recognised overseas pension scheme.

9.3.3 Employer deductions

If an employer pays a contribution in respect of a member of an overseas scheme, the employer may be able to claim a deduction. The following conditions must be observed:

a. contributions must be made to a qualifying overseas pension scheme (the scheme must be a QOPS when the contribution is paid); and
b. the employee must be a relevant migrant member.

Contributions may alternatively be deductible under the provisions relating to employer-financed retirement benefit schemes (see **Chapter 12**).

Law: FA 2004, Sch. 33, para. 2
Guidance: PTM 111200

9.3.4 Migrant member

The individual is a relevant migrant member if:

a. he was not tax resident in the UK when he became a member of the scheme. In other words he was a member of the scheme before he became UK resident;
b. contributions are made to the scheme by, on behalf of, or in respect of the individual during a period of UK tax residence which began when he was a member of the scheme. In other words, he did not leave the scheme and re-join when he came to the UK;
c. the individual was entitled to tax relief on contributions to the scheme in the overseas country in which he was resident immediately before coming to the UK (even though contributions may not have been made), or has been so entitled in any overseas country where he was then resident in the 10 years before he became UK tax resident; and
d. he has been notified by the scheme manager that information concerning his benefit crystallisation events will be given to HMRC.

Law: FA 2004, Sch. 33, para. 1, 4; *The Pension Schemes (Relevant Migrant Members) Regulations* 2006 (SI 2006/212); *The Registered Pension Schemes (Extension of Migrant Member Relief) Regulations* 2006 (SI 2006/1957)
Guidance: PTM 111200

9.3.5 Migrant member relief – what is an overseas scheme?

For a scheme to be an overseas scheme it must be a pension scheme (as we describe in **Chapter 1**) that is established outside the UK and is not a registered pension scheme (see **9.4.2**). The scheme need not be restricted to providing the benefits required of a registered pension scheme.

Normally, a scheme will be treated as established in the country where its registered office and main administration is or, if there is no registered office, where its main administration is. The scheme's location of main administration is where the scheme's decisions are made. In the case of a trust-based scheme, that would normally be determined by reference to where the scheme trustees are resident.

It must also meet the following conditions:

- It must be regulated as a pension scheme in the country or territory in which it is established or, if there is no body by which it could be so regulated, then certain conditions must be met. It can be an occupational pension scheme (including a public sector scheme), a personal pension scheme or a social security scheme. A scheme is regulated in a country or territory if it is subject there to supervision by the national authorities that are responsible for ensuring that pension schemes are administered soundly in order to protect members' interests.
- It must be recognised for tax purposes by the country or territory in which it is established, as described at **6.9.6**.

There are different (more streamlined) rules for schemes set up by an international organisation such as the United Nations.

Law: FA 2004, s. 150(7) and *The Pension Schemes (Categories of Country and Requirements for Overseas Pension Schemes and Recognised Overseas Pension Schemes) Regulations* 2006 (SI 2006/206)
Guidance: PTM 111400

9.3.6 Relevant non-UK schemes and pension flexibility

It could be said that there is far too much jargon and terminology in respect of overseas aspects of pension planning. The legislation that introduced "pension flexibility" in 2014 refers to "relevant non-UK schemes" as a generic term. To quote the legislation:

"A scheme is a relevant non-UK scheme if:

(a) relief from tax has been given in respect of contributions paid under the scheme by virtue of Schedule 33 (overseas pension schemes: migrant member relief),

(b) relief from tax has been so given at any time after 5th April 2006 under double tax arrangements,

(c) a member of the scheme has been, or members of the scheme have been, exempt from liability to tax by virtue of section 307 of ITEPA 2003 (exemption for provision made by employer for retirement or death benefit) in respect of provision made under the scheme at any time after 5th April 2006 when the scheme was an overseas pension scheme, or

(d) there has been a relevant transfer at any time after 5th April 2006 when the scheme was a qualifying recognised overseas pension scheme."

Most of the terms used in this definition are described elsewhere in this chapter.

ToPA 2014 provides that the tax charges that apply when a member withdraws an uncrystallised funds pension lump sum from a relevant non-UK scheme shall be the same as if the lump sum had been taken from a registered pension scheme.

A payment from a relevant non-UK scheme may be taxed as a withdrawal if tax is due, but cannot immediately be collected in the UK because of a double taxation agreement, but where overseas tax has been collected from a withdrawal it will be set off against the UK liability.

From 6 April 2017, tax charges under FA 2004, Sch. 34 will apply to payments referable to a member's ring-fenced transfer fund (the equivalent of a relevant transfer fund prior to 6 April 2017). Sch. 34 no longer applies once the UK-relieved and transfer funds have been exhausted. Similarly, if the scheme is an employer-financed retirement benefit scheme, it will be taxed under EFRBS provisions when these funds have been exhausted.

From 6 April 2017, the time limit during which the member payment provisions apply is extended to 10 years from when the member was last UK resident.

The money purchase annual allowance may apply where an individual is, or has been, a currently-relieved member of a currently-relieved non-UK pension scheme and flexibly accesses pension rights under that non-UK pension scheme. Where benefits are flexibly accessed part-way through a tax year, the appropriate fraction applied to the allowance is the same as for a registered scheme.

The *Taxation of Pensions Act* extends regulation-making powers in respect of the annual and lifetime allowances (that apply to registered schemes) to non-UK schemes. The Act also requires any payment of uncrystallised funds pension lump sum from a non-UK scheme to be taken into account as a BCE 6, but the value of any prior BCE 8 or pension commencement lump sum (also BCE 6) is to be disregarded in these circumstances.

Law: FA 2004, s. 242 (amended by FA 2017, s. 1), Sch. 34, para. 1(5); ToPA 2014

9.3.7 What is a QOPS?

A QOPS must be an overseas scheme (as described at **9.4.2** below) and must not have been excluded from being a qualifying recognised overseas pension scheme (QROPS). The scheme manager must also meet three conditions:

- the manager must have notified HMRC that it is an overseas pension scheme and, if required, have provided supporting documentation. If documentation is required HMRC would normally ask for a copy of the letter of tax approval or a letter from the tax authority confirming that status. But if the country in which the scheme is established does not have a system of tax approval then a letter from the tax authority confirming that the scheme is resident there, and a copy of the scheme's rules, may be required instead;
- the manager must have undertaken to notify HMRC if it ceases to be an overseas pension scheme; and
- the manager must have undertaken to provide to HMRC, by 31 January next following the end of the tax year in which the benefit crystallisation event occurs, the following information:
    1. the name and address of any relevant migrant member in respect of whom there has been a benefit crystallisation event in the tax year;
    2. the date, amount and nature of the benefit crystallisation event.

ToPA 2014 introduced a new requirement that a scheme manager must provide an undertaking to HMRC to comply with any prescribed benefit crystallisation information requirements. "Benefit crystallisation information requirements" includes prescribed information requirements relating to when an individual first flexibly accesses his pension rights. This is in order to trigger the money purchase annual allowance.

Law: FA 2004, Sch. 33, para. 5

9.4 What is a qualifying recognised overseas pension scheme?

9.4.1 The four main conditions of a QROPS

In order to be able to transfer benefits from a UK registered pension scheme to an overseas scheme without the payment being treated as an unauthorised payment, the receiving scheme must be a "qualifying recognised overseas pension scheme" (QROPS).

A QOPS will not necessarily be a QROPS, but a QROPS will be capable of qualifying as a QOPS. HMRC maintain an updated list of QROPS on their website, but the list is not exhaustive as schemes may choose not to be represented on the list.

A transfer of rights from a UK registered pension scheme to a QROPS is a BCE 8 and any lifetime allowance charge that may arise is charged at a rate of 25%.

The rules regarding QROPS are designed to strike a balance between freedom of cross-border movement (especially within the EU) and anti-avoidance.

HMRC tell us that to be a QROPS, a scheme must meet "four incremental definitions", as follows:

- it must be a pension scheme;
- it must be an overseas pension scheme (as defined);
- it must be a recognised overseas pension scheme (ROPS – as defined);
- the recognised overseas pension scheme must then become a qualifying recognised overseas pension scheme (this "elevation" being primarily dependent on reporting requirements).

The *Taxation of Pensions Act* 2014 was notable for introducing "pension flexibility" (as it was called) to registered pension schemes as well as a significant change in the way tax legislation dealt with death benefits. Less publicised were the parallel measures in respect of certain overseas schemes (particularly QROPS) and non-registered schemes. The 2014 legislation in respect of QROPS was partly enabling, but its theme was to tax flexible benefits as if they were deriving from a registered scheme and also to apply anti-avoidance restrictions and appropriate information requirements.

Law: FA 2004, s. 150, 169
Guidance: PTM 112000

9.4.2 Overseas pension scheme

To be an overseas pension scheme, the scheme must be established outside the UK (and must not be a registered pension scheme). It may be a scheme established by an international organisation. Schemes established by an international organisation outside the UK will be overseas pension schemes. An international organisation is defined by legislation and includes, for example, the UN and the EU.

From 6 April 2017 the requirements of an overseas pension scheme that is not set up by an international organisation are amended.

Of more common relevance, an overseas pension scheme may be a personal pension scheme or an occupational pension scheme that meets two main conditions: the "regulatory requirements test" and the "tax recognition test". Overseas public service schemes (set up to provide benefits for employees based in the overseas territory) do not have to meet the regulatory requirements test (below).

The regulatory requirements test

Until 5 April 2017, this test was met if the scheme satisfied one of three conditions:

1. it was an occupational scheme and was established in a country that regulated pension schemes and the scheme was so regulated; or
2. the scheme was not an occupational scheme, but was established in a country that regulated pension schemes and the scheme was so regulated; or
3. there was no regulator and the scheme was established in the EU, Iceland, Liechtenstein or Norway. The rules must

have required 70 per cent of the member's tax-relieved funds to have been allocated to providing an income for life no earlier than 55 (or earlier if the member had to have stopped working because of ill health).

From 6 April 2017, there are two changes to these requirements. The first distinguishes between occupational schemes and other schemes such as personal pension schemes, and the second abolishes the "70% rule".

For occupational schemes, if there is a regulator in the country in which the scheme is established, then it must be regulated by that regulatory authority. If there is no such regulator, the scheme will pass the test.

Similarly, if the scheme is not an occupational scheme and there is a relevant regulator, the scheme must be regulated by that authority. However, if there is no regulator, then to pass the regulatory requirements test, the scheme must have been established in the EU, Norway, Liechtenstein or Iceland. The non-occupational scheme may also pass the test if there is a financial services regulator (rather than a pensions regulator) that regulates the provider in the setting up and running of pension schemes and the scheme is regulated by that regulator.

The tax recognition tests

There is no change to the tax recognition tests from 6 April 2017 and they continue to apply to overseas public service schemes.

There are three tax recognition tests, all of which must be met:

1. The scheme must be open to residents of the country in which the scheme is established.
2. In the country of establishment, there is a system of taxation of personal income tax under which tax relief is available on pensions and one of three tests is met:
    - tax relief is not available to the member on his own contributions or, if he is an employee, by his employer (in respect of earnings to which benefits under the scheme relate),

- the scheme is liable to taxation on its income and gains, and is a complying superannuation plan as defined in s. 995-1 (definitions) of the *Income Tax Assessment Act* 1997 of Australia, or
- all or most of the benefits paid by the scheme to members who are not in serious ill-health are subject to taxation.

3. This requires that the scheme is approved or recognised by, or registered with, the relevant tax authorities – as a pension scheme in the country or territory in which it is established.

Law: FA 2004, s. 150(1), (7) *The Pension Schemes (Categories of Country and Requirements for Overseas Pension Schemes and Recognised Overseas Pension Schemes) Regulations* 2006 (SI 2006/206) as amended by *The Registered Pension Schemes and Overseas Pension Schemes (Miscellaneous Amendments) Regulations* 2012 (SI 2012/884) and by *The Pension Schemes (Categories of Country and Requirements for Overseas Pension Schemes and Recognised Overseas Pension Schemes) Regulations* 2017 (SI 2017/398)

Guidance: PTM 112200

9.4.3 Recognised overseas scheme

In order for a scheme to be a qualifying recognised overseas pension scheme (QROPS – see **6.9.7**) it must meet the requirements of a recognised overseas pension scheme (ROPS). A ROPS is a scheme that is an overseas pension scheme (above) that meets certain additional requirements.

Those additional requirements were amended by regulation with effect from 6 April 2017. Those additional requirements are as follows:

Residence requirement

Where tax relief in respect of benefits paid from the scheme is available to a member of the scheme who is not resident in the country or territory in which the scheme is established, the same or substantially the same tax relief must:

- also be available to members of the scheme who are resident in the country or territory; and

- apply regardless of whether the member was resident in the country or territory:
    - when the member joined the scheme; or
    - for any period of time when he or she was a member of the scheme.

Transfer funds requirement

The benefits payable to the member under the scheme, to the extent that they consist of the member's relevant transfer fund or ring-fenced transfer funds:

- are payable no earlier than they would be if pension rule 1 in section 165 applied; or
- if payable earlier, are only payable in circumstances in which they would be authorised member payments if they were made by a registered pension scheme.

This is known as the pension age test.

Until 5 April 2017, a recognised overseas pension scheme was an overseas pension scheme that met the benefits tax relief test, the pension age test and one or more other requirements. The benefits relief test required that tax relief:

- was also be available to members of the scheme who were resident in the country or territory; and
- would apply regardless of whether the member was resident in the country or territory:
    - when he joined the scheme; or
    - for any period of time when he was a member of the scheme.

Overseas public service pension schemes, and schemes set up by international organisations, did not have to meet the benefits tax relief test or the pension age test.

To be a recognised overseas pension scheme, unless the scheme was established by an international organisation or was a public service pension scheme, the following tests (reproduced from PTM 112300) had to be met:

> ***The benefits tax relief test***
>
> This required that where tax relief in respect of benefits paid from the overseas pension scheme was available to members of the scheme who were not resident in the country or territory in which the scheme was established, the same or substantially the same tax relief must:
>
> - also have been available to members of the scheme who were resident in the country or territory; and
> - have applied regardless of whether the member was resident in the country or territory:
>   - when the member joined the scheme; or
>   - for any period of time when they were a member of the scheme.
>
> ***The pension age test***
>
> There is a change to the pension age test from 6 April 2017.
>
> This test sets the earliest age from which benefits can be paid to the member. It applies to any QROPS and any member of a QROPS who takes benefits on or after 6 April 2015. Benefits payable to the member, to the extent that they relate to the transfer, must not be payable earlier than normal minimum pension age unless the member is retiring due to ill-health or the lump sum would be payable under the lump sum rule if derived from a registered pension scheme.
>
> The obligation may be met by a scheme rule or the legislation of the country.
>
> If the scheme rules do not contain the required restriction, and the scheme is not prohibited by the law of the country in which the scheme is established from paying benefits before normal minimum pension age, the scheme cannot be a ROPS and so cannot be a QROPS.

Other requirements

To be a ROPS, the overseas scheme must have met one of the tests below (reproduced from PTM 112300).

"Test 1

This is a test of location / scheme type. At least one of the following bullet points must be satisfied:

- the scheme must be established in a Member State of the European Union, Norway, Liechtenstein or Iceland, or
- the scheme must be established in a country or territory, other than New Zealand, with which the UK has a Double Taxation Agreement that contains exchange of information and non-discrimination provisions, or
- the scheme must satisfy the requirement that, at the time of the recognised transfer in, the transfer is made to a pension scheme which is a KiwiSaver scheme as defined in section 4(1)(interpretation) of the *KiwiSaver Act* 2006 of New Zealand.

Test 2

This test requires that, at the time of the recognised transfer into the overseas pension scheme, all three of the following sub-requirements are met:

- the rules of the scheme are such that the pension benefits (and any associated lump sum) payable to the member under the scheme, to the extent that they relate to the transfer, are payable no earlier than normal minimum pension age or earlier retirement on grounds of ill-health,
- the rules of the scheme are such that membership of the scheme is open to persons resident in the country or territory in which it is established, and
- if the scheme is established in Guernsey and is an exempt pension contract or an exempt pension trust

under s. 157E of the *Income Tax (Guernsey) Law* 1975, then the scheme must not be open to non-residents of Guernsey."

9.4.4 ROPS to QROPS

In order for a ROPS to be a QROPS, certain steps must be taken and further conditions met.

The scheme manager is the person (or the persons) administering or responsible for the management of the ROPS. The scheme manager of the ROPS must:

- notify HMRC:
    - that the scheme is a ROPS, and
    - state in which country or territory the scheme is established;
- provide such evidence as HMRC may require to show that the scheme is indeed a ROPS (which may include supplying a copy of the scheme rules); and
- undertake to:
    - inform HMRC if the scheme ever ceases to be a ROPS, and
    - comply with any prescribed information requirements that fall on the scheme manager, including answering information notices and providing HMRC with certain information on payments made in respect of certain scheme members.

The initial requirements are set out in the APSS251 form, which collects information and undertakings, as well as providing information on when supporting details need to be supplied. If further evidence or information is required on receipt of the APSS251, HMRC will write to the scheme manager.

Law: FA 2004, s. 169
Guidance: PTM 112100

9.4.5 The effect of QROPS status and loss of status

QROPS status does not confer an overseas pension scheme with the same combination of UK tax exemptions that a registered pension scheme enjoys. In particular, it does not affect the pension scheme's liability to UK tax on any income it has from UK property.

If a QROPS invests in an unauthorised unit trust, any gains accruing to that unit trust remain chargeable if the overseas scheme is exempt from capital gains tax or corporation tax on such gains only by reason of its residence.

QROPS status does not directly affect every aspect of the pension scheme and is principally of relevance to the transfer of UK tax-relieved pension savings and to the treatment of payments from such schemes. For example, there is no change to the UK tax treatment of any pension income from a QROPS – this is treated in the same way as a pension from any other pension scheme outside of the UK.

If a scheme that is a QROPS stops being a QROPS, whether voluntarily or otherwise, it can no longer receive a recognised transfer under FA 2004, s. 169.

Existing members of such a pension scheme at the time of loss of status are not prevented by the tax rules from continuing as members of the ongoing scheme. They may receive benefits that were due under the QROPS from the sums that had transferred in from the originating RPS when the scheme was a QROPS, in the same way as they would if QROPS status had continued. The loss of status will not of itself incur member payment charges.

Guidance: RPSM 13104050

9.4.6 Qualifying recognised overseas pension scheme – transfers

In order to be a *recognised transfer* and therefore an authorised payment, the scheme must also be *qualifying* to accept a transfer value from a UK registered pension scheme. To be qualifying, the receiving scheme must undertake to provide specified information to HMRC (and any further information HMRC may request).

HMRC maintain and publish a list of QROPS. However, the member and scheme administrator have a general obligation to check if a scheme is recognised as being a QROPS by HMRC. The list only reflects that the administrator has declared that the scheme meets the requirements of a QROPS and HMRC may subsequently override this. Alternatively, some schemes may request that they do not appear on the list and HMRC must respect the confidentiality of the scheme. If the transferring administrator has acted diligently and in good faith, but turns out not to have met the requirements, HMRC may waive the scheme sanction charge.

HMRC may withdraw QROPS status because of failure to provide information. In those circumstances, any future transfers to the scheme from registered pension schemes will be unauthorised payments, but the scheme may continue as an overseas or recognised overseas pension scheme and benefits accrued may be paid in the normal way. There are no unauthorised payment charges for losing "qualifying" status.

The scheme manager of a QROPS that receives a transfer from another overseas pension scheme must check whether or not the transferring member has a UK tax-relieved fund or a relevant transfer fund included in the transfer. This is in order to establish if the receiving QROPS may have to provide information to HMRC about payments that may yet be made out of the receiving QROPS. The scheme manager should ask the individual to declare whether or not the transferred funds include any amounts that have received UK tax relief or have originated in a UK registered pension scheme. If so, more detailed information will need to be obtained by the QROPS scheme manager to establish if the individual will have a relevant transfer fund in their receiving scheme. The important point here is that a further onward transfer does not "shake off" HMRC interest.

As an anti-avoidance provision, the reduced money purchase annual allowance will be triggered if a flexible pension payment (such as an uncrystallised funds pension lump sum or flexi-access drawdown payment) is taken from an arrangement that is or has been a

QROPS. This is to prevent transfers from registered schemes to a QROPS to circumvent the operation of the lower allowance.

Law: FA 2004, s. 150(1), (7); ToPA 2014; *The Pension Schemes (Categories of Country and Requirements for Overseas Pension Schemes and Recognised Overseas Pension Schemes) Regulations* 2006 (SI 2006/206) as amended by *The Registered Pension Schemes and Overseas Pension Schemes (Miscellaneous Amendments) Regulations* 2012 (SI 2012/884)
Guidance: PTM 112010-112800

9.4.7 Overseas transfer charge – FA 2017

This text relies heavily on guidance published by HMRC:

- Guidance: *Pension Tax for Overseas Pensions* (3 January 2017 version); and
- Policy Paper: *Qualifying recognised overseas pension schemes: charge on transfers* (8 March 2017):

Until 8 March 2017, recognised transfers to QROPS were tax-free within the lifetime allowance. Any excess over the lifetime allowance was subject to the lifetime allowance charge at a rate of 25%. This rule remains in place, but has been modified by the introduction of the overseas transfer charge, which is essentially aimed at minimising tax avoidance through offshore transfers from registered pension schemes.

From 9 March 2017, funds transferred to a QROPS from a registered pension scheme will be taxed at 25% unless one of the conditions below applies:

- both the member and the QROPS are resident in the same country at the date of transfer;
- the member is in one EEA country and the QROPS is resident in another EEA country at the date of the transfer;
- the QROPS is an occupational scheme sponsored by the member's employer;
- the QROPS is an overseas public service pension scheme and the member is employed by one of the employers participating in the scheme; or

- the QROPS is a pension scheme established by an international organisation and the individual is employed by that international organisation.

UK tax charges will apply to a tax-free transfer if, within five years, an individual becomes resident in another country.

UK tax will be refunded if, within five tax years of the tax charge, an exemption applies.

The scheme administrator of the transferring scheme and member are jointly and severally liable for the overseas transfer charge, which requires the administrator to deduct the charge at source. This applies to scheme managers of former QROPS that make transfers out of funds that have had UK tax relief if the scheme is a QROPS on or after 14 April 2017 and at the time the transfer to the former QROPS is received.

Payments out of funds transferred to a QROPS on or after 6 April 2017 will be subject to UK tax rules for five years after the date of transfer regardless of where the member is resident.

Law: FA 2017, Sch. 4, Pt. 2 (amending FA 2004, Pt. 4)

9.4.8 Transfers – changes in FA 2013

The conditions for transferring to QROPS were modified under the provisions of FA 2013 and supporting regulations. Section 53 of the Act enables HMRC to make regulations requiring accurate information to be provided to HMRC in certain circumstances, which are widely drawn. It includes sanctions for non-compliance (essentially loss of QROPS status) if non-compliance is significant (i.e. described in the legislation) and prejudices the collection of tax. QROPS status may also be withdrawn if there is no scheme manager.

Section 54 harmonises the reporting forms and inspection powers for QROPS with those for registered schemes. It includes a power to request documents that are 10 years old (before the notice). The provisions relate to new and existing QROPS and schemes that have ceased to be QROPS.

The consequent regulations provide much of the detail:

- Basic details of the QROPS must be re-notified to HMRC every five years, as must changes to information already provided. This measure is effective from 1 April 2015. Basic details include address and contact details of the scheme manager.

- Basic information must be provided to HMRC when the scheme makes a payment in respect of a member. This includes the scheme details and details of the relevant member including National Insurance number. This measure is part of an attempt to track transfer values that are transferred on to another scheme that is not as restricted as the QROPS.

The information to be provided by the overseas scheme to HMRC appears in the *Pension Schemes (Information Requirements – Qualifying Overseas Pension Schemes, Qualifying Recognised Overseas Pensions Schemes and Corresponding Relief) Regulations* 2006 (SI 2006/208) and *The Registered Pension Schemes and Overseas Pension Schemes (Electronic Communication of Returns and Information) Regulations* 2006 (SI 2006/570) as amended:

- the name and address of the scheme and the country or territory in which it is established;
- confirmation whether or not the scheme is regulated in the country or territory in which it is established and, if so, the name and address of the regulator and the reference number, if any, allocated by that regulator;
- in the case of a scheme falling within reg. 3(4) of the *Pension Schemes (Categories of Country and Requirements for Overseas Pension Schemes and Recognised Overseas Pension Schemes) Regulations* 2006 (70 per cent of funds to provide an income no earlier than normal minimum pension age etc.), evidence demonstrating that it fulfils the requirement set out in that paragraph; and
- any other evidence required in writing by HMRC.

When a qualifying recognised overseas pension scheme makes, or is treated under the relevant provisions as making, a payment in respect of a relevant member, it must provide to HMRC:

- the name and principal residential address of the relevant member;

- the relevant member's National Insurance number, if any; and
- the date, amount and nature of that payment.

This paragraph is subject to two qualifications:

(1) at the date of the payment more than ten years has elapsed beginning with the date on which the relevant transfer fund in respect of the relevant member came into existence; and

(2) the relevant member to whom the payment is made or treated as made is a person to whom the member payment provisions do not apply.

In the case of a payment by way of a pension the obligation applies only to the first such payment.

The information required by this paragraph must be provided:

- within 90 days beginning with the day on which the payment is made or is treated as made; or
- by such other time as may be agreed between HMRC and the scheme manager.

Where the scheme manager is a company it must provide the names and addresses of the directors of the company to HMRC if required to do so in writing, and within such time as may be specified, by HMRC.

Where there is a transfer to a qualifying recognised overseas pension scheme of sums or assets which have at any time been held for the purposes of, or representing accrued rights under, a registered pension scheme from a registered pension scheme or another qualifying recognised overseas pension scheme, the following information must be provided:

- the date of the transfer;
- the name and address of the tax authority for the scheme in the country or territory in which it is established and the reference number, if any, allocated by that tax authority;
- confirmation of the basis on which the scheme satisfies the requirements imposed by the *Pension Schemes (Categories of Country and Requirements for Overseas Pension Schemes*

and Recognised Overseas Pension Schemes) Regulations 2006, reg. 2 and 3;

- if a scheme satisfies reg. 2(2) of those Regulations solely because it fulfils the requirement in reg. 2(2)(c)(ii), or if a scheme satisfies reg. 3(1)(b) solely because it fulfils the requirement in reg. 3(4), evidence demonstrating that it fulfils the requirement set out in paragraph (2) or (4), as the case may be;
- the name, address, contact details and legal status of the scheme manager;

The information required under paragraph (1)(a) to (f) must be provided:

(a) five years after the date of the HMRC letter advising the QROPS of the reference number that had been allocated to it, and

(b) at the end of every succeeding period of five years.

The five-year requirement does not apply if the transfer reference number was reported before 1 April 2010 and less than 15 years have since elapsed.

- the name and address of any bank and details of any bank account which the scheme has used in relation to the transfer;
- details of the sums or assets transferred;
- where information is required from a scheme which is a transferee, the way that the sums or assets have been applied by the scheme;
- where the transfer is from a registered pension scheme, the name and address of that scheme;
- the name, principal residential address, date of birth and, if any, the national insurance number of the member who is connected with the sums or assets;
- where the member referred to in sub-paragraph (f) is a person to whom the member payment provisions do not apply by virtue of paragraph 2 of Schedule 34, the date that the member ceased to be resident in the United Kingdom;

- the name and address of the body that regulates the scheme and the reference number, if any, issued to the scheme by the regulator;
- the name and address of the tax authority that administers the scheme and the reference number, if any, issued to the scheme by the authority;
- evidence to show that the scheme met at the time of the transfer and continues to meet the requirements specified in regulations 2 and 3 of the *Pension Schemes (Categories of Country and Requirements for Overseas Pension Schemes and Recognised Overseas Pension Schemes) Regulations* 2006; and
- any other evidence relating to the transfer as may be required by HMRC.

This information required must be provided:

- within 90 days beginning with the day on which the requirement is notified by HMRC; or
- by such other time as may be agreed between HMRC and the scheme manager.

A pension scheme which ceases to be a qualifying recognised overseas pension scheme must, within 30 days beginning with the day on which the cessation takes place ("the cessation date"), provide to HMRC:

- the value at the cessation date of the relevant transferred sums or assets pertaining to each relevant transfer fund under the scheme; and
- the name, principal residential address, date of birth and, if any, the National Insurance number of each member in respect of whom there is a relevant transfer fund under the scheme at the cessation date.

For the purposes of s. 169(4), if at any time after a pension scheme has provided HMRC with information in accordance with the above it becomes apparent to the scheme that:

- there is a material change affecting that information; or
- the information is incomplete or contains a material inaccuracy,

the scheme must – within 30 days of the change becoming apparent or an alternative period agreed with HMRC – provide to HMRC details of the change, the complete information or correction of the inaccuracy.

No obligation arises in respect of a former QROPS if at the time the relevant obligation arises:

(i) more than ten years have elapsed beginning with the date on which the relevant transfer fund in respect of the relevant member came into existence; and

(ii) the relevant member to whom the payment is made or treated as made is a person to whom the member payment provisions do not apply; or

(iii) there is no relevant transfer fund.

When a QROPS or former QROPS makes, or is treated under the relevant provisions as making a payment in respect of a relevant member, the scheme manager of the QROPS or former QROPS must provide to HMRC:

(a) the name, principal residential address, date of birth, contact details, the National Insurance number or, if he does not have one, the tax identification number, if any, of the relevant member, and if the relevant member has ceased to be resident for tax purposes in the UK, the date that residence ceased;

(b) the name, address and contact details of the QROPS or former QROPS and of the scheme manager;

(c) the date, amount and nature of the payment and if as a result of the payment no relevant transfer fund remains, a statement to that effect;

(d) if the payment is made to a pension scheme, the name and address of the recipient and, if the recipient is a registered pension scheme or a QROPS, the reference number allocated to that pension scheme by HMRC;

(e) where the relevant member has died and the payment is made to an individual, the name, principal residential address, date of birth and the National Insurance number or, if he does not have one, the tax identification number, if any, of that individual; and

(f) where the relevant member has died and the payment is made to a person who is not an individual, the name and address of that person.

An amendment included in *The Registered Pensions Schemes (Provision of Information) (Amendment) Regulations* 2013 (SI 2013/1742) requires individuals who are not UK resident and want to transfer their UK pension savings overseas to notify their UK scheme administrator of the date they ceased to be UK resident. The scheme administrator will then have to report that information to HMRC.

FA 2013 and regulations change the period in which HMRC can demand documents under an information notice from six to ten years.

Regulations introduced in 2015 require the QROPS or member to meet the information requirements of a registered pension scheme when the member opts for flexi-access drawdown. This includes providing information within 91 days of a "trigger event" in order to ensure the operation of the money purchase annual allowance.

Law: *The Registered Pensions Schemes and Overseas Pensions Schemes (Miscellaneous Amendments) Regulations* 2013 (SI 2013/2259); *The Overseas Pension Schemes (Miscellaneous Amendments) Regulations* 2015 (SI 2015/673)

Failure to comply

A scheme may be excluded from being a qualifying recognised overseas pension scheme if HMRC decide that there has been a significant failure to comply with the information reporting requirements set out at and that, as a consequence, it is inappropriate for tax relief to be given on contributions to the qualifying overseas pension scheme.

A failure will be significant if, for example, a substantial amount of information has not been provided or if the failure to provide any information is likely to result in serious prejudice to the assessment or collection of tax. Any contributions made to the scheme after the date on which it ceases to be a qualifying overseas pension scheme will not receive tax relief.

Loss of QROPS status has most often been reported in the context of transfers from UK registered pension schemes (although it remains unusual). Those cases suggest that status has been withdrawn because of lack of reporting under the regulations and because membership of the scheme was not available in fact to local residents.

The cases of status withdrawal and the tightening of requirements by regulation suggest that HMRC will only tolerate genuine overseas schemes for migrant members and for those who wish to move abroad. HMRC's patience has undoubtedly been tested by schemes set up under the direction of UK based companies solely to transfer rights offshore and which in the past have depended to some degree on lack of HMRC oversight.

Law: FA 2004, s. 150(7), Sch. 33, para. 5(1); FA 2013, s. 53, 54; *The Pension Schemes (Category of Country and Requirements for Overseas Pension Schemes) Regulations* 2006 (SI 2006/206); *The Pension Schemes (Application of UK Provisions to Relevant Non-UK Schemes) Regulations* 2006 (SI 2006/207); *The Pension Schemes (Information Requirements – Qualifying Recognised Overseas Pension Schemes and Corresponding Relief) Regulations* 2006 (SI 2006/208); *The Pension Schemes (Categories of Country and Requirements for Overseas Schemes and Recognised Overseas Schemes) (Amendment) Regulations* 2007 (SI 2007/1600); *The Registered Pension Schemes and Overseas Pension Schemes (Miscellaneous Amendments) Regulations* 2012 (SI 2012/884); *The Pension Schemes (Categories of Country and Requirements for Overseas Pension Schemes and Recognised Overseas Pensions Schemes)(Amendment) Regulations* 2012 (SI 2012/1221); *The Registered Pensions Schemes and Overseas Pension Schemes (Miscellaneous Amendments) Regulations* 2013 (SI 2013/2259)

Guidance: PTM 112010-112800

9.5 Qualifying non-UK pension schemes (QNUPS)

The *Inheritance Tax (Qualifying Non-UK Pension Schemes) Regulations* 2010 (SI 2010/51) exempt qualifying non-UK schemes (QNUPS) from inheritance tax. The definition of QNUPS is similar to that of QROPS except that:

- there is no requirement for a double taxation agreement to exist with the provider's territory if it is outside the European Economic Area; and
- there is no need for the scheme to make the declaration to HMRC required of a QROPS to keep HMRC informed of its status. So, the QNUPS closely resembles a registered overseas pensions scheme: all QROPS will qualify as QNUPS, but not all QNUPS will qualify as QROPS.

The attraction is that transfer from a UK scheme to a qualifying recognised overseas scheme is a benefit crystallisation event, but is an authorised payment. It will also fall outside the estate for inheritance tax purposes. A qualifying non-UK pension scheme (QNUPS) falls outside the estate for IHT purposes, but transfer from a UK registered scheme to a QNUPS is an unauthorised payment. Broadly speaking, inheritance tax is chargeable on worldwide assets less liabilities of an individual who is UK domiciled, and chargeable on UK assets of somebody who is overseas domiciled. QNUPS are therefore attractive if an individual is UK resident and overseas domiciled, or overseas resident and UK domiciled.

Recent HMRC statements and enhanced legislation and proposed legislation cast doubt on whether the transfer from QROPS to QNUPS can be successful subject to the practical sanctions available to HMRC if an individual moves abroad permanently. QNUPS should be seen primarily as a means of accruing benefits rather than as a vehicle for tax-efficient transfers from UK registered pension schemes.

However, HMRC have clarified that there is no time limit on unauthorised payment charges arising in respect of taxable property and this is reinforced by the proposed new legislation. In any case, the scheme may be wary of provoking HMRC and being removed from QROPS status.

At all times, care should be taken to consider the investment aspects, overseas tax aspects and the cost of the exercise. The member will also wish to consider how well protected are the arrangements in the new country of residence.

9.6 Double taxation agreements and tax relief

9.6.1 *Introduction*

The UK has a number of bilateral double taxation agreements or treaties with other countries. The objective of such an agreement is primarily to prevent an individual paying tax twice on the same income or transaction. Some of the agreements include provisions, usually in the pensions article, that provide relief from UK tax on contributions made to a pension scheme that is tax-recognised in the other country by, or in respect of, a member who comes to work here.

Although such provisions tend to be broadly similar, the particular conditions that have to be met to qualify for relief on pension contributions can vary from agreement to agreement. The text of each agreement is contained in a statutory instrument that – together with ICTA 1988, s. 788, TIOPA 2010, s. 5(2), and FA 2006, s. 173 – gives it the force of law. Information about particular agreements appears in statutory instruments and on the HMRC website (go to *Tax Treaties in Force*).

Generally, agreements containing such provisions enable individuals to receive UK tax relief on contributions made by them, and on contributions made on their behalf by their employer, as if the contributions to the overseas pension scheme were made to a UK registered pension scheme. Agreements may also provide for employers to claim a deduction for contributions made to an overseas pension scheme in respect of eligible employees.

The lifetime allowance and annual allowance provisions will apply in respect of contributions made to overseas pension schemes after 5 April 2006 that have received tax relief under a double taxation agreement or treaty. Member payment charges can also apply to certain payments from overseas schemes to UK tax resident (and recently tax resident) individuals out of funds relating to contributions made after 5 April 2006 that have received tax relief under a double taxation agreement.

If contributions made to an overseas pension scheme by an individual or an employer after 5 April 2006 do not qualify for tax relief under a double taxation agreement they may receive migrant member relief or transitional corresponding relief instead if the relevant conditions are met

Relief for individuals on contributions to an overseas pension scheme under a double taxation agreement is generally given on the same basis as on contributions to a UK registered pension scheme.

If the conditions for UK tax relief specified in a particular double taxation agreement are met, a member of an overseas pension scheme is entitled to relief on the contributions he makes to that scheme. Relief on personal contributions to the UK scheme or the overseas scheme or a combination of both is restricted by the annual limit for relief: the greater of £3,600 and 100 per cent of UK taxable relevant earnings in the tax year of payment.

Like migrant member relief, the relief at source option of claiming tax relief on contributions is unavailable.

Employees will not be liable to income tax on contributions made to an overseas pension scheme on their behalf by their employer. Some double taxation agreements will allow UK employer contributions to an overseas pension scheme to be treated as a deduction against profits for tax purposes.

Law: FA 2004, Sch. 34
Guidance: PTM 113000

9.6.2 FATCA – US agreement

The *Foreign Account Tax Compliance Act* is a piece of US legislation designed to prevent US taxpayers from evading tax by the use of foreign bank accounts and investments. The Act requires US persons to report financial accounts they hold outside the United States and for foreign institutions to report to the Internal Revenue Service about their account holders and investors. The basis of this requirement is that, unlike many countries, the United States taxes citizens rather than residents.

Some countries have refused to endorse US demands under the Act, but the UK has complied and agreed that the authorities will collect and pass on information under an inter-governmental agreement.

From 1 July 2014, where a non-US financial institution fails to comply with the registration and reporting requirements, any investment income made to it from the US will normally be subject to an additional 30% withholding tax. A non-US financial institution may include a funded pension scheme.

UK registered pension schemes are effectively exempted from the registration and reporting requirements to be established by HMRC. However, they will need to provide evidence of their exempt status to any payer of income sourced in the US. This will take the form of the trustee or scheme manager filing a completed form (W-8BEN-E) with its investment managers and/or custodian or, where the scheme invests directly into US stocks and bonds, with that US payer.

9.7 Tax charges and non-UK schemes

Not surprisingly, those overseas schemes that enjoy tax reliefs similar to those that apply to UK registered schemes will in principle attract the tax charges that apply to UK registered schemes, and in similar circumstances. The charges will only extend to funds derived from UK tax relieved contributions. The most significant of the charges are the annual allowance charge and the lifetime allowance charge.

The annual allowance charge applies to an individual who is a currently-relieved member of a currently-relieved non-UK pension scheme as if the scheme were a registered pension scheme.

A pension scheme is a currently-relieved non-UK pension scheme in relation to a tax year if it is not a registered pension scheme and if one or both of the following conditions is met:

a. relief from UK tax is given in respect of individual or employer contributions paid to it during the tax year. That includes contributions that have received migrant member relief and employer contributions in respect of which an employee is tax exempt. It also includes contributions that have received transitional corresponding relief. The contributions must have been made after 5 April 2006.
b. any of its members has been exempt from liability to tax in respect of provision for retirement or death benefits made by his or her employer at any time during the tax year when it is an overseas pension scheme. Such provision must have been made after 5 April 2006.

Members are exempt from tax on their accrual of benefits in the scheme as a benefit in kind. So (b) provides that the annual allowance charge provisions will apply even where no contributions have been made to the scheme during the tax year, for example because of a contributions holiday or because the scheme is unfunded.

An individual is a currently-relieved member of a currently-relieved non-UK pension scheme in relation to a tax year if:

- any of the relieved contributions mentioned at (a) were paid by or in respect of him to the scheme, or
- he is the member, or one of the members, who has been exempt from liability to tax as mentioned at (b).

The mechanics of measuring contributions to a currently-relieved non-UK pension scheme against the annual allowance are the same as for contributions to a UK registered pension scheme except that the input period will always be the UK tax year. If the annual allowance is exceeded, the member is charged at his or her marginal rates of UK income tax.

Guidance: PTM 113100, 113200

Temporary periods of non-residence

Anti-avoidance rules introduced on 6 April 2015 apply when the member is temporarily non-resident to:

- any drawdown pension paid from a flexi-access drawdown fund to a member;
- any drawdown pension paid from a flexi-access drawdown fund to a dependant;
- the taxable part of an uncrystallised funds pension lump sum;
- any withdrawals from a fund where the individual was entitled to flexible drawdown before 6 April 2015.

The rules apply to anyone who left the UK in 2013-14 or later and returned in 2015-16 or later.

The pension will be taxed when the member becomes UK resident again if the total of relevant withdrawals during the period of temporary non-residence was more than £100,000.

The rules will be the same whether payment is made from a registered pension scheme or a relevant non-UK scheme.

If a payment is made other than in sterling, it will be converted to a sterling equivalent by using the average exchange rate for the year ending 31 March for all payments in the tax year containing that 31 March.

Where the value of withdrawals exceeds £100,000 under s. 579B, all of the withdrawals are treated as taxable pension income in the period of return to the UK, not just the excess over £100,000.

Law: ToPA 2014, Sch. 1, para. 80

9.8 Lifetime allowance

The lifetime allowance charge was originally described as a "recovery" charge. Although the expression is now little used it helps to describe its application. It is applied to registered pension schemes and recovers tax reliefs in respect of benefits that exceed the lifetime allowance.

The principle is extended to members of overseas pension schemes that have enjoyed UK tax relief (a relieved member of a relieved non-UK pension scheme). Only the funds that have enjoyed UK tax relief since 6 April 2006 are measured against the lifetime allowance. This introduces the concept of the relevant relieved amount which is defined in the legislation as:

- the total pension input amounts that have arisen in relation to that scheme in each tax year after 5 April 2006 in respect of the individual; plus
- the pension input amount that would have applied if the period beginning on 6 April in the tax year in which the benefit crystallisation event occurs, and ending immediately before the benefit crystallisation event, was a full tax year.

At each benefit crystallisation event the amount crystallised is reduced by any excess over the untested portion of the relevant relieved amount in order to determine the crystallised amount to be tested against the individual's lifetime allowance. The untested portion of the relevant relieved amount is the total relevant relieved amount less all the amounts previously crystallised in respect of the individual under the relieved non-UK pension scheme.

HMRC have provided the following example.

HMRC example

Carmine has a fund value of £2 million. On 6 January 2007 he became a relieved member of a relieved non-UK pension scheme. That is the only scheme of which he is a member. His benefits crystallise on 6 July 2012, at which point he has been a relieved member of the relieved non-UK pension scheme for five and a half years. The amount crystallised is £200,000 and there have been no previous benefit crystallisation events from the scheme.

His pension input amounts for the previous six tax years (2006-2007 to 2011-2012) amount to £300,000 and his pension input amount for the period from 6 April 2012 to 6 July 2012 is £15,000. The untested portion of his relevant relieved amount at the date of the benefit crystallisation event is therefore £315,000. As the amount crystallised does not exceed his relevant relieved amount it is not reduced and so the whole of the crystallised amount of £200,000 is tested against his lifetime allowance of £1.85 million. So he is not liable to a lifetime allowance charge.

Two years later Carmine has another benefit crystallisation event. His pension input amounts for those two years were nil. The amount crystallised is £150,000. The untested portion of his relevant relieved amount is £115,000 (£315,000 less £200,000). The amount crystallised is reduced by £35,000, the excess over the untested portion of his relevant relieved amount, so only £115,000 is tested against Carmine's unused lifetime allowance. Again, he is not liable to a lifetime allowance charge.

A year later Carmine has another benefit crystallisation event. His pension input amount for that year was nil. The amount crystallised is £50,000, but no amount is tested against his lifetime allowance. That is because there is no longer any untested portion of his relevant relieved amount so the £50,000 is reduced to nil by the £50,000 excess.

A consequence of this principle is that if a member joins such an overseas scheme after 5 April 2006, enhanced protection may be lost as it there is benefit accrual to such a scheme when membership pre-dates 6 April 2006.

In normal circumstances a transfer from a UK relieved scheme to an overseas scheme will be a transfer from a UK registered pension scheme to a qualifying recognised overseas pension scheme. The transfer is an authorised payment and will trigger a BCE 8. If there is a transfer of sums or assets from a relieved non-UK pension scheme to a qualifying recognised overseas pension scheme by a relieved member this will not be a BCE 8 if it is a block transfer and there will therefore be no measurement against the lifetime allowance. A block transfer is a transfer of rights in respect of two or more members from the same scheme to the same scheme as part of the same transaction.

The lifetime allowance charge in respect of an overseas scheme will be the liability of the member: there is no joint liability of administrator and member as is the case with a registered pension scheme. The lifetime allowance charge is unaffected by relieving measures such as double taxation treaties.

As a general rule, benefits must be paid according to the same rules as apply to a registered pension scheme (the pension rules). The main exception is that a money purchase scheme that offers a scheme pension need not first offer a lifetime annuity option.

There are a number of other "modifications" to terms used in the legislation in respect of registered pension schemes to make the parallel rules adaptable to overseas schemes.

Guidance: PTM 113400

10. Death benefits and inheritance tax

Much of the content of this chapter, broadly from paragraph 10.3 onwards, has been adapted from a chapter in John Woolley's book, *Financial Planning with Trusts*, also available from Claritax Books. I am very grateful to the author for allowing me to reproduce his wording (and to adapt it where necessary to fit the context of this book).

10.1 Introduction

Inheritance tax is a tax on transfers of value on death or occasionally on lifetime transfers, especially where the transfer is part of a discretionary settlement. The fundamental basis of the charge to inheritance tax is the loss to the estate of an individual, usually on death and occasionally during his or her lifetime.

There are many allowances and exemptions. The most important are:

- potentially exempt transfers: gifts that are excluded from the deceased's estate if they survive for seven years after making the gift;
- gifts from normal expenditure: gifts that are made from income, on a regular basis, and that do not reduce the donor's standard of living, are excluded from the estate;
- allowances against the values of agricultural and business property, where the donor has a significant interest, reduce the value of the gift;
- miscellaneous small gifts of cash, for certain purposes and within certain amounts, are excluded from the estate;
- gifts between spouses or civil partners are excluded from the estate;
- the "nil rate band" refers to the bottom band of the estate value which is taxed at a rate of zero per cent. Each individual has a nil rate band (£325,000 in 2017-18), but the balance of any band not used is automatically transferred to the surviving spouse or civil partner. This situation may typically arise because the gift on the first

death is made to a surviving spouse or civil partner and is therefore exempt.

Having identified the size of the taxable estate after excluding allowances and exemptions, there are generally four rates of inheritance tax. The first rate is zero per cent and above the "nil rate band" the charge is to tax at 40 per cent. There is also a charge to tax at 20 per cent on lifetime gifts, which may be increased if death is within seven years. From 6 April 2013, if a testator gifts at least 10 per cent of the estate to charity, the rate of inheritance tax reduces to 36 per cent.

The IHT charge to tax is based not on the gain to donees but on the loss to the estate of the donor. This a difficult principle to apply to pensions where we must distinguish between pension fund assets, that are usually purchased by a trust in order to deliver rights, and the value of those rights, which involves consideration of the income payable on retirement and for how long it will be paid.

There is no charge to capital gains tax on the death of an individual and the acquisition price of the asset is "rebased" on death of the owner. This is unlikely to be relevant to pension planning.

The establishment of a trust serves four main purposes in respect of pension funds:

- it will exclude the assets from the estate for IHT purposes (although rights will remain);
- it will allow the rights to be passed to beneficiaries without waiting for the administration of the estate;
- it will allow lump sums occasioned by death to be held for the benefit of minor children until they are able to take care of their own affairs; and
- as a requirement of a funded occupational scheme, it is a practical way of keeping pension fund assets outside the control of the sponsoring employer.

Law: IHTA 1984, s. 3, 5, 8, 10

10.2 Pension schemes and IHT

10.2.1 The particular problems of pension benefits

The problem that confronts the pension adviser is that gifts with reservation are not generally regarded as gifts at all by the legislation and remain in the estate. A pension scheme seeks to provide a death benefit for successors whilst "reserving" a pension for the member. The *Inheritance Tax Act* 1984 allows some exemptions for registered pension schemes.

For people who have valuable pension plans with a reasonable investment value, trusts can play an important role in reducing the impact of potential IHT liabilities on the pension fund. Registered pension schemes enjoy reliefs from inheritance tax that might otherwise apply to discretionary trusts and transfers of value, but there are occasions when the tax might apply. Furthermore, the financial planner will wish to consider how lump sum death benefits should be treated when they have been paid.

As we considered in **Chapter 1**, all funded occupational pension schemes and some personal pension plans are established under a trust. Others are contract-based and benefits may be assigned to a trust for later distribution. Trusts are a means of preserving the value of assets for subsequent generations by moving the value of assets outside the estate.

10.2.2 "By-pass" trusts and discretionary disposal

Trusts may also help to preserve the fund for future generations by giving protection against the claims of creditors and ex-spouses of family members. It is therefore important that people with large pension funds are also appraised of the benefit of so-called "by-pass trusts". The importance of these is, however, likely to be reduced now that ToPA 2014 has reduced the application of inheritance tax (see **Chapter 5**) in favour of an income tax-based regime.

By-pass trusts allow lump sum benefits payable from pension schemes to be paid to a trust for the benefit of beneficiaries. So, they do not refer to the trust under which the pension fund has been established, rather the vehicle to which the pension arrangement may pay death benefit lump sums.

As such, the death benefit will be paid to the trust under the discretionary disposal rules. Under those rules, the member expresses a wish as to the person to whom the lump sum should be paid on his or her death, and the trustees nominate. The courts will not interfere with the discretion of the trustees, but they may wish to ensure that the exercise of the discretion has been undertaken properly.

The discretionary disposal rules do not therefore bind the trustees and, if they did, any disposal would be regarded as a gift falling within the estate.

It is axiomatic that in order for a lump sum to be payable to the by-pass trust, the trust must be included within the "list" of available beneficiaries. Most scheme rules are drafted widely enough to allow such a payment, but by no means all.

The reason the phrase "by-pass" has been attributed to these trusts is that funds are kept outside the estate of a beneficiary (particularly a surviving spouse) and so by-pass that person's estate, yet he or she still has access via the trustees to the funds representing the investment of the pension fund death benefits.

10.3 Increased HMRC interest

Due to the considerable size of some pension funds, HMRC have, over the last ten years, taken a much greater interest in the value of a deceased member's pension fund and the potential IHT that may apply.

Following the introduction of the flexi-access pension rules from 6 April 2015, the impact of IHT and other taxes on death benefits will normally be less onerous. However, there will still be occasions when IHT can be a material consideration, such as when somebody who is in serious ill-health transfers his pension benefits or declares a trust over the death benefits, or in cases where somebody exercises complete control over who receives death benefits. Furthermore, there will be ongoing future IHT considerations if a by-pass trust is established and receives death benefits.

To help them gather information on these plans, HMRC have introduced a comprehensive questionnaire (IHT 409) which acts as an appendix to the main IHT 400 death account. IHT 409 captures information on the value of pension funds on a person's death and details of any significant transactions he has made in respect of pension funds over the last two years. The notes to the IHT 409 were revised by HMRC in September 2015 and, unfortunately, these do not therefore cover the concessions announced to flexi-access drawdown benefits in the Autumn Statement in December 2015.

The IHT rules that apply to pension plans are complicated although, fortunately, the position has eased following important changes made on 6 April 2011. These changes mean that:

a. there is no longer a compulsion for a pension scheme member to buy an annuity by age 75 at the latest; and
b. an income tax charge (marginal rates) now applies to lump sum benefits paid on the death of a member with uncrystallised benefits who is aged 75 or over. If the lump sum is paid to a trust that is not a bare trust, or to a company, a partnership or a limited liability partnership (i.e. paid to a non-qualifying person) the lump sum will be subject to the special lump sum death benefit charge at a rate of 45%. The special lump sum death benefit charge is also applicable if the lump sum is distributed to a non-qualifying person outside a two-year window: that is within two years of the scheme administrator learning of the death or, if earlier, within two years from the date on which it would have been reasonable for him to have learned of the death.

This has enabled the Government to remove the application of IHTA 1984, s. 3(3) – the omission to exercise a right rule – to pension schemes.

Law: IHTA 1984, s. 3(3), 151

10.4 The structure of a pension scheme

In general, a registered occupational pension scheme will be established by means of a trust deed and scheme rules. The trustees or scheme administrator will, scheme rules permitting, be able to pay death benefits to any person who falls within the class of discretionary beneficiaries set out in the scheme rules / trust deed – including the trustees of a separate independent trust.

A personal pension scheme can be constituted by a declaration of trust, a deed poll or a contract (arrangements established by deed poll or contract are not regarded by HMRC as having been written under a trust, but they may assigned to an individual trust). Underlying this would be scheme rules and the document evidencing the member's rights - normally a policy if the plan provider is a life office.

Typically, the person who makes the decision as to who receives the lump sum death benefits would be the scheme administrator (or scheme trustees) and they would choose to benefit the appropriate person from the list of eligible discretionary beneficiaries.

The "power to appoint" is a discretion and cannot be delegated unless the trust deed says so. In most cases, the member will be asked to express a wish as to the person to whom the death benefit should be paid, but the trustee or administrator actually nominates the beneficiary. If the member were to nominate, then exemption from inheritance tax would be withdrawn. Under the rules that apply to the National Employment Savings Trust, the member is required to nominate rather than simply express a wish.

HMRC have suggested that the form of words is not as important as what actually transpires in this context. So, if the member is asked to nominate a beneficiary, this will not trigger an exposure to IHT if the trustees retain a discretion as to the person to whom they should pay the benefit. In other words, a document will be treated as an expression of wish if the trustees retain the discretion even if it is called a nomination.

There are two downsides to this. Firstly, the scheme administrator may make a payment of death benefits to persons the member would not have wished to benefit. To a degree this objection can be overcome by the member completing the expression of wish and giving this to the scheme administrator. However, this is not binding on the scheme administrator and, whilst there is an expectation that the member's wishes will be followed, there is no guarantee.

The second downside is inheritance tax. If benefits are paid to, say, the deceased member's spouse, they will form part of his or her taxable estate even though he/she may not need the cash.

To overcome these problems, the member can declare a personal trust during his lifetime (frequently called a pilot trust) to which the trustees / scheme administrator could appoint death benefits. It would then be the trustees of that personal by-pass trust who decide who benefits, and the member can give those trustees an expression of wish setting out whom he would wish to benefit. This approach can also give opportunities for ongoing inheritance tax planning. We will look at these trusts in more detail below.

10.5 The IHT implications on pension funds

There are general and special IHT rules that apply to pension funds.

10.5.1 General IHT rules as regards an interest in a pension fund

Whilst the member is alive, even though the scheme may be subject to a discretionary trust, the fund representing the member's pension fund rights will not be subject to the IHT periodic or exit charges that generally apply to relevant property trusts (IHTA 1984, s. 58).

Under IHTA 1984, s. 151, an interest in a pension or annuity under a registered pension scheme that comes to an end on a person's death will not be taken into account in valuing the deceased's estate for IHT purposes.

The right a deceased had to take a pension commencement lump sum (PCLS) instead of a pension is not regarded as part of the deceased's estate for IHT purposes.

In Statement of Practice 10/86, HMRC confirmed that the gift with reservation rules would not apply to trusts of approved pension schemes. This means that if the effect of a trust was to hold retirement benefits for the member and death benefits for beneficiaries of a discretionary trust, no gift with reservation would arise.

HMRC have confirmed that this practice continues to apply to registered pension schemes. Moreover, the income tax pre-owned assets tax (POAT) rules do not apply to registered pension schemes because the settlor would not retain an interest under the trust for the purposes of ITTOIA 2005, s. 624(1) (see s. 627(2)(c)).

Where the payment of a pension/annuity does not cease on the death of the member (eg. where the pension has been guaranteed for a set period and the member dies before the end of that period), the value of the right to receive the remaining payments should be included as an asset of the estate for IHT purposes. For this purpose the value taken is the open market value of the outstanding annuity payments. This problem may be avoided if the continuing instalments of pension for the balance of the guarantee period can be paid at the discretion of the scheme administrator (see below).

Amounts should no longer be included in a person's taxable estate on death in respect of pension funds as a result of the IHT "omission to exercise a right" legislation. This applies equally to crystallised and uncrystallised rights (IHTA 1984, s. 12(2)).

Any death benefits payable under the plan will be treated as part of the deceased member's taxable estate if the deceased had a general power of appointment over those benefits or the deceased's estate had a right to death benefits.

IHT should no longer apply if the payment of lump sum death benefits depends on the date of death of the member. An overview of the position on this is as shown immediately below.

An IHT liability can still arise when a person who is in serious ill health pays a large contribution, declares a trust of death benefits or transfers a pension plan and does not survive that transaction by two years.

Death before age 75

Prior to 6 April 2015, if lump sum death benefits were paid by the Scheme Administrator within the relevant two-year period of a member's death, those death benefits would have been free of inheritance tax (IHTA 1984, s. 58(2A)) and income tax where death occurred prior to age 75 and the payment was made from uncrystallised funds. Following provisions introduced by ToPA 2014, the relevant two-year period requirement for IHT exemption on the payment of death benefits has been removed and so, in effect, no IHT liability will arise whenever death benefits are paid. However, if death benefits are paid outside of the relevant two-year period from uncrystallised funds and the member died under age 75, whilst there will not be an IHT charge and no test against the deceased member's remaining lifetime allowance, those benefits will be taxed under PAYE when paid out to an individual as an income or a lump sum, or as a lump sum taxed at 45% when payment is made to a trust. To avoid death benefits paid as income from being subject to income tax, the fund would need to be designated to drawdown within two years of the member's death.

Death on or after age 75

As regards payments made on the death of a member who was age 75 or more, prior to 6 April 2015, no IHT would apply (whenever the payment was made) and this remains the position post 5 April 2015. Prior to 6 April 2015, the death tax of 55% would have applied.

Whilst there is no relevant two-year period, IHT liability or test against the deceased member's remaining lifetime allowance on death of a member who has attained age 75, any death benefits paid as a lump sum or as a flexi-access drawdown pension will be taxed on the recipient under PAYE. Likewise a lump sum paid to a trust will be taxed at 45%.

It should be borne in mind that this is only an overview of the taxation issues that arise on pension death benefits.

Law: IHTA 1984, s. 58, 151; ITTOIA 2005, s. 624(1), 627(2)(c)

10.5.2 Special IHT rules in relation to pension schemes: overview

One of the tax implications that arises from the introduction of "flexible pensions" is that the death benefits payable under registered pension schemes are generally no longer subject to IHT. Of course, if a pension scheme member dies at age 75 or more, lump sum or drawdown death benefits will be subject to income tax. This also applies to benefits paid following the subsequent death of a beneficiary who has become entitled to income drawdown death benefits following the death of the pension scheme member.

Despite this, there are still three other situations in which inheritance tax may be relevant to registered pension schemes:

- if a person makes substantial contributions to a pension scheme;

- if a pension scheme member declares a personal integrated trust over death benefits under a plan; and
- if a pension scheme member transfers his pension plan to another pension provider.

However, in all of these cases, HMRC will usually treat the transfer of value that arises as being of negligible value. This is on the basis that the pension scheme member will eventually vest the benefits under the plan and use those benefits for his own purposes. Consequently, the benefit arising to others is small as will be the loss to the individual's estate. The one exception to this is in cases where the individual is in serious ill health and unlikely to live long enough to draw benefits. In those cases, there will be an actuarial measurable loss to the estate which could result in a transfer of value for IHT purposes under IHTA 1984, s. 3(1).

To help taxpayers, HMRC adopt a rule of thumb for these purposes that says that they will only treat a transfer of value as possibly arising if the individual makes the transfer when he or she is in serious ill health and dies within two years. In such circumstances, a return will need to be made in boxes 17-21 of IHT 409. This is the pension supplement to the IHT 400 (the IHT return on death).

This whole area has become very much more relevant to pension transfers due to the introduction of flexible pensions and the need that people sometimes have to transfer their plans to other pension providers to access such flexibility.

10.5.3 Special IHT rules: contributions

Normally when a person makes a pension contribution, the prime intention will be to enhance their retirement provision. Therefore, even though death benefits are subject to a discretionary trust, the actuarial likelihood of him dying before retirement is remote and so any transfer of value that arises when the contribution is paid will be negligible.

However, the situation changes if, when the contribution was paid, the member knew he was in serious ill heath. In such cases, there will be a measurable loss to the estate. In these circumstances HMRC adopt a "two-year test". This means that, in general, they will only consider such cases as possibly giving rise to a transfer of value if the member dies within two years of making the contribution. In other words, if the member survives for two years HMRC will assume (unless there is clear evidence to the contrary) that the member was in normal health at the time of the contribution, so there is no transfer of value. In this respect Box 22 of IHT 409 (the pension supplement to the inheritance tax account on death) requests details of contributions paid in the two years before death.

The question then arises as to whether IHTA 1984, s. 10 can provide relief. This section states that there will be no transfer of value in cases where there was no intention by the transferor to confer a gratuitous benefit, i.e. when the contribution was paid.

In this respect, HMRC take the view that the protection of IHTA 1984, s. 10 would not be available and so a measurable transfer of value could arise under s. 3(1).

However, in cases where the member paid the contribution when in ill health but without the member knowing of that ill health, it is submitted that the s. 10 relief can apply.

This issue is obviously more likely to be relevant in cases of larger contributions as any transfer of value arising on smaller contributions may well be covered by the annual exemption, etc.

Example 1

Archie, aged 61, knowing he is in serious ill health, decides to pay a substantial contribution of £25,000 to his personal pension plan under which death benefits are subject to a personal discretionary trust. He dies four months later.

Because Archie was in serious ill health when he made the contribution a transfer of value will take place. Archie will not be helped by the s. 10 exemption ("no intention to confer a gratuitous benefit") as he knew he was in serious ill health when he paid the contribution. A part of this contribution will therefore give rise to a loss to his estate that can be actuarially determined. This will be a chargeable lifetime transfer.

Example 2

Sally, aged 57, who believes she is in excellent health, pays a contribution of £40,000 to a personal pension plan. Two and a half years later and out of the blue she has a heart attack and dies. Even if she was actually in poor health when she made the contribution, the s. 10 exemption should apply because at the time she made the contribution she had no reason to believe that she was likely to die before drawing retirement benefits. In any event, as she survived the contribution by two years, HMRC are unlikely to investigate the case and no entry is needed on form IHT 409.

Example 3

Bob is aged 68. He pays a contribution of £50,000 to his personal pension plan under which death benefits are held subject to a discretionary trust. At the time of the contribution he has lung cancer but doesn't realise this until some four months later. He dies 15 months after making the contribution. The payment of the contribution could give rise to a chargeable lifetime transfer. Because Bob died within two years of the contribution it is reportable on form IHT 409. However, because he was unaware of his illness when he made the contribution his personal representative may be able to claim that any transfer was covered by the s. 10 exemption ("no intention to confer a gratuitous benefit").

Even if an individual does die within two years of making a contribution, knowing he is in serious ill health at the time of the contribution, the question arises as to whether IHTA 1984, s. 12 would help him.

Section 12 provides that a disposition is not a transfer of value if it is allowable in computing the transferor's profits or gains for the purposes of income tax. Payments of contributions to a registered pension scheme may be allowable for income tax purposes but the allowance is in the form of a deduction or set off against the "relevant UK earnings" of the person making the contribution. HMRC take the view that relief under s. 12 is therefore not available in this scenario – the payment of the contribution is not allowable in computing the contributor's profits for income tax purposes. Rather the contribution is or may be a deduction from "relevant UK earnings" and these are calculated after computing the person's profits for income tax purposes.

Law: IHTA 1984, s. 3(1), 10, 12

10.5.4 Special IHT rules: lifetime transfers of death benefits to a trust

Where a member of a pension scheme transfers his death benefits to a trust he may be considered to have made a transfer of value under IHTA 1984, s. 3(1).

In most cases, any transfer of value will have a nominal value because the member will be in good health and it is likely that he will survive to draw his retirement benefits, at which time the death benefits will lapse.

In this respect (and assuming there is no evidence to the contrary), provided the member survived the transfer by two years HMRC will assume that the member was in normal health at the time of the transfer and no further investigation will be necessary. If a member makes such a transfer and does die within two years, Box 17 in IHT 409 will need to be completed.

This provision could apply to a situation where an individual places a retirement annuity policy in trust or (depending on the circumstances) declares a personal (integrated) trust of the death benefits of a personal pension plan. In both of these cases, if the member is in ill health, careful thought should be given before declaring the trust.

Sensible planning would suggest that the trust should be established at the start of the arrangement when the value for all purposes is negligible if regular contributions are to be paid, the member is more likely to be in good health, and future contributions may be of a regular nature.

Law: IHTA 1984, s. 3(1)

10.5.5 Special IHT rules: pension transfers

From time to time a number of people will consider the transfer of their pension rights from one pension scheme to another – perhaps with a view to increasing investment choice, improving investment performance and/or reducing administration costs.

However, a note of caution needs to be sounded on making a pension transfer from an inheritance tax standpoint.

Where the pension scheme member knows he is in serious ill health, the transfer may give rise to inheritance tax problems. This may mean that, by making the transfer, the member goes from a position of freedom from inheritance tax (on current pension funds) to one of liability to inheritance tax (on new pension funds).

HMRC's view on transfers

To many it is not that clear why a transfer of value should arise in the case of a pension transfer because in virtually all cases the individual will be transferring from one plan where death benefits are held under a discretionary trust to another plan where death benefits are held under a virtually identical discretionary trust.

So how can a transfer of values arise in such a case?

In the *Inheritance Tax Manual*, at IHTM 17072, HMRC explain their reasoning on this as follows:

> "A pension scheme member has a statutory right to transfer their pension fund from one scheme to another. When this type of transfer is made, the member surrenders their rights under the first scheme in return for rights under the second. A person can do this regardless of their rights to benefits under the first scheme. This includes the situation where there is an existing irrevocable nomination in relation to death benefits, for example, where the death benefits have been assigned on discretionary trusts. The second scheme is not subject to directions given in relation to the first scheme.
>
> The funds do not rejoin the member's estate during transit. What is in the estate at this point is the right to determine the terms of payment of death benefits in the second scheme. This right has value because the member could direct the payment to their own estate. If payment is not directed to the estate then there may be a loss to the estate depending on the member's health at the time.
>
> If a person is in normal health at the date of the transfer then the loss to the estate is nominal. If they are in ill-health at the date of the transfer then the loss may be significant.
>
> Details of any transfers made within the 2 years before the death should be reported on the IHT409 (IHTM17014)."

The reality of the situation is that the new pension plan will include trusts of the death benefits which will exclude the member as a beneficiary and so, according to the HMRC rationale, a transfer of value will occur under IHTA 1984, s. 3(1).

In practice, however, HMRC will only treat this as a transfer of value which has more than a nominal value if the member is in serious ill health when making the transfer. As with the position on contributions, it seems that HMRC will, in general, assume that the member was in good health at the time of the transfer unless he dies within two years of the transfer, in which circumstances HMRC will require Boxes 17 to 21 of the IHT 409 death return to be completed.

This whole issue is particularly relevant at the current time because more people will be transferring their pension benefits in order to access flexi-access benefits. Where such people are in ill health, the IHT implications will need to be considered.

Section 10 defence

(1) The general position

Legal personal representatives who are in this situation will find that the only way they can resist a claim is to establish that in entering the transaction, the taxpayer had no intention of conferring a gratuitous benefit on another and so the exemption in IHTA 1984, s. 10 applies. This is not easy. An example of a situation in which the defence may be available is where the individual did not know that he or she was in ill health at the time the transfer was made.

HMRC make the point that s. 10 only applies to a transfer if it is shown that the transfer was not *intended* to confer *any* gratuitous benefit on any person. This places the burden of proof on the taxpayer (usually the personal representatives following a death) to show that the transferor had *no* gratuitous intent when the transfer took place. Making a transfer between pension schemes *solely* to achieve a better rate of annuity *for the benefit of the individual* would normally satisfy this provision. But *any* element of gratuitous intent would mean that s. 10 could not apply.

HMRC do, however, accept that in certain circumstances a s. 10 defence can be available – for example if somebody who is in ill health makes a transfer and then immediately vests benefits under the new plan. In such a case there is clearly no intention to confer a gratuitous benefit on transfer. Unfortunately, not all cases will be as clear cut.

However, HMRC have confirmed that when a person transfers and immediately vests all of their benefits, the s. 10 exemption (no intention to confer a gratuitous benefit) will apply. Where not all benefits are vested immediately the IHT position will depend on the circumstances of the case.

This can provide a solution for people in ill health who want to transfer their pension plan to maximise death benefits for a spouse. Provided they are prepared to accept some income tax on encashment of the whole pension plan after transfer (or they are entitled to a full ill-health commutation) death benefits can then be left to the surviving spouse, free of IHT, under the member's will.

Even if the member did die within two years and a return is made under IHT 409, if the member did not know he was suffering from a life-threatening illness when he made the transfer, there is an argument to say that the s. 10 exemption (no intention to confer a gratuitous benefit) should apply.

As will be appreciated, the transfer of pension benefits for people in this position could have serious IHT consequences. The moral therefore is very clear – if an individual is in serious ill health and is concerned about inheritance tax, a transfer of pension rights to a new plan should only be undertaken with extreme caution. Two further important points needs to be considered in relation to this.

First, this issue is particularly relevant at the current time because more people will be transferring their pension benefits in order to access flexi-access benefits. Where such people are in ill health, the IHT implications will need to be considered. However, HMRC have confirmed that when a person transfers and immediately vests all of their benefits, the s. 10 exemption (no intention to confer a gratuitous benefit) will apply. Where not all benefits are vested immediately the IHT position will depend on the circumstances of the case.

In cases where a section 3(1) transfer does occur, it will be necessary to ascertain the size of the transfer of value. This will clearly depend on the value of the fund on transfer and the member's then mortality. For members who are of an age to draw benefits, it will also be possible to make a deduction in respect of any retained rights to the member under the new scheme – this will include the right to a PCLS and the present value of any net guaranteed annuity he or she would be entitled to. Where the transfer is made to a pension plan offering flexi-access benefits and that person is aged at least 55, it is thought that a deduction can be made for the PCLS and any net (of income tax) pension fund.

(2) The Staveley case

This area of taxation was recently examined in the Courts in the case of *Mrs Staveley deceased*, which is therefore the second important consideration.

Mrs Staveley owned a s. 32 pension plan which she transferred into an AXA personal pension plan. Unfortunately, the transfer took place at a time when Mrs Staveley knew she was in serious ill health and, on her death a short time afterwards, HMRC claimed IHT on the basis that there had been:

- a transfer of value under s. 3(1) of IHTA 1984, which reduced her taxable estate at the time of transfer; and
- an omission to exercise a right with the intention of deliberately increasing the estate of another under s. 3(3). This led to a lifetime transfer of value occurring immediately before death. This is on the basis that Mrs Staveley could have taken retirement benefits but chose not to. Thus the value of the pension fund increased and this passed free of IHT under the discretionary trust.

The beneficiaries under Mrs Staveley's Will were her two sons. They were also the nominated beneficiaries who ultimately received the death benefits under the AXA pension plan on her death at the discretion of the pension scheme trustees.

The case was unusual in its facts because it was clear that Mrs Staveley's prime reason for making the transfer was to prevent her ex-husband directly or indirectly getting any benefit at all from her pension plans on her death. This could have happened under the s. 32 policy before 2006 because surplus funds would be returned to the employer company of which her ex-husband was a substantial shareholder. Following the changes made in FA 2004, Mrs Staveley's adviser confirmed that all of the funds on death after April 2006 would pass to her beneficiaries (her sons) via her estate. However, there was evidence that Mrs Staveley did not trust this outcome and still believed that there was a risk that her husband would get an indirect benefit. This risk could be eliminated by making the transfer.

This case was an appeal to the Upper-Tier Tribunal (UTT) from a decision by the First-Tier Tribunal (FTT). It is necessary to consider the decisions on section 3(1) and 3(3) separately.

Section 3(1)

As stated above, HMRCs general stance in these cases (i.e. under s. 3(1)) is that a pension transfer will not generally give rise to a transfer of value because the value of the gifted (death) benefits is negligible. But, if it is made at a time when the planholder is in serious ill health, and knows that, and dies within two years, then a lifetime transfer of value can arise.

The estate claimed that no transfer of value should arise under s. 3(1) because of the exemption in s. 10 that there was "no intention to confer a gratuitous benefit".

In this case the FTT found in favour of the taxpayer's estate.

HMRC appealed against this decision. The UTT started by considering the law.

(i) Was there a disposition under section 3(1)?

Section 3(1) provides that a transfer of value is a disposition made by a person which reduces the value of his estate. Section 3(3) states that a disposition can include a deliberate omission to exercise a right.

Both parties agreed that there was a disposition for the purposes of s. 3(1). Under the s. 32 policy, Mrs Staveley had the right to dispose of the death benefits. It did not matter that following transfer to the AXA plan, she no longer had that right because it was then the AXA Scheme Administrator who made that decision.

Section 10 states that a disposition is not a transfer of value if it is shown that it was not intended and not made in a transaction intended to confer a gratuitous benefit on any person and it was made either:

- in a transaction at arm's length between persons not connected with each other; or
- on terms that might be expected between such persons.

For these purposes, "transaction" includes a series of transactions and any associated operations.

(ii) Did the Section 10 defence apply?

Here there were a number of factors to consider.

(a) Did the transfer intend to confer any gratuitous benefit?

Here the FTT said that the signing of the letter of wishes could not be the conferring of a gratuitous benefit because her sons would already benefit from the proceeds of the plan under her will. The UTT disagreed with this view. In their opinion the existence of an expectant benefit under a will cannot prevent the conferring of a lifetime benefit of substantially the same interest and to the same beneficiaries as under the will.

Irrespective of this point on the need for a pre-existence of a benefit, the FTT also decided, based on an interpretation of the facts, that in making the transfer of funds from the s. 32 policy to the AXA PPP, Mrs Staveley did not intend to confer a gratuitous benefit on any person. Her sole intention was to prevent surplus pension funds reverting to Morayford Ltd and thus being used for the benefit of her ex-husband.

HMRC argued that the FTT were wrong to reach this conclusion based on the facts of the case and so there was an error of law. This argument was dismissed by the UTT. Quoting *Edwards v Bairstow* (1956) AC 14, the UTT agreed with the FTT that the transfer of the s. 32 policy to the AXA PPP, was not motivated by an intention to confer a gratuitous benefit on her sons (although that may have been a motivating factor behind her decision not to take retirement benefits).

Further, for s. 10 to apply, if the disposition is made in a transaction or series of transactions, none of those transactions must be made with the intention of conferring a benefit. HMRC argued that Mrs

Staveley's omission to take benefits needed to be taken into account in this respect because that omission was an intention to confer a benefit. The UTT disagreed with this argument and supported the FTT decision that a "transaction" did not include an omission. Therefore this omission was not relevant to Mrs Staveley's intention.

(b) Associated operations

An omission can be an associated operation. Could this mean that the intention behind Mrs Staveley not accessing the pension fund had been to confer a gratuitous benefit on the sons?

This required the UTT to consider existing case law in *IRC v Macpherson* (1989) 1 AC 159.

Having done so, the UTT decided that the transfer to the AXA PPP and the motivation for it were found to be entirely separate to the omission to take lifetime pension benefits and any intention in that respect. Therefore, the FTT were correct to say that the transfer and omission were unconnected and not part of any scheme to confer benefit on Mrs Staveley's two sons.

(c) Arm's length transaction

Did the existence of the expression of wishes (and its gratuitous intention) mean that the transaction could not be regarded as at arm's length?

The UTT thought not – the test is whether the transaction is "between" unconnected persons. In this case, although the two sons were named in the expression of wish, it could not be said that the transaction was between Mrs Staveley and her sons – the parties to the transfer were Mrs Staveley and AXA – who were unconnected parties.

Summary

The UTT approved the decision of the FTT that s. 10 would provide a defence. In doing so, they said:

> "What the FTT concluded was that Mrs Staveley's sole motive in making the transfer was to exclude the possibility of her ex-husband benefiting. The finding that that was her sole motive can also be understood as a finding that, but for that risk, Mrs

> Staveley would not have made the transfer, but would have allowed the status quo to endure, and for her sons to benefit, as she had planned, under her will.
>
> In our judgment, therefore, the FTT was entitled on the evidence to find, as it did, that the disposition by the transfer of funds from the s 32 policy to the AXA PPP was not intended to confer a gratuitous benefit on any person. The FTT did not, contrary to HMRC's submission, shut its eyes to the desired destination of the death benefits; to the contrary it clearly took that factor into account."

The UTT went on to say:

> "Agreeing with the FTT, therefore, we find that it has been shown that the disposition by the transfer of funds to the AXA PPP was not intended, and was not made in a transaction intended, to confer gratuitous benefit on any person, and that it was made in a transaction at arm's length between persons not connected with each other. The transfer was accordingly, by virtue of s 10 IHTA, not a transfer of value for the purpose of s 3 IHTA 1984."

Section 3(3)

On the question of an omission to exercise a right, HMRC had previously won the case in front of the FTT.

For section 3(3) to apply the omission must be deliberate and lead to an increase in the estate of another person – those persons being Mrs Staveley's sons in this case.

Before the UTT, the representatives of the estate did not dispute the fact that Mrs Staveley had expressed a deliberate omission to take lifetime benefit. However, there was a challenge on the basis that her omission did not amount to a disposition which was required for the provision to apply. In effect, the estate representatives argued that the increase in the estates of Mrs Staveley's sons (who benefitted from death benefits under the AXA personal pension plan) was not sufficiently connected to the non-payment of benefits to Mrs Staveley. In this connection, the Estate argued that the sons benefitted because of the exercise of a discretionary power by the Scheme Administrator. Whilst the Scheme Administrator was likely to exercise this in favour of the beneficiaries named under the letter of wishes, there was no guarantee that they would follow this instruction.

In this respect, the UTT said:

> "In our judgment, the proximate cause of the increase in the estates of the two sons was the exercise of the discretion of the Scheme Administrator. Their estates were increased 'by' the exercise of that discretion, and not by the omission of Mrs Staveley to exercise her right to take lifetime benefits. There would have been no increase in the value of the son's estates but for the omission to take those benefits, but the test is not a 'but for' test and it was not the omission which had the effect of increasing the sons' estates; it was the exercise of the Scheme Administrator's discretion. It follows, therefore, that the conditions of s 3(3) are not satisfied with respect to Mrs Staveley's omission, and that omission cannot be treated as a disposition or as a transfer of value within s 3(1)."

The UTT therefore accepted the taxpayer's arguments and HMRC lost on both counts.

Comment

This case could be of considerable importance in determining the future IHT treatment under s. 3(1) of transfers of pension schemes. Of course, since FA 2011, the omission to exercise a right rule in s. 3(3) is no longer relevant to registered pension plans (see IHTA 1984, s. 12(2ZA) and 12A).

HMRC frequently challenge pension transfers made by people in seriously ill health under s. 3(1). It would now seem that, irrespective of ill health, if it can be shown that the sole reason for the transfer was something other than to confer a gratuitous benefit on another person, then no lifetime transfer of value should arise for IHT purposes (even if such a benefit is a consequential result). Much will depend on the facts of each case. Such reasons might include commercial aspects, such as a transfer to reduce plan charges, or to gain access to a greater range of investment funds or to access pension flexibility. It is not certain how easy this will be to demonstrate and how far one needs to go to distance the pension transfer from the payment of death benefits that are free of IHT.

HMRC have not, it seems, changed their view on the s. 10 defence following this case, which they regard as having been decided on its own particular facts. They may well appeal against the UTT decision.

As will be appreciated, the transfer of pension benefits for people in ill health could have serious IHT consequences. The moral therefore is very clear – if an individual is in serious ill health and is concerned about inheritance tax, a transfer of pension rights to a new plan should only be undertaken with extreme caution.

Law: IHTA 1984, s. 3(1), 10
Case: *HMRC v Representatives of Staveley (deceased)* UKUT 4 (TCC)

10.6 Lump sum death benefits

10.6.1 Introduction

It is common for the rules of a registered pension scheme to provide for the payment of death benefits as a lump sum or as a pension to a dependant.

Following provisions introduced in TOPA 2014, it is now possible under flexi-access drawdown for drawdown death benefits to be paid to a wide range of beneficiaries. Prior to 6 April 2015, income drawdown death benefits could only be paid to people who were dependants of the scheme member. Now flexi-access drawdown benefits can be paid to people who are dependants, nominees or successors – see below.

On the death of the member of a DC / money purchase pension scheme, flexi-access drawdown funds can be used to provide benefits to a dependant or a nominee. On the death of the dependant or nominee, a successor can become entitled to the pension fund, and this process can be continued through the generations until the funds are exhausted – either because they are all taken as income drawdown benefits or a lump sum is paid out on the death of a beneficiary, thereby extinguishing the fund.

It should be borne in mind that whilst a person may be named as somebody who can benefit on a member's/beneficiary's death, it will be the Scheme Administrator who will normally make the final decision as to who should receive death benefits and, after discussion with the beneficiary concerned, whether he or she will be paid in the form of an income or a lump sum. This discretion is very important because it enables IHT freedom to be retained on the death benefits.

Following the removal of the need for a pension scheme member to buy an annuity at the latest by age 75, this lump sum can be paid at any time before the member has bought an annuity. This means that a lump sum death benefit can be paid for somebody in drawdown – be it capped drawdown or flexible drawdown.

From 6 April 2012, protected rights are abolished and benefits that have arisen as a result of an individual having contracted out of the additional state pension are paid in the same way as other pension benefits.

On the basis that a lump sum is payable, how this will be paid will depend on the scheme rules. In general, it will be in one of two ways:

- The lump sum death benefit can be paid to one or more of the eligible range of beneficiaries included in the rules at the discretion of the scheme administrator/trustees. The range of beneficiaries is normally very widely drawn and will frequently include not only the member's spouse and relatives but also the trustees of a trust (say a pilot trust), any person specified in writing by the member, and charities.
- If the member has declared a trust of the pension plan under which the death benefits of a pension plan are held for the benefit of a discretionary class, the lump sum will be paid to the trustees of that trust. This is what is known as an "integrated trust" and effectively means that the trustees of that personal trust will then take over responsibility for deciding who receives the benefits.

The payment of lump sum death benefits requires consideration of both income tax and inheritance tax consequences.

10.6.2 The taxation of lump sum death benefits: income tax

In the event of the payment of a lump sum on the death of a member of a registered pension scheme on or after 6 April 2011, the following tax rules apply:

a. If death occurs after the member has attained age 75, the lump sum death benefits will be subject to a 45 per cent tax charge (the special lump sum death benefit charge) if paid to a non-qualifying person (trustee other than of a bare trust, company, partnership or member of a limited liability partnership). This charge was abolished from 6 April 2016 where payment is to individuals for their own benefit and the lump sum is taxed as pension income at marginal rates of income tax.
b. If death occurs before age 75, the death benefits will generally be tax-free within the lifetime allowance (the exception being if the benefit is paid to a non-qualifying person and is not paid within two years of the administrator learning of the member's death or within two years of when it would have been reasonable for him or her to have learned of the death if earlier). Payment outside the two year period to a non-qualifying person will introduce the special lump sum death benefit charge (45% in 2017-18).

There will be no inheritance tax payable in any of the above circumstances – see below.

Where a member has elected for an annuity to be paid for a minimum guaranteed period, and dies during that period, the present value of the remaining guaranteed pension payments will normally be added to the deceased's estate and be subject to income tax / inheritance tax as appropriate. However, where the rules of the scheme/annuity policy enable the payments to be made at the discretion of the scheme administrator these may be paid out free of IHT under that discretion to any one or more of the potential beneficiaries.

Law: F(No.2)A 2015, s. 21-22

10.6.3 Lump sum death benefits: inheritance tax – general rules

Pension plans are normally constituted by a discretionary trust and any payment out of a discretionary trust to a beneficiary would normally suffer inheritance tax by way of an exit charge under the inheritance tax regime. However, under IHTA 1984, s. 58, in the past, it has been possible for the Scheme Administrator to pay lump sum death benefits from a registered pension scheme free of inheritance tax if paid, broadly, within the relevant two-year period of death. Failure to pay within this time scale could have meant that the protection from the IHT charges would cease to have effect and later payments may be subject to the unauthorised payment charges. With effect from 6 April 2015, the new rules are as follows:

- Where the member dies under age 75, payments will be free of inheritance tax irrespective of whether they are paid inside or outside the relevant two-year period. However, whilst payments made outside of the relevant two-year period are not subject to IHT or an unauthorised payment charge, they will be subject to PAYE assessed on an individual recipient or at 45% SLSDBC payable by the Scheme Administrator if paid to a trust.
- Payments made in respect of a member who has died at age 75 or later will not be subject to an IHT or an unathorised payment charge but will be subject to PAYE assessed on an individual recipient or at 45% SLSDBC payable by the Scheme Administrator if paid to a trust.

Law: IHTA 1984, s. 58

10.6.4 Inheritance tax and flexi-access pensions

The introduction of flexi-access pensions has meant that the inheritance tax rules need to be reconsidered as regards this new breed of pensions.

Naming a dependant, nominee or successor

Under the previous registered pension regime, for death benefit payments to be free of inheritance tax, the Scheme Administrator needed to retain discretion as to who should benefit on the member's death. How does this sit with the new rules that permit the naming of a dependant, nominee or successor who will be entitled to flexi-access drawdown death benefits?

In this respect HMRC have confirmed that the nomination of a dependant, nominee, or successor by a pension scheme member/beneficiary will not cause the member/beneficiary to be treated as making a transfer of value for IHT purposes on death provided:

a. the member/beneficiary does not have power under the scheme rules to choose irrevocably the beneficiary who should be entitled to death benefits on his/her death; and
b. the Scheme Trustee/Scheme Administrator has a discretionary power to choose who should receive death benefits.

So, for example, even though the pension scheme member may have nominated a person to receive income drawdown death benefits, the Scheme Administrator could still override this nomination and pay lump sum death benefits.

There could also be cases where the Scheme Administrator has, in effect, no option but to follow the member's nomination if it is desired to pay flexi-access income drawdown benefits. Say, for example, that a scheme member has named a dependant to be entitled to flexi-access drawdown death benefits. If the Scheme Administrator wants to pay flexi-access drawdown benefits, the Scheme Administrator may have to pay benefits to that dependant (because there are no other dependants). Here HMRC take the view that provided the Scheme Administrator has the option to pay an alternative benefit (i.e. a lump sum), and can determine who would receive such alternative benefit, the member would not be treated as making a transfer of value of his fund on his death.

This official view is now embodied in IHTM 17052.

10.6.5 Lump sum death benefits: cases where IHT can still apply

Since 6 April 2011, the provisions in IHTA 1984, s. 3(3) – omission to exercise a right – no longer apply to the payment of death benefits from a registered pension scheme. This rule created substantial complications and its application was not necessarily helped by the High Court decision in *Fryer*. Section 3(3) can now be largely ignored in relation to pensions plans.

HMRC are reconsidering the position in the light of the pension changes in April 2015 and whether a legislative change should be made to put the position beyond doubt. Any legislative change could apply retrospectively back to the introduction of IHTA 1984, s. 12(2ZA) in 2011.

It would seem that this particular problem will not arise in cases where the beneficiary entitled is a nominee, dependant or successor (i.e. after the member's death).

There are therefore now two circumstances when IHT can apply to lump sum death benefit payments.

Deceased's estate has a right to death benefits

Any death benefits payable to the deceased's estate or personal representatives as of right at the date of death form part of the deceased's estate for IHT purposes.

There is an exception to this rule where an annuity becomes payable to a dependant of the deceased but the deceased had the option of taking the lump sum instead. So, for example, if an annuity becomes payable on the death to the widow, widower, surviving civil partner or dependant and the deceased had the option of taking a lump sum instead, that lump sum is not treated as part of the death estate.

To avoid a charge under this provision, it is important to make sure that the trustees / scheme administrator have discretion over the payment of death benefits. This will avoid the death benefits being treated as part of the deceased's estate even if the trustees exercise their discretion in favour of the deceased's estate.

General power of appointment

If the deceased pension scheme member had a general power of appointment over the death benefits, or a power of nomination which binds the scheme trustees or personal representatives as to whom to pay the death benefits to, including his own estate, then under IHTA 1984, s. 5(2), the lump sum will be treated as forming part of the deceased member's taxable estate. The exception to this is if the deceased member had irrevocably exercised the power of appointment during his lifetime while he was in good health.

So, for example, in a case where:

- the death benefits are held on discretionary trusts with the settlor having the power to appoint benefits, and

- the settlor is a beneficiary or can add himself as a beneficiary,

then because the deceased had power to appoint funds to himself or his own estate, the death benefits will be treated as forming part of his estate under IHTA 1984, s. 5(2).

This provision will also apply in cases where the deceased had an unfettered power to sign a nomination which binds the trustees of the pension scheme to make the payment of the death benefits to the person named by the deceased. Here the death benefits will be treated as an asset of the estate.

An unfettered power to nominate in this context means that the deceased could nominate to anyone he wished including his personal representatives. Care must be taken not to confuse a binding nomination with a non-binding letter of wishes as these are sometimes called nominations. A non-binding letter of wishes will not give rise to a problem in this respect *(unless they are badly drafted so that, for example, the pension scheme member has the right to revoke an existing expression of wishes up until his death and, if he did so without indicating another person, the death benefits would be paid into the member's estate).*

Therefore problems will not arise in this area provided:

a. the member cannot appoint death benefits under the trust and/or the member is not a beneficiary under the trust; or
b. the death benefits are distributed at the trustees' discretion even if the distribution is in line with a non-binding letter of wishes expressed by the member to the trustees.

Law: IHTA 1984, s. 3(3), 5(2)
Case: *Fryer v HMRC* [2010] UK FTT 87 (TC)

10.6.6 Lump sum death benefits: IHT and flexi-access pensions

The introduction of flexi-access pensions has meant that the inheritance tax rules need to be reconsidered as regards this new breed of pensions.

Naming a dependant, nominee or successor

Under the previous registered pension regime, for death benefit payments to be free of inheritance tax, the scheme administrator needed to retain discretion as to who should benefit on the member's death. How does this sit with the new rules that permit the naming of a dependant, nominee or successor who will be entitled to flexi-access drawdown death benefits?

In this respect HMRC have confirmed that the nomination of a dependant, nominee or successor by a pension scheme member/beneficiary will not cause the member/beneficiary to be treated as making a transfer of value for IHT purposes on death provided:

a. the member/beneficiary does not have power under the schemes rules to irrevocably choose the beneficiary who should be entitled to death benefits on his/her death; and
b. the scheme trustee/scheme administrator has a discretionary power to choose who should receive death benefits.

So for example, even though the pension scheme member may have nominated a person to receive income drawdown death benefits, the scheme administrator could still override this nomination and pay lump sum death benefits.

There could also be cases where the scheme administrator has, in effect, no option but to follow the member's nomination if it is desired to pay flexi-access income drawdown benefits. Say, for example, that a scheme member has named a dependant to be entitled to flexi-access drawdown death benefits. If the scheme administrator wants to pay flexi-access drawdown benefits, he may have to pay benefits to that dependant (because there are no other dependants). Here HMRC take the view that provided the scheme administrator has the option to pay an alternative benefit (i.e. a lump sum), and can determine who would receive such alternative benefit, the member would not be treated as making a transfer of value of his fund on his death.

This official view is now embodied in IHTM 17052.

IHT exit charges on payments to beneficiaries

HMRC have also confirmed that the naming of a dependant/ nominee who is entitled to flexi-access drawdown death payments, followed by the scheme administrator exercising his discretion in his or her favour, would not give rise to an IHT exit charge from the discretionary trust as regards the whole fund. This is on the basis that a flexi-access drawdown fund is an arrangement under which property is held for the purposes of a registered pension scheme. It is therefore within IHTA 1984, s. 58(1)(d), and is not relevant property. Any payment out of a flexi-access drawdown fund is therefore not an exit from a relevant property trust.

There would also be no IHT exit charge on payments of flexi-access income drawdown death payments out of a trust of a registered pension scheme, even if paid more than two years after the members death.

IHT on payments made more than two years after the member's death

Previously if benefits from an uncrystallised pension plan were paid out of a registered pension scheme on the death of somebody under age 75 more than two years after a member's death, an IHT exit charge could have arisen. This provision in FA 2004, s. 168(1) has been amended by ToPA and so IHTA 1984, s. 58(2A) will provide relief in these circumstances. Of course, the 45% special lump sum death benefit charge could apply in these cases.

Section 3(3) – omission to exercise a right

Since 2011, the omission to exercise a right rule in IHTA 1984, s. 3(3) has not applied to a member's entitlement to tax free cash and pension payments under a registered pension scheme, due to the introduction in 2011 of an exemption in IHTA 1984, s. 12(2ZA) to remove an inheritance tax charge under the "omission to exercise a right" rules.

It was assumed that under the new regime inheritance tax would not apply to death benefits. However, some commentators queried this analysis, stating that s. 3(3) could still apply in cases where the member died having designated his pension fund to drawdown. This was on the basis that the s. 12(2ZA) exemption applied to the member's right to elect to crystallise the plan and so draw benefits. The exemption did not apply to the member's rights to draw the funds having gone into drawdown, i.e. where the funds had already been designated to drawdown but just hadn't been fully drawn at the point of death.

From the contents of private correspondence with HMRC, it appeared that technically there could be a problem and that this legislation might still apply to certain cases where a member died with drawdown benefits. Fortunately, FA 2016 has now introduced a new s. 12(2A) to IHTA 1984. This provides that no omission to exercise a right can arise in respect of somebody who dies with income drawdown rights be he a member, dependant, nominee or successor. This new provision applies for any deaths that occur on or after 6 April 2011.

Section 12(2A) of IHTA 1984 means that s. 3(3) will not apply to benefits held in a registered pension plan – irrespective of whether the member is or is not in drawdown. This will also be the case where the beneficiary entitled is a nominee, dependant or successor (i.e. after the member's death). The change applies retrospectively back to the introduction of IHTA 1984, s. 12(2ZA) in 2011.

This, in effect, confirms that most income drawdown plans will be free of IHT on a member's/beneficiary's death.

10.6.7 Lump sum death benefits: IHT summary

So, in summary the main IHT implications of using flexi-access income drawdown death benefits are that:

(a) the value of the pension fund will not, in general, be in the estate of a named beneficiary under FAD – be that a dependant, nominee or successor;

(b) where a beneficiary draws payments from the FAD account, there will be no IHT exit charge on these payments – irrespective of when they are made.

By leaving pension death benefits via FAD, it is possible to transfer the value of a large pension scheme down the generations free of IHT – provided the family are prepared to accept some of the possible drawbacks of this (see later).

If it is desired to pay out a lump sum, then rather than making a payment to an individual beneficiary, there can sometimes be advantages in the pension scheme trustees making a payment to a trust rather than to an individual beneficiary. By using an appropriate trust, this will enable them to by-pass a beneficiary's (say a surviving spouse's) taxable estate yet still give that spouse access to the trust fund. We examine the advantages of the so-called "by-pass trust" further below.

If the scheme administrator makes a lump sum death benefit to the trustees of a by-pass trust which is a potential beneficiary under the scheme rules, this will be tax free if the member died under age 75. If he or she died age 75 or over, the payment will be taxed at 45%. Income and capital gains on investments in the trust will be taxed in the normal way in later years and IHT implications will arise at the 10-year anniversaries.

Law: IHTA 1984, s. 58

10.7 By-pass trusts

By-pass trusts are designed to allow assets to be distributed to children or other beneficiaries without the inheritance tax charge that would arise if the pension lump sum death benefit eventually fell into the surviving spouse's or civil partner's estate.

Some firms of lawyers and pension providers offer a "by-pass" trust in connection with pension lump sum death benefits.

The trust is established during the member's lifetime (having confirmed that the rules of the scheme allow the lump sum to be paid to a trust).

A by-pass trust is normally established in one of two ways:

- the member declares a trust of the lump sum death benefits on his death (an integrated trust); or
- the member sets up a lifetime pilot discretionary trust for a nominal amount – say £10. The scheme administrators follow a letter of wishes to add to this trust on the member's death.

On the death of the member, the lump sum is paid to the trust and the trust may then lend money to the spouse or civil partner.

Alternatively, the spouse or civil partner may have self-investment powers and even use of trust assets as if the owner. The trust is repaid from the estate of the spouse or civil partner when he or she dies. It then distributes the proceeds to children.

An alternative approach would be for the spouse to give the money to children in the hope of surviving the seven-year term during which an inheritance tax charge might otherwise be made.

There are variations on the design and this is only a general description.

10.8 By-pass trusts: IHT implications after death of settlor

10.8.1 Introduction

As this is a discretionary trust, special IHT charging rules apply. Under these rules there may be a potential IHT charge:

- on every 10-year anniversary of the trust – "the periodic charge"; or
- whenever property leaves the trust (e.g. when capital is advanced to a beneficiary) – "the exit charge".

Whilst the rules on the IHT treatment of discretionary trusts have been under review, the Government announced in the 2014 Autumn Statement that no substantial changes are to be made to the current system.

10.8.2 Periodic charge

Periodic charges at 10-yearly intervals may be applied to the value of the assets in the trust. The rate of inheritance tax charged will be determined by considering an assumed transfer by an assumed transferor. In this calculation, it will be necessary to take account of:

- the value of the property in the trust on the 10-year anniversary plus the value of any related settlements (i.e. same-day settlements) when they were established (the assumed transfer); and
- the settlor's cumulative total immediately before he made the trust (assuming no property has been added to the trust) and any sums paid out of the trust in the 10 years prior to

the anniversary (the cumulative total of the assumed transferor).

Special rules apply for inheritance tax when property moves between different relevant property trusts.

When property moves from one discretionary ("relevant property") trust to another then, for IHT purposes, that property will be treated as continuing to be comprised in the original trust (IHTA 1984, s. 81).

Exactly the same principle applies to transfers of pension rights between trust-based pension schemes.

This means that if the lump sum death benefit originates from a pension scheme which was subject to a discretionary trust (as opposed to a deed poll when different rules apply), HMRC will apply IHTA 1984, s. 81.

HMRC take the view that the deceased pension scheme member is the settlor of the benefits which are held for him on the discretionary trusts of the pension scheme and so the trust began when he became a member of the scheme. The settlor is considered to be the member even in the case of a non-contributory scheme. The reason for this is that pension benefits and rights are the product of sums paid into the pension fund by the employer as deferred or delayed remuneration for the employee's current work (see *Parry v Cleaver and The Halcyon Skies*). The 10-year anniversary date for the recipient discretionary trust will then run from the date the member joined the pension scheme and established the initial discretionary trust.

The trust will have begun when either:

- the member joined the current pension scheme, if there have been no transferred benefits; or
- the member joined the pension scheme from which benefits were transferred to the current pension scheme.

Thus it will be necessary to determine the chargeable transfers the settlor made in the seven years before he joined the current pension scheme or the transferring scheme, if earlier, in order to calculate the amount of any periodic charge.

The date the by-pass trust is actually established can effectively be ignored because the value of property then transferred would be nominal if a £10 pilot trust was used, or negligible (assuming the member was in good health), if an integrated trust was used.

Example – Polly

Polly joined her current trust-based pension scheme on 1 August 2012 and subsequently executes a pilot by-pass trust for a nominal amount. If a lump sum death benefit is paid to the pilot trust, for IHT purposes the pilot trust will, to all intents and purposes, be treated as commencing when Polly joined her current pension scheme.

Example – Belinda

Belinda joined her current trust-based pension scheme on 1 August 2012 and subsequently executes a pilot by-pass trust for a nominal amount. As part of the amount that established her new pension scheme she transfers the benefits from her trust-based pension plan with Transinternational Life which she set up on 1 June 1987. On her death, if lump sum death benefits are paid to the pilot trust, the cash representing the transferred amount would be treated as being held in a trust created on 1 June 1987.

In calculating the IHT charge, it is necessary to remember that there would not have been any periodic or exit charges prior to the payment of the death benefits because the death benefits were held subject to a registered pension scheme which is exempt from these charges (IHTA 1984, s. 58).

In cases where:

- the settlor has not made any chargeable transfers in the seven years before he joined the current pension scheme or an earlier pension scheme (as appropriate);
- no payments have been made out of the trust in the previous 10 years; and
- there has been no added property,

there will be no liability provided the value of the trust fund at the time of the periodic charge does not exceed the nil rate band applicable at the 10-year anniversary. Any excess over the then nil rate band will suffer IHT at an effective rate of 6% with a credit for any time during that 10-year period that the property was still in the registered pension scheme.

Example – Harold

Harold, who had made no previous chargeable lifetime transfers at that time, joined a trust-based pension scheme on 5 October 1995 and transferred benefits to his current trust-based pension scheme on 1 May 2014 to which no further contributions are paid. He executed a pilot by-pass trust on 10 July 2012 for a nominal amount. He dies on 1 October 2014 and the scheme administrator exercises his discretion to pay death benefits to the pilot by-pass trust on 5 October 2014.

The first 10-year anniversary charge would have arisen on 5 October 2005 but at that time the death benefit had no value (because Harold was still alive) and, in any event, because Harold was still a member of the pension scheme the exemption in IHTA 1984, s. 58 would apply.

The second 10-year anniversary charge will arise on 5 October 2015. If the value of the trust fund on 5 October 2015 is £425,000 (and the nil rate band then £325,000) the IHT charge would be £100,000 @ 6% and so equal £6,000. This equates to 1.41% of the total value of the trust fund. However, this rate would be reduced to take account of the fact that during the 10-year period, the property in the trust was only outside the pension scheme for four out of the 40 quarters, namely from 5 October 2014 to 5 October 2015. The rate would be 4/40ths of 1.41% and would therefore be 0.141%. The IHT payable at the 10-year anniversary would therefore be £425,000 at 0.141% which equals £600.

Numerically the IHT would be calculated as follows:

- £100,000 @ 6% x 4/40 (the period of time the trust property has been relevant property).
- The IHT charge would therefore be £600.

- So the main rate of 1.41% of the value of the trust has been reduced to 0.141% to reflect the period of time the death benefits were "inside" the pension scheme (and not subject to IHT).

Law: IHTA 1984, s. 58, 81

Cases: *Parry v Cleaver* [1970] AC1; *The Halcyon Skies* [1976] WLR 514

10.8.3 Exit charge

The calculation of an exit charge depends on when the property leaves the trust (i.e. when the exit occurs).

Exit occurring after a 10-year anniversary

If the exit occurs after a 10-year anniversary, when a periodic charge was made, the exit charge is based on the rate of IHT paid at that last periodic charge with no discount in the rate for the period of time the trust fund was not relevant property in the previous ten years.

Example – Harold

Harold's trustees distribute £200,000 from the trust fund on 5 October 2017.

The tax charge is £200,000 @ 1.41% x 8/40 = £564.

Two points should be noted here:

- The amount of any exit charge occurring after the first 10 years will depend on:
    - the rate of IHT charged at the last 10-year anniversary periodic charge (if any) but disregarding any reduction in the rate on account of the fact that the property in the trust was not relevant property for the whole of the prior ten years; and
    - the length of time (in quarters) that the property has been in the trust since the last periodic charge.

  This means that the rate applied in the above example is 1.41%.

- There is a quarterly discount that, in effect, reduces the tax charge by reference to the number of full quarter periods over the ten-year period that the property has been in a discretionary trust since the last 10-year anniversary. Here the property has only been in the trust for two years out of the ten-year cycle and so the discount is 8/40.

Exit occurring before the first 10-year anniversary after death

Where property is distributed *before* the first 10-year anniversary after death, one might think that no IHT will arise because the rate of IHT payable at the last 10-year anniversary was zero as the benefits held in the pension scheme were not then relevant property.

Unfortunately HMRC do not agree with this and, on the basis of IHTA 1984, s. 69(2)(b) and 69(3), state that a recalculation must be made of the hypothetical tax charge that would have arisen at the last 10-year anniversary using the value of death benefits when they became relevant property (i.e. the full value on the member's death). This will establish the notional tax charge at the last 10-year anniversary and the exit charge will be based on that.

Law: IHTA 1984, s. 69(2)(b), 69(3)

10.8.4 HMRC consultation

For some years the Treasury and HM Revenue and Customs have been looking at ways of simplifying the IHT rules that apply to discretionary trusts. To that effect, three consultative documents have been issued over the last four years putting forward proposals to change the system. Each set of consultative document proposals was met by strong criticism from the Representative Bodies of Tax Associations. The Government announced in the 2014 Autumn Statement that they would not proceed with the proposals in the latest consultative document that was issued on 6 June 2014 and proposed the implementation of a settlement nil rate band.

Instead, changes would be made to remove inconsistencies in the legislation and counter certain tax avoidance strategies based on a settlor adding property on the same day to a number of existing settlements. These are known as the "same day transfer" rules and new legislation dealing with this was originally published in the Finance Bill 2015 in the shape of a proposed new section 62A of IHTA 1984. The draft legislation was removed from the *Finance Bill* 2015 in order to include a £5,000 *de minimis* rule.

The question arises as to whether the same day transfer rule could apply where lump sum death benefits from a pension scheme are paid to an existing by-pass trust.

As regards the payments of death benefits out of a trust-based pension scheme into a by-pass trust, it is thought that the new rules would have no impact because the trust will be treated as starting when the pension scheme began and any payment made to the trust which enhances its value is *not* a further transfer of value – just an increase in value of existing property. This will not necessarily be the case with a contract-based scheme where no initial trust was established when the member joined the scheme. The payment of a lump sum death benefit from a contract-based pension scheme to a pilot by-pass trust may therefore be an addition and so, if it went to several trusts, a same-day addition, but it would seem difficult to term this as a "transfer of value" (a pre-requisite for the new s. 62A to apply). Perhaps in these cases, the best approach would be to ensure that any addition is not made to more than one trust.

10.8.5 Trust-based pension schemes

It will clearly be easy to determine when either of these by-pass trusts actually commenced. However, the date of commencement of the by-pass trust will not necessarily be important for IHT purposes as regards calculating IHT at a later date on any lump sum death benefits paid to the trust, or assets representing those death benefits.

The reason for this complexity is that when a person joins a trust-based pension scheme (not a contract-based pension scheme) he will, at that time, be treated as creating a trust of his pension scheme benefits. (For contact-based schemes see below). If a member subsequently dies and lump sum death benefits are paid to a by-pass trust, IHTA 1984, s. 81 will apply to mean that those lump sum death benefits, and assets representing them, will be treated for IHT purposes as being comprised in a trust that commenced when the pension scheme member joined the pension scheme and not when the by-pass trust was established.

This means that in cases where the scheme administrator pays the lump sum death benefits:

- out of a trust-based pension scheme that the member joined before 7 June 2014;
- to a by-pass trust established after 6 June 2014,

the lump sum death benefits and assets representing them will be treated for IHT purposes as being comprised in a pre-7 June 2014 discretionary trust. This, in turn, means that the trust of those benefits/assets will *prima facie* be entitled to a full nil rate band. The assets representing the nominal original gift used to establish the by-pass trust will be subject to the new post 6 June 2014 rules.

Of course, if the individual joins a trust-based pension scheme after 6 June 2014, the trust will be treated as a post 6 June 2014 trust for IHT purposes.

Further complications can of course arise if a transfer has been made from one trust-based pension scheme to another. In general, the s. 81 chain will remain as regards the transferred funds but, if further contributions have been made to the new scheme, then that would have created a new trust in itself and so there would then be two trusts for IHT purposes. It would therefore be necessary to determine when each trust commenced so as to determine their respective treatment under any new IHT rules.

10.8.6 Contract-based schemes

The above treatment does not apply in the case of a contract-based scheme. Examples of a contract-based pension scheme would be a personal pension established under a deed poll or an old retirement annuity policy. There the pension scheme member will not be treated as creating a trust when he joins the pension scheme. Instead, if death benefits are paid to a by-pass trust, the start date of that actual by-pass trust and the date of addition of other funds will determine the IHT treatment of the benefits held in the trust (i.e. inclusive of the death-in-service payment).

It follows that if a by-pass trust has been established before 6 June 2014 and funds are paid to it after 6 June 2014 from a contract-based scheme, those funds will be treated as an addition to a pre 7 June 2014 trust. The funds representing the addition will be subject to the new rules as a separate fund within the same trust. The original trust date will be used for calculating 10 year charges and exit charges.

Where the by-pass trust is established after 6 June 2014, so it is taxed under the new rules, any additional funds paid to it after 6 June 2014 from a contract-based scheme will be treated as swelling the value of that original trust for IHT purposes.

If a person establishes an integrated trust of their death benefits under a contract-based scheme then the date of the trust creation (as opposed to the date of joining the scheme) will be all important for the purposes of any new IHT provisions. In these circumstances, a trust of the death benefits under the scheme will exist from the moment the trust is executed and the value of the trust property will increase on the member's death.

Obviously, much depends on the precise details of any final legislation. However, on the basis that the proposals in the consultative document are largely adopted, it will be important to determine when any trust commenced.

The forestalling proposals in the consultative document prevent people from establishing new trusts and benefiting from the current IHT discretionary trust rules which mean that each trust can benefit from a full nil rate band. However, many people may be unaware that they have already created a discretionary trust by joining their trust-based pension scheme before 7 June 2014 and so, if that trust continues into the future after their death, it will be entitled to a full nil rate band.

11. Transitional protection

11.1 The need for transitional measures

The pension tax regime changed radically on 6 April 2006 (A-Day). For most people, the rules became simpler, but for those who wished to indulge in more sophisticated planning or who had acquired substantial funds, it appeared that one set of complicated rules was replaced by another.

As is always the case with pension reform, the challenge is most acute when the legislators address the issue of existing rights. It is generally regarded as being unfair to reduce benefits or rights that have already accrued or indeed to reduce allowances and limits on which current savings strategies have been based.

Schedule 36 of FA 2004 therefore included a substantial text on transitional protection. Transitional protection covered the following main areas:

- amalgamation of all tax-advantaged pensions schemes and public service schemes into one tax regime;
- harmonisation of scheme rules with the new statutory framework;
- protection of early pension ages to prevent early pensions being regarded as having been paid too early and therefore unauthorised;
- protection of already accrued large funds from the standard lifetime allowance tax charge;
- protection of already accrued large pension commencement lump sums from unauthorised payment charges; and
- protection of previously purchased investments and improvements to investments from new unauthorised payment and scheme sanction charges.

Law: FA 2004, Sch. 36

11.2 Previous regimes: a summary

The differences between the "old" and "new" regimes can be summarised. Under the tax regime prior to 6 April 2006:

- There were a number of regimes for different types of product, but the main distinction was between personal pension schemes (and retirement annuity contracts) and occupational pension schemes.
- The tax reliefs were the same for each regime and the same as now. What was different was the way in which the tax relief was limited.

  Personal pension schemes – contributions

  - Contributions were limited to a percentage of "net relevant earnings". The percentage was higher the older the member.
  - Net relevant earnings were capped for these purposes (starting at £60,000 in 1989 and thereafter indexed with prices and rounded up to the nearest £600).
  - Retirement benefits could be taken at any time between the ages of 50 and 75 although those employed in special occupations could take benefits from an earlier age agreed with HMRC.
  - The retirement lump sum was limited to 25 per cent of the fund when it is crystallised.
  - The retirement benefit was otherwise unlimited.
  - Premiums to a pension term assurance policy could qualify for tax relief.
  - The death benefit could be paid as a pension or lump sum which was unlimited.

  Retirement annuity contracts

  - These were not issued after 30 June 1988 (although contributions could have continued).
  - They were contract-based (deferred annuities).

- They were subject to similar rules to those for personal pension schemes.
- Maximum relievable contributions depended on age, but using a different scale from the later personal pension schemes.
- There was no facility to pay contributions other than from the individual planholder.
- The lump sum was calculated as three times the residual pension (so it increased with age and interest rates).

Occupational schemes (retirement benefit schemes)

The tax regime went through a number of changes between 1970 and 2006. The following describes the last such regime:

- Schemes were mainly trust-based (particularly if they were being funded).
- The tax rules primarily restricted emerging retirement benefits.
- The maximum benefit for an individual depended on his or her years of service with the employer (a pension of up to two-thirds of final remuneration after 20 years' service).
- The lump sum was based on a multiple of final remuneration based on service, but further restricted to maintain the link with related pension.
- Maximum benefits were inclusive of benefits accrued in previous occupations.
- There was a further limit on personal relievable contributions (15 per cent of remuneration).
- Lump sum and income death benefits were restricted to a multiple of pay or member's pension.
- Pensionable remuneration was capped from 1989.

11.3 The transitional provisions

The two main areas that we will explore in this chapter are the implementation of the lifetime allowance and the protection of retirement lump sums.

11.3.1 Lifetime allowance

For most individuals, the main control on output from registered pension schemes from 6 April 2006 is the standard lifetime allowance (SLA). Benefits are only measured against the lifetime allowance when there is a benefit crystallisation event (BCE). BCEs only apply after 5 April 2006.

The lifetime allowance was set at £1.5m in 2006-07 with a provision that it would increase in stages over the next five years to £1.8m in 2010-11. It remained at £1.8m in 2011-12 and then reduced to £1.5m in 2012-13. It fell further to £1.25m in 2014-15 and to £1 million in 2016-17 (and 2017-18). From 2018-19, the lifetime allowance will increase each year with increases in the Consumer Prices Index.

The reductions in 2012-13, 2014-15 and 2016-17 were accompanied by the facility for the member to claim fixed protection (FP) or (2014-15 and 2016-17 only), individual protection (IP). Fixed protection was unavailable if the member already enjoyed enhanced or primary protection (see below). FP 2012 ensures that the member is entitled to an "underpinned" lifetime allowance: the greater of £1.8m and the current SLA (£1m in 2017-18). In 2014-15 (FP 2014), the underpinned lifetime allowance is the greater of £1.5m and the standard lifetime allowance (i.e. £1.5m). In 2017-18 (FP 2016), it is the greater of £1.25m and the standard lifetime allowance (i.e. £1.25m).

IP 2014 allowed further benefit accrual without jeopardising the protection and protects the value of the accrued benefit up to £1.5 million (at 5 April 2014). So, if the value of the member's benefits was £1.45m at 5 April 2014, the protected amount is £1.45m. If the value was £1.55m, the protected value is £1.5m. IP 2016 protects the accrued value to £1.25m.

Neither fixed nor individual protection is classified as transitional protection in the legislation. Transitional protection refers to protection from the lifetime allowance tax charge which accompanied the change to the new tax regime implemented on 6 April 2006. (See **3.12** for further text about fixed and individual protections.)

11.3.2 Primary and enhanced protection

There are two types of protection from the lifetime allowance charge that the individual could have claimed at any time before 6 April 2009. They are "primary" and "enhanced" protection. It was possible for the individual to claim both enhanced and primary protection and in many cases this was the appropriate cause of action: if enhanced protection was lost, this would trigger primary protection.

It would be useful to draw "thumbnail" sketches of each type of protection although they should be read with caution because the detailed rules are fairly convoluted.

Enhanced protection

Enhanced protection protects the total of all registered pension scheme benefits in respect of an individual from the charge providing that:

- there is no further (beyond 5 April 2006) benefit accrual;
- the individual does not enter into any new arrangements other than to transfer rights;
- transfers are only "permitted" or "permissible".

Particular features of enhanced protection are:

- no minimum required value;
- no maximum protected value;
- the loss of enhanced protection is not retrospective;
- the protection is at member rather than scheme level so it covers (or not) all pension provision for an individual.

Primary protection

Primary protection protects the total value of all registered scheme benefits to a monetary limit in respect of an individual from the charge providing that the total value of the member's benefits at 5

April 2006 was more than £1.5m. The amount protected is the value of the benefits at that date increased to the same extent as the SLA. This requires some etymological dexterity since the SLA reduced in 2012. The rule is now that the protected amount will increase with the SLA, but will not reduce with it (so it is an underpinned allowance). The lifetime allowance for anyone who claimed primary protection is therefore the value of benefits at 5 April 2006 increased by 20 per cent (derived from £1.8m/£1.5m x 100%). By way of example, if the value of benefits was £2m at 5 April 2006 and the member claimed primary protection, the protected allowance in 2015-16 would be 1.8/1.5 x £2m = £2.4m. It would have risen to this figure in 2010/11, but would not have reduced with the subsequent reduction in the lifetime allowance.

Primary protection will not be lost unless the application of a pension debit on dissolution of marriage reduces the value of benefits below £1.5m.

Law: FA 2004, Sch. 36, para. 7-17

11.3.3 Valuing the benefits for transitional protection

Probably the most difficult aspect of the transitional protection rules is a hangover from the previous regime, namely the valuation of benefits. The value of an individual's pension rights at 5 April 2006 is the aggregate value of crystallised and uncrystallised rights at that date.

Crystallised rights

The value of crystallised rights is fairly straightforward. It is the pension received at that time multiplied by 25. So, a pension of £10,000 at that date equates to a value for these purposes of £250,000. The figure is higher than the usual valuation factor of 20 because any lump sum taken is ignored. This caused some anomalies at the time because some pre-April 2006 pensions did not allow a lump sum to be taken, chief among these being protected rights pensions derived from contracting out rules and some AVC pensions.

If the individual was in receipt of a drawdown pension, the pension to be taken into account is the maximum allowable withdrawal at 5 April 2006 rather than the pension that was actually being taken.

In order to determine the value of the crystallised pension commencement lump sum, the total value of crystallised benefits (i.e. the pension multiplied by 25) is divided by 4. The result bears no direct relationship to the lump sum that was actually taken.

Law: FA 2004, Sch. 36, para. 10
Guidance: PTM 088300

Uncrystallised rights

The legislation specifies how uncrystallised rights under different types of arrangement are to be valued at 5 April 2006. It lists:

a. cash balance arrangements;
b. other money purchase arrangements;
c. defined benefit arrangements; and
d. hybrid arrangements (i.e. a combination of any of the above).

The basis of the calculation is that the value represents the value of benefits if they were being taken on that day, but without any actuarial reductions that would normally be made by the scheme to reflect early payment. For the purposes of the valuation only, it is assumed that benefits would be available notwithstanding that the member may not yet have reached normal pension age. Specific conditions apply to each option.

Cash balance scheme

If the scheme is a cash balance scheme or a defined benefit scheme, the valuation must assume that the member has reached an age at which no early retirement deductions would apply and that the member was in good health (so there would be no enhancement).

Law: FA 2004, s. 212(4), 277; Sch. 36, para. 8
Guidance: RPSM 03101080 (webarchives.nationalarchives.gov.uk)

Defined benefit scheme

If the scheme is a defined benefit scheme, the benefit will have been expressed as a pension and perhaps a separate lump sum. In that case, a relevant revaluation factor must be applied to the pension which must be added to the lump sum. The value is therefore ((accrued pension x RVF) + lump sum). If the lump sum is only an option provided by commutation (as is usually the case with private sector schemes), the pension is taken as the pension before commutation and the lump sum in the formula is nil. RVF is the relevant revaluation factor which is usually 20, but higher if agreed with HMRC because the rate of pension increase is exceptionally high.

Law: FA 2004, s. 212(6), 277; Sch. 36, para. 8
Guidance: RPSM 03101090 (webarchives.nationalarchives.gov.uk)

Other money purchase scheme

If the scheme is an "other money purchase scheme" (i.e. not a cash balance scheme) the valuation represents the value of the accrued funds, that is the market value of assets or funds representing those assets and the value of cash.

Law: FA 2004, s. 212(5); Sch. 36, para. 8
Guidance: RPSM 03101070 (webarchives.nationalarchives.gov.uk)

Hybrid scheme

If the scheme is a hybrid scheme (i.e. in effect incorporating an "underpin"), the valuation method yielding the highest result is used. If appropriate, the revaluation factor is applied to a defined benefit.

Law: FA 2004, s. 212(7); Sch. 36, para. 8
Guidance: RPSM 03101100 (webarchives.nationalarchives.gov.uk)

11.3.4 Retirement benefit schemes

Retirement benefit schemes and buy-out policies were subject to limits on emerging benefits before 6 April 2006. For the purposes of transitional protection and determining values, any sums that exceeded HMRC limits at 5 April 2006 are ignored. Furthermore, if an individual was a member of more than one retirement benefit scheme in respect of the same employment, each was required to be calculated separately to the others and then, if necessary, proportionately cut back.

There is a difficulty with the calculation of benefits under a retirement benefit scheme whether it is a defined benefit or money purchase scheme. Put very simply, if pensions at normal retirement date accrue at a faster rate than 1/60 of final remuneration for each year of service, then they will be reduced proportionate to time if they are taken "early" (n/ns x p, where n is actual service, ns is potential service and p is the maximum pension that would have been available at normal retirement date). There are other (rarer) circumstances when this reduction may apply.

Rather than burdening oneself with the detail, it is worth considering:

- few people will be undertaking this calculation now: the ultimate values will be available;
- even given the methodology, it would be difficult to calculate the figures from ground level because different schemes were subject to different tax regimes and scheme rules;
- there were occasional difficulties when HMRC rules conflicted with DWP rules in relation to money purchase schemes (in which case DWP rules prevailed);
- the deadline for claiming enhanced or primary protection was 5 April 2009, by which time the claimant had to submit form APSS 200 which included values at 5 April 2006;
- the methodology can be found at RPSM 03101530 onwards.

11.4 Primary protection

Primary protection works by "modifying" the individual's standard lifetime allowance. The result is achieved by determining a "primary protection factor" and applying it at each subsequent benefit crystallisation event (BCE).

The factor is found through the simple:

(RR – SLA)/SLA

where:

RR is the value of the individual's pension rights at 5 April 2006; and

SLA is £1.5m.

For example, suppose the value of funds was £3m. The factor is (£3m-£1.5m)/£1.5m = 1.

When there is a BCE, the individual's lifetime allowance is obtained by the formula (SLA + (1 x SLA) in this case. If the lifetime allowance has increased to £1.8m, the individual would be able to call on a lifetime allowance of (£1.8m x 2) = £3.6m, assuming no previous BCEs.

Note that although the value of primary protection rights increases to the same extent as the standard lifetime allowance, it does not reduce with it. So, although in 2016-17 the lifetime allowance is £1m, primary protection is based on a figure of £1.8m which is where it peaked (until now) in 2010-11.

If a pension debit is on divorce awarded against an individual who enjoys primary protection, the amount of the debit is deducted from the value of benefits protected at 5 April 2006. If the value then goes below £1.5m (the 2006 standard lifetime allowance), primary protection is lost. If it does not fall below £1.5m, the factor is recalculated with effect from that date although it does not affect BCEs that may have taken place between 5 April 2006 and the date of the debit.

Example (provided by HMRC):

Kevin has notified protected pension rights of £3 million. His personal lifetime allowance is twice the standard lifetime allowance.

In June 2010, his protected pension rights are reduced by a pension debit of £300,000. His £3 million pension rights on 5 April 2006 are deemed to have reduced to £2.7 million because of the £300,000 pension debit. This causes a recalculation of his protected pension rights which reduces his personal lifetime allowance to 1.8 x the standard lifetime allowance. From 6 April 2012, the 1.8 factor applies to a lifetime allowance of £1.8 million for so long as the lifetime allowance is below this figure.

Kevin crystallises his benefits in December 2016 when the standard lifetime allowance is £1 million. Kevin can crystallise benefits valued up to £3.24 million (£1.8m x 1.8) without being subject to the lifetime allowance charge.

Law: FA 2004, Sch. 36, para. 7-11
Guidance: PTM 092300

11.5 Enhanced protection

11.5.1 What is enhanced protection?

Subject to having notified HMRC appropriately by 5 April 2009 and not subsequently jeopardising a claim, enhanced protection will prevent the lifetime allowance charge applying to any funds of the individual regardless of their size. Enhanced protection would usually have been claimed with primary protection in case the former failed and the latter was then able to offer a (reduced) measure of protection.

Again, if a valuation before 5 April 2006 revealed a "relevant excess", the excess was required to be surrendered for the claim to be valid.

The following surrenders of rights did not count as a surrender of relevant excess:

- a surrender for the purposes of a pension sharing order;
- a surrender to increase prospective rights for a dependant of the member;
- a surrender by means of a transfer of rights to another arrangement;
- a surrender that was an assignment; and
- a surrender of rights held prospectively by the individual as a dependant of a scheme member.

Law: FA 2004, Sch. 36, para. 12-17
Guidance: RPSM 03104010-03104040 (webarchives.nationalarchives.gov.uk); PTM 092100

11.5.2 Losing enhanced protection

Enhanced protection will be lost where:

- relevant benefit accrual occurs in relation to a registered pension scheme of the member;

- there is a transfer from an arrangement that is not a permitted or permissible transfer;
- a new arrangement is established for the member other than:
    - solely to accept a transfer of rights from another arrangement,
    - as part of a retirement benefits compliance exercise,
    - as part of an age-equality compliance exercise,
    - where an arrangement receives an impermissible transfer;
- the member notifies HMRC that he does not wish enhanced protection to apply.

Law: FA 2004, Sch. 36, para. 12(2); *The Registered Pension Schemes (Enhanced Lifetime Allowance) Regulations* 2006 (SI 2006/131), reg. 4
Guidance: PTM 092400

11.5.3 New arrangements

An arrangement is set up as part of a retirement-benefit activities compliance exercise if all the following conditions are met.

1. The new arrangement is set up in connection with the cancellation of rights under an old arrangement relating to the individual.
2. The old arrangement is held under a registered pension scheme that is an occupational pension scheme and has some members who have not accrued retirement benefits, but only have the prospective right to pension and/or lump sum death benefits. To comply with PA 2004, s. 255 (which describes the requirements for membership of a retirement benefits scheme, discussed in **Chapter 1**) those members whose rights consist only of prospective (lump sum and/or pension) death benefits are removed from the scheme. The old arrangement is cancelled to enable the scheme to comply with s. 255.
3. Both the old and new arrangements relating to the individual are in respect of the same employment and

there are prospective rights to pension death benefits under both arrangements.

4. The prospective rights to death benefits conferred under the new arrangement are not significantly different from the rights conferred under the old arrangement.

If the prospective rights to death benefits remain in the original registered pension scheme, and the member's prospective pension benefits are moved out instead, this will not satisfy the requirements for a retirement-benefits activities compliance exercise. Unless the transfer of the prospective pension benefits is a permitted transfer the new arrangement will cause loss of enhanced protection.

Law: FA 2004, Sch. 36, para. 12(2)(c), (2A)-(2C)
Guidance: PTM 092420

11.5.4 Impermissible transfers

The following are impermissible transfers into a money purchase arrangement that is not a cash balance arrangement:

- a transfer of sums or assets from an arrangement under a registered pension scheme not relating to the individual (except as a direct consequence of a pension sharing order);
- a transfer of sums or assets which were held otherwise than by a pension scheme.

There is an impermissible transfer if at any time after 5 April 2006 there has been a transfer or payment to a hybrid arrangement and that hybrid arrangement later becomes an "other money purchase arrangement".

There is an impermissible transfer if at any time after 5 April 2006 a defined benefits arrangement or a cash balance arrangement for an individual becomes a money purchase scheme for that individual under that scheme.

Law: FA 2004, Sch. 36, para. 12(2)(aa), 17A
Guidance: PTM 092420

11.5.5 Relevant benefit accrual

Relevant benefit accrual is easy to describe in relation to a money purchase scheme: it is simply the payment of further contributions. For cash balance and defined benefit schemes, the test is, broadly speaking, to determine whether there has been any increase in benefits that can be attributed to contributions (rather than, for instance, transfer values) and whether that increase exceeds inflation.

Relevant benefit accrual occurs when the total value of

- the benefit crystallisation events; and
- permitted transfers to other money purchase arrangements

paid from cash balance and/or defined benefits arrangements in respect of the same employment, or from arrangements related to the employment. are more than the "appropriate limit".

The "appropriate limit" is the greater of:

- the indexed amount; and
- the earnings recalculation amount.

The indexed amount

The value of the pension rights on 5 April 2006 are increased by an indexation percentage to the date of the benefit crystallisation event or of the "permitted transfer". The indexation percentage is the greatest of:

- an average annual increase of five per cent from 5 April 2006;
- for guaranteed minimum pensions in respect of contracted-out accrual before April 1997, the increase in that guaranteed minimum pension; and
- the percentage increase in the Retail Price Index from April 2006 to the month in which the benefit crystallisation event or the permitted transfer occurs.

The total value of benefits crystallised/transfers made is compared to the indexed amount to see whether or not relevant benefit accrual has occurred.

The earnings recalculation amount

This is the value of the pension rights in the arrangement on 5 April 2006 uprated by "the earnings re-calculation value". The value of the pension rights on 5 April 2006 is calculated using pensionable earnings up to that date. Under the earnings re-calculation value, earnings paid after 5 April 2006 can be used to increase the value of pension rights on that date.

The earnings recalculation value is set at the point of the first benefit crystallisation event or permitted transfer to an other money purchase arrangement.

The test of benefit accrual differs from the similar test for fixed protection. Loss of fixed protection is immediate whereas loss of enhanced protection may only be discovered when benefits are taken or the member leaves service by virtue of the earnings recalculation amount.

Care should be taken with the definition of benefit accrual. It may be a consequence of delaying retirement beyond normal scheme pension age.

Law: FA 2004, Sch. 36, para. 13, 15
Guidance: PTM 092430

11.5.6 Permitted transfers

A transfer can only be a permitted transfer if:

- All or part of the sums and assets or pension rights under an arrangement are transferred to one or more other money purchase arrangements under a registered pension scheme or a recognised overseas pension scheme. So any type of arrangement may transfer to an other money purchase arrangement. Pension rights may be transferred to other money purchase arrangements under more than one scheme.
- All or part of the sums and assets or pension rights under a defined benefits or cash balance arrangement are transferred to a defined benefits or cash balance arrangement under a registered pension scheme or a recognised overseas pension scheme, but only:

- where the transfer is made in connection with the winding up of the original pension scheme containing the cash balance or defined benefits arrangement, and the receiving cash balance or defined benefits arrangement relates to the same employment as the transferring arrangement that is being wound up, or
- where the transfer is made in connection with a relevant business transfer. A relevant business transfer is a transfer of all or part of a business or undertaking from one person to another that involves at least 20 employees, and if both parties to the business transfer are companies they are not treated as members of the same group for the purposes of CTA 2010, Pt. 5, or
- where the transfer is made as part of a retirement-benefit activities compliance exercise (i.e. to meet a statutory obligation).

- Sums and assets being used for the provision of a scheme pension (crystallised benefits) are transferred to an insurance company as a result of the winding up of the transferring pension scheme (a section 32 / buy-out policy).

  Where defined benefit or cash balance pension rights are transferred to a money purchase arrangement, the value of the sums and assets received by the money purchase arrangement are actuarially equivalent to the rights being transferred.

  Where the transfer is permitted because the original scheme is being wound up, the receiving scheme relates to the same employment (if it is not a buy-out policy).

Law: FA 2004, Sch. 36, para. 12(7), (8) *The Taxation of Pension Schemes (Transitional Provisions) Order* 2006, Article 35 (SI 2006/572)

Guidance: PTM 092420

11.5.7 *Effect of losing enhanced protection*

If an individual loses a successful claim for enhanced protection, the loss is not retrospective. However, if there have been events that would have been benefit crystallisation events had the individual not claimed enhanced protection, then if there are any BCEs after loss of protection, it is assumed that the earlier events used some of the individual's lifetime allowance. For these purposes, it is assumed that the lifetime allowance was set at the then standard lifetime allowance.

Example

Jean made a successful claim for enhanced protection in 2006. In 2011 when the standard lifetime allowance was £1.8 million, she crystallised benefits valued at £450,000. She enjoyed enhanced protection so there was no measurement against the lifetime allowance.

In 2013 she lost her enhanced protection and in 2016 crystallised £800,000 (when the standard lifetime allowance had reduced to £1 million). She must take into account that she used 25 per cent of the lifetime allowance in 2011 in addition to the proportion of allowance used in 2016.

11.6 Lump sum protection

The lump sum in this case refers to what is now described as the pension commencement lump sum. The general rule is that the maximum allowable is 25 per cent of the total retirement benefits being crystallised, subject to a cap of 25 per cent of the lifetime allowance. The lump sum is deemed to be taken at the same time as the member becomes entitled to the related pension although there is some flexibility as to when payment actually has to be made.

11.6.1 *Rules before 6 April 2006*

That was not always the case, however. Before 6 April 2006, the lump sum rules could be summarised thus:

- the maximum lump sum under a personal pension scheme was 25 per cent of the value of benefits coming into payment;

- the maximum lump sum under a retirement annuity contract was three times the residual pension;
- the maximum lump sum under a fund that enjoyed protected rights (derived from contracting out and since abolished) was nil;
- the maximum lump sum paid under an occupational scheme varied according to the relevant tax regime, but in its last incarnation was 2.25 x the available initial pension, which was itself determined by reference to years of service with the employer and capped final remuneration.

11.6.2 Rules after 5 April 2006

From 6 April 2006, the pension commencement lump sum in respect of a scheme that started before that date will be calculated as:

- 25 per cent of total benefits being crystallised and subject to being "capped" by the available lifetime allowance;
- in the case of a personal pension scheme or retirement annuity contract, 25 per cent of total benefits being crystallised, but without the lifetime allowance cap if the member has enhanced or primary protection; or
- in the case of an occupational scheme only, any percentage of total benefits being crystallised based on the valuation at 5 April 2006 and without the lifetime allowance cap if the member has enhanced or primary protection.

11.6.3 Two bases of lump sum protection

There are two bases of lump sum transitional protection:

1. Lump sum protection when the member has claimed enhanced or primary protection and the value of lump sum rights at 5 April 2006 was more than £375,000 (so it might be more or less than 25 per cent of total benefits). There are two elements to this: this form of protection will not be available, for instance, if although the member has enhanced or primary protection, the value of lump sums did not exceed £375,000 in 2006. This protection is

available only at member level. It applies to aggregate benefits from all schemes.

2. Lump sum protection when (1) above does not apply and the lump sum relating to a scheme represents more than 25 per cent of total benefits from that scheme or more than 25 per cent of the standard lifetime allowance. So, the protection is at scheme level and may apply to more than one scheme of the same member. In this case, no claim is required to be made and protection, if it applies, is automatic.

Note that if the pre-6 April 2006 rules did not allow or restricted a lump sum, the lump sum cannot be protected (there is no lump sum to protect) or the restriction removed.

Guidance: PTM 063240, 063250

11.7 Valuing benefits at 5 April 2006

In calculating the value of lump sums at 5 April 2006, the lump sums of both crystallised and uncrystallised benefits at that date are taken into account for this purpose. If the benefits have crystallised, the lump sum is deemed to be 25% x (25 x the pension in payment at that date). If the pension is a drawdown pension, the maximum available withdrawal is used in the calculation.

For personal pension schemes and retirement annuity contracts, the uncrystallised value of benefits is the value of assets (or funds) and cash held in the relevant arrangements and the lump sum is usually assumed to be 25 per cent of that value. In fact, the lump sum may be restricted by certificates issued on transfer of benefits from an occupational scheme to a personal pension scheme before 6 April 2006 and which were designed to ensure that there could have been no lump sum advantage from moving from one regime to another.

Under an occupational scheme, the lump sum is determined by the scheme rules as limited by HMRC limits. The legislation (FA 2004 Sch. 36, para. 25) describes it thus:

"6. The amount is the amount of any lump sum to which the individual would have been entitled under the arrangement on 5th April 2006 on the assumption that the individual became entitled to the present payment of a lump sum under the arrangement on that date.

7. In calculating an amount in accordance with sub-paragraph (6) the valuation assumptions apply but as if the reference to such age (if any) as must have been reached to avoid any reduction in benefits on account of age in paragraph (a) of section 277 were to the relevant age; and for this purpose "the relevant age" is:
    a. if on 10th December 2003 the terms of the arrangement made provision for a reduction in the amount of benefits payable in respect of rights under the arrangement on account of the holder of the rights being below a particular age, that age, and
    b. otherwise, 60."

Note that freestanding AVCs and some main scheme AVCs were unable to provide lump sums prior to 6 April 2006, but they may be able to offer lump sums of up to 25 per cent of total value under the general rules (i.e. with no transitional protection).

Law: FA 2004, s. 277, Sch. 36, para. 25

11.8 Occupational schemes – lump sum valuation

The maximum permitted lump sum allowed under an approved occupational scheme is the maximum lump sum that a scheme could pay to an individual in good health on 5 April 2006. In arriving at the maximum permitted lump sum, assume that:

- if the individual were in the employment to which the arrangements related on 5 April 2006, the individual is deemed to have left the employment on that date (this is important because the benefit is calculated by reference to service with the employer, not just in the scheme); and
- HMRC would permit immediate payment of lump sum benefits on 5 April 2006 to an individual of whatever age. By way of example, the fact that the deemed payment of the lump sum would be to an individual aged, say, 40 should not be taken as being an action that would cause HMRC to withdraw approval.

What this means is that the calculation of the maximum lump sum will be derived from the greater of:

a. Actual service/potential service x the maximum available lump sum; and
b. 3/80 x years of service x final remuneration (as defined).

The maximum available pension will depend on the regime under which the scheme was established and/or the date the member joined the scheme. It could be as much as 1.5 x final remuneration.

The calculation is complicated if there have been retained benefits. These are benefits that have accrued before the accrual under scheme under consideration. The objective of the retained benefit rules is to ensure that the limit on benefits does not distinguish between one period of service in one scheme and a series of consecutive periods of service. The rules need not apply if the member is a 1987 or 1989 member or if earnings were less than £25,000 in the last year of employment. Further information on this especially difficult area can be found at RPSM 03105100.

If the member has primary protection and the value of the lump sum at 5 April 2006 exceeds £375,000, the protection will allow the pension commencement lump sum to represent the value at 5 April 2006 plus increases to the same extent as the lifetime allowance. However, the lump sum is now described as "underpinned" because it does not reduce with the lifetime allowance. The practical consequence of this in 2016-17 is that the lump sum reflects the increase in lifetime allowance until 2010-11 (20 per cent), but does not reflect the reduction in the allowance (to £1m in 2016-17).

A feature of member-specific lump sum protection that derives from primary protection is that the lump sum may be taken from any scheme in any proportion. This is a valuable option and, for example, would allow an aggregate lump sum to be taken from money purchase benefits if the commutation rate applying to a defined benefit scheme is unattractive.

If the member has claimed and retained enhanced protection, then member-specific lump sum protection will be available if the value of the lump sum at 5 April 2006 exceeded £375,000. It may be worth remembering here that (unlike primary protection) enhanced protection did not require the value of benefits to exceed the standard lifetime allowance.

The protected lump sum is the lump sum as valued at 5 April 2006 as a proportion of the total value of the member's scheme benefits. So, if the lump sum at that date was 30 per cent of the value of benefits, it will continue to be 30 per cent whatever the later value.

If a member registered for primary or enhanced protection, but did not enjoy lump sum protection, then when the lifetime allowance reduced to £1 million on 6 April 2016, he or she retained an entitlement to a pension commencement lump sum of up to 25 per cent of £1.5 million (i.e. not £1 million). However, for the purposes of calculating available lifetime allowance on a second or subsequent BCE, it is assumed that the amount already crystallised has been revalued to reflect the higher, underpinned lifetime allowance (from £1 million to £1.5 million).

Law: FA 2004, Sch. 36, para. 25-28
Guidance: PTM 063250

11.9 Enhanced protection: mixing the rules

HMRC advice in the *Registered Pension Schemes Manual* was that if enhanced protection has been claimed, the member does not then have the option of using the standard rules if they would produce a better result because notification of enhanced protection has changed the lump sum. However, if the scheme administrator pays a lump sum that does not exceed the "standard" lump sum, although the payment will be an unauthorised payment, the administrator will not be subject to the scheme sanction charge.

Law: FA 2004, Sch. 36, para. 30
Guidance: RPSM 03105220 (webarchives.nationalarchives.gov.uk)

11.10 Stand-alone lump sums and enhanced protection

A pension commencement lump sum cannot be paid where all the benefits are being paid in lump sum form. This is because FA 2004 requires a pension commencement lump sum to be paid in connection with a related pension.

Where on 5 April 2006 an individual's total uncrystallised rights in all relevant pension arrangements could have been taken entirely as a lump sum benefit the individual can still receive all his benefits in lump sum form if certain conditions are met.

A stand-alone lump sum may be payable to an individual with enhanced protection where:

- On 5 April 2006 all the member's rights under all schemes could have been paid out as a tax free lump sum. In making this test it is assumed that the member has left employment and that HMRC rules would have allowed the immediate lump sum payment on 5 April 2006 whatever the member's age. In valuing the lump sum right it should also be assumed that if the member was not old enough to take an unreduced lump sum under the scheme on 5 April 2006, the benefit should normally be calculated assuming the individual to be 60 years of age. This is modified if a different age was specified under the arrangement on 10 December 2003 as the age at which no reduction would apply to the payment of an immediate benefit, in which case the individual should be assumed to be that age.
- All the benefits are paid out from a pension scheme at the same time as a single BCE (BCE6).
- The member has reached the normal minimum pension age (or any earlier protected pension age he may have under the scheme) or is taking benefits earlier due to ill-health.

Payment of a stand-alone lump sum is a benefit crystallisation event if it occurs before age 75. After that age, the lump sum is not subject to a BCE (it will have been tested at age 75 under BCE 5B) and will ordinarily be tax-free. A stand-alone lump sum otherwise falls within BCE 6 (just as a pension commencement lump sum does). The stand-alone lump sum is not liable to income tax.

There is no set upper limit on the amount of stand-alone lump sum whilst the member has valid enhanced protection.

Law: *The Taxation of Pension Schemes (Transitional Provisions) Order* 2006, *Articles* 25-25D (SI 2006/572)

Guidance: RPSM 03105202 (webarchives.nationalarchives.gov.uk); PTM 063130

11.11 Scheme-specific lump sums

11.11.1 Introduction

Lump sum protection is available where the conditions for member-specific lump sum protection are unavailable. This will arise when either the member has not claimed primary or enhanced protection or the value of lump sum rights at 5 April 2006 was no more than £375,000 (or both).

The facility, which does not have to be claimed, allows the member a pension commencement lump sum of more than 25 per cent of total benefits attaching to a scheme at a BCE. The measure, as we saw above, includes deemed lump sum rights in respect of benefits crystallised before 6 April 2006.

Scheme-specific lump sum protection is unavailable to personal pension schemes and retirement annuity contracts unless a personal pension scheme has received a block transfer after 5 April 2006. (The requirement for two members to transfer as part of the same transaction is suspended if the transfer took place from a money purchase scheme on or after 19 March 2014, but before 6 April 2015 where entitlement to benefits arises before 6 October 2015.)

Law: FA 2004, Sch. 36, para. 31-34
Guidance: PTM 063230

11.11.2 Trivial lump sum and lump sum protection

However a scheme-specific protected pension commencement lump sum may also be paid in connection with a trivial lump sum (not a trivial commutation lump sum).

A lump sum is a trivial lump sum if:

- it is not more than £10,000;
- when paid the member is aged at least 60;
- when paid the member has available lifetime allowance (there needs to be available lifetime allowance after payment of the pension commencement lump sum). Where the lump sum is paid after age 75 the amount of lifetime allowance used up by a BCE 5 or BCE 5B that occurred in relation to the member is ignored for the purpose of

calculating the amount of available lifetime allowance. But lifetime allowance is used up by any event occurring in relation to the member after reaching age 75 if it would have been a benefit crystallisation event but for the fact that it occurred after age 75;

- apart from any pension in payment before 6 April 2006 it extinguishes the member's entitlement to benefit under the scheme;
- it is paid in connection with a scheme-specific protected pension commencement lump sum, and no later than one month after payment of that pension commencement lump sum; and
- since the payment of the pension commencement lump sum:
    - no contributions have been made to the scheme in respect of the member,
    - no recognised transfer has been made into or out of the scheme in respect of the member, and
    - no annuity or scheme pension has been purchased by sums or assets held by the scheme for the benefit of the member.

Where the payment of a scheme-specific protected lump sum leaves a very small amount in respect of the member to provide a pension this provision allows the total rights under the scheme to be paid in lump sum form. The pension commencement lump sum will be tax free. The trivial lump sum is classed under the tax legislation as a special kind of trivial commutation lump sum through commutation of crystallised rights (so not a BCE). This means that the whole trivial lump sum will be taxable at the member's marginal rate of tax.

Example

Andy has a protected lump sum of £100,000. The value of his total rights under his pension scheme is £108,000. On 1 June 2016 Andy has available lifetime allowance of £101,000. Andy's pension scheme pays the whole of his rights to him as lump sums on 1 June 2016. £100,000 is paid as a PCLS and is not taxable. After paying the

PCLS Andy still has £1,000 available lifetime allowance. The remaining £8,000 can be (and is) paid to Andy as a trivial lump sum. The whole £8,000 is taxable and PAYE is applied to this trivial lump sum.

Although scheme-specific lump sum protection does not have to be claimed, a number of conditions must be met in order for it to be retained, most (but not all) of which relate to transfers of benefits to other registered pension schemes.

Law: *The Taxation of Pension Schemes (Transitional Provisions) Order* 2006, Article 23C (SI 2006/572)

Guidance: PTM 063130

11.11.3 Conditions for scheme-specific lump sum protection

The legislation refers to the "pension condition" and conditions A and B having to apply. The pension condition is that the member becomes entitled to all benefits under the scheme (rather than arrangement) on the same day. This precludes phased retirement and taking the lump sum from one scheme and pension from another if the lump sum is to remain protected. It would therefore be unwise to take the lump sum and *then* transfer funds to a drawdown plan, perhaps because it would apparently save time or because the original scheme does not offer a drawdown option!

There are exceptional rules when the scheme offers more than one type of arrangement (such as money purchase and defined benefit), but one lump sum.

Condition A

Condition A simply refers to the types of pension scheme to which the protection may apply (retirement benefit schemes and buy-out policies) and explains that the application is to schemes under which the lump sum before 6 April 2006 exceeded 25 per cent of total benefits.

Condition B

Condition B refers to protection of lump sums on transfer:

> "Condition B is met if the individual is a member of the pension scheme ("a transferee pension scheme") as a result of:

a. a block transfer from the pension scheme ("the original pension scheme") in relation to which condition A is met to the transferee pension scheme, or

b. a block transfer to the transferee pension scheme from a pension scheme that was a transferee pension scheme in relation to the original pension scheme by virtue of the previous application of paragraph (a) or the previous application (on one or more occasions) of this paragraph."

The "block transfer" has already been defined by the legislation at this point as a transfer of rights in respect of two or more individuals from the same scheme to the same scheme as part of the same transaction (not necessarily at the same time). Partial transfer to or from more than one scheme will not meet the definition. The member must not have been a member of the new scheme for more than 12 months. To cater for a specific set of circumstances, the definition will also include a single individual who is the last left in a scheme from which there has been a block transfer.

Block transfers imply transfers to or from personal pension schemes or retirement benefit schemes. Buy-out policies and retirement annuity contracts are single member schemes and unable to meet the requirements of a "block" transfer.

The requirement for two members to transfer as part of the same transaction is suspended if the transfer took place from a money purchase scheme on or after 19 March 2014, but before 6 April 2015 where entitlement to benefits arises before 6 October 2015.

Due to an anomaly in the way the legislation was drafted, only one lump sum for each scheme may be protected. So, if a scheme is protecting a lump sum based on accrual to 5 April 2006 in that scheme, or if the scheme is protecting a lump sum as a consequence of having received a valid block transfer, only one lump sum may be protected on subsequent receipt of transfer sums. The practical lesson from this is simply to ensure that transfers that include protected lump sums should be transferred to schemes of which the individual has (a) not been a member for more than 12 months and (b) does not already hold a protected lump sum. Such might be the dangers of "consolidation".

The amount of the lump sum that is protected, the value, is difficult to access if it was not recorded in 2006.

Law: FA 2004, Sch. 36, para. 31
Guidance: RPSM 03105520-03105523; PTM 063130, 063150

11.11.4 Valuation

For a single arrangement in respect of an employment, the value of uncrystallised lump sum rights and the value of uncrystallised rights are again based on the value of those benefits at 5 April 2006 assuming that the individual took benefits at that date. If the value exceeds the then HMRC limits, the values are limited by those HMRC maxima. The main assumptions are that the member was in good health and left employment on that date and that the usual valuation assumptions apply (such as the multiple of 20 to be applied to defined benefit pensions).

If the member has more than one arrangement under one scheme or in respect of the same employment, the valuation assumptions are applied to each arrangement and then, if appropriate, reduced proportionately. The reduction may be necessary when the total of lump sums payable exceeds the maximum permitted lump sum or, indeed, the maximum permitted pension.

In each case, the legislation requires us to apply a deduction from the value of the lump sum rights. This is derived from a proportion of the excessive lump sum found by applying the formula:

V/AV

where:

> **V** is the value of the uncrystallised lump sum or pension rights under the arrangement, and
>
> **AV** is the total value of the uncrystallised lump sum rights or pension rights under all the arrangements in respect of the employment being pensioned.

HMRC example

Mike has benefits in 3 money purchase arrangements for his single employment. The total fund value is £645,000 split as follows.

- Scheme A = £120,000
- Scheme B = £500,000
- Scheme C = £25,000

All schemes provide lump sums by commutation. Scheme A provides a lump sum of 3/80ths salary for each year of service. Schemes B and C both potentially provide the maximum permitted lump sum that can be paid under HMRC limits. The lump sum entitlement under the schemes on 5 April 2006 is as follows

- Scheme A = £110,000 (91.67%)
- Scheme B = £150,000 (30%)
- Scheme C = £25,000 (100%)

Mike can only protect what he is actually entitled to. The funds in scheme C are less than Mike's HMRC maximum permitted lump sum, but as there is only £25,000 actually available to provide benefits the lump sum entitlement is the fund value of £25,000.

Mike's HMRC maximum benefits are a pension of £100,000 pa and a lump sum of £150,000. The total scheme funds will not provide excessive pension benefits but the total lump sum entitlement of £285,000 is £135,000 more than the HMRC maximum permitted lump sum. The £135,000 excess will be apportioned across all 3 schemes using the formula

Scheme lump sum – (excess lump sum x scheme lump sum/total lump sums)

Scheme A = £110,000 – (£135,000 x £110,000/£285,000) = £57,895

Scheme B= £150,000 – (£135,000 x £150,000/£285,000) = £78,947

Scheme C= £25,000 – (£135,000 x £25,000/£285,000) = £13,158

This gives LS rights apportioned between the schemes as follows

- Scheme A = £57,895 (48.25%)
- Scheme B = £78,947 (15.79%)
- Scheme C = £13,158 (52.63%)

Schemes A and C will have protected lump sum rights. As the adjusted lump sum rights under scheme B are now below 25% scheme B will not be protected. The normal lump sum rules under paragraphs 2 and 3 Sch. 29 FA 2004 will apply to scheme B.

Law: FA 2004, Sch. 36, para. 32
Guidance: PTM 063140

It is too easy to become buried under a mass of formulae and abbreviations when considering protected lump sums, and reference will frequently be made to the *Registered Pension Schemes Manual* and *Pensions Tax Manual*. Until this point, we have considered the protection of lump sums accrued to 5 April 2006. The full "story" extends to the protected lump sum and the value of lump sums in respect of accrual and investment returns after that date. The rules have changed significantly on three occasions, but for crystallisations after 5 April 2006, the appropriate formula for calculating the protected lump sum is:

(VULSR x ULA/FSLA) + ALSA

where:

VULSR is the value of the individual's uncrystallised lump sum rights under the scheme on 5 April 2006;

ULA is the greater of £1.8 million and the standard lifetime allowance when benefit entitlement arises. This resulted from the last change and acknowledges the introduction of an underpinned lifetime allowance which for these purposes in 2017-18 assumes that the lifetime allowance has increased to £1.8 million since 2006-07, but has not reduced;

FSLA = £1.5 million; and

ALSA is the amount found by the formula

(LS + AC – (VUR x CSLA/FSLA))/4, where:

CSLA is the current standard lifetime allowance, or £1.8 million if the individual has fixed protection 2012 (£1.5 million if fixed protection 2014, £1.25 million if fixed protection 2016);

LS is the amount of pension commencement lump sum actually paid;

AC is the amount actually crystallised by becoming entitled to a pension in connection with which the pension commencement lump sum is paid, or the amount of the trivial lump sum paid.

ALSA cannot be a negative value.

Where a scheme pension is paid from a money purchase arrangement AC will be the scheme pension purchase price, i.e. the value of the sums and assets made available to provide the scheme pension. Where the member becomes entitled to the connected pension after reaching age 75 although there is no actual benefit crystallisation event AC is the amount that would have crystallised had there been such an event.

VUR is the value of the individual's uncrystallised rights under the scheme on 5 April 2006.

The following examples have been provided by HMRC.

Example 1 – Benefits taken on or after 6 April 2012

Ruth had a protected lump sum right of £50,000 in a retirement benefit scheme on 5 April 2006. The value of her total rights under the scheme (the fund from which her benefits, including lump sum, will be provided) was £100,000 on 5 April 2006.

Ruth took her lump sum under the scheme in August 2016 when the standard lifetime allowance was £1 million and she did not have fixed protection at that time. At this point the value of her rights under the scheme had fallen to £80,000.

Ruth's lump sum rights in August 2016 are in principle made up of two elements, the revalorised amount of the lump sum rights as at 5 April 2006 and the ALSA lump sum. In Ruth's case the revalorised lump sum is £50,000 x (£1.8 million/£1.5 million) = £60,000.

The amount of the ALSA is the minimum zero, calculated as:

[£80,000 – (£100,000 x £1 million/£1.5 million)]/4

So Ruth could be paid a pension commencement lump sum from the scheme of £60,000.

Example 2 – Benefits taken on or after 6 April 2012

The facts are the same as those for Example 1 above after 6 April 2012 above except that the value of Ruth's rights under the scheme in August 2016 is £160,000.

The value of the revalued amount of the lump sum rights as at 5 April 2006 is unchanged from Example 1 so the revalued lump sum is £60,000.

However, the ALSA lump sum now has an actual value as Ruth's scheme rights have increased by more 60% whilst her standard lifetime allowance between 6 April 2006 and August 2016 has fallen by £250,000. The amount of the ALSA lump sum will be £23,333:

[£160,000 – (£100,000 x £1 million/£1.5 million)]/4

So Ruth can be paid a pension commencement lump sum from the scheme of £83,333, being £60,000 (the revalorised 5 April 2006 lump sum rights) plus £23,333 (the ALSA lump sum).

Example 3 – Benefits taken on or after 6 April 2012

The facts are the same except that total value of benefits is now £118,000 and Ruth applied for fixed protection by 5 April 2013 and this is still valid.

The value of the revalued lump sum rights as at 5 April 2006 is unchanged from Example 1 and is £60,000.

Since Ruth has fixed protection, CSLA is replaced in the ALSA formula by her underpinned lifetime allowance of £1.5 million since this is greater than the standard lifetime allowance of £1 million for August 2016. The amount of the ALSA lump sum will be £4,500:

£118,000 – (£100,000 x £1.5 million/£1.5 million)/4

So Ruth can be paid a total pension commencement lump sum from the scheme of £64,500.

Example 4 – Benefits taken on or after 6 April 2012

The facts are the same as those for Example 3 above except that the value of Ruth's rights under the scheme in August 2016 is £160,000.

The value of the revalued amount of the lump sum rights as at 5 April 2006 is unchanged from Example 3 so the revalued lump sum is £60,000.

However, the ALSA lump sum now has an actual value as Ruth's scheme rights have increased by more 60% which exceeds the increase in her standard lifetime allowance between 6 April 2006 and June 2016. The amount of the ALSA lump sum will be £15,000 calculated:

[£160,000 – (£100,000 x £1.5 million/£1.5 million)]/4

So Ruth can be paid a pension commencement lump sum from the scheme of £75,000, being £60,000 (the revalued 5 April 2006 lump sum rights) plus £15,000 (the ALSA lump sum).

What this formula is doing is indexing pre-2006 uncrystallised lump sum rights and adding to them 25 per cent of the difference between the actual value of rights crystallising and 25 per cent of the indexed value of those rights (from 6 April 2006). The effect on a money purchase scheme is that:

- if investment returns easily outperform the underpinned lifetime allowance, the lump sum will reduce significantly as a proportion of the pre-2006 fund, but will increase significantly as a proportion of the post 2006 fund;
- further contributions (after April 2006) will increase the lump sum as will investment returns.

We have already seen that a transfer of rights that is not part of a block transfer will jeopardise scheme-specific lump sum protection. However, the member may transfer part of his or her rights. In these circumstances, there will be no protection for the rights that are transferred, but protection will be retained for the reduced value of benefits that are not transferred. In those circumstances, the value of protected lump sum rights is reduced by 25 per cent of the value of rights transferred.

Finding the maximum allowable pension commencement lump sum under a defined benefits arrangement that provides lump sum benefits by commutation is more complex – unless the scheme uses a lump sum commutation factor of 20:1. However, it is unusual to find a defined benefit scheme offering a lump sum that exceeds 25 per cent of benefits and which may therefore be protected. RPSM 03105612 gives an example of paying a protected lump sum of more than 25% from a defined benefits arrangement.

Law: FA 2004, Sch. 36, para. 34
Guidance: PTM 063130

11.11.5 Stand-alone lump sums

There are circumstances in which a stand-alone lump sum may be paid (as is the case with member-specific protection above). The lump sum is not a pension commencement lump sum because, by definition, there is no related pension. The conditions mirror those for enhanced and primary protection lump sums:

- the member has reached the normal minimum pension age (or any earlier protected pension age enjoyed under the scheme) or is taking benefits earlier due to ill-health;
- the entitlement to the lump sum is a single benefit crystallisation event that crystallises all of the member's rights under the scheme that had not crystallised before 6 April 2006;
- there has been no relevant benefit accrual for the individual under the scheme after 5 April 2006;
- the member did not have lump sum rights of more than £375,000 on 5 April 2006 where either primary or enhanced protection applies when the lump sum is paid;
- on 5 April 2006, all the member's uncrystallised rights under the scheme and any other employer-sponsored schemes or buy-out policy relating to the same employment could have been paid out as a tax free lump sum; and
- the total value of the member's uncrystallised lump sum rights lump sum provided under all registered employer-sponsored schemes and buy-out policies relating to the same employment (calculated as per the previous bullet point) was within pre-6 April 2006 HMRC limits.

Payment of a stand-alone lump sum is a benefit crystallisation event (BCE 6).

Where a scheme under which a member has the right to a stand-alone lump sum receives a transfer from a registered pension scheme the member will lose the right to payment of a stand-alone lump sum unless

- the transfer comes from a scheme where immediately before the transfer the member had the right to the payment of a stand-alone lump sum;
- all of the member's uncrystallised rights are transferred from the transferring scheme to the receiving scheme; and
- the receiving scheme has not paid out a stand-alone lump sum or a pension commencement lump sum to the individual before the transfer was made.

A transfer in from a non-registered pension scheme will trigger the loss of the right to a stand-alone lump sum.

Law: *The Taxation of Pension Schemes (Transitional Provisions) Order* 2006, Articles 25-25D (SI 2006/572)

Guidance: RPSM 03105640-03105642 (webarchives.nationalarchives.gov.uk)

12. Employer-financed retirement benefit schemes

12.1 Background

It is indeed ironic that one of the more difficult areas of pensions is that of employer-financed retirement benefit schemes or EFRBS. EFRBS are schemes that have not registered for tax purposes (or have de-registered) and were not automatically registered by the transitional provisions implemented on 6 April 2006. An employer-financed retirement benefit scheme is a scheme which is not a registered scheme (i.e. it is a non-registered scheme) that provides or includes provision for "relevant benefits".

The rules have changed back and forth over the years since their genesis in 1989 with the introduction of funded unapproved retirement benefit schemes (FURBS) and unfunded unapproved retirement benefit schemes (UURBS).

There was a major change in the emphasis of the tax rules in 2006 when the burden of tax shifted from employer contributions to the distribution of benefits. An understanding of the pre-2006 rules is necessary because there were transitional reliefs. The last major change was in 2011 when rules were introduced to curb avoidance through third-party vehicles.

There are two important features of these schemes:

- they do not attract the tax reliefs available to registered schemes and therefore are not so "restricted" by allowances; and
- they are employer sponsored and continue to benefit from some member protections under DWP legislation. Tax is not therefore the only consideration when assessing their suitability.

In the context of tax rules, they fall more into the camp of settlements. However, their traditional grouping with other forms of pension provision is largely due to DWP member protections that apply in part to these arrangements.

Generally, an EFRBS will be used to top up benefits under a registered pension scheme (these arrangements were introduced when the earnings cap came in for tax relievable pension schemes in 1989), but with the introduction of further anti-avoidance measures they are competing with other forms of remuneration such as share incentive schemes and cash bonuses, not to mention various offshore solutions.

Guidance: EIM 15000-15438

12.2 The 2011 changes

A significant amendment to the taxation of remuneration was introduced by Part 7A of FA 2011 to "tackle arrangements involving trusts or other vehicles used to reward employees that seek to avoid or defer the payment of income tax or NICs" (sometimes described as "disguised remuneration" or "remuneration through third parties"). Its application in the context of pensions includes the provision of earmarked retirement benefits through an EFRBS.

At this stage it might be useful to determine exactly where EFRBS sits on the taxation landscape and where Part 7A applies

Most EFRBS will now be taxed under Part 7A because, by their nature, they involve trusts as a means of rewarding employees.

EFRBS may be taxed under Part 6 (Chapter 2) of ITEPA 2003, but if they are taxable under Part 7A, Part 6 will not apply. The scheme will remain an EFRBS. Relevant benefits provided under an EFRBS from rights accrued since 6 April 2011 will in practice always be subject to Part 7A. "Accrued" in this context is likely to mean paid or where there is a "relevant step" (see below).

Registered pension schemes are specifically exempted from the provisions of both Part 7A and Part 6.

Unfunded schemes were not affected by the 2011 measures unless they promised a benefit through a third party which was backed by some form of security held by the employer. This is because unfunded schemes provide a payment directly from the employer and not generally through a trust.

The legislation ensures that where a third party makes provision for what is, in substance, a reward or recognition or loan in connection with the employee's employment, an income tax charge arises. The value of the provision is based on any sum of money made available or on the higher of the cost or market value where an asset is used to deliver the reward or recognition. The amount concerned counts as a payment of employment income and the employer is required to account for PAYE accordingly.

When this principle is applied to pension schemes, it may refer to earmarking benefits for a member in a scheme which is designed not to so earmark benefits when initially established and funded.

There are special rules for unregistered retirement benefit schemes in addition to the general rules about remuneration through third parties.

Law: FA 2011, Sch. 2; ITEPA 2003, Part 7A; ITEPA 2003, Pt. 6, Ch. 2

12.3 EFRBS as third-party remuneration (Part 7A)

The legislation does not prevent the use of EFRBS, but it can make them less attractive. The legislation treats certain steps taken by the employer (in anticipation of contributions to third party arrangements such as EFRBS) as if they were already "relevant steps" taken by a relevant third person. If the other statutory conditions are met, such steps will give rise to Part 7A income.

However, the legislation does not apply unless an employer has given a "relevant undertaking" (for a contribution). The steps which are deemed to be relevant steps are:

- earmarking employer sums or assets with a view to a contribution being made later; and
- with a view to taking a later step.

What this means in practice is that the contribution to an earmarked benefit provided under an EFRBS is subject to tax and National Insurance when the benefit is paid, as may be a transfer of assets between one EFRBS and another. To the extent that the benefit has been provided by a contribution that has been subject to income tax, it will be tax-free if paid as a lump sum. This mirrors the taxation of funded unapproved retirement benefit schemes before 6 April 2006.

The 2011 rules are designed to cover many forms of remuneration or benefit provided through a third party, not just EFRBS (to which this book will restrict itself).

Law: ITEPA 2003, s. 386-400 (as amended)
Guidance: EIM 15010

12.4 Unfunded schemes

It is also worth noting the part played by unfunded schemes. They are not that common. They offer a promise of future income to be paid directly from the employer's resources. As such, they avoid the provisions of ITEPA 2003, Pt. 7A, which prescribes the rules for funded schemes written under trust. On the other hand, they are unable to offer the same level of security as a funded trust-based scheme (because they are dependent on the facility of the ex-employer to pay).

Unfunded schemes are not generally taxed until the income is paid to the member. Any premium paid by the employer to insure the benefit against the possibility of loss on the employer's insolvency will be taxed as a benefit (FA 2004, s. 248 amending ITEPA 2003, s. 307).

An unfunded unapproved retirement benefit scheme (UURBS – the term is still used by HMRC) may be consolidated and rolled into a registered scheme, but the input will normally count towards the annual allowance and the fund will use part of the lifetime allowance.

For IHT purposes, the UURBS is a relevant property trust and on the face of it subject to periodic and exit charges. However, HMRC accept that there is no value in the trust, so no charge can arise. If income is paid, it is not an interest in possession trust.

The government announced in the 2012 Budget Statement that it would not be taking action to curb the use of unfunded, non-registered schemes, but will continue to monitor their take-up (HMRC *Pensions Newsletter* 53, April 2012).

In its 2015 summer Budget, the Government announced informal consultation with a view to including legislation in FA 2016 to "tackle the use of" unfunded employer-financed retirement benefit schemes to avoid a tax advantage on remuneration. More specifically, this refers to National Insurance.

12.5 Transactions that generate liability

The legislation identifies three transactions that could generate a liability: earmarking, payment or transfer, or making an asset available. It is easy to see why the new rules were introduced like this. Imagine an individual being enrolled in a scheme in which benefits are not earmarked until taken. The member then borrows money from the scheme with an indeterminate repayment date. At no stage was it possible under the pre-2011 rules to identify when tax would be paid on what was clearly a benefit. The new rules may tax an earmarked contribution, a loan from the scheme (third party) or a benefit provided by the scheme. The *Finance Act* 2017 proposes a new tax on loans which will tighten this control further.

Under the original 2006 regime, based more on tax-privileged allowances than limits, the government saw no place for a second set of tax reliefs applying to non-registered schemes. Prior to 6 April 2006, unapproved retirement benefit schemes offered relevant benefits and enjoyed limited tax advantages. They could be funded or unfunded and were mainly applicable to individuals whose earnings exceeded the permitted maximum (earnings cap).

If an unapproved scheme met the requirements of an employer-financed retirement benefit scheme after 5 April 2006, then it became an employer-financed retirement benefit scheme. There was some element of protection for funds built up prior to A-Day in funded unapproved retirement benefit schemes (FURBS).

Contributions to employer-financed retirement benefit schemes do not count towards use of the annual allowance and the fund will not count towards the lifetime allowance.

Law: ITEPA 2003, s. 554A
Guidance: EIM45025

12.6 The *Finance Act* 2017

The *Finance Act* 2017 introduced further anti-avoidance measures under the disguised remuneration rules. The rules are mainly aimed at employment-benefit trusts, but they have a technical relevance to EFRBS. Guidance is promised by HMRC for late 2017.

The legislation:

- introduces "new relevant steps" of transferring, releasing or writing off a loan;
- introduces measures to prevent double taxation where relevant steps might otherwise "overlap";
- covers the interaction between an accelerated payment notice and Part 7A; and
- covers transfers of employment-related loans to a new employer.

This summary relies heavily on an HMRC draft guidance document published on 20 March 2017.

Law: ITEPA 2003, Pt. 7A; FA 2017, s. 15, Sch. 6

12.7 Employment income through third parties

The term "employer-financed retirement benefit scheme" covers a range of benefits (including retirement benefits) that may be provided directly or through the medium of a third party such as a trust (of which the employer may be a trustee). The rules we consider here are to do with funded trust arrangements.

In fact, the 2011 rules are complicated. They attempt to counter avoidance through a number of vehicles such as employee benefit trusts (which do not enjoy DWP legislative protection), not just EFRBS. The result is that the rules are not so very different from how they were prior to 6 April 2006 when the incidence of tax was on contributions and scheme investments and benefits were generally tax-free. What has changed is the scope of the rules beyond so-called retirement benefit schemes and the anti-avoidance structure.

12.8 The structure of the rules

Put very simply, if the arrangements provide what is in substance a reward or recognition or loan in connection with the employee's current, future or former employment then a charge to income tax on what is regarded as remuneration will arise. This is known as

Part 7A income referring to the appropriate legislation (Part 7A of ITEPA 2003) and will be taxed under the PAYE process.

Where there is a conflict or possibility of double-charging, occasioned by other legislation dealing with remuneration (such as Part 6), Part 7A prevails if it is applicable.

On the other hand, relevant benefits provided under an unfunded scheme, where the employer pays the benefit directly from company funds to a retiring or retired employee, will normally not pass through any third parties. Such benefits will continue to be taxed as remuneration, but under a separate heading.

A feature of the legislation is that it offers very significant discretion to HMRC.

Law: ITEPA 2003, Part 7A
Guidance: EIM45001

12.8.1 The gateway

Turning to the legislation, we see that the legislators have used their predisposition to use metaphors to explain when the tax charge could arise. In order for Part 7A to apply (i.e. the tax charge):

- the arrangement must "come through the section 554 gateway". This is a set of conditions to be met before the benefit can be considered by HMRC as Part 7A remuneration;
- if it does, a "relevant third person" who is likely to be the trustee must have taken a "relevant step"; and
- the relevant step must be connected with the arrangement.

The gateway in respect of EFRBS comprises seven conditions:

1. there is an undertaking that the contribution will be paid;
2. the contribution is paid to a scheme that is not UK registered;
3. in connection with the arrangement, a third person is to pay "relevant benefits" from the contribution;
4. the provision of relevant benefits is a relevant step;
5. no relief is given (to the member) on the contribution;
6. there is no relief under a double taxation treaty;

7. the contribution is not provision under an overseas pension scheme in respect of which A is exempted from tax under the benefits code.

Law: ITEPA 2003, s. 554A
Guidance: EIM45025

12.8.2 Who is a relevant person?

They are referred to in the legislation and guidance as A, B and P.

A is usually an employee (or former or prospective employee for whom the benefit is being made available).

Any person on this list is a "relevant person":

- A;
- a person "linked" with A;
- a person chosen by A;
- a person chosen by a person linked with A;
- a person within a class of persons chosen by A; or
- a person within a class of persons chosen by a person linked with A.

Any other person not listed above is a "relevant person" if:

- the relevant third person (P) is taking a step on A's behalf;
- P is otherwise taking a step at A's direction or request;
- P is taking a step on behalf of a person linked with A; or
- P is otherwise taking a step at the direction or request of a person linked with A.

B is A's employer.

P is the person taking the step.

Relevant person: a person who will benefit from the steps being taken (e.g. A above).

Relevant step: an action which can give rise to a Part 7A tax charge on earned income.

Relevant third person: the person who takes the step. In general, a "relevant third person" means any person other than A or B (the employee and the employer in this context). So, a "relevant third person" does not have to be connected with either A or B.

Whether a contribution to an EFRBS is to be treated as income under these rules will depend ultimately on whether a relevant step has been taken and when it was taken. A relevant step is taken by a relevant third person if the person:

- pays a sum of money, transfers an asset, or grants a lease which is likely to have an effective duration exceeding 21 years; and
- does so in favour of a "relevant person".

There are some significant exceptions in the case of retirement benefit schemes, the most notable of which are registered pension schemes.

Law: ITEPA 2003, s. 554A
Guidance: EIM45090

12.8.3 What are "relevant benefits"?

Relevant benefits include benefits paid:

- on or in anticipation of retirement;
- on the death of an employee or ex-employee;
- after the death of the (ex-)employee in connection with past service;
- on, or in anticipation or in connection with, any change in the nature of the service of the employee;
- to any person under a pension sharing order.

The definition of "retirement" in this context is problematic. It requires the employment to have ended and for the local inspector of taxes to be satisfied that early retirement benefit is not, in fact, compensation for loss of office. A payment made to compensate for termination of employment due to ill-health will not be regarded as a relevant benefit and will not be charged to tax.

The exceptions will prevent Part 7A income arising to the extent that the relevant step is in respect of sums of money and assets derived from "taxed" contributions to an EFRBS paid before 6 April 2006.

They shelter from Part 7A certain lump sums paid from certain schemes where the lump sums are paid out of rights accruing before 6 April 2011 and the capital cost of annuities.

Such lump sums remain chargeable to income tax as employment income.

Relevant benefits in this context do not include pension income taxed under ITEPA 2003, Pt. 9 (registered pension schemes) or benefits taxed under FA 2004, Sch. 34 (non-UK schemes).

The exceptions will prevent most transfers of sums and assets from giving rise to Part 7A income to the extent that they derive from employer contributions paid before 6 April 2006 to schemes that HMRC accepted as corresponding to approved pension schemes. The exclusion is restricted to transfers made to other schemes accepted as corresponding to approved schemes or to non-UK pension schemes.

Law: ITEPA 2003, Part 7A
Guidance: EIM 15010

12.8.4 Loans

A loan can represent a "relevant step", but there are some significant exceptions such as loans made on commercial terms and other loans made as part of the remuneration package, short-term loans to exercise share option schemes and loans made under employee car ownership schemes.

However, there may be a tax charge if the short-term loans described here are repaid late.

In certain circumstances, a "relevant third person" will take a relevant step if the person makes available a sum of money or asset.

The four circumstances are where the person makes available a sum of money or asset:

- for use as security for a loan made (or to be made) to a "relevant person";
- for use in some other way as security for the meeting of any liability (or the performance of any undertaking) which a relevant person has or will have;

- under an arrangement which permits its use as security for a loan made (or to be made) to a relevant person; or
- under an arrangement which permits its use in some other way as security for the meeting of any liability (or the performance of any undertaking) which a relevant person has or will have.

In this context, making available means making available from the start (and, from the date the legislation is effective, not continuing to make available).

So-called "section 615(3) schemes" fall within the scope of Part 7A. These are described in **Chapter 9**.

12.9 Taxation of EFRBS since 6 April 2011

There are three stages to consider.

12.9.1 Contributions

The payment of an earmarked contribution or earmarking of benefits (such as on allowing a transfer to another scheme or taking benefits) will generate a charge to income tax. The "reward" is treated as remuneration and may be subject to income tax and National Insurance. To the extent that contributions have suffered tax, or have been paid by the employee, lump sum benefits are payable without liability to income tax. Contributions to employer-financed retirement benefit schemes do not count towards the annual allowance and the fund will not count towards the lifetime allowance. This is described in more detail above. If the contribution is not earmarked initially, the tax charge will apply when the benefit is earmarked.

The case of *Forde and McHugh Ltd v HMRC* (Supreme Court – February 2014) raises some questions about the liability of contributions to National Insurance. This would have application to the pre-2006 regime (unapproved retirement benefit schemes) and the post 5 April 2011 regime (remuneration through third parties). The *Social Security Contributions and Benefits Act* 1992 as amended, requires a charge to National Insurance "where in any tax week earnings are paid to or for the benefit of an earner". The court held that a transfer of cash and assets to an unapproved scheme in 2002 did not constitute "earnings". The Court had difficulties with the argument that the transfer to a trust could be given the natural meaning of earnings and also the practical difficulty of valuing what it saw as a contingent benefit (the member might die before taking the retirement benefit). Little discussion of the case has yet been available. The case has no direct application between 2006 and 2011 because the incidence of taxation had fallen on the benefits rather than the contribution in this period. As such, a National Insurance liability would fall on the benefit if the member continued to be employed, but not if he or she had retired.

Law: ITEPA 2003, Part 7A

Case: *HMRC v Forde and McHugh Ltd* [2014] UKSC 14

Guidance: EIM 15010

12.9.2 Investments

The investments will be held in a discretionary trust and the usual tax charges that apply to discretionary trusts will apply.

IHT

There is a possible charge at (currently) six per cent on each tenth anniversary (the periodic charge). Periodic IHT charges are chargeable under IHTA 1984, s. 64(1) and the exit charges are chargeable under s. 65(1). The settlor is the member even if the scheme is funded by the employer. No IHT charge will arise in respect of pre-6 April 2006 contributions that have been "ring-fenced" or in respect of contributions/benefits from that date that are subject to income tax.

The chargeable value will be based on the value of the trust property and the value of property that has transferred from the trust in the previous ten years. There may also be an exit charge when property stops being subject to the trust. It will be based on the charge at the previous ten-year anniversary reduced to allow for the unexpired term (of ten years).

From 6 April 2006, IHT reliefs only apply to registered pension schemes and s. 615(3) schemes (These are a special type of overseas scheme that the government has proposed abolishing in the 2017 Budget Statement. It is established under trust as an occupational pension scheme by employers working primarily outside the UK, for employees who work wholly outside the UK. The section refers to ICTA 1988, s. 615). This means that property held in an EFRBS is treated as relevant property held in a normal discretionary trust. A charge to IHT can therefore arise on failure to take retirement benefits (an omission to act in anticipation of death which enhances the beneficiary's estate at the expense of the member), on the member's death and periodically (as well as on "exit").

HMRC takes the view that a disposition in connection with an EFRBS may constitute a gift with reservation. It cites *IRC v Eversden* (2002).

The two-year exemption period for distribution of death benefits does not apply to EFRBS.

Income tax

Income tax is paid on investments by the trustees as if they owned the assets absolutely.

Capital gains tax

There may be a CGT liability on transfer of an asset to the trust or from it.

Within the trust, the usual rates of tax will apply, depending on the income tax rate of the member. If the investments are collectives, the annual exemption will be half of the standard annual exemption, but this is reduced further if there is more than one trust (the exemption is divided by the number of trusts to a minimum of 10% of the standard exemption).

12.9.3 Benefits

If the benefits are paid as a lump sum, they will be tax-free to the extent that the relevant funds have already been subject to income tax when paid or earmarked. If paid as an income they will be subject to income tax.

Law: IHTA 1984, s. 64(1), 65(1); ITEPA 2003, Pt. 9

Case: *CIR v Eversden* (2003) 75 TC 340

12.10 Transition

Pre-commencement rights are available in respect of contributions paid before 6 April 2006 by virtue of FA 2004, Sch. 36, para. 53-56. The paragraphs deal with the situations:

- where contributions continue to an employer-financed retirement benefit scheme after 5 April 2006; and
- where no such contributions continue.

For continuing contributions, the relevant para. 54 applies if all the income and gains accruing to the scheme are taxed and the lump sum is payable to one or more of a range of people (the member, relative of the member, personal representatives, ex-spouse or other person designated by the employee) or the scheme was established before 1 September 1993 and has been unamended since then.

Where the pre-commencement rights are available, any lump sum paid as a retirement benefit that has derived from taxed employer contributions will be free of income tax to the extent that the fund does not exceed the value of assets on 5 April 2006 increased in line with the RPI. Any excess will be subject to tax. In undertaking the calculation, the fund in respect of member contributions (which is tax-free if paid as a lump sum) must be deducted.

If no contributions are made to such an arrangement after 5 April 2006, the full fund is available tax-free, assuming that contributions were originally taxed.

The general protection from inheritance tax (IHTA 1984, s. 151) will continue to apply to a proportion of the value of assets in the scheme. The protected amount (which is scheme specific) is the adjusted commencement value as a percentage of the value at the relevant time (pre-6 April 2006 accrual). The adjustment to the commencement value requires the value to be increased in line with the RPI, but reduced by relevant payments (expenses, payments chargeable to income tax).

Law: FA 2004, Sch. 36, para. 53-56; IHTA 1984, s. 151

12.11 Excepted group life policies

There are special rules for non-registered group life schemes that, for these purposes, should be identified as "excepted" and "non-excepted" group life schemes.

An excepted group life policy is a type of non-registered policy which is intended to provide death benefits in respect of more than one member.

Employer contributions are deductible if the local inspector considers them to be incurred wholly and exclusively for the purposes of trade and they are not assessed on the member.

The policy is excepted from the general provisions of ITTOIA 2005, Pt. 4 which deal with charges to tax on policy gains. There is therefore no charge to income tax or CGT on benefits. Applying a complicated logic to pre and post 6 April schemes established before 6 April 2006 and after 5 April, there will usually be no IHT liability on a periodic basis or exit if the policy has no surrender value at date of settlement and at the ten-year point. The exceptions explained by HMRC are where death occurs before the ten-year anniversary and the proceeds have not been distributed, or if the employee was terminally ill at the ten-year anniversary.

There is no liability to NICs on the contributions or the benefit.

The excepted group life policy is therefore relatively tax efficient and avoids the paperwork associated with registered schemes. However, in order to be an excepted policy, the legislation requires a number of conditions to be met:

- the benefit must be payable on death before the life assured reaches 75 and any exclusions in cover must apply to all members (strictly, individuals insured under the policy);
- the calculation of lump sum benefits must be calculated on the same basis for all insured individuals and limitations must be applied to all;
- a surrender value cannot exceed the amount of premiums refundable by reference to unexpired paid-up period;
- no other benefits are payable other than in accordance with these three conditions;

- benefits may only be paid to an individual or trust beneficially entitled to them or to a charity on their behalf;
- no benefit may be paid directly or indirectly to another life assured under the policy or anyone connected with that other life assured;
- tax avoidance by the policyholder or a person beneficially entitled under the policy must not be the purpose or main purpose of the policy.

A non-excepted group life policy may fall into one of two categories: a relevant life policy (ITEPA 2003, s. 393B) or a group life policy that is not a relevant group life policy and which is an employer-financed retirement benefit scheme.

Relevant life policies would qualify as excepted group life policies were it not for the addition of ill health, disability or accidental death benefits and the restriction to one life assured. These policies are similarly free of tax on contributions and benefits except that there will be a chargeable event for income tax purposes on payment of death benefits.

There are significant tax disadvantages to policies that are not excepted or even relevant life policies and fall under the heading of an employer-financed scheme (EFRBS) as defined above.

Employer contributions are not taxed, but the employer will only be able to claim a deduction when (and if) the benefit is paid. There should be liability to National Insurance on contributions. If the life assured has left service, there is no liability on the benefit. If the benefit is payable before the life assured's 75th birthday, and would qualify as an authorised payment under a registered scheme, then 25 per cent of the benefit is not subject to NICs even if the life assured had not left service. Otherwise, the benefit is subject to Class 1 NICs.

Assuming that the policy would have no surrender value there would, in effect, be no liability to inheritance tax unless the sum assured was awaiting distribution when the periodic charge fell due. If the scheme provided a "return of fund", however, there would be charges on exit and a ten-year periodic charge. An exception relates to benefits that accrued before 6 April 2006.

Law: ITEPA 2003, s. 393-400; FA 2004, s. 245-249; ITTOIA 2005, s. 480-482

Table of primary legislation

Table of statutory instruments

Index of cases

General index

Printed and bound in Great Britain by
Marston Book Services Limited, Oxfordshire